FROM THE EYE
OF THE STORM
Regional Conflicts
and the Philosophy of Peace

VIBS

Volume 29

Robert Ginsberg

Executive Editor

Associate Editors

a volume in

Philosophy of Peace

POP

Joseph C. Kunkel, Editor

FROM THE EYE
OF THE STORM
Regional Conflicts
and the Philosophy of Peace

WITHDRAWN

Edited by

Laurence F. Bove
Laura Duhan Kaplan

Amsterdam - Atlanta, GA 1995

Cover design by Chris Kok based on a photograph, © 1984 by Robert Ginsberg, of statuary by Gustav Vigeland in the Frogner Park, Oslo, Norway.

∞ The paper on which this book is printed meets the requirements of "ISO 9706:1994, Information and documentation - Paper for documents - Requirements for permanence".

ISBN: 90-5183-870-0 (CIP) (bound)
©Editions Rodopi B.V., Amsterdam - Atlanta, GA 1995
Printed in The Netherlands

CONTENTS

SECTION II
AMERICA'S HOMEFRONT

SECTION III
DESERT STORM ASSESSMENTS

EDITORIAL FOREWORD

This volume inaugurates a Special Series in the Philosophy of Peace. The volume brings together a set of papers that examine peace and militarism in regional conflicts. A number of the authors, writing after Operation Desert Storm in the Persian Gulf, address either the confrontation with Iraq or broader Middle Eastern issues. The volume's title, *From the Eye of the Storm*, recalls the well-publicized Desert Storm; at the same time, the title connotes a reflective calm capable of interpreting the actions swirling around in what has been called a warist or militarist culture.

Most of this volume's contributors are members of Concerned Philosophers for Peace (CPP), which was founded in 1981. CPP's original purpose was to encourage philosophers to lend their voices and special talents to concerns being raised nationally about the superpower nuclear arms race. In the subsequent years, we have urged each other to teach courses on war and peace, to share syllabi and resources, to analyze critical terms, to utilize ethical, social-political, and human nature theories, to write papers, and to help educate ourselves and others on the worldwide dangers posed by weapons of mass destruction. Today, CPP members number over 500 in the United States and Canada.

The *Concerned Philosophers for Peace Newsletter* has been published since our inception, and CPP meets annually for an extended weekend conference. Contributors to CPP's first conference in 1987 stressed the ethical and political orientations of the United States and the Soviet Union, various implications of possessing and using nuclear weapons, and peacemaking proposals for the Reagan-Gorbachev years. Several members had been to the Soviet Union and could articulate the strengths and weaknesses on both sides of the nuclear debate.

The dramatic changes that took place in Eastern Europe and the now former Soviet Union beginning with the collapse of the Berlin Wall caught us unprepared. Some members found whole manuscripts upon which they had been working outmoded by the unfolding events. That would have been a small price to pay had nations begun to live in peace with their neighbors. But recent conflicts have shown that while the world may have given up its superpower clashes, nations have not surrendered their implements of war. The world, more secure than in the past, is still insecure.

Philosophers concerned about issues of war and peace have been reworking their conceptions and extending their analyses to wars that involve sophisticated conventional weapons. Such weapons are no less deadly for those killed, no less destructive of the environment, and no less depleting of the world's natural resources. Nuclear arsenals, as well as chemical and biological weapons of mass destruction, are still produced and deployed, although the major powers have signed a global chemical weapons treaty which soon will go into effect. Peacemaking issues have broadened from halting a nuclear holocaust to stopping warfighting as a means of settling international disputes. There is also the need to explore the causes of war and to address the institutionalized violence in societies that spills over into the overt violence of wars.

Philosophy of Peace as a Special Series explores socio-political and ethical perspectives, such as just war doctrine, realism, consequentialism, Marxism, pacifism, and the ethics of care. It addresses conventional warfare, the problems of nuclear proliferation, and the continued reliance on nuclear deterrence in the post-cold war world. The series also examines covert and overt violence as found in sexism, racism, and classism. The editors welcome manuscripts probing positive and negative aspects of peacemaking, and ones studying how to understand or reduce the apparently intractable problems of violence ranging from domestic violence to international war.

From the Eye of the Storm is timely as the first volume in this new series and will make a valuable addition to the Value Inquiry Book Series, which was begun under the executive editorship of Robert Ginsberg and published by Rodopi. We thank all the editors associated with this volume for their support in its publication.

Joseph C. Kunkel
Executive Secretary, 1989–1995,
Concerned Philosophers for Peace

Editor, Philosophy of Peace

PREFACE: PARADIGMS FOR THE PHILOSOPHY OF PEACE

Laurence F. Bove and Laura Duhan Kaplan

Throughout the twentieth century, tempests of violence and war have relentlessly swept personal, social, and political tragedies through the human family. The traditional metaphor for the academic life, the "ivory tower," implies that philosophers live in peaceful seclusion from these trials. However, the authors of this volume prefer to live in the transient calm of "the eye of the storm." They have come to realize that the continued use of violence in human affairs cries out for analyses that can lead to new behaviors. As such, they represent a growing tradition and body of literature emerging as a new branch of philosophical study: the philosophy of peace.

Philosophy at the end of the twentieth century appears ready to recapture the relevance to current events it enjoyed in the classical era. Pragmatism, utilitarianism, and existentialism, all of which express the tendency to remain close to the experiential world, are now standard components of the philosophical curriculum. Participation in the civil rights, anti-Vietnam war, ecological, and feminist movements have been formative experiences for many of today's philosophers. These philosophers recognize that contemporary social conflicts partially determine who people are, which ethical appeals will move them, and to which discourses they will respond. They recognize that the analysis of conflicts reveals the epistemological and ontological boundaries operating within and between cultures. Therefore, the philosophy of peace has much to offer beyond discussions of the ethics of nonviolence and war. In this book alone, philosophers of peace identify and critically evaluate cultural myths about women, death, Christianity, Islam, patriotism, politicians, globalism, the media, the economy, enemies, revolutionary causes and, of course, war and peace.

Philosophers of peace evaluate the myths they uncover using a variety of hermeneutical approaches. Here we will describe two approaches. The first hermeneutic sees through the lens of an inclusive theoretical perspective which is normative for all. The second assumes a commitment to pluralism and synthesizes different theoretical and cultural perspectives.

The just war tradition, which informs no less than six chapters of this book, exemplifies the first approach. Just war theory accepts war as a fact of life, and prescribes limits to its destructiveness by enumerating the ethical criteria for entering and conducting war. Just war theory has demonstrated remarkable consistency since Augustine of Hippo first articulated it in the fifth century, partially because its logical classification of actions is easily adapted to national and international law and policy. As a hermeneutic, just war theory identifies actions in terms of the theory's categories and evaluates them according to each category's guidelines.

The second is a postmodern hermeneutic, exemplified perhaps by Foucault's structuralist analyses of how history, culture, and gender affect the ways we experience violence, oppression, and other forms of injustice. This approach, which informs no less than eight chapters in this book, explores the ways in which religious myths, stereotypes, and political discourse can encourage or discourage our participation in violent conflict. Philosophers using this approach are content to arrive at partial clarifications. They recognize that since action, experience, and thought are intertwined, inquiry must proceed through a dialogue among theories, practices, persons, and the social forces which affect them. No theoretical orientation dominates, as every theory's cultural role can be analyzed from the perspective of some other theory. The power of this approach comes from its similarity with real thinking as well as its commitment to pluralism.

Both approaches complement each other and contribute to the philosophy of peace. The first approach makes systematic inquiry into war and peace possible. It exemplifies the enlightenment ideal of one scientific paradigm guiding all inquiry. This ideal demonstrates how guidelines and rigor are possible in philosophical analysis and suggests that the amorphous task of cultural and ethical analysis results in unified knowledge. The second approach encourages the multicultural study of local and international conflict. Motivated by the challenge to make sense of a diverse global village, philosophers of peace in the second tradition develop interpretive frameworks that synthesize and evaluate an increasingly complex range of cultural data. They also accept the ongoing responsibility of revising those frameworks as new knowledge is discovered. The two approaches to inquiry in the philosophy of peace are relevant to the actual practice of conflict resolution. The first articulates an unshakable moral commitment to restraint from (and, failing that, restraint in) war, while the second explores new ways of understanding and resolving conflicts, some of which lead people towards war.

To return to the metaphor of the storm: a meteorologist observing from the eye of a hurricane keeps moving to avoid being destroyed by the storm. In the same way, the philosophy of peace continues to evolve, lest its deliberations be coopted by a warist culture in which violence is a Machiavellian tool of survival (as several chapters in this book argue has been the fate of just war theory). The editors of this book are committed to the postmodern approach to inquiry into the philosophy of peace, defined as a conversation between all paradigms of research and practice. We affirm this approach for six reasons.

First, since a goal of the philosophy of peace is to bring theory to bear upon personal action, it is a form of what Socrates called wisdom. Wisdom requires a commitment to avoiding mere sophistry and to allowing experience to inform intelligent theorizing. The postmodern approach to the philosophy of peace invites attention to various levels of experience.

Second, since a goal of the philosophy of peace is to better international relations, the philosophy of peace should examine the understandings other nations have of their and our behaviors. The rich cultural achievements of various peoples and countries become both objects of study and resources for models of improved international relations.

Third, as the philosophy of peace recognizes that the use and abuse of political and economic power are central causes of war, it must seek to understand more comprehensively the nature of that power. Postmodernism builds upon the insight that a comprehensive analysis of power must include the voices of the (academically as well as socially) marginalized and disenfranchised. While the philosophy of peace is an activity performed by an intellectual elite, it must also embrace an openness which can challenge that elitism, or it will be characterized by the closedness and classism which lead to war.

Fourth, philosophers of peace writing on the phenomenology of violence have suggested that the disconnection of actions from consequences have often made organized acts of violence possible. Resisting the lure of this disconnectedness in intellectual discourse, a postmodern philosophy of peace acknowledges that actions have complex and subtle social consequences which should be studied.

Fifth, the power of those who use the dominant political and military discourses to set national agendas is more easily maintained when their opponents think and act in isolation from one another. Because the postmodern approach to the philosophy of peace, as we have defined it, includes multiple paradigms, it encourages collaboration and cooperation between all those who work for peace.

Sixth, postmodern methods of inquiry provide the tradition of nonviolence with expanded intellectual tools for using understanding and the methods of compassion to resolve conflicts among. many traditions and peoples. We are reminded of what Martin Luther King, Jr., envisioned—the creation of a new world house, one which affirms new ways of being together. Our task, now, is to make that house a home.

We see *From the Eye of the Storm* as a postmodern inquiry into the philosophy of peace. The authors of this volume are a diverse group, bringing to their work strong backgrounds in analytic philosophy, phenomenology, poststructuralism, philosophy of religion, legal studies, and feminist philosophy. Their chapters include analyses of the historical and conceptual contexts of specific regional conflicts and of the cultural and psychological foundations of our attitudes towards violence, as well as suggestions for practical nonviolent solutions and new paradigms for peaceful cooperation. The chapters in Section I explore our understandings of patriotism and militarism and the effects these understandings have on our political, social and ethical views. The essays in Section II focus on how foreign policies affect the American homefront, dealing specifically with conscientious objection, media ethics and foreign investment. Section III is a series of detailed inquiries into the ethics of the recent Persian Gulf War with Iraq. Section IV explores the perspectives of participants in the ongoing violence in the Middle East. Section V explores the ethical and political responses of Latin American peace activists to political instability. Finally, Section VI offers five brief chapters about the ethics and historical context of recent events in Bosnia, Somalia, and the Mideast.

ACKNOWLEDGMENTS

Many hands, hearts and minds contributed to the production of this book. Above all, we would like to thank the authors of the chapters for their cheerful, thoughtful and timely responses to our deadlines, our queries and our sometimes heavy-handed editing. This book is as much theirs as it is ours.

We would like to thank the members of the organization Concerned Philosophers for Peace (CPP), who introduced us to one another and who nurtured our interest in the philosophy of peace. Joseph Kunkel, Executive Director of CPP, provided us with moral and administrative support throughout the project. Together with James Sterba, Duane Cady, and Robert Holmes, he helped us make appropriate publication decisions and negotiate a contract. Sheldon Cohen, with the support of the Philosophy Department of the University of Tennessee at Knoxville, hosted the CPP conference at which the idea for this book was born. Members of the CPP Executive Committee who helped make that conference possible include Duane Cady, James Sterba, William Gay, Richard Werner, Joseph Betz, Michael Fox, Paula Smithka, Ron Hirschbein, and Ernest Partridge. We are grateful for permission to include the article by Linda Rennie Forcey, "Women as Peacemakers: Contested Terrain for Feminist Peace Studies," *Peace & Change* 16:4 (October 1991), 331–354, reprinted by permission of Sage Publications, Inc.

Our editor at Rodopi, Robert Ginsberg, encouraged us with his unflagging enthusiasm for peace studies and for our work in this area. Linda Weiner Morris of *educational publishing resources*, our freelance copy editor and desktop publisher, worked swiftly and accurately to prepare the manuscript for publication and to draft a bibliography and index. She helped us recognize numerous details that go into manuscript preparation that we might have otherwise overlooked. Computer assistance at earlier stages was provided by Joey Council and Charlotte Simpson at the University of North Carolina at Charlotte, who helped us organize the files; and by Alan Plastow and Paula Roski at Walsh University, who spent hours of their precious time helping us translate files into Word Perfect to prepare them for copy-editing. UNC Charlotte Teaching Assistant Meg Blazek helped us condense an early version of the index.

Secretarial assistance was provided by Linda Miltner and Martha Capeta at Walsh University and by Vicki Griffith and

Travis Snead at the University of North Carolina at Charlotte. Without their help typing manuscripts, corresponding with authors, photocopying papers, fielding telephone calls and sending faxes, our scholarly work would not be possible. A special thanks is due to William Gay, Chair of the Philosophy Department at the University of North Carolina at Charlotte, for his administrative assistance when one of us was busy with a family emergency during a crucial stage in manuscript preparation.

Finally, we thank our spouses, Penny Bove and Charles Kaplan, for lovingly providing ideas, editorial assistance, encouragement and childcare during the many stages of this project.

Laurence F. Bove
Walsh University

Laura Duhan Kaplan
University of North Carolina at Charlotte

SECTION I

Conceptual Foundations

INTRODUCTION

The chapters in Section I challenge the prevailing militarist paradigm of the life of nations. The premise of this paradigm is the view that humans are naturally aggressive, and its conclusions include the following. A sovereign nation should declare war when its boundaries, opportunities or freedoms to act are threatened. The best way for a nation to forestall such challenges is to threaten aggression, by building and deploying a strong military arm. These efforts to prevent war will be limited by human nature, so waging war can be morally justified. Citizens who support their countries' wars are praised as "patriotic." But, as the authors of the essays in this section suggest, perhaps humans are not naturally aggressive. Perhaps nations with shared values can negotiate rather than threaten. Perhaps a fair distribution of economic resources can forestall nations' desires to challenge other nations. Perhaps a belief in the moral superiority of nonviolence can replace the prevailing view that war is an ethical means of protecting national sovereignty. And perhaps patriotism can be decoupled from the uncritical acceptance of war.

In "Militarism in the Modern State and World Government: The Limits of Peace through Strength in the Nuclear Age," William C. Gay recognizes that nations can prosper without the use of military force. To support his vision, he appeals to Émile Benoit-Smullyan's (1946) and Joseph Neyer's (1947) proposals for avoiding nuclear war. Gay rejects Benoit-Smullyan's proposal to pursue world peace by designating the United Nations as the supreme military power. Instead, he affirms Neyer's view that moving beyond militarism entirely is desirable, and that this move will require the cultivation of shared values on a global scale.

In "A Demilitarized Concept of Patriotism," Stephen Nathanson argues that it is possible for citizens to be patriotic without uncritically supporting their leaders' military domination of other countries. Nathanson argues for a moderate, morally acceptable form of patriotism in which citizens desire that their countries prosper and flourish, but reserve the right to question their leaders' choices of ends and means.

David E. Johnson, in "The Concepts of Militarism," questions both the ends and the means of American foreign policy. The goal of American foreign policy, he claims, is to preserve an unjust economic status quo which assures first world prosperity at the expense of the third world. The use of military power to achieve that goal is justified by the false and immoral—but expedient—beliefs "it is appropriate for some people to dominate other people" and "if you want to ensure peace prepare for war."

In "Augustine's Stance on War," Warren Harrington shows that Augustine's articulation of the criteria of a morally justified war is grounded in Roman expediency rather than in Christian ethics. According to Harrington, Augustine's political commitments to Rome motivated him to ignore Christianity's commitment to nonviolence, and instead to develop an idiosyncratic interpretation of Christian scripture which supported Roman militarism.

Finally, Linda Rennie Forcey, in "Women as Peacemakers: Contested Terrain for Feminist Peace Studies," examines the arguments presented by various feminist authors for and against the view that while men are naturally aggressive warriors, women are naturally nurturing peacemakers. Recognizing that theory underlies praxis, Forcey calls for feminist pacifists to give up the need for a single correct description of women's interest in peace and be willing instead to try a variety of approaches to making peace.

Forcey's concluding advice should be heeded by all those who theorize about the causes of and cures for war.

MILITARISM IN THE MODERN STATE AND WORLD GOVERNMENT: THE LIMITS OF PEACE THROUGH STRENGTH IN THE NUCLEAR AGE

William C. Gay

> Those who favor complete nuclear and conventional disarmament (must) admit that their recommendation is inconsistent with national sovereignty.
>
> —Jonathan Schell, *The Fate of the World*

> Humanity has no alternative but...to learn to live with politics, to live in the world we know: a world of nuclear weapons, international rivalries, recurring conflicts, and at least some risk of nuclear crisis.
>
> —Harvard Nuclear Study Group, *Living With Nuclear Weapons*

1. Maintenance of National Sovereignty and the Capacity to Wage War

Despite their differences, Jonathan Schell and the Harvard Nuclear Study Group operate within the metaphysical parameters of Hobbesian political theory.[1] Specifically, both Schell and the Harvard Group recognize a necessary connection between the maintenance of national sovereignty and the capacity to wage war. If in our political metaphysics we premise that the capacity to wage war is necessary for maintaining national sovereignty, then those of us living in the modern world have only two political options: we can embrace national sovereignty, in which case we must also embrace the capacity to wage war *or* we can reject the capacity to wage war, in which case we must also reject national sovereignty. This supposed dilemma is not new, but it was more conspicuous in the 1980s when concern over the nuclear arms race led large numbers of people to re-evaluate governments and their weapons policies.[2] Now, in the 1990s when so many people, especially Americans, are relishing in what they take to be the successes of the New World Order, this linkage of military capability and the nation state is not as readily perceived as a dilemma. In other words, throughout the 1980s and so far in the 1990s, this connection is largely taken for granted, whether viewed as a problem or an asset.

In his book *From Warism to Pacifism*, Duane Cady exposes the extent to which warism permeates our culture.[3] His concern is to show how warism functions as the primary obstacle to pacifism. I am stressing how both warists and pacifists, despite their disagreement on whether war is inevitable, often concur in taking it for granted that the state and the capacity to wage war go hand in hand. When this link is also considered, assessment of the problem of war occurs within the parameters of reflection on the benefits and dangers associated with the modern state.

Schell provides the argument for eliminating sovereignty and war, and the Harvard group provides the argument for retaining both. If nuclear war might entail biocide or only genocide, the choice appears to concern values, not facts.[4] Schell contends "the nuclear powers put a higher value on national sovereignty than they do on human survival."[5] Since most people probably more highly value survival of the species, Schell has stacked the deck against the system of national sovereignty. The Harvard group begs the value question when they assert "securing national sovereignty is a moral goal worth pursuing; indeed all nations pursue it."[6] By holding to the same metaphysical premise as Schell but affirming a different fundamental value, the Harvard group holds out arms control as our best hope.

The peculiarity of our supposed dilemma can be highlighted by considering the *logical* possibilities before making metaphysical commitments. Four situations are possible in relation to sovereignty and war: (1) we can have both sovereignty and war—the Harvard group and many advocates of world government accept this situation; (2) we can have neither sovereignty nor war—Schell and most anarchists advocate this option; (3) we can have war but not sovereignty—the Hobbesian state of nature illustrates this situation; and (4) we can have sovereignty but not war—this prospect at the level of national and world government is focus of this essay.

In relation to the four possibilities, the fundamental *political* question is whether there is a necessary connection between the maintenance of national sovereignty and the capacity to wage war. If the connection is necessary and one embraces the state, then the foundations are set for the militarism of the modern state. Likewise, if the connection is necessary but one wishes to avoid the potential consequences of standing military organizations, then the basis is set for abandoning the modern state. As is widely known, contract theory from Hobbes through Rousseau myopically coupled sovereignty and war and the resulting orientation toward nation states is termed *Realpolitik*—"political realism." While modern history does show a rather constant conjunction of sovereignty and war, Hume taught us to be sceptical about positing a necessary connection in our metaphysics (e.g., if sovereignty, then war). Unless stronger support is offered for their contentions, the positions of the Harvard group and Schell may well illustrate two sides of the same coin.

I maintain that political entities with sovereignty (i.e., nation states and world government) are contingent (historical) and that whether they require war is also contingent (historical). I am not here interested in pre-modern cases of war without sovereignty. Instead, in seeking to pass between the horns of the dilemma of sovereignty with war and neither sovereignty nor war, I am interested in envisioning sovereignty without war. Since the option I am advocating is still political, its pursuit requires consideration of how to go beyond Hobbesian assumptions regarding the state. In this regard, the issue of world government arises. At this level, however, the same assumption is often made.

Within the framework of Hobbes, order requires force; more specifically, political order (often termed peace) requires military force. We are all too familiar with the slogan, "Peace through Strength." In the 1980s, we became well aware of the manner in which its domestic version really had as its goal peace through *national* strength. Several of the critiques of the nuclear state argued that the pursuit of such strength by several nations could lead to an Apocalyptic version of the Hobbesian war of all against all. Some proposed that the way out is to attempt the same solution at the international level. In blunt terms, we were told that the solution is a world government, but one that maintains control of the primary instruments of war—whether nuclear or only conventional. In other words, the solution is to be found in peace through *supernational* strength. These suggestions are not new, even in the nuclear age—nor is the critique of them. To make this point, I will review a very illuminating set of essays in *Ethics* that appeared *at the beginning of the nuclear age.*

2. The Relation of Military Strength and Government

The maintenance of national sovereignty does not necessarily imply nationalism, and the capacity to war does not necessarily imply militarism. However, in the twentieth century, whether one looks at regional conflicts or global wars, it is difficult to separate one from the other. And, increasingly, it is difficult to separate consideration of regional conflicts from the prospect of escalation to global war. These potential, though fortunately not always actual, connections have been especially acute since the beginning of the nuclear age. As a result, the philosophical assessment of the relation of military strength and government has been an on-going concern since the mid-1940s.

In July 1946, *Ethics* published its first article on the atomic bomb. This article, "An American Foreign Policy for Survival," was written by a social scientist, not a philosopher.[7] Émile Benoit-Smullyan, the author of the article, was then working in the U.S. Department of Labor. He subsequently taught at the Associated Colleges of New York and is more widely known within sociology for his work on Durkheim.[8] One year after the publication of Benoit-Smullyan's article, *Ethics* published "Is Atomic-Fission Control A Problem in Organizational Technique?"[9] This essay was written by the philosopher Joseph Neyer as a response to Benoit-Smullyan's argument. And, as far as I have been able to determine, Neyer's article is the first philosophical critique of a previous article on atomic weapons. Since both articles treat the atomic bomb from a social scientific point of view, it is appropriate that Neyer's Ph.D., which he received from Rutgers in 1942, was in philosophy and sociology. Neyer had held a Rockefeller fellowship in 1946–1947 before coming back to Rutgers as an Assistant Professor of Philosophy in 1947.[10]

The article by Benoit-Smullyan reflects what was then and still is today the political establishment's orientation toward *Realpolitik*, and the article by Neyer may well be the first attempt by a philosopher to expose and criticize the Hobbesian assumptions that inform the political establishment's approach to the atomic bomb. However, Neyer's criticisms are directed primarily at the latter half of Benoit-Smullyan's article. The first half of Benoit-Smullyan's article provides a critique of the national approach to the control of atomic energy, specifically of the effort by the U.S. to guarantee its atomic superiority. This part of his article is as timely today as the second half is now dated. Neyer's article also provides still timely criticisms of some approaches to world government and of U.S. policy toward foreign countries.

A. Benoit-Smullyan on the Limits of Peace Through Strength

Benoit-Smullyan hypothesized right away that atomic weapons would alter war. He projected that within a few years "only a defense that was practically 100 percent effective could prevent the complete destruction of our cities," and he believed that such an effective defense would not be possible (280). The relation between atomic bombs and war was such that the institution of war itself would have to be eliminated if civilization is to be preserved. We have to eliminate war, along with atomic weapons, because "you cannot prevent war simply by preventing atomic Armament, and, once war starts, you cannot prevent atomic Armament" (282). For Benoit-Smullyan, world government was the only way to avoid a nuclear arms race. He accurately foresaw that "an atomic armament race, if it gets well under way, will acquire a sinister impetus of its own and will be very hard to stop" (290).

The first half of Benoit-Smullyan's article is devoted to a critique of pursuing peace through *national* strength by the U.S. and through *international* strength by the U.N. His critique is based on the general principle that "a government can prevent war only if it possesses overwhelming physical force relative to the force available to a potentially rebellious faction" (284). Benoit-Smullyan's critique of peace through national strength of the U.S. is based on a rejection of the view that superiority in atomic weapons provides an effective form of deterrence. He captures the emergence of the theory of nuclear deterrence when he notes, "some of our military ad visers...have pinned their faith on keeping ahead in the atomic armament race and on having more and better bombs than other nations. According to this view, our defense against attack would be our ability to deliver an even stronger counterattack" (280). The reasons he gives suggest that ability to inflict great harm does not guarantee that one will not suffer great harm. Hence, in the atomic age national strength does not guarantee peace.

The pursuit of peace through international strength by the U.N. is equally flawed, according to Benoit-Smullyan. First, international control of fissionable material would require inspection, and only the ability to "inspect *everything* would guarantee compliance. Since such inspection would undercut the safeguarding of military secrets, if not national sovereignty itself, some governments will not accept it" (281). Secondly, such an approach to preventing atomic war is actually only a delaying mechanism, since once war breaks out atomic weapons can be re-introduced. Although many years later Jonathan Schell (in *The Abolition*) will see in this prospect a form of nuclear deterrence that does not rely on (as yet) stockpiled nuclear weapons,[11] Benoit-Smullyan realized, even when the U.S. was the only nation with atomic bombs, that such a situation would only lead to another and rather bizarre race. He notes, "the signatory nations would...put themselves in as advanced a state of preparedness for the rapid production of atomic weapons as treaty restrictions would permit." Not only would nations still possess the knowledge of how to produce nuclear weapons, they also would maintain at least some of the most vital technological installations necessary for their re-introduction into military arsenals.

The relevance of his observation to the current situation in Iraq should be obvious. Even if Iraq's capability to produce nuclear weapons has been crippled, if not destroyed, the knowledge remains. Likewise, it would be extraordinarily naive to believe that Iraq will stop short of imposed limits on re-development of technologies needed for the production of nuclear—and chemical—weapons. We would probably be wise to apply a similar scepticism in our assessment of how successful other "peace treaties" will be for the settlement of other regional conflicts.[12]

According to Benoit-Smullyan, world government (i.e., a *supernational* authority) is the political solution for the prevention of war. He notes that in pursuing such a world government we must be careful that it entails neither less nor more than is necessary. In this regard, he does not believe that effective world government presupposes "the development of an extensive moral and psychological sense of world community" (284). It is on this point that Neyer will disagree. Nevertheless, Benoit-Smullyan's insistence that worthwhile world government only needs to do what is necessary is also a cogent response to those who argue that we must have global justice before we can have global peace. For him, the critical issue is maintaining life, not attaining justice. Those who insist on full justice fail to recognize "the necessity of keeping the patient *alive* until the more fundamental or more far-reaching remedies can be applied." To support his point, he again raises the question of his critics and then answers it with an example that may catch his readers off guard:

> But can peace be found where there are prejudices, antipathies, and gross
> instances of exploitation and where no uniformity exists in living standards,

educational levels, and ways of thinking? The fact that all these sources of
dissension are found within the borders of the United States, and often in an
extreme form, suggests that they do not necessarily lead to war if there is a
common government established to enforce peace. (284)

We could have peace—and injustice—on a global scale if we had a
world government that could prevent war.

Until now, this possibility for world government could not be
realized because the requisite level of overwhelming force could not
be obtained. For Benoit-Smullyan, a world government which has
sole possession of atomic bombs could prevent war and would be
able to do so without relying on vast armies. At the level of world
government, but not at the level of national government, Benoit-
Smullyan believes nuclear deterrence can work. He states, "It is
essential, however, *in the interest of preventing the use of atomic
weapons*, that the world government possess them and be willing to
use them under certain specified conditions" (285). He believes that,
on humanitarian grounds, world government would use atomic
weapons only if "absolutely necessary," and he believes that, in light
of the rigorous exercise of inspection, "there is only the remotest
likelihood that the bomb would ever be used." Hence, though he
does not say so, Benoit-Smullyan is himself an advocate of peace
through strength. His position amounts to advocating peace through
supernational strength by a world government which has exclusive
possession of atomic weapons.

For Benoit-Smullyan the real issue is not whether we need world
government. The real issue concerns the implementation of world
government. The remainder of his article is devoted to the elabora-
tion of a supposedly minimalist world government. Actually, his
model looks like the U.S. constitution writ large in that it is based on
a balance of power among executive, legislative, and judicial
branches. After giving many details on and arguments for his model,
he ends by proposing that U.S. foreign policy while still cultivating
national strength, should also include efforts toward the type of
minimalist world government that "would actually assure survival
and not merely postpone the inevitable day of disaster" (289).

B. Neyer on the Relation of Shared Values to Effective Law

In his response to Benoit-Smullyan's argument, Neyer zeros in
on its basic assumption. Benoit-Smullyan, like other exponents of
Realpolitik, is looking for an organizational device that will provide

a political solution to the problems raised by the atomic bomb. Though Benoit-Smullyan accuses those he criticizes as looking for a technical solution when a political one is needed, Neyer views Benoit-Smullyan as operating on the same level. In proposing a supernational organization, Benoit-Smullyan is actually saying that an international organization to control atomic fission is *not yet* the correct organizational device. For Neyer, those who seek to find some way to put adversaries under a system of enforceable law are looking for a political solution (290). Even if they are not actually fighting, they are constantly prepared to fight, and there is no authority that can intervene to stop them.

Benoit-Smullyan's critique of peace through international strength suggests that the U.N. is not the proper organizational device. Benoit-Smullyan's model for world government is simply another attempt at a political solution. Neyer tries to expose the insufficiency, by itself, of any organizational device. When Benoit-Smullyan dismissed the need for psychological and moral changes, he was presuming that government can operate like a machine. You get the proper machinery for government, and it can crank out the results you want. Benoit-Smullyan's proposed machinery for world government is one of checks and balances, and he uses U.S. history to argue that we need not fear that one branch of world government will expand itself beyond its proper limits. Neyer responds that even in the U.S. there has been "legislation by adjudication," as well as the usurpation of powers of Congress by several of our presidents. But that is not the more telling point. Neyer concedes that the process of checks and balances has worked fairly well in the U.S., but he denies that its effectiveness is a function of its status as an organizational device. Yes, it is machinery, but, for machinery to operate, there have to be the right kind of people behind it. And he does not mean just the few good people you need to turn the wheels of state. Neyer is referring to the broad cultural base, the tradition, that lies behind our political system.

Neyer makes his criticism quite clear when he says:

> the system of "checks and balances" is not a "machinery" which, once created and set going, operates of itself and in a vacuum. It receives not only .
> its energies but also its directions from a live tradition and a communal substance....It is on such stuff that our guaranty against tyranny reposes—not on ingeniously manufactured machinery. This is not to say that the machinery counts for nothing but that it is meaningless apart from the

social structure and the inherited and developing system of values shared by the individuals within the structure. (291)

The dissolution of the Soviet Union and the independence movements in Eastern Europe show the relevance of this observation. While the governments retained the capacity to wage war—even against their own citizens—they had cultivated insufficiently the requisite level of shared values. As Gene Sharp has remarked, the ability to govern ultimately rests on the will of the people.[13]

Neyer is quite perceptive regarding the origin of the view that what we need is merely the proper machinery. Thomas Hobbes foisted that view on modern political thinking. He abstracted people from other communities and only gave them the qualities of selfishness and fear. They need security, and they latch onto the machinery of the Leviathan—which incidentally, when originally mentioned in the book of Job, was described as a monster. At any rate, Hobbes views people and their government in mechanistic terms. The same can be said for the *Realpolitik* that is based on his philosophy. As Neyer notes, "In such an abstract view, law is meaningless where the military power for its enforcement is absent" (292).

In essence, Neyer contends that Benoit-Smullyan's proposals "assure that a satisfactory 'political' solution can be worked out in advance of a sociological solution." Instead of political technique, we need social technique. Instead of our current political science, we need a new type of social science. Neyer does not want to impose moral values; he wants them to develop and believes a proper social science can help. At this level, his view is very much like Dewey's.[14] Neyer, like Dewey, saw how morality and values get presented as separate from science and technology. Just as Dewey wants values to operate within science and technology, even so Neyer wants the shared values of the world community to operate within any world government that is to be viable.

Though Neyer does not endorse the full range of the philosophy of George Gurvitch, he draws on Gurvitch's October 1941 article in *Ethics* to make his point. Neyer states:

law is related to "forms of sociality" —to community. The coercive agencies must themselves be in a position to recognize the validity of the law—which is to say, they must exist in vital relation with the community....the force of law is always something beyond the physical coercion of the law. Law is the

crystallization and the routinization of values whose appeal and power is
already felt by the members of a living community. (292–93)

Without this vital connection, the leaders of a world government may
well act beyond their limited roles, and the device of checks and
balances may be a mere technicality which holds little or no sway.

For Neyer, our survival will take time. There is no quick fix, no
political fix. Our choice lies between political techniques of
increasing physical strength or social techniques of developing
cultural values. Benoit-Smullyan showed the ineffectiveness of
national strength and international strength, and Neyer showed the
ineffectiveness of supernational strength. So, for the long run, the
only viable choice is social, not political.

Neyer realizes that the shared values needed for world
community do not require "a miraculous creation *ex nihilo*." That is
what Benoit-Smullyan's proposal would require. These values
already exist. In our foreign policy, Neyer contends, "We must cease
acting in such ways as choke the growth" (293). Moreover, we need
to use our technology for peace, not war: "All science finds its uses
for peace as well as for war; the choice is ours." Neyer suggests,
"every step taken, through the intelligent use of the new technology
of communication, toward the increase of mutual understanding
among peoples of the globe is a step toward world government in its
only valid meaning." Neyer sees a role for application of the physical
sciences in developing communication technologies and a role for
the application of social sciences in developing symbolic activities.
Regarding the latter, he recommends that instead of using social
science to subjugate people by means of "the mass-suggestion
technique of a Goebbels," we can use it for "the liberation of
personality and the strengthening of democracy."

Neyer's suggestion might help end the dualisms that concerned
Dewey. We do not need an external moral authority to resolve the
problem. Neyer, like Dewey, has little use for those "who speak in
vague language of the need for 'spiritual and moral' reformation."
His stand is that of science, but of reformed science. Neyer calls for
an applied social science infused with shared values and oriented
toward peace.

3. Alternatives to Militarism and Nationalism

I have tried to show that programs of "peace through national
strength" and "peace through supernational strength" are products of

the political metaphysics which links sovereignty and the capacity to wage war. I have done so by recalling Benoit-Smullyan's critique of the former and Neyer's critique of the latter. In my closing remarks, I wish to reflect on the lessons we can learn from them.

Militarism and nationalism are historical phenomena. Regardless of whether they ever played a positive role, the real issue is whether they have played out their historical viability. What is obvious is that a global nuclear war could end modern states and most everything else. Hence, even those who believe the modern state can continue to rely on militarism and nationalism also need to pursue arms control. Regarding the relation of sovereignty and war, the advice of the Harvard group is rational but it is myopic. Probably, the modern state can be maintained longer by means of the capacity to wage war, including nuclear war, but it cannot be maintained indefinitely by this means. The balancing of sovereignty and war, even aided by arms control, cannot be permanent. Those caught up in the anti-nuclear movement decided we cannot risk that arms control will create a sufficient lull before the next and perhaps final war. However, while those who reach this conclusion are also rational, they need not necessarily adopt Schell's disavowal of national sovereignty. Nuclear and conventional disarmament is inconsistent with the modern state of *Realpolitik*, but not with the form of state based on shared cultural values as conceived by Neyer.

Once we abandon the quest for a solution in some political technique, we need to begin taking steps to forge effective social techniques for the creation of shared global values. Whether our concern is the decades old problem of nuclear weapons or the centuries old problem of conventional war, we need to look beyond the militarism of both national and world government in the quest for peace.

NOTES

1. Detailed critiques of the Hobbesian assumptions of Schell and the Harvard group are presented in several essays in "Philosophy and the Debate on Nuclear Weapons Systems and Policies," a special, double-issue of *Philosophy and Social Criticism* 10:3–4, edited by William C. Gay. See, too, various essays in *Issues in War and Peace*, edited by Joseph C. Kunkel and Kenneth H. Klein (Wolfeboro, NH: Longwood Academic, 1989) and *In the Interest of Peace*, edited by Kenneth H. Klein and Joseph C. Kunkel (Wakefield, NH: Longwood Academic, 1990). For even more recent assessments of Hobbesian assumptions by American and Russian philosophers, see the first part of *On the Eve of the 21st Century: Perspectives of*

Russian and American Philosophers, edited by William C. Gay and T.A. Alekseeva (Lanham, MD: Rowman & Littlefield, 1993).

2. For a more detailed critique of other public and governmental presumptions, see my essay "Nuclear War: Public and Governmental Misconceptions," in *Nuclear War: Philosophical Perspectives*, edited by Michael Allen Fox and Leo Groarke, (New York: Peter Lang, 1985), 11–25.

3. Duane Cady, *From Warism to Pacifism: A Moral Continuum* (Philadelphia: Temple, 1989).

4. Their argumentation regarding this premise has similarity to the much earlier debate between Bertrand Russell and Sidney Hook. See my essay, "The Russell-Hook Debates of 1958: Arguments from the Extremes on Nuclear War and the Soviet Union," in *In the Interest of Peace*, 79–95.

5. Jonathan Schell, *The Fate of the Earth* (New York: Knopf, 1982), 210. (The quote from Schell cited at the beginning of this section is from p. 218.)

6. The Harvard Nuclear Study Group, *Living with Nuclear Weapons* (Cambridge: Harvard University Press, 1983), 244. (The quote from the Harvard Group cited at the beginning of this section is from p. 19.)

7. Émile Benoit-Smullyan, "An American Foreign Policy for Survival," *Ethics* 56, 280–90. Subsequent references (in the section titled "Benoit-Smullyan on the Limits of Peace Through Strength") are given as page numbers in parentheses in the text. Quotations without parenthetical citation appear on the same page as the previous citation.

8. See bibliographic data in *An Introduction to the History of Sociology*, edited by Harry Elmer Barnes (Chicago: The University of Chicago Press, 1948).

9. Joseph Neyer, "Is Atomic-Fission Control a Problem in Organizational Technique?" *Ethics* 57 (July 1947), 289–96. Subsequent references (in the section "Neyer on the Relation of Shared Values to Effective Law") are given as page numbers in parentheses in the text. Quotations without parenthetical citation appear on the same page as the previous citation.

10. *Directory of American Scholars: A Bibliographical Directory*, 3rd ed., edited by Jaques Cattell (New York: R.R. Bowker Co., 1957), 547–48.

11. Jonathan Schell, *The Abolition* (New York: Knopf, 1984).

12. Kant makes a similar point in the very first of his "Preliminary Articles" in *Perpetual Peace*. See Immanuel Kant, *Perpetual Peace and Other Essays on Politics, History, and Morals*, translated by Ted Humphrey (Indianapolis: Hackett, 1983), 107.

13. Gene Sharp, *Social Power and Political Freedom* (Boston: Porter Sargent, 1980).

14. John Dewey, "Dualism and the Split Atom: Science and Morals in the Atomic Age," *The New Leader* 28 (November 1945), 1 and 4. Reprinted in *Concerned Philosophers for Peace Newsletter* 7 (April 1987), 5–7.

A DEMILITARIZED CONCEPT
OF PATRIOTISM

Stephen Nathanson

For many people, war and patriotism are inextricably connected. As a result, enthusiastic patriots often seem enamored with war, seeing it as an opportunity to show one's devotion to one's country. Conversely, people who abhor war frequently reject patriotism, seeing it, as Tolstoy did, as "the root of war."[1]

As one who abhors war, I am sympathetic with antiwar critics who have denounced patriotism. Nonetheless, I think they are mistaken in their belief that war and patriotism are essentially linked and that patriotism (by virtue of its links with war) is necessarily evil. In this essay, I want to sketch a form of patriotism that is not subject to the criticisms of Tolstoy and other antiwar opponents of patriotism.[2] I do not deny that there are forms of patriotism that are open to their criticisms, but I do deny that every form of patriotism is vulnerable to their charges.

In his critique of patriotism, Tolstoy identifies a number of features as central to patriotism and argues, quite correctly, that these features are dangerous and immoral. The features he emphasizes are:

1. Belief in the superiority of one's country
2. A desire for dominance over other countries
3. Exclusive concern for one's own country
4. No constraints on the pursuit of national goals
5. Automatic support of one's country's military policies

These qualities are dangerous because the belief in superiority, coupled with the desire for dominance, leads to *aggressive* policies. The exclusive concern for one's own country involves either hostility or indifference to others, and this in turn leads to *ruthless* pursuit of one's own goals because no constraints are recognized on what one may do on behalf of the nation. Finally, automatic support of policies, in the spirit of "my country, right or wrong," leads to *passive* acceptance of immoral decisions by citizens.

My view is that while these are all recognizable traits of a familiar kind of patriotism, they are not essential features of patriotism itself. One kind of evidence for my view is linguistic. Our repertoire of words for describing forms of national attachment includes not only the word "patriotism" but also words like "chauvinism," "jingoism," and "xenophobia." The attitudes named by these latter terms are clearly related to patriotism in important ways, but these distinct terms call our attention to certain excesses that patriotism is liable to and differentiate these excesses from patriotism itself.

While patriots must love their country and think well of it, chauvinists have an excessive love for and an inflated conception of their country's worth. While patriots must want their country to flourish and must be concerned about its defense, jingoists are overeager to engage in conflicts and wars with others. While patriots feel a special connection with their fellow citizens, xenophobes have developed an unnecessary hostility to people who are citizens of other lands.

What is perhaps most significant about terms like "chauvinism" and "jingoism" is that they are parts of ordinary language. Their presence in the language reveals an awareness that patriotism may have different forms and that some forms of patriotism are extreme and excessive. It suggests that extreme forms of patriotism are undesirable and that patriotism needs to be moderated in certain ways if it is to be a virtue.

1. Moderate vs. Extreme Patriotism

We can see what a moderated form of patriotism would look like by returning to the undesirable features listed above and replacing each of them with a related but more reasonable alternative.[3]

A. Superiority

Patriots need not believe in the superiority of their country. All that is required is that they have a special affection for their own country. Tolstoy correctly notes that a belief in national superiority is a stupid belief.[4] Reasonable patriots will know that their country is not best, but they will love it nonetheless. They will love it not because it is "objectively" the best but simply because it is their own country. It is familiar to them. It contains the values and ideals they have been brought up to feel attached to. Their sense of self is tied up with its language, culture, history, and natural features.

In answer to the question "Why does one love one's country?" a character in Bertolt Brecht's play *The Caucasian Chalk Circle* gives the following explanation:

Because the bread tastes better there, the air smells better, voices sound
stronger, the sky is higher, the ground is easier to walk on. Isn't that so?[5]

While these lines explain love of one's country in a quasi-objective
fashion, the idiosyncratic and personal nature of the experiences that
are described calls attention to their subjectivity. It calls attention to
the fact that for people in other countries, their bread will taste better,
their air will smell better, etc. It highlights the relational ties between
people and their countries and so undercuts any presumption to
objective superiority.

In describing a moderated patriotism, then, we can substitute the
quality of special affection or love of one's country for the
chauvinist's absurd conviction that one's country is objectively
superior to all others.

B. Dominance

Patriots need not desire that their country dominate over others.
All that they need to desire is that their own country prosper and
flourish, that its citizens live well, and that its ideals are realized.

In some conflict situations, it may be that one's country can only
flourish if it dominates over others. In a war, for example, the victory
of one country requires the defeat of another. This "zero-sum"
situation, however, is not representative. There are many forms of
flourishing that do not require dominance. A country can be secure,
for example, if it has sufficient strength to resist aggression. It need
not have the power to conquer all others.[6] Likewise, a country can
meet the economic needs of its citizens and provide them a decent
standard of living without having the highest per capita gross
national product. Finally, a country need not possess the greatest
number of artists and thinkers, so long as it possesses enough
creative people to sustain a culture that enriches its citizens.

Patriots will want their country to possess the things that are
needed to sustain a viable way of life. Achieving this, however, does
not require that the country be better than other countries in these
respects. Dominance is not a goal to which patriots must be
committed.

C. Exclusive Concern

Patriots must care about their country and their fellow citizens.
They need not, however, be hostile or indifferent to other countries
and peoples. Caring for one person or group is perfectly compatible

with having concern about others. Caring may have its limits, but it is not exclusive, and greater degrees of care for some people may coexist with limited but genuine concern for others.

The idea that patriotism requires exclusive concern for one's own country is undermined by many facts. No one thinks, for example, that it was unpatriotic of Americans to donate money to relieve famine victims in Ethiopia. Even those who believe "charity begins at home" can see that the extreme suffering of people who live beyond our borders requires some kind of humane response.

Likewise, however cynical one's view of foreign policy ideals may be, it remains true that the defense of other peoples' well-being is often put forward as a rationale for foreign policy decisions. John Kennedy proclaimed that "the world cannot exist half slave and half free." Lyndon Johnson claimed to be protecting the rights of the Vietnamese to self-determination. Jimmy Carter promoted human rights as an important component of foreign policy. George Bush has spoken of a "new world order."

These professions of global ideals may or may not be genuine. I cite them because they express concern for people who are not citizens of our own country, and, even if we interpret them cynically, those who professed these goals assumed that American citizens would share them. They certainly did not think that there was any inconsistency between a commitment to our country and a commitment to these broader, humanitarian goals.

Patriotism, then, requires a strong concern for one's own country, but it does not require that this concern be exclusive. It does not rule out a concern for people of other countries.

D. Ruthless Pursuit of National Goals

Ruthlessness, as I have already noted, arises out of a lack of concern for others. When we are hostile or indifferent to others and only care about ourselves, then we will feel that it is legitimate to do anything whatsoever in pursuit of our goals. We may trample on the rights and interests of others because they do not matter to us. Their well-being does not enter into our calculations.

This may be the attitude of the xenophobe, but as we have just seen, patriots need not have an exclusive concern for their own country, and if their concern is not exclusive, they will be concerned about the effects of their actions and policies on others. One way that this concern is reflected is in the recognition of constraints on what one may do in pursuit of the national interest.

These constraints take a number of forms. Among the primary constraints is the disavowal of aggressive war as an instrument of policy. One may not kill people simply because they are in one's way. Likewise, one may not simply plunder the resources of others, even if one has a legitimate need for those resources. These and other limits on the means that we adopt to pursue our interests grow out of a recognition that we share a common humanity with people of other countries and that they, too, are ends in themselves, not simply means to the satisfaction of our needs and desires. We may not think that these moral ideals and constraints are sufficiently recognized or acted on, but there is nothing in our conception of patriotism that rules them out. Patriots may well want their nation to pursue its good within the limits of moral rules and principles.

E. Automatic Acceptance

If patriots have special affection and concern for their own country, then they will want to support actions and policies that promote its well-being and its national ideals. They need not, however, be committed to the ideas expressed by the slogan "my country, right or wrong."

Criticism of one's own country's policies and actions is entirely compatible with a patriotic attitude. Indeed, genuine patriotism requires that one criticize government policies in some situations. Such criticism may arise because one believes that actions by the government are likely to harm the country rather than benefit it. If, as a patriot, one is concerned about the well-being of one's country and if one believes that the government has adopted a policy that will harm the country, then one's patriotic commitment will show itself in efforts to criticize and alter the policies. It would be an odd patriot who would acknowledge that the government's policies were harmful to the country and yet think that it was wrong to criticize them. Supporting one's country is not the same as supporting all the policies that public officials adopt or pursue.

One may also criticize government policies because they are insufficiently attentive to the rights of people in other countries. If we grant that patriotism need not involve an *exclusive* concern for the well-being of one's own nation and if we grant that there are moral constraints on what a nation may do in pursuit of its goals, then a patriot may well criticize a national policy because it violates these moral constraints. Wanting our country to do what is right, we may criticize its policies because they violate moral principles and ideals that we believe the country should follow. Patriotism does not require passive acceptance of the particular policy choices and decisions that public officials make.

2. Forms of Patriotic Concern

We are now in a position to see that patriotism need not have the features that Tolstoy attributes to it and thus that it need not be open to the criticisms he makes. Moderate patriotism involves the following features:

1. Special affection for one's country
2. Desire that one's country prosper and flourish
3. Special but not exclusive concern for one's own country
4. Support of morally constrained pursuit of national goals
5. Conditional support of country's policies

People who possess these traits would be patriots but would not be chauvinists, jingoists, or xenophobes. They would be specially attached to their country without believing that it is best, without wanting it to dominate over others, and without feeling hostile toward others. However strong their sense of attachment to their own country, their patriotism would be moderated by their recognition of the humanity of people in other countries.

As I indicated above, I do not want to deny that chauvinism, jingoism, and xenophobia are forms of patriotism. My view is that because of their extremity, they are bad forms of patriotism. Nonetheless, they embody genuine forms of attachment to one's country. Both the moderate and extreme forms that I have described are species of a more general class of patriotic attitudes. Having described both of these special forms, it is worth having a general description of the more inclusive category of patriotism.

There are in fact two senses of the word "patriotism." In its most usual sense, "patriotism" is the name of a set of attitudes that a person may possess. In a second sense, it is the name for a certain kind of ideal or principle. This second sense, which stresses the "ism" in patriotism, is the general principle that patriotic attitudes are valuable and that we should take steps to encourage and promote patriotic attitudes in people.

The second sense of "patriotism" presupposes that we understand patriotism in its attitudinal, psychological sense. We can best define the general class of patriotic attitudes by listing the features that all patriots must possess. These features are:

1. Special affection for one's own country
2. A sense of personal identification with the country
3. Special concern for the well-being of the country
4. Willingness to sacrifice to promote the country's good

Any person with these four features is a patriot. Other attitudes, such as exclusive or nonexclusive concern, the belief or disbelief in national superiority, etc., are traits that patriots may or may not possess. These four attitudes, however, are essential.

Without special affection, a person would lack the love of country that is most frequently cited as the heart of patriotism. Beyond that, patriots feel a sense of identification with their country, a sense of "my-ness" that gives rise to feelings of pride when the country acts well or shame when it acts badly. One can only feel these attitudes about one's own country.[7] Normally, special affection and personal identification give rise to a special concern about the nation's well-being, and together, all of these traits generate a willingness to act on the country's behalf, even if this requires some sacrifice by a person. If such willingness to act and sacrifice is lacking, that would call into question whether the affection and concern that a person expresses are genuine. A person who merely professed these attitudes but was unwilling to act on them would be a hypocrite, not a patriot.

We can use this definition, then, as a criterion for the genuineness of patriotism, while continuing to remember that it is not a criterion for the goodness of patriotism, since both extreme and moderate patriotism possess the required traits.

The definition is also helpful in differentiating the patriot from the universalist. A universalist will be committed to the equal worth of all human beings and to equal activity on behalf of all people. Universalists might feel special affection for their own country and a special identification with it simply because it is the place where they have grown up. Nonetheless, they would not be specially committed to its well-being since, ultimately, they regard national boundaries and other differentiations among people as arbitrary. Hence, they would be committed to acting on behalf of any or all people and not primarily concerned with people of their own nation. They would only act on behalf of their own country if it had, so to speak, the best case (i.e., the greatest need or the most pressing rights) or if, given practical limits, it were the only country they were able to help.

3. Is Moderate Patriotism Defensible?

My main goal in offering a definition of patriotism and in distinguishing different forms of patriotism has been to describe a form of patriotism that would not be subject to the criticisms of Tolstoy and others who see patriotism as an impediment to peace and human cooperation. Does the moderate patriotism I have sketched achieve this?[8]

Tolstoy's main criticisms can be bluntly and concisely summarized. Patriotism, he argues, is stupid, immoral, a sham, and the cause of war.

Moderate patriotism, however, is not stupid because it is not committed to a false belief in the superiority of one's own nation. Nor is it immoral, since it recognizes that people in other countries have rights and that there are moral constraints on what any country can do to promote its own good.[9]

Whether moderate patriotism is a sham or not depends in part on whether those who espouse it are sincere in what they say. Tolstoy believed that all patriotism was an instrument of propaganda to generate support for unworthy government policies and for maintaining the power of public officials.[10] There is no doubt that patriotism is frequently used in this way. Nonetheless, moderate patriotism is much less useful for these purposes than is extreme patriotism. Since moderate patriotism permits and even encourages a critical attitude to government policies, it is not useful for bolstering either unjustified policies or the power of political officials. Like any other ideal (love, charity, religious devotion, etc.), patriotism may be invoked for ulterior motives or manipulated for evil purposes. The moderate patriotic conception, however, contains some built-in safeguards against these abuses that other forms of patriotism lack.

Finally, for all these reasons, moderate patriotism is not war-like or belligerent. It does not include the qualities of extreme patriotism that are conducive to war. Having excised the belief in superiority, the desire for dominance, exclusiveness of concern, and nonrecognition of moral constraints on national actions, moderate patriotism permits the pursuit of legitimate national goals by morally legitimate means but does not encourage belligerence, hostility, or aggression. It is, therefore, compatible with a commitment to international cooperation and the nonviolent solution of conflicts between nations. Because this is true, patriotism is not essentially or necessarily militaristic.

For these reasons, we can accept the validity of Tolstoy's arguments as they apply to extreme patriotism while rejecting them as a refutation of moderate patriotism. There is no reason to reject patriotism per se, though there are many reasons to reject the extreme forms of patriotism.

NOTES

1. For Tolstoy's criticisms, see his essays "On Patriotism" and "Patriotism, or Peace?" in *Tolstoy's Writings on Civil Disobedience and Non-Violence* (New York: New American Library, 1968.) Randolph Bourne also links war and patriotism in his powerful essay, "The State," in *War and the Intellectuals*, edited by Carl Resek (New York: Harper and Row, 1964). For the suggestion of a different view, however, see Bourne's "Trans-National America," reprinted in the same volume.

2. I develop and defend this view more fully in my book, *Patriotism, Morality, and Peace* (Lanham, MD:Rowman & Littlefield, 1993). This essay is a version of Chapter Three. I have also discussed these issues in the following papers: "In Defense of 'Moderate Patriotism'," *Ethics* 99, 535–552; "On Deciding Whether a Nation Deserves Our Loyalty," *Public Affairs Quarterly* 4, 287–298; and "Patriotism and the Pursuit of Peace," in *In the Interest of Peace*, edited by K. Klein and J. Kunkel (Wakefield, NH: Longwood Academic, 1990), 315–323..

3. For a succinct statement of a similar view, see the article on "patriotism" in Aldous Huxley, *An Encyclopedia of Pacifism* (New York: Garland Publishing, 1972), 87–88.

4. Tolstoy, *Writings*, 74f.

5. Translated by Eric Bentley (New York: Grove Press, 1966), 21.

6. For a brief discussion of defense strategies that aim to provide security without threatening others, see Harry Hollins *et al.*, *The Conquest of War* (Boulder, CO: Westview Press, 1989), chap. 7.

7. Cf. Andrew Oldenquist, "Loyalties," *Journal of Philosophy* 79, 173–93.

8. For the argument that moderate patriotism is defective because it is too critical, too conditional, and too constrained in its support of the nation, see Alasdair MacIntyre, "Is Patriotism a Virtue?" *The Lindley Lecture* (Lawrence, KS: University of Kansas Press, 1984). I reply to these "conservative" criticisms in "In Defense of 'Moderate Patriotism'" and in *Patriotism, Morality, and Peace*, chaps. 5 and 6.

9. Paul Gomberg argues that moderate patriotism is immoral and supports a more universalistic view in "Patriotism Is Like Racism," *Ethics* 101, 144–150. I reply to his objections in "Is Patriotism Like Racism?," *APA Newsletter on Philosophy and the Black Experience* 91:2, 9–11.

10. Tolstoy, *Writings*, 77.

THE CONCEPTS OF MILITARISM

David E. Johnson

1. The Role of Philosophy

A cursory glance at the morning paper discloses that our world is
besieged by regional struggles. As a result of these regional conflicts,
humanity is in great danger. I believe that any regional conflict has
the potential to expand into a nuclear confrontation. Tactical nuclear
weapons are even more attractive to military planners for use against
a regional power that cannot retaliate in kind than against a global
power that can retaliate in kind. Now that the U.S.S.R.'s client-
states, like Iraq, have lost their strategic nuclear umbrella, U.S.
military strategists may be even more tempted to use tactical nuclear
weapons against such states.

Einstein prophesied dangers from nuclear weapons.

> Our world faces a crisis as yet unperceived by those possessing the power to
> make decisions for good or evil. The unleashed power of the atom has
> changed everything save our modes of thinking, and thus we drift toward
> unparalleled catastrophe. We scientists who unleashed this immense power
> have an overwhelming responsibility in this world life-and-death struggle to
> harness the atom for the benefit of mankind and not for humanity's
> destruction.[1]

Reflecting on this passage as a philosopher, I am led to two
questions. What responsibility do philosophers bear *as philosophers*
in "this world life-and-death struggle?" Second, what can philosophers possibly do to benefit humanity and not increase the likelihood
of humanity's destruction?[2]

A helpful connotation of "philosophy" for my purposes comes
from the root meaning of the word "philosophy": "love of wisdom."
I contend that wisdom may be recognized by its fruits. Using this
criterion, I would argue that the global society in which we find
ourselves today provides clear evidence that we are not living wisely.
Crises in society and in nature, including war, starvation, unnecessary deaths (40,000+ children a day world-wide), spouse and child
abuse, erosion and pollution provide ample illustration of the
practical consequences of our stupidity. What, if anything, can
philosophers do about these problems? Are the crises too big for one
philosopher, or all philosophers, to do anything about? Are the crises
of a nature that philosophy is not the discipline to deal with them?

No! I agree with Einstein that we lack the fruits of wisdom and have the crises we do because of how we think (what we believe). If that diagnosis is correct, then philosophy is precisely the discipline to deal with part of what ails us.

As philosophers, we bear the responsibility of our *privilege* of having been educated in the language and skills of philosophy. We have been entrusted with skills in a powerful medium, and we must use those skills with care and caring.

2. Positive and Negative Peace

Those in power also have the power to define the world. They have the power to define concepts, to allocate prestigious words to their own thinking, and to stamp out the thinking of others through words that have a negative connotation.[3]

I am interested in the conceptual frameworks in which "peace" occurs. In what follows I will use "peace" in two senses: negative peace, meaning the absence of direct violence, and positive peace, meaning the absence of indirect or structural violence.[4] Discussions about policy generally focus on attaining negative peace because it is easier to observe that direct violence is not happening than to observe that conditions are promoting greater life expectancy or better quality of life. Further, in the scheme of things it would seem that negative peace must be achieved as a foundation on which to build positive peace. However, there are concepts, including equity, health, mutuality, respect and justice, that correlate with positive peace; and there are other concepts, including growth, greed, oppression, development, sexism, racism, classism, and militarism, that are obstacles to positive peace. It is obvious to me that the international or overseas military policies of the United States contribute to increased structural violence at home, that is, they reduce positive peace at home.

The world has been almost totally militarized.[5] By "militarization," I do not mean merely armed with nuclear weapons, or even armed with conventional weapons. Rather, militarization is a process in which increasing segments of our lives become dependent upon the military as an institution and as a way of thinking.[6] For example, an entire community can become economically dependent on a nearby military base so that members of the community cannot tolerate the thought of closing the base. Therefore, I do not think that "disarmament" is a sufficiently broad or deep category with which to grapple with the mentality of militarism in our world. There are thousands of defence and strategy intellectuals who are grappling with disarmament. My concern with that focus is that even if we achieve massive nuclear disarmament (for instance, down to some sort of minimum deterrent), a disarmed military will still be a military. That is, there will still be an institution with the belief that violence is certainly the last and probably the best means of resolving conflicts. For instance, superpowers will still try to keep others from going to war by threatening them with superior military power. In fact, given the way our world is organized, negative peace depends on a context of militarization.

3. A Critique of "Peace Through Strength"

How has this massive militarization been justified? Let us turn to two of our basic militaristic beliefs and the justifications offered for them. The first belief is that peace can only be achieved through a strong military. The second is that it is morally acceptable for some people to dominate others, particularly by the use of military force, thereby making them economically dependent. I want to analyze how we do think by examining these two crucial beliefs, and then point out how we could think by presenting an alternative vision of the future.[7]

The first belief is summed up in the slogan, "Peace Through Strength." Ronald Reagan illustrated this approach to the abolition of war with his reliance on what he alleged was an ancient Roman maxim, "If you would have peace, prepare for war." This "Peace Through Strength" approach tries to keep hot war from breaking out by deterring one's opponent through fear.[8] We see the continued growth of militarization exemplified in huge military budgets and a lively arms trade. Note that here we are dealing with "negative peace."

One argument against this "Peace through Strength" approach is that it in fact has not achieved its stated aims. The Reagan program, enacted at great cost to the American economy and increased suffering for many of the American people, has proved to be unworkable. We have less peace (both positive and negative) and security now than in 1980. Instead, this approach has massively produced the fruits of unwisdom. The natural and social worlds have become less sustainable, and the features of society that make it worth defending have decreased in value and amount. Factors in domestic as well as international society that led to more violence have increased, including (1) more poverty, (2) an increasing gap between haves and have-nots, and (3) a shaky economy that makes many men and women feel less secure. The only benefit I see from the Reagan program is that by bankrupting the U.S. economy, it has begun to open more people's eyes to the absurdities of that program. From that heightened awareness hopefully we will see more and more people stand up to oppose the slide into social and environmental destruction by calling for the abolition of war and an end to the militarization of our lives.[9]

A second argument against the "Peace through Strength" approach is that it has opened us to greater risk of annihilation through the chance of technical or human failure of the process of preparing for war. Technical failure can be illustrated in our recent lives by the Chernobyl accident and the explosion of the shuttle Challenger. Both of these technical systems were touted publicly by their governments to be models of safety and freedom from accident. Human failure can be seen in the insanity of autocratic leaders, including Hitler and Stalin. But the western democracies are not immune to the problem of human failure either, as illustrated by the end of the career of Secretary Forrestal, which was characterized by severe mental illness leading to suicide. People subject to emotional breakdown *can* have their finger on the button in countries with very diverse political systems. Instead of enhancing security *and peace*, with this approach people's lives are degraded, the quality of life goes down, and the natural environment degenerates.

4. Domination of the "Other"

The use of our great military power to provoke and engage in regional conflicts rests on the moral acceptability of dominating those who are different from us. By "dominate" I mean to control and/or exploit the lives of other people as well as the natural environment for one's narrow advantage. The underlying assumption of domination is that difference denotes inferiority.[10] A few examples of the application of this assumption to nature by many humans include: the conclusion often drawn from the biblical story of Genesis that human beings have the right (or god-given privilege) to dominate the planet earth and all the other species on it,[11] Descartes' soul/body distinction in which matter does not or cannot think, and the vehement rejection of Darwin's theory by much of the religious community as soon as it was perceived to imply continuity among species. In our present culture the world over, most men in general and the military in particular regard women as "other" and inferior.[12] And the perception of women as close to nature has intensified the domination of both. Consider what Fritjhof Capra has to say about the metaphors of the new Baconian science.

> The terms in which Bacon advocated his new empirical method of investigation were not only passionate but often outright vicious. Nature, in his view, had to be 'hounded in her wanderings,' 'bound into service,' and made a 'slave.' She was to be 'put in constraint,' and the aim of the scientist was to 'torture nature's secrets from her.' Much of this violent imagery seems to have been inspired by the witch trials that were held frequently in Bacon's time. As attorney general for King James I, Bacon was intimately familiar with such prosecutions, and because nature was commonly seen as female, it is not surprising that he should carry over the metaphors used in the courtroom into his scientific writings. Indeed, his view of nature as a female whose secrets have to be tortured from her with the help of mechanical devices is strongly suggestive of the widespread torture of women in the witch trials of the early seventeenth century. Bacon's work thus represents an outstanding example of the influence of patriarchal attitudes on scientific thought.[13]

The assumption that "anything on planet earth different in kind from me is inferior to me or to my kind" can be observed in the attitudes of colonizing Europeans and Americans to indigenous people, at about the same time as the rise of modern science under the impetus of Bacon. The people of the metropolitan nations who set out to establish colonies neither knew nor understood the cultures of the indigenous people whom they dominated by means of weapons, deceit, alcohol and disease.

I suspect that the indigenous people were regarded as inferior because of their closeness to nature—that is, their evolved ability to live in harmony with nature.[14] For instance, the aboriginal in Australia had evolved over tens of thousands of years to a fine-tuned harmony with nature.[15] European cultures, highly artificial, which, to me, means increasingly separated from nature, felt superior to cultures highly natural—to the point of regarding them as sub-human or non-human.

It is widely documented and acknowledged that militaries, in order to motivate their troops to kill fellow human beings, present enemies as sub-human, as in the cases of the gooks of VietNam, the Huns of World War II, and the evil empire of the Cold War. The aboriginal Australian writer Kevin Gilbert has pointed out that the activity of bombing Hiroshima and Nagasaki were regarded by the scientists involved in the Manhattan Project as "experiments." Perhaps the scientists believed they could destroy innocent people and pollute nature, including genes, because their superiority in intellect and technology supposedly gave them the "right" to do so.[16] These intertwined beliefs, that the other is inferior and that the superior should dominate, have produced many of the fruits of militarism's un-wisdom that we suffer, suffer under, and suffer from today.[17] If militarism casts the "other" as sub-human, then it stands to reason that those who operate from the perspective of militarism often feel no qualms about deliberately keeping third world peoples in poverty in order to enhance their own prosperity.

5. Domination of the Poor by the Rich

The Australian historian Humphrey McQueen writes about a "world civil war" between the rich and the poor.[18] This observation has been borne out in U.S. foreign policy. When George Kennan was head of the State Department Policy Planning Staff in 1948, he explicitly stated that we are going to have to use our military powers to perpetuate an imbalance in the distribution of the world's resources.

> We have about 50 percent of the world's wealth but only 6.3 percent of its population. In this situation, we cannot fail to be the object of envy and resentment. Our real task in the coming period is to devise a pattern of relationships which will permit us to maintain this position of disparity without positive detriment to our national security. To do so we will have to dispense with all sentimentality and day-dreaming; and our attention will have to be concentrated everywhere on our immediate national objectives. We need not deceive ourselves that we can afford today the luxury of altruism and world benefaction...we should cease to talk about vague and—for the Far East—unreal objectives such as human rights, the raising of living standards, and democratization. The day is not far off when we are going to have to deal in straight power concepts. The less we are then hampered by idealistic slogans, the better.[19]

Kennan is clear that the military might of the rich nations must be used to maintain the status quo of an inequitable distribution of the world's resources. Of course, following Clausewitz's concept of the relation of diplomacy and warfare, we first use diplomacy under the guise of third world development. Then, if the third world does not appreciate that doctrine, we come in with our military to enforce our material (economic) advantage.

We have devised a "pattern of relationships...to maintain this position of disparity without positive detriment to our national security." The rich nations acquire most of the world's resources by bidding more for them in the international marketplace. Inappropriate development produces Hilton hotels and export plantations that benefit the third world rich, the transnational corporations and consumers in rich nations.

This inappropriate development does not "trickle down" any wealth to the poor people in the Third World. (One billion people are desperately poor, at least 500 million are hungry, and living standards in the poorest half of the world's people are not improving much.) Instead, the rich nations prop up dictatorships that are willing to perpetuate economies that benefit the rich nations. When any move is made by poor people to change to an approach to development that would primarily benefit the poor, that move is branded as subversion, usually "communist," and military aid is sent to stamp it out.[20] This is one of the ways in which the militarism of the "overdeveloped" nations contributes to regional conflicts, including conflicts in Palestine, Nicaragua, El Salvador, and South Africa. Our willingness to dominate those who are different results in the impoverishment of those who are different. And this poverty results in a definite lack of positive peace.

As far as I can see, there are only three options in the distribution of the world's resources. One, we can maintain the status quo. The consequence will necessitate participating in regional conflicts like those we are in now. Second, standards in the third world can be raised to equal those in the first world. On this option the resources of the planet will be exhausted in a short time unless we are able to find a "technological fix" that will enable all of us on planet earth to meet our needs. Third, we can reduce the standard of living in the first world in order to distribute more resources to the third world. This raises the issue, which I will not discuss here, of how to assess social or distributive justice.[21] But at least we can recognize injustice in the sense of a great disparity in meeting people's basic needs for clean water, inexpensive food, basic health services and education.

Ted Trainer writes, "Our affluent life-styles require us to be heavily armed and belligerent, i.e., to guard the empires from which we draw resources...we cannot expect to achieve a peaceful world until we achieve a just world, and we cannot do that until rich countries change to much less extravagant living standards." I agree with Trainer: if you want peace, you have to prepare for peace. The best way I can think of to promote peace is to work for justice.

6. Conclusion

This paper has shown that negative peace depends on a context of militarism; that militarism rests on rejecting and dominating those who are different; and that this domination in turn results in poverty, that is, a lack of positive peace. For the sake of humanity and of the environment, it is necessary to abolish various causes of violence in our lives.[22] As individuals and small groups, philosophers can promote the humanizing of people and the reclamation of the environment by doing more forcefully and publicly what philosophers have done through the ages: asking critical questions, scrutinizing fundamental beliefs (our own and those of the society in which we live), and analyzing the concepts in which those beliefs are stated in order to assist the process of clarification which will benefit all of us.[23]

NOTES

1. Quoted in Dorothy Green and David Headon, eds., *Imagining the Real: Australian Writing in the Nuclear Age* (Sydney: ABC Enterprises, 1987), 7.

2. The topic of this book is very timely because humankind (in terms of peace) and the environment (in terms of degradation) are in crisis because of regional conflicts. Some have labelled the decade of the 1990s the "turn-around decade" in the sense that if we do not start to reverse these unwise trends during the 1990s, we may not have another chance. I want to deal with the question, "How can philosophy benefit humanity and the natural environment?" I will answer: "By analyzing the conceptual foundations of militarism."

3. Birgit Brock-Utne, *Educating for Peace* (New York: Pergamon Press, 1985), 147. An example she gives of male bias in naming what women do is Marx and Engels subordinating reproduction (making babies) to production (e.g., making weapons), 21. Sarah Hoagland points out that 'feminine' is defined so that a woman who remains submissive to men is characterized as "normal," while a woman who gets angry and fights back is characterized as "insane" or "mad," or trivialized by

such comments as "You're so cute when you're angry." Sarah Lucia Hoagland, *Lesbian Ethics* (Palo Alto, CA: Institute of Lesbian Studies, 1988), 178.

4. Birgit Brock-Utne, *Feminist Perspectives on Peace and Peace Education* (New York: Pergamon Press, 1989), 44–65. Brock-Utne goes into a much more detailed analysis of the phrase "positive peace" than is possible in this short paper.

5. I am indebted to discussions with Cynthia Enloe and to reading her *Does Khaki Become You?* (Boston: Pandora, 1988), for clarifications about the process of militarization.

6. Maryland Sane/Freeze released information in October 1991 that indicated that residents of Maryland paid more in taxes to support the federal defense budget than they paid to support the State of Maryland. In late 1991 and early 1992 there were large cuts in jobs and social services in Maryland.

7. Some might argue that presenting visions of a better society is not a proper function of philosophy. However, philosophers have traditionally used their creative imaginations to offer visions of alternative futures, going back at least as far as Plato in the *Republic*.

8. This approach also assumes that the opponent will play by our rules of rational behavior, which some, for example, Saddam Hussein, apparently will not.

9. I contend that one perfectly legitimate function of philosophy is illustrated in the way Socrates went about doing philosophy. He tried to increase the awareness of those with whom he talked about the assumptions in their thinking. These included assumptions made by the individual as well as assumptions generally held in their culture.

10. Philosophical support for this can be found in Plato, Aristotle, Kant, Hegel's master/slave morality, and Nietzsche's will-to-power. In other words, our own discipline has contributed to the position I am arguing against.

11. This is one interpretation of the creation story in the Judeo-Christian tradition in the book of *Genesis*.

12. Mary Daly quoting George Gilder on training in Marine Corps boot camp: "From the moment one arrives, the drill instructors begin a torrent of misogynistic and anti-individualist abuse. The good things are manly and collective; the despicable are feminine and individual. Virtually every sentence, every description, every lesson embodies this sexual duality, and the female anatomy provides a rich field of metaphor for every degradation. When you want to create a solidary group of male killers, that is what you do, you kill the women in them. That is the lesson of the Marines. And it works." Mary Daly, *Gyn/Ecology* (Boston: Beacon Press, 1978), 358.

13. Fritjhof Capra, *The Turning Point* (London: Fontana Paperbacks, 1982), 40–41.

14. "Savages" = df uncultivated, wild, uncivilized, in primitive state; brutally cruel or barbarous person. *The Concise Oxford Dictionary of Current English*, 5th ed. (London: Oxford University Press, 1964), 1118.

15. Wildlife rangers in Australia (e.g., at Ayer's Rock) are adopting ancient aboriginal practices of land management because of their success in providing a sustainable life for the inhabitants. This fact was disclosed to me in conversations with park rangers in Australia in August 1990.

16. Brian Easlea, *Fathering the Unthinkable: Masculinity, Scientists and the Nuclear Arms Race* (London: Pluto Press, 1983).

17. Need it be the case that acknowledging differences and boundaries involve antagonisms? In common parlance we chat about the "war of the sexes." In fact the "warfare" metaphor seems to be an important way of conceptualizing in the present age—consider the "war on poverty" and now the "war on drugs" in the U.S.

18. Green and Headon, *Imagining the Real*, 85.

19. Policy Planning Study 23, 24 February 1948, FRUS 1948, 1 [part 23]. Quoted in *In These Times*, 10–16 October 1990.

20. The position outlined here is presented in the writings of Australian scholar, Ted Trainer, University of New South Wales.

21. For instance, look at the obstacles thrown in the way of such a definition by Walter Kaufmann, *Without Guilt and Justice* (New York: Dell Publishing, 1973).

22. Moves in this direction will involve dealing with the interconnected "-isms" of domination, including sexism, racism, classism, and militarism.

23. Do philosophers form a community? Does a relatively small grouping of philosophers like Concerned Philosophers for Peace form a community? Is there something philosophers as a group can do? That may be difficult because we tend to regard ourselves as individuals. Judging from the annual business meetings of the divisions of the American Philosophical Association, I am not sure we could reach consensus on any proposed course of *action.*

AUGUSTINE'S STANCE ON WAR

Warren Harrington

St. Augustine of Hippo's writings have influenced for centuries the moral values of Western Europe. He was pivotal in the tradition of thinking about just war since he was the first major Christian philosopher to justify war and participation in it. Augustine's views on war were taken over entirely by St. Thomas Aquinas. Together, these two giants of Latin Christian thought have influenced religious and secular ethicists and legists down to our own time.

As just war thinking has reached its limits in the twentieth century's experience of war, the time is ripe to review Augustine's stance and develop a critique. At present, other weaknesses in Augustine's moral thought are under examination. For example, his well known concept of "original sin" is widely questioned and his views on marriage and sex are under attack. A critique of his stance on war is in order and a step in that direction is the aim of this paper.

1. Christianity's Stance Before Augustine

For its first three centuries, the Christian movement relied on the power of prayer, the power of persuasion, and the power of moral example to promote its own growth and to resolve external and internal conflicts. Christians did not serve in the Roman military and chose at times to die as martyrs rather than worship the genius of Caesar and the state. A typical view of war held by Christians before Augustine is represented in a text from Origen's *Contra Celsum*. Origen defends the Christians against a charge of lack of patriotism and service to the Emperor and gives us insight into how early Christians understood their obligations to the state and Emperor.

> At appropriate times we render to the Emperors divine help, if I may so say, by taking up even the whole armor of God. And this we do in obedience to the apostolic utterance which says:
>
> I exhort you, therefore, first to make prayers, supplications, intercessions, and thanksgivings for all men, for emperors, and all that are in authority.
>
> Indeed, the more pious a man is, the more effective he is in helping the emperors—more so than soldiers who go out into lines and kill all the enemy troops that they can. [1]

Origen clearly holds that the traditional non-violent service of the Christians is more effective of the public good than is fighting in the front lines of war. What happened to change this view so prevalent among Christians of the first four centuries and Augustine's role in the change of outlook needs to be considered.

2. Origins of Augustine's Stance

A major factor contributing to this shifting view seems all too obvious: the Empire became officially Christian and ambitious politicians became Christian for career purposes. Likewise the Church's leaders became men of stature in Imperial affairs. So too with Augustine. His education shaped him to admire Rome and tolerate her wars. Augustine was a bright and ambitious pupil who benefitted from the best education available in his day. As a student of rhetoric, preparing with his father's encouragement for a career in public service, he made his way from the remote town of Thagaste in North Africa to the liveliest center of the western empire, Milan, where he established himself for a time as professor of rhetoric. Nothing in his autobiographical *Confessions* indicates that he had any doubts in his formative years about imperial ways and policy. He thought little of Christianity and regarded it as intellectually dull. After his conversion he inclined to private life, but it was not accorded him; he was called to be Bishop of Hippo in his native North Africa. While his talents were many, he was forced to absorb the Christian heritage speedily and he lacked ability in Greek which cut him off from much of the earlier Christian literature of great thinkers.

Augustine very quickly became a powerful insider in the official church of the empire who could use the art of rhetoric he had learned before becoming a Christian in service of pastoral and imperial ends, and toward the same ends invoke the aid of imperial force in governance of his church. Augustine's rhetorical training is evident on every page he wrote. An equally extensive training in interpreting the Christian heritage of opposition to war is not evident.

Augustine's thought on war is not systematic. His scattered remarks are those of a pastor who wanted to help soldiers and policy makers for the Empire. Much of what Augustine wrote on war and being a soldier is buried in discussions of other topics. It will be necessary for us, therefore, to pay careful attention to Augustine's disparate thoughts on war in order to see how he resolved tensions between commonly accepted Imperial views, on which he was raised, and opposing Christian attitudes with which he was becoming familiar. Key texts are found in his *Contra Faustum* and *De Civitate Dei* and in letters of pastoral advice. These texts contain somewhat lengthy reflections on the topic of war or the role of the soldier. All of these texts date from the later part of Augustine's life when he bore pastoral responsibility as a bishop and when he had the backing of the imperial authorities. In a certain sense Augustine was a functionary in the imperial order whose right to war he advocated.

3. *Contra Faustum*

Augustine's method at this time was to turn first to Roman common sense and then to probe the Christian Scriptures from that vantage point. He settles the essential question of the rightness of war using Roman common sense. Next he suggests that a Christian religious obedience is involved in war. Finally, he turns to a reading of the Christian Scriptures, interpreting them in such a way as to pose no obstacle to common sense's verdict and in ways which appear to gainsay their obvious intent.

In the *Contra Faustum* of 397, two years after becoming Bishop of Hippo, Augustine begins his discussion of war by appealing to a common understanding of the rightness of it. "A monarch should have the power of undertaking war if he thinks it advisable, and soldiers should perform their military duties in behalf of the peace and safety of the community" (22:74).[2] Augustine is not attempting here to persuade as much as to state the obvious. He is drawing on common sense. His understanding of war's morality seems rooted in the high value he finds in the "peace and safety of the community."

Augustine's Roman roots and his attitudes towards death and soldiering can be seen in comments about war's evil made in this same treatise of 397. "What is the evil of war?" he asks. "Is it the death of someone who will die soon in any case, that others may live in peaceful subjection? This is mere cowardly dislike not any religious feeling" (22:74). These rhetorical questions and this dismissive judgment against those who mourn the physical evil and death of war arise easily out of Augustine's background. Antiquity's pessimism about the brevity of life colors Augustine's attitude here and he readily praises a Roman soldier's courage and disdains cowardice. He does not seem to advert to the courage of earlier Christians in refusing Imperial service. Further we note that he has a sense that peace may involve a subjection and that the need to avoid such subjugation is a value which justifies loss of a soldier's life.

Not only is war not morally wrong, for Augustine, at this stage, war rights moral wrongs.

> The real evils in war are love of violence, revengeful cruelty, fierce and implacable enmity, wild resistance and the lust of power and such like; and it is generally to punish these things, when force is required to inflict the punishment, that, in obedience to God or some lawful authority, good men undertake wars. (22:74)

For purposes of punishing moral evils, Augustine thinks, good men obediently undertake wars. This is the first place in which Augustine suggests that war may be obedience to God.

This claim that good men make war in obedience to God places Augustine at variance with preceding centuries of Christian tradition in accord with which Christians had refrained not only from participation in war but also from holding public office for fear of being required to participate.[3] Augustine offers no rationale for his claim, however, and we are left to wonder what is the basis for it.

As new bishop and pastor, Augustine next turns to texts of the Scripture, wherein he claims to find no contradiction of his stance. Augustine uses, for example, the text in Luke which tells of John the Baptist's advice to Roman legionaries that they be content with their pay. The Gospel text itself makes no reference to the rightness of the career of a soldier. It simply reports John's advice to those who already were embarked on such a career. Augustine argues, however, that if the soldier's career were evil, John the Baptist would have told them to throw away their arms, give up the service and never strike, wound or disable anyone. Augustine's is, of course, an argument from silence, a claim of what surely would have been and not an argument rooted in what actually is said.

A modern biblical scholar approaches the text quite differently. Today, the key question brought to Luke's text asks about Luke's purpose and intention in telling the story.[4] Augustine seems to be interested in the intention of John the Baptist, a personage whose purpose can be discerned only indirectly from the various and not always consistent accounts in the gospels. The modern reading of Luke's text focuses on its function in Luke's narrative. Therein, this story portrays John as very demanding of his followers, yet setting a moral goal which even Roman legionaries would be capable of enfleshing. Luke contrasts John's demands with the extremely more demanding ethic of Jesus as presented in the Sermon on the Plain, Chapter 6. Luke's point seems to be that the follower of Jesus must go beyond the justice of John the Baptist which is consistent with Caesar's justice and adopt the teaching of Jesus which demands imitation of the divine compassion. From this perspective, the scripture implies that obedience to Roman authority is not a high enough moral performance. I recognize that it is anachronistic to hold Augustine to the standards of twentieth century redaction criticism but it is equally anachronistic to repeat Augustine's interpretation in support of war and military service. Augustine uncritically accepted the Imperial view of war and could not see the thrust of opposition in the entire gospel of Luke.

Augustine seems not to have entertained thoughts of alternative solutions for the moral evils on his list. The search for non-violent solutions to conflict and non-punitive reversals of evil attitudes and intents does not arouse his energy. There seems further an implication that, in the conduct of a war of punishment, its good and godly obedient wagers would be free from moral evil themselves. He failed to see that the scriptures he used to support his views can also be read as pointing towards moral alternatives to war.

4. Letter to Marcellinus

Marcellinus, Imperial Commissioner at Carthage, wrote Augustine for help in discussions about several topics of the faith with Volusian, a Pagan senator from Carthage. Marcellinus is seeking a letter marked by "that shining splendor of Roman eloquence" (Letter 136:1) for which Augustine is famous. One concern is with the uniqueness of Jesus: how, the Pagans ask, might he differ from magicians such as Apollonius and Apuleius? Another concern is about the proper role of sacrifice, and another about the charge that Jesus' preaching and doctrine were not adaptable to the customs of the state, especially war. Of particular concern are the teaching about turning the other cheek and the principle, "Render to no one evil for evil" (Rom. 12:17). Volusian and his friends ask, "Who would not wish to return evil, as the law of war allows, to the ravager of a Roman province?" Are these Christians truly loyal supporters of the Emperor and his right to make war?

Augustine wrote the letter to Marcellinus in 412, a year before he began work on *The City of God*. In it, he argues against a literal reading of the text on turning the cheek and not rendering evil for evil. Instead, he offers a psychological explanation. The text on not rendering evil is to be understood as calling for "refraining from the passion of revenge—in other words, choosing, when one has suffered wrong, to pardon rather than punish the offender, and to forget nothing but the wrongs done to us" (138:9). Thus, use of force without revenge is "not rendering evil for evil."

These precepts pertain rather to the inward disposition of the heart than to the actions done in the sight of others, requiring us, in inmost heart, to cherish patience along with benevolence, but in the outward action to do that which seems most likely to benefit those whose good we ought to seek (138:11). Thus the teaching does not rule out forceful, even coercive, actions if they have practical value. Punishment is even justified, so long as it is not vengeful.

Augustine next claims that the Christian teachings are in accord with the noblest ideals and performance of Roman tradition. Augustine asks how it was possible that the Republic of Rome was able to grow and prosper, to move from obscurity and poverty to greatness and opulence, if the leading men lived by a code of vengeance. To the contrary, argues Augustine, Rome's founders and benefactors were men who "when they had suffered wrong, would rather pardon than punish the offender" (138:9). Indeed, turning the cheek was practiced by Rome's forebears and has practical, persuasive value. Turning the cheek is done, Augustine reminds Marcellinus, "that a wicked man may be overcome by kindness." One senses here Augustine's wish to promote Christianity as the official religion.

On the basis of this interpretation of the scriptural teaching, Augustine turns to the conduct of war and calls for an ethic of good intention and benevolent design. If the Commonwealth observes the precepts of the Christian religion, even its wars themselves will not be carried on without benevolent design that, after the resisting nations have been conquered, provision may be more easily made for enjoying in peace the mutual bond of piety and justice (138:14).

5. Letter to Boniface

In a letter written approximately 418, Augustine urged Boniface, the Count of Africa, an Arian Goth and professional general, to remain a soldier despite his inclination to monastic life. Augustine needed the force Boniface represented against the Donatists, a dissident Christian group with which he was in conflict. Augustine's letter speaks in terms of the ideal for the Christian soldier.

The soldier as peace-maker is Augustine's theme when he asks Boniface to be mindful that his very bodily strength is a gift from God and faith is to be kept with the enemy against whom war is waged. "Peace should be the object of your desire; war should be waged only as a necessity, and waged only that God may by it deliver men from the necessity and preserve them in peace. Let necessity, therefore, and not your will, slay the enemy who fights against you" (189:6). For Augustine, necessitated war, conducted with the proper interior dispositions, takes precedence as a Christian practice over the freely chosen life of a monk. He paved the way for an ethic of correct *interior dispositions* to overcome centuries of Christian insistence on *practice* of alternatives to violence.

6. *City of God*

In the famous Book XXII of *City of God*, written in 425, Augustine treats war in the context of a discussion of the divine permission of evil in order that greater good may come. His attention in Book XXII is directed to eternity and his effort to understand evil is conducted *sub specie aeternitatis*.

In *City of God*, Augustine argues that, on the basis of the state's natural right to permanent existence, it has a right to engage in war. Here Augustine draws on Cicero's *De Re Publica*, in which Cicero asserted that the Roman republic is naturally immortal and that Roman conquest brings greater safety. Here Augustine says "death is not natural to a republic as to a man, to whom death is not only necessary, but often even desirable. But, when a state is destroyed, obliterated, annihilated, it is as if (to compare great things with small) this whole world perished and collapsed"(XXII,6). To prevent this cataclysmic evil, the lesser evil of war is therefore justified.

Again, Augustine's view, following Cicero's, seems particularly Romano-centric. A claim to natural permanence for the state is not historically convincing. Quite to the contrary, states come and go in history. Nor is a claim of the rightness of the state's continued existence defensible.

7. Summary

Augustine, educated for a life of public service in the late Roman Empire, sees war as morally right. In his view, the monarch may wage war on his own authority. The soldier is to obey dutifully without question for the safety of the political community, which has an unquestionable right to exist. War's moral rightness further derives from its being a punishment for moral evils of enemies. In that sense, war carries out the will of God. If the interior motives of policy makers are untainted by the desire for revenge, their actions do not contradict Christian teachings on nonviolence. Benevolent intention confers rightness on acts of war. A soldier's duty is to obey without question and he may regard his role as one of peace maker.

This stance has the ring of nobility and high purpose but seems remarkably removed from the actualities of war and the likely motives of participants. It may be possible for an Augustine to slay without ignoble motives but such a trait is not common.

It is questionable whether the decision to make war is rightly made by a monarch. It is questionable whether soldiers must obey blindly. It is questionable that one side only in war deserves punishment. It is questionable that the evils of war are willed by God. It is questionable that interior motives make acts of war right. A major purpose of Augustine clearly is to assure his readers that war and being a soldier are consistent with the teaching of the Christian scriptures, but it is questionable whether Augustine's hermeneutic is adequate. For all that Augustine's virtue and genius may be admired, for all his influence in the Middle Ages and later, his role in providing guidance in contemporary discussions of the morality of war is severely limited and criticizable.

NOTES

1. Origen, *Contra Celsum*, translated by Henry Chadwick, VIII: 73.

2. Citations of Augustine follow standard book or chapter divisions and paragraph divisions found, for example in the series *The Fathers of the Church* (Washington: Catholic University Press, 1947).

3. Origen, *Contra Celsum*, VIII: 75.

4. Among many redactional studies are Richard J. Cassidy, *Jesus, Politics and Society: A Study of Luke's Gospel* (Maryknoll, NY: Orbis, 1978) and *Political Issues in Luke–Acts* (Maryknoll, NY: Orbis, 1983), and J.M. Ford, *My Enemy Is My Guest: Jesus and Violence in Luke* (Maryknoll, NY: Orbis, 1984).

WOMEN AS PEACEMAKERS: CONTESTED TERRAIN FOR FEMINIST PEACE STUDIES

Linda Rennie Forcey

This end-of-the-century decade is one of global transformation and destabilization. For peace studies optimists it holds the promise of a more peaceful world order; if not this decade, or the next, then perhaps in three or four. In the past decade, on the other hand, we have witnessed throughout the world numerous regional wars and low-intensity conflicts, unparalleled "peacetime" military expenditures, and unparalleled concentration of wealth in many countries including the United States. As for the latter, we are told that there has been "no parallel upsurge of riches...since the late nineteenth century."[1] The gap between rich and poor has widened virtually everywhere, placing mothers and children in increasingly precarious economic positions and allowing tens of thousands of children each day to die of preventable causes throughout the world. And it is men, with few exceptions, who continue to rule and lead, to hold the positions of responsibility in the public realm.

What is going on? Where are the voices of women, the caretakers of the world, the hands that rock the cradles? The connection between women and peace is ancient; peace is often symbolized as the mother, the preserver of life, the angel in the house. Appeals to peace have often been made in the name of children, and we have a long history of women as peace activists. Is it not women who possess the special peacemaking skills for a new, more peaceful, and more just world order? These are among the questions that place peace researchers squarely in the center of the contemporary feminist debate about the nature and power of women and the social construction of gender.

But do women have something special to say about a new more peaceful world order? Do they have special peacemaking skills based on their roles as nurturers that can be universalized? Or is the very asking of such questions part of the age-old trap of oversimplifying the notion of "woman," denying her differences with other women and with men, and thereby lessening her power? Most important for me as a feminist peace researcher, peace educator, and peace activist, what are the political implications of these questions? With which theories and strategies can women best be mobilized for peace?

What I have to say here is prelude to a study of women thinking about peace and implications of such thoughts for the peace studies classroom. This article outlines the feminist theoretical debate among three groups: (1) those arguing that women's differences from men should be minimized in the fight for equity in education, employment, and the law (the equality position); (2) those holding that women, for any number of reasons related to their nurturing'qualities and mothering responsibilities, are essentially different from men—essentially nicer, kinder, gentler (the essentialist position); and (3) those arguing that because language itself is socially constructed, no categories of women are natural or inevitable and attempts to categorize must be resisted (the poststructuralist position).

When we integrate feminist theoretical perspectives with feminist peace research in the interdisciplinary field of peace studies, we find, not surprisingly, that the feminist theoretical debate is replicated in feminist peace research. At present feminist peace research takes the essentialist standpoint, emphasizing the caring, relational, mothering qualities of women. This feminism remains, currently, an important new catalyst to challenge militarism by the posing of a set of questions very different from those traditionally asked by (mostly male) practitioners in both international relations and peace studies. It should be noted, too, that while feminist peace researchers generally take an essentialist position, they are not comfortable with this label. They clearly acknowledge the dangers and pitfalls of such polarized thinking.

After considering feminist analyses of women's diverse experiences as peacemakers and nonpeacemakers at levels from the familial to the international, I conclude that the argument that women because of their nurturing capacities are essentially different from, and perhaps on some levels better at peacemaking than, men should be neither dismissed out of hand nor embraced as the truth. Rather, I argue for a more complex picture, one that sees the essentialists and their poststructural critics as part of the changing social construction of gender. I argue that both positions are politically vital catalysts for developing strategies for change: a "don't throw the baby out with the bath water" position.

My article, therefore, calls, first, for feminist appreciation of the contribution of an essentialist viewpoint to peace research, activism, and pedagogy; second, for feminist appreciation of the importance of the poststructuralist critique of essentialism; and, third, the need to move beyond the debate with a finely tuned appreciation of a variety of approaches and a tolerance for ambiguity and more than a little theoretical untidiness.

1. Defining the Terms

For those readers unfamiliar with the language of either feminism or peace studies, definitions of mothering, feminism, and peace studies are used in the discussion to follow are in order.

Mothering is a socially constructed set of activities and relationships involved in nurturing and caring for people.[2] It is also the main vehicle through which people first form their identities and learn their place in society. As Sara Ruddick points out, mothering is the procedure by which children learn "mother-tongue," a special language in which children assimilate "a sense of what can be named and what must remain secret; what is unavoidably given and what can be changed; who is to be feared and whose authority is only a sham."[3] At the heart of mothering as it is commonly understood in contemporary Western society is an ethic of caring—of knowing, feeling, and acting in the interests of another. Although mothering usually refers to the thoughts and activities of women who have willingly assumed the responsibility for the caring, nurturing, and socialization of their biological, adopted, or step children, the process of defining mothering is not this simple or clear-cut. I have all "caring labor" in mind when I speak of mothering—from birthing labor to all kinds of teaching, to care of the disabled and of the frail elderly.[4] This is because all women, and some men too, have in one way or another internalized the socially constructed mandates of mothering in their given societies at any given point in time.

As for feminism, the general working definition with which I am comfortable takes as proven the historical oppression of women and stresses the interrelationship of theory and practice to eliminate it. As Virginia Sapiro tells us:

> Feminism is both a way of thinking about the world, and a way of acting in it…[It] is a perspective that views gender as one of the most important bases of the structure and organization of the social world. Feminists argue that in most known societies this structure has granted women lower status and value, more limited access to valuable resources, and less autonomy and opportunity to make choices over their lives than it has granted men. Feminists further believe that although this gender-based world may be organized around biological facts such as the exclusive capacity of men to

create sperm and the exclusive capacity of women to bear children, gender inequality is due to the social construction of human experience, which means that it should be possible to eradicate it.[5]

Feminism, as I view it, is both a way of viewing the world and an evolving social movement. As noted previously, feminism does not embrace one theoretical approach, but rather several. This article will focus on the contributions of (1) the essentialist viewpoint that holds that women are essentially different from men (nicer, kinder, gentler) and should be so regarded in analyses of peace, power, and gender and of (2) its feminist critics (post-structuralists and others) who argue that essentialists have been oblivious to the social construction of language itself, leaving women resistant to change and insensitive to the diverse experiences among women.

Finally, peace studies, as defined by one widely accepted guide, is a relatively new, interdisciplinary field that "analyzes the causes of war, violence, and systemic oppression, and explores processes by which conflict and change can be managed so as to maximize justice while minimizing violence." It includes "the study of economic, political and social systems at the local, national and global levels, and of ideology, culture, and technology as they relate to conflict and change."[6] One of its primary and most controversial assumptions centers on the interrelationship of peace research, peace education, and peace action.[7]

There are within the field, of course, widely divergent definitions of peace, much controversy over issues of an "implicit ideological bias," and even more worry about the "activist orientation" of peace studies curricula. My definition focuses on the values, norms, and institutions of peace. It incorporates such concepts as structural violence, racism, sexism, class, religious and ethical perspectives, international law, and global cooperation. It leans toward the proactive and methodologically qualitative bent of many, if not most, of the over three hundred university peace studies programs.[8]

As a feminist, I would have to say that peace studies so broadly and positively defined can have no meaning unless it is in the context of feminist thought, particularly that of the social construction of gender and mothering. Militarism has shaped our economic priorities for the past forty years; its use of the resources and capital of this country has depleted medical, educational, and social programs, thus creating a new poverty class composed primarily of mothers and children. When the concept of peace implies that every human being regardless of sex has the right to a life that includes fulfillment of basic human needs, then much of feminist research can also be considered peace research. Much of peace research, therefore, must focus on the intrinsic value of caring, of mothering as we have come to understand it.

2. Feminist Theory and Women as Peacemakers

The gentle, caring, and peacekeeping qualities attributed to women have not always been celebrated by feminists. Virginia Woolf, the harbinger of much in contemporary feminist thought, described her relationship with Coventry Patmore's *Angel in the House* like this:[9]

> It was she who used to come between me and my paper when I was writing reviews. It was she who bothered me and wasted my time and so tormented me that at last I killed her. You who come of a younger and happier generation may not have heard of her—you may not know what I mean by The Angel in the House...She was intensely sympathetic. She was immensely charming. She was utterly unselfish. She excelled in the difficult art of family life. She sacrificed daily. If there was chicken, she took the leg; if there was a draught, she sat in it—in short she was so constituted that she never had a mind or wish of her own, but preferred to sympathize always with the minds and wishes of others. Above all...she was pure.[10]

In what has been referred to as "liberal feminism," the "equality position," or Stage 1 of the contemporary feminist movement, the angel in the house was, if not squashed, at least repressed. That is to say, the caring, peacekeeping aspects of women's activities were not the focus. Mothers certainly were not the focus. Building on the work of Simone de Beauvoir in the late 1940s and Betty Friedan in the early 1960s, feminists saw the glorification of mothering as an instrument of women's oppression.[11] Feminists called for the right not to mother, documented the darker side of the mothering experience, and advocated a more equitable sharing of the responsibilities for child rearing in the struggle for job equity. They argued that the institution of motherhood as currently defined was harmful to children and to mothers themselves. In fact, until the early 1970s, feminists tended to deny any important differences between women and men, thereby playing down the central role of nurturing in gender identity.

Many feminists theorists outside the liberal camp rather than focusing on the joys of mothering began to analyze the inequities of home labor. Radical, Marxist, and socialist feminists showed how capitalism combined with patriarchy made both home labor and market labor gender specific, with women's status both economically and psychologically disadvantageous. They argued that most women's work as currently carried on in home and market, including child care, helped to perpetuate male domination and capitalist production.[12]

Although there was only a most tenuous relationship between feminist and peace research until the mid-1970s, portrayals of women as peace activists generally reflected this feminist theoretical position. Most peace researchers were neither women nor feminists, and many feminists considered peace studies a diversion from the main task of liberating women. It was left primarily to a few feminist scholars (most of whom would not have called themselves peace researchers) to acknowledge the role of earlier pioneers such as Bertha von Suttner, Jane Addams, Emily Greene Balch, and members of the Women's Peace Party and the Women's International League for Peace and Freedom (WILPF). Their major objective is to show that some women did play a role in social and political history and could be counted among men for equal citizenship.

By the mid-1970s, however, a number of scholars had begun to argue that the first wave of feminist theorizing had invalidated ways of knowing that seemed characteristically womanly. This second wave seeks to discover and validate women's lives in the concrete labors of their daily experiences. The perspective (later to be labeled essentialist) assumes a separate female world, one in which women are essentially different from men—more caring, more cooperative, more peaceful.

With a psychoanalytic lens, sociologist Nancy Chodorow, for example, argued that women, because of the ways in which they were mothered, are more caring, more nurturing, less differentiated, more preoccupied with relationships than men. In fact, they spend their lives nurturing in one way or another and reproduce daughters who do the same.[13] Carol Gilligan, while acknowledging her intellectual debt to Chodorow, takes the celebration of traditional female virtues a step further. Challenging developmental theorists like Freud, Piaget, Erikson, and Kohlberg, she regards the nurturing traits so frequently associated with mothers as strengths rather than weakness. In fact, women with their mothering and caring labor are, in a certain sense, more moral than men. Women know that in a world that extends through an elaborate network of relationships, the fact that someone is hurt affects everyone who is involved, complicating the morality of any decision and removing the possibility of a clear or simple solution. Thus, morality, rather than being opposed to integrity or tied to an ideal of agreement, is aligned with the "kind of integrity" that comes from "making decisions after working through everything you think is involved and important in the situation," and taking responsibility for choice. In the end, morality is a matter of care. [14]

A growing number of feminists agreed with Gilligan that because of maternal practices women have developed an ethic of care quite different from men's. It is a way of thinking characterized by such descriptive words as receptivity, relatedness, responsiveness, connectedness, intuitiveness, ambiguity, ambivalence, feelings, empathy, and caring.[15] It is a way of thinking that, actually and not just theoretically, should socialize each new generation to nonviolent behavior and to a peaceful world order.

Male violence, according to Gilligan, stems from problems in communication and men's lack of knowledge about human relationships. "If aggression is tied, as women perceive, to the fracture of human connection, then the activities of care...are the activities that make the social world safe, by avoiding isolation and preventing aggression rather than by seeking rules to limit its extent." In this light, she contends, "aggression appears no longer as an unruly impulse that must be contained but rather as a signal of a fracture of connection, the sign of a failure of relationship."[16]

Among feminists concerned with peace studies and peace education strongly influenced by Nancy Chodorow and Carol Gilligan were Betty Reardon, Birgit Brock-Utne, Nel Noddings, and Sara Ruddick.[17] With the Freeze movement and increased peace activism in the early eighties, they and others began to turn to issues involving peace, but their research was of a very different kind from that being done by the World Policy Institute and male-dominated established journals such as the Journal of Peace Research and the Journal of Conflict Resolution. Their perspective grew out of the realization that the process of conducting corrective and compensatory research had shown that the scientific method itself was tightly structured around such conventions mirroring ideal traits of Western white males as objectivity, freedom from values, and abstract reasoning.

Betty Reardon's influential monograph, *Sexism and the War*

System, growing out of her experiences with the World Policy Institute and the World Order Models Program in the 1970s and early 1980s, is representative of this second stage of feminist thinking.[18] Contending that within the field of peace studies most researchers have viewed women's issues as secondary or collateral to the central concerns of peace, she calls for an integration of feminist scholarship with peace research whereby the need for inner psychic transformation on a personal level is appreciated as much as the need for global political and economic change. She develops a feminist peace paradigm focused on the *yin* and *yang* aspects of being, contrasting such characteristics as gentleness and strength, receptivity and dominance, caring and competing.

One of Reardon's central metaphors is mothering: conception, labor, birth, and nurture. She writes of humane and fulfilling human relationships, personal change, vulnerability, and pastoral images of peace:

> The lion can lie down with the lamb in a nurturing rather than devouring relationship, only if each is able to transform its reality by transforming itself. These transformations are what peace studies should be about.[19]

Reardon and other feminist peace researchers see an unhealthy imbalance toward male principles in modern society, leading to war, aggression, greed, and other embodiments of "manly" aspects, rather than the more conciliatory and constructive "womanly" aptitudes. "If the world itself seems under siege, and if that siege holds any community and all children hostage, the effort of world protection may come to seem a 'natural' extension of maternal work,"writes philosopher Sara Ruddick.[20] The logical extension of the argument is that the world would be a safer place if the female element were stressed. Clearly, according to this view, mothers should find war a contradiction and global peace an integral part of their maternal work.

But, as Reardon, Brock-Utne, Noddings, Ruddick, and most essentialist thinkers readily acknowledge, women often support wars enthusiastically and vigorously. Noddings points out that "Women...too want to belong...An important virtue of the good woman...is her generous support of her man's conception of honor."[21] Ruddick, however, calls this maternal trait "inau thenticity," and she laments that mothers all too often believe that their children's interests depend on their country's military strength, even though they may hate wars in general. She finds that very few mothers "take the world as an object of extended maternal care."[22] She, too, fears the temptation to celebrate the caretakers while forgetting their failures. She also fears an emergent self-righteousness that while condemning violence forgets to tend to its root causes.[23]

In the final analysis, most feminist peace researchers cautiously yet hopefully conclude that it is women or mothers with a feminist consciousness and politics who are most likely to become truly effective peacemakers. For example, Ruddick writes: "By increasing mothers' powers to know, care, and act, feminism actualizes the peacefulness latent in maternal practice." It is her belief that "feminism is already conjoined with a peace politics that is marked by its double origins in women's traditional work and feminists' resistance to abuse against women."[24]

3. Feminist Criticism of Women as Peacemakers

Not all contemporary feminists are as sanguine about the nurturing attributes of women as the theorists discussed above. As bell hooks writes:

> The resurgence of feminist interest in motherhood has positive and negative implications for the feminist movement. On the positive side there is a continual need for study and research of female parenting which this interest promotes and encourages....On the negative side, [by] romanticizing motherhood, employing the same terminology that is used by sexists to suggest that women are inherently life-affirming nurturers, feminist activists reinforce central tenets of male supremacist ideology.[25]

Critics argue that essentialist theory has an exaggerated focus on the differences between men and women. British feminist Lynne Segal, striking her central theme as to the inadequacy of polarized thinking about men and women, writes: "This has meant a minimal interest in conflicts and contradictions as they are experienced within feminine identity, a false universalizing of our own gender categories and a disregard for other social practices (outside mother-daughter bonding) as they impinge upon gender identity.[26] We need to be asking a different set of questions, Segal and others assert. How else can we explain diverse historical and cultural forms of femininity and masculinity? How else can we explain mothers who send their sons to war? How else can we explain women's behavior that does not conform to maternal thinking? How else can we explain the angry, sad, and bitter stories of mothers? How else can we understand the lives of women who do not wish to be mothers?

Even on the familial level the record of women as being inherently more life affirming appears to be mixed. For generations we have been reading from the male perspective about the pathological implications of these mothering qualities—with mothers being blamed for all "social deviations" of their children from mental illnesses to juvenile delinquency to matters of life-styles and sexual orientation. While the essentialist viewpoint has done much to modify this unwarranted assignment of responsibility to women alone, it has not left mothers with a sense that they are standing on terra firma. Jane Flax, criticizing Ruddick's "maternal thinking" thesis argues that "important things like rage, frustration, aggression, sexuality, irrational intense love and hate, re-experiencing of one's own childhood, blurring of body boundaries, conflict between demands of a child, one's mate, other children and other work are missing."[27] And Lynne Segal writes, "The weight of one's own children can mean a contradiction of social vision, an envy and resentment of the welfare of others....While it may be true that women are more concerned about peace and a better world...this does not necessarily mean that women are any less nationalistic, racist, or committed to class privilege than men."[28]

My own conclusions from a study of mothers of sons (120 mothers with sons age fifteen and older) are that on the familial level, women's perceptions of their roles as peacemakers are far more ambivalent, complex, and conflict ridden than one might conclude from a reading of Chodorow, Gilligan, Reardon, Noddings, or Ruddick.[29] Although most of the women with whom I spoke identified themselves as peacemakers within the family, some expressed ambivalence and often downright anger with their roles, especially when it was between father and son. They would say: "To be in the same room with them is to set my stomach churning. I am sick to death of it"; or "I've lied for my son so many times just to keep the peace that I hardly know how to stop!"[30]

When women define peace in the family as merely the absence of conflict, as many in my study did, their communications with sons become limited to the inconsequential or noncontroversial. They feel impelled to sweep differences under the carpet, at tremendous cost to their own self-esteem, growth, and peace of mind, as well as that of their children. For example, a mother poignantly described how her fear of confrontation made it doubly difficult for both her and her son to come to terms with his homosexuality. Two women told me they could not bear to burden their sons with the knowledge of their battles with cancer. Another described how she could not bring herself to ask her son about his experiences in Vietnam, thereby shutting herself out of a part of her son's life both he and she needed to share.[31] In what they considered to be the line of duty, I concluded that many mothers opted for a limited honesty and openness—one that suppresses anger and hides the self.

In the public sphere, as we have seen, most feminist peace researchers themselves readily acknowledge that the record regarding women's support of national wars is problematic at best. Women as well as men are committed to what they regard as "the national interest." Jean Elshtain writes, "The woman of republican militancy is no mere victim of events; rather, she is empowered in and through the discourse of armed civic virtue to become an author of deeds—deeds of sacrifice, of nobility in and through suffering, of courage in the face of adversity, of firmness in her, and not just her polity's 'right.'"[32]

Furthermore, in my study of mothers and sons, I discovered many women who encouraged their sons to join the military not at all for reasons of patriotism but rather because they view the military as the only available means of shifting the mothering responsibility—be it psychological, social, or economic—from themselves along.[33] Similarly, Barbara Omolade points out that African American women have a legacy of support of war because the military represents economic opportunity and social status for black men, and now black women too. "Few black women can live outside the dilemmas posed by this predicament. Which war zone does she protect her son from: the military or the street?"[34]

What about ordinary women outside the United States who by no choice of their own are participants in national political conflicts? An emerging literature is providing portraits of women who have sacrificed bravely and fought fiercely for principles beyond the familial.[35] For example, Marjorie Agosin tells a moving story about the *arpilleristas*, women in Chile who make the small appliqued and embroidered wall hangings that portray the suffering of women and their families under the repressive military dictatorship of Pinochet. It was the upheaval in their personal lives (the arrests, "disappearances," exiles, and deaths of their sons and loved ones) that obliged them to take political action and learn to speak as a collective voice. As one woman put it, "Because of all this suffering we are united. I do not ask for justice for my child alone, or the other women just for their children. We are asking for justice for all.[36]

Another example of this emerging literature are the ten essays in *Women and Political Conflict*, edited by Rosemary Ridd and Helen Callaway, describing women's experiences in the war in Cyprus, the Islamic revolution in Iran, the national struggle in Northern Ireland, the ideological conflict within an Israeli kibbutz, the Breton separatist movement in France, and the struggle by Turkish migrants in West Berlin to maintain their ethnic identity. It needs to be pointed out, however, that while rich with portraits of courageous women, this book, like others, concludes that these women see themselves as powerless beyond their genius to survive, and, the editors argue, "in terms of the wider political systems, must be seen as relatively so."[37]

As I have written elsewhere, these books give voice to women whose lives have been turned upside down by political conflict.[38] The stories serve to remind those of us who care about women's and peace issues that the terrible cost of war and political conflict is paid by women as well as men; that women have used their informal powers to express their political will bravely and even heroically. The books also remind us how cautious we must be about embracing a theoretical perspective that celebrates "mothering" values and virtues while minimizing the fact that this gender construct falters before broader power structures. The experiences of many women involved in conflict throughout the world illustrate that the force of what women as nurturers do on the interpersonal level—whether in the family or the workplace—is painfully problematic in the global arena.

In addition, what about the women who choose to be part of their country's political and military conflicts? What about the growing numbers of women, including mothers, serving in the U.S. military since 1973, for example? The National Organization for Women (NOW) supports the move for women to be eligible for combat on the perfectly rational ground of professional opportunity equity. Congresswoman Pat Schroeder, for example, has written a bill to adopt a Pentagon group's suggestions that the army test women in combat roles. Also, syndicated columnist Ellen Goodman has come down on the side of women in combat, arguing that "any war that isn't worth a woman's life isn't worth a man's life." And what about the voices of the eager young American women, who served in the Persian Gulf War pleading for the privilege of combat duty?

With this growing literature on women's relationship to issues of peace and war, it has become clearer than ever that men throughout the world continue to have greater access to power, wealth, and privilege than women have. However, it also has become clearer that feminists are having increasing difficulty coming to agreement on the theories and strategies needed to explain and challenge these inequities. Feminist peace theorizing now fluctuates ambivalently around two views: one, increasingly supported by feminist men in the field, that focuses on the identification of essential psychological or sociological differences between men and women and another that acknowledges the distortion and disadvantages of the first. It grapples with this difference-versus-equality debate on both theoretical and strategic levels. The tension, writes Anne Phillips, is "built into the feminist project. Men and women are different; they are also unequal; feminists will continue to debate and disagree over how far the inequality stems from the difference, and how far the difference can or should be eliminated."[39]

That it is time, however, to move beyond the difference-versus-equality debate is the emerging consensus at least outside the peace studies field. As long as women find themselves in the political context of these present times, comments historian Ruth Milkman:

> Feminist scholars must be aware of the real danger that arguments about "difference" or "women's culture" will be put to uses other than those for which they were originally developed. That does not mean we must abandon these arguments or the intellectual terrain they have opened up; it does mean that we must be self-conscious in our formulations, keeping firmly in view the ways in which our work can be exploited politically.[40]

Joan Scott, taking Milkman's point further, argues that the equality-difference debate can be an intellectual trap, one out of which feminists must move: "When equality and difference are paired dichotomously, they structure an impossible choice. If one opts for equality, one is forced to accept the notion that difference is antithetical to it. If one opts for difference, one admits that equality is unattainable." How then, Scott asks, "do we recognize and use notions of sexual difference and yet make arguments for equality?" The only response, she answers, is a double one: "the unmasking of the power relationship constructed by posing equality as the antithesis of difference, and the refusal of its consequent dichotomous construction of political choices."[41] Feminists need to recognize that the antithesis of difference is not equality but sameness; the antithesis of equality is not difference but inequality.

The analytic perspective Scott and many contemporary feminist social scientists find most valuable for moving beyond the difference-versus-equality debate is poststructuralism. This approach, based on the borrowings from the humanities, with its attack upon the methodological assumptions of modern science, on the one hand, and its questioning of the status of all knowledge on the other, is providing a major challenge to the essentialist standpoint in the fields of international relations and peace studies.[42] In this context, it is referred to as "the third debate"—a loosely defined and evolving cluster of attitudes toward theory and practice that takes into account a whole range of analytical approaches and "for all its heterogeneity has a number of thematic connections that help to identify it and explain its overarching critical purpose."[43]

Poststructuralism does not have one fixed meaning; rather, it is applied to a wide range of theoretical positions derived from the work of Derrida, Lacan, Kristeva, Althusser, and Foucault.[44] In its myriad aspects, it can be defined as a broadly interdisciplinary approach that disputes the underlying assumptions of most social sciences—epistemological foundations, the Enlightenment heritage (faith in the idea of progress and rationality), and a social science methodology modeled after the hard sciences with its search for generalizations, simplifications, and verifications. Rather than focusing on personality, behavior, attitudes, goals, and choices, it turns attention to language, symbols, alternative discourses, and meaning. It holds that knowledge is grounded in language and language does not reflect "reality." And it is language itself that creates and reproduce a world that is never definitive but always in transition.[45]

It is really easier to say what poststructuralism is not, than what it is. This is partly because it resists definition on empirical grounds and partly because it is still in its infancy. Poststructuralism's positive identity has yet to be formed. Its proponents do agree that it aims "to destablize and render open to question all claims to an absolute foundation."[46]

In her discussion of the contribution poststructuralism can offer contemporary feminism, linguist Chris Weedon articulates a specific version that is able to address the questions of how social power is exercised and how social relations of gender, class, and race might be transformed. This is not to say that the differences among forms of poststructuralism are not important; but rather, that they are not equally productive for feminism.[47] Poststructuralists, according to

Weedon, deny the assumption that women and men have essential natures. They refuse to "fall back on general theories of the feminine psyche or biologically based definitions of femininity which locate its essence in processes such as motherhood or female sexuality." This does not, however, "rule out the specificity of women's experiences and their difference from those of men, since, under patriarchy, women have differential access to the discursive field which constitutes gender, gendered experience and gender relations of power in society."[48]

I choose to focus on poststructuralism's more moderate, feminist adaptation from an international relations perspective as a useful framework for understanding power and for developing strategies for peace and change. Preferring the term postmodernism to poststructuralism, political scientist Christine Sylvester (who probably would not see herself as a peace researcher) defines this approach as

> a form of critical theory which questions secure knowledges and practices and seeks to open up policy processes to those who have been spoken for and "protected" by purveyors of certitude and security. It is a community—of radical doubters, tolerant dissenters, neo-anarchists, seekers of knowledge at the hyphens of lived experience. Unabashedly pro-women, it also is alert to other groups historically silenced within the master discourses of androcentric modernity.

From this position, Sylvester challenges the theses of essentialists like Brock-Utne, Reardon, Chodorow, and Ruddick, arguing that women are not naturally opposed to war and for peace and that peace and war are all of a piece, rather than negations of each other. At this moment in time, she argues, that piece is patriarchal. It is patriarchy itself that damages and distorts women's perspectives as well as men's: women may be embracing (and calling our own) peacemaker images that reflect and serve the prevailing gender order, leading to a denial that liberation brings pain, confusion, and loss. She questions the value of what she calls "establishment-supporting gender expectations" for the end of patriarchal society as we now know it.[50]

Clearly influenced by poststructuralism, Carol Cohn's widely discussed essay, "Sex and Death in the Rational World of Defense Intellectuals," is another example of new directions toward which feminist peace research may be turning. Cohn considers how the language of the defense intellectuals is a reflection of the ideas that express and construct men's power in relation to women. It is a language tenaciously rooted in and around us, reinforcing sexism and militarism.[51] Cohn describes her own transformative process, that of learning the language, while participating in a Harvard-MIT summer program on nuclear weapons designed for college teachers, followed by a year as a participant observer at the Center for Defense Technology and Arms Control. The language (she calls it technostrategic) is clearly masculine, based on a uniquely male rational conceptual system that excludes human beings and connections. Her own transformation went through several stages:

Stage 1: learning to listen to white men in ties discussing clean bombs and clean language, missile size, fathers, sons and virgins, domestic bliss, male birth and creation, God and nuclear priesthood.

Stage 2: learning to speak the language (noting the allure of power and white male privilege) and feelings of control, escape from thinking of oneself as victim.

Stage 3: learning to dialogue and finding that it could not be done in English (she notes, for example, that the word 'peace' is not part of the vocabulary, one must use 'strategic stability' instead).

Stage 4: feeling the terror as she realized that she herself was being transformed, that not only was she speaking in this language—she was thinking in it.

The transformative process Cohn describes is truly a dilemma for feminist peace researchers, one for which Cohn offers no simple answers. The dilemma is this: women will not be listened to by those in power if they cannot speak the language—yet the very process of learning the language leaves them unable to speak their concerns, that is, to stay connected to human lives. Cohn suggests that the language itself may not really articulate the "rational strategies" upon which nuclear weapons development and deployment decisions are in fact made. Rather, technostrategic discourse might be functioning more as a gloss, an ideological curtain to hide the actual reasons for these decisions. She believes women have two tasks: one is a deconstructive project that involves first learning and then deconstructing the language ("beating the boys at their game"); the other is a reconstructing project to create "alternative visions of possible futures"—with "diverse voices whose conversations with each other will invent those futures."[52]

4. The Feminist Challenge for Peace Studies

The challenge for feminist peace researchers, as I see it, is to recognize such dilemmas as those highlighted by Sylvester and Cohn. It is to acknowledge the tension between needing to act as women who value mothering and caring labor and needing an identity not overly determined by our gender. The challenge is about difference and equality; it dramatizes women' differences from men and from each other—and it sees the necessity of sometimes making common cause. It is about resisting claims that some categories (like mothering) are natural and inevitable. It is to remember that, as literary critic Ann Snitow points out, "in a cruel irony that is one mark of women's oppression, when women speak as women they run a special risk of not being heard because the female voice is by our culture's definition that-voice-you-can-ignore." And it is to remember that, again as Snitow puts it, "the alternative is to pretend that public men speak for women or that women who speak inside male-female forums are heard and heeded as much as similarly placed men."[53]

This is not to argue that poststructuralism offers the only acceptable theoretical approach to feminist peace research. On the contrary, I fear there is a danger that rigidly self-defined poststructuralist advocates, particularly those on the extremely skeptical side, can lessen the critical and constructive voices of women for peace. As Marx put it, "The philosophers have only interpreted the world...the point, however, is to change it." If we can do nothing more than acknowledge the multi-dimensionality of all reality, then where does this leave us? It is difficult, to say the very least, to be both part of this community of radical doubters and a feminist peace activist.

There is a special urgency, poignancy, if you will, to the feminist debate within the field of peace studies. First, to argue that women are essentially different (more nurturing, caring) is to valorize women's experiences as peacemakers. As is true with all oppressed groups, this feeling of difference is a powerful consciousness-raising tool to promote solidarity for collective action. Second, humanist aspirations for a more peaceful world, where peace by definition must include an ethic of caring and a valuing of caring labor, are at the heart of the peace studies endeavor. The central question, as Ann Snitow phrases it, is "How can the caring that belongs to mother travel out to become the responsibility of everyone?"[54]

Furthermore, peace studies in a sense can be seen as a critique of one of the most male-dominated of the social sciences fields, international relations. Feminist peace research, therefore, is at an earlier stage than feminist thought emerging from the fields of literature, philosophy, history, sociology, psychology, and anthropology. For peace researchers, a feminist perspective that focuses on caring, nurturing, feeling, intuiting, emphasizing, and relating remains an important new catalyst to challenge militarism. This contribution of essentialist thinking to the field of international relations and the peace endeavor is refreshing, comforting, energizing, and affirming for women. Thus it is with more than a little ambiguity and hesitation that I myself have come to see its limitations and weaknesses, and the need to move on. Who among us can say that there could ever be too much caring in this violent world? But move on we must.

Feminist peace researchers must be both radical doubters and believers. As Lynne Segal has put it, "What guarantees we have...come from women's and men's engagement in a whole variety of political campaigns against militarism and arms production, and more."[55] The challenge is to work for change, while questioning any tendency to paint over the diversity of lived experiences for the sake of clarity and coherence. The challenge is about moving beyond the difference-versus-equality debate to a finely tuned appreciation of both that allows a pragmatic tolerance for ambiguity and more than a little theoretical untidiness.[56]

NOTES

1. See conservative political analyst Kevin Phillips's description of wealth in the Reagan aftermath in *The Politics of Rich and Poor* (New York: Random House, 1990).

2. This is the definition agreed upon by Evelyn Nakano Glenn, Elsa Barkley Brown, and myself as organizers of "Contested Terrains: Construction of Mothering," a conference held at the State University of New York at Binghamton, 12–13 October 1990. This approach is closely linked to feminist theoretical work on the concept of gender as a central organizing feature of political, cultural, and social life developed over the past fifteen years. We agree with Mary Belenky, Blythe Clichy, Nancy Goldberger, and Jill Tarule (*Women's Ways of Knowing* [New York: Basic Books, 1986], 137–38) that "all knowledge is constructed...that answers to all questions vary depending on the context in which they are asked and on the frame of reference of the person doing the asking."

3. Sara Ruddick, *Maternal Thinking: Toward a Politics of Peace* (New York: Ballantine Books, 1989), 35.

4. I agree with Ruddick's position, in her path-breaking *Maternal Thinking*, that mothering is hard to define precisely. She takes the position, however, that while maternal work is central to caring work, it is not the whole and should not be made to stand for it. I find the lines between "caring labor" of most women and mothering to be fuzzier. See also Nancy Hartsock, *Money, Sex, and Power* (New York: Longman, 1983) and Nel Noddings, *Caring: A Feminine Approach to Ethics and Moral Education* (Berkeley: University of California Press, 1984).

5. Virginia Sapiro, *Women in American Society* (Palo Alto: Mayfield, 1986), 440–41.

6. Daniel C. Thomas, ed., *Guide to Careers and Graduate Education in Peace Studies* (Amherst: The Five College Program in Peace and World Security Studies, 1987), 5.

7. COPRED (The Consortium on Peace Research, Education and Development) by its very title illustrates this point.

8. This is my sense of the field based on my work with COPRED and the Peace Studies Association. Others may disagree, particularly in the grayer area of conflict resolution. George A. Lopez has developed a useful conceptual map of peace studies for those beginning or developing peace studies programs. It includes three areas of substantive foci: causes and consequences of violence; methods for reducing or resolving violent conflict; and the values, norms, and institutions of peace, in "Strategies for Curriculum Development," in *Peace and World Order Studies,* edited by Daniel Thomas and Michael Klare (Boulder, CO: Westview, 1989), 76.

9. Coventry Patmore, *The Angel in the House* (New York: E. P. Dutton, 1876).

10. Virginia Woolf, "Professions for Women," in *Collected Essays* (London: Hogarth Press, 1966), 2:285, as quoted in Noddings, *Caring*, 59.

11. Simone de Beauvoir, *The Second Sex* (New York: Random House, 1974); Betty Friedan, *The Feminine Mystique* (New York: Dell, 1963). I discuss their contributions to mothering more fully in my *Mothers of Sons: Toward an Understanding of Responsibility* (New York: Praeger, 1987).

12. See, for example, Margaret Benson, "The Political Economy of Women's Liberation," *Monthly Review* 21; 13–25; Lise Vogel, "The Earthly Family," *Radical America* 7; 9–50; Maxine Molyneux, "Beyond the Housework Debate," *New Left Review* 116:3–27; Martha E. Gimenez, "Structuralist Marxism on 'The Woman Question,'" *Science and Society* 42:301–323. For a history of the contributions of early radical feminists see Alice Echols, *Daring to Be Bad: Radical Feminism in America, 1967–1975* (Minneapolis: University of Minnesota Press, 1989).

13. Nancy Chodorow, *The Reproduction of Mothering* (Berkeley, CA; University of California Press, 1978).

14. Carol Gilligan, *In a Different Voice* (Cambridge, MA: Harvard University Press, 1982), 147.

15. Belenky, *et al.*, *Women's Ways of Knowing.*

16. Gilligan, *In a Different Voice*, 43.

17. See, for example, Birgit Brock-Utne, *Education for Peace: A Feminist Perspective* (New York: Pergamon, 1985) and *Feminist Perspectives on Peace and Peace Education* (New York; Pergamon, 1989); Noddings, *Caring*; and Ruddick, *Maternal Thinking*.

18. Betty A. Reardon, *Sexism and the War System* (New York: Teachers College Press, 1985).

19. Betty A. Reardon, "Toward a Paradigm of Peace," in *Peace: Meanings, Politics, Strategies*, edited by Linda Rennie Forcey (New York: Praeger, 1989), 25.

20. Ruddick, *Maternal Thinking*, 81.

21. Noddings, *Caring*, 203.

22. Ruddick, *Maternal Thinking*, 81, 113.

23. Ibid., 135.

24. Ibid., 242.

25. bell hooks, *Feminist Theory from Margin to Center* (Boston: South End Press, 1985), 135.

26. Lynne Segal, *Is the Future Female?* (London: Virago, 1987), 148.

27. Jane Flax, "Theorizing Motherhood," *Women's Review of Books* 1:9, 13.

28. Segal, *Is the Future Female?*, 16.

29. Forcey, *Mothers of Sons*.

30. Ibid., 86.

31. Ibid., 91.

32. Jean Bethke Elshtain, *Women and War* (New York: Basic Books, 1987), 93.

33. Forcey, *Mothers of Sons*, 117–35.

34. Barbara Omolade, "We Speak for the Planet," in *Rocking the Ship of State: Toward a Feminist Peace Politics*, edited by Adrienne Harris and Ynestra King (Boulder, CO: Westview, 1989), 184.

35. See, for example, Rosemary Ridd and Helen Callaway, eds., *Women and Political Conflict: Portraits of Struggle in Times of Crisis* (New York: New York University Press, 1987); Marjorie Agosin, *Scraps of Life: Chilean Arpilleras* (Toronto: Williams-Wallace, 1987); Elene Fourtouni, *Green Women in Resistance* (Chicago: Lake View Press, 1986); Daniela Gioselfi, *Women on War* (New York: Simon & Schuster, 1988).

36. Agosin, *Scraps of Life*.

37. Ridd and Callaway, *Women and Political Conflict*, 214.

38. Linda Rennie Forcey, "When Women Fight?," *Women's Review of Books* 5:8–9.

39. Anne Phillips, ed., *Feminism and Equality* (New York: New York University Press, 1987), 22.

40. Ruth Milkman, "Women's History and the Sears Case," *Feminist Studies* 12 (1986), 394–95.

41. Joan Wallach Scott, *Gender and the Politics of History* (New York: Columbia University Press, 1988), 172.

42. See Pauline Roseanu, "Once Again into the Fray: International Relations Confronts the Humanities," *Millennium: Journal of International Studies* 19,

83–105, for a cautious overview of poststructuralists' challenge to international relations.

43. Jim George, "International Relations and the Search for Thinking Space," *International Studies Quarterly* 33, 270. See also Yosef Lapid, "The Third Debate: On the Prospects of International Theory in a Post-Positivist Era," *International Studies Quarterly* 33, 235–54; Roseanu, "Once Again into the Fray."

44. Jacques Derrida, *Of Grammatology* (Baltimore, MD: Johns Hopkins University Press, 1976); Julia Kristeva, *The Kristeva Reader* (Oxford: Blackwell, 1986): Louis Althusser, *Lenin and Philosophy and Other Essays* (London: New Left Books, 1971); and Michel Foucault, *Les Mots et les choses* (Paris: Gillimard, 1966), *The Birth of a Clinic* (London: Tavistock, 1973), and *Discipline and Punish* (Harmondsworth: Penguin, 1979).

45. Rosenau, "Once Again into the Fray," 86.

46. Ibid., 102.

47. This is the position taken by Chris Weedon, *Feminist Practice and Poststructuralist Theory* (New York: Blackwell, 1987), 20. Here I have chosen to use the term poststructuralism rather than postmodernism for convenience and because there is considerable overlap, with some even finding the terms synonymous. See, for example, R.R.J. Walker, "Genealogy, Geopolitics and Political Community: Richard K. Ashley and the Critical Social Theory of International Politics," *Alternatives* 13 (1988), 86.

48. Weedon, *Feminist Practice,* 167.

49. Christine Sylvester, "Feminist Postmodernism, Nuclear Strategy, and International Violence," paper delivered at the International Studies Association Conference, London, 1 March 1989.

50. Christine Sylvester, "Patriarchy, Peace and Women," in *Peace: Meanings, Politics, Strategies*, edited by Linda Rennie Forcey (New York: Praeger, 1989).

51. Carol Cohn, "Sex and Death in the Rational World of Defense Intellectuals," in *Peace: Meanings, Politics, Strategies*, edited by Linda Rennie Forcey (New York: Praeger, 1989), 39–72. This article originally appeared in *Signs: Journal of Women in Culture and Society* 12, 687–718.

52. Cohn, "Sex and Death," 64.

53. Ann Snitow, "A Gender Diary," in *Rocking the Ship of State: Toward a Feminist Peace Politics*, edited by Adrienne Harris and Ynestra King (Boulder, CO: Westview, 1989), 40.

54. Ibid., 52.

55. Segal, *Is the Future Female?*, 201.

56. This essay, published as "Women as Peacemakers: Contested Terrain in Feminist Peace Studies," *Peace and Change* 16:4 (October 1991), 331–354, is reprinted by permission of Sage Publications, Inc.

SECTION II

America's Homefront

INTRODUCTION

Dedicated to values of freedom, democracy, and free enterprise, the government and citizens of the United States repeatedly face challenges which ask us to examine the difference between what we aspire to be and what we actually are. The essays in this section explore critical questions that result from balancing the tasks of maintaining a free democratic society with the herculean burden of supporting, opposing or resolving armed conflicts around the world. No areas more clearly evidence these challenges than the law, the media and the economy.

In "The Need for a Reevaluation of the Treatment of Conscientious Objection under the Laws of the United States," Michael Seng reviews current procedures and issues concerning the laws which govern those who conscientiously oppose the use of force in settling disputes. He shows how recent legal cases involving refugees, who base their claims for asylum upon religious, moral or political claims, demonstrate that our policies and laws could be altered to give greater protection to United States citizens who object to specific conflicts. His arguments allow for reasoned and socially acceptable ways to recognize judicially some form of 'selective' conscientious objection. He sees, as we embark on a new post cold war world, that protecting the rights of conscientious objectors strengthens the First Amendment's right to dissent and sustains the need for the free expression of ideas that are so necessary to a strong democracy.

In "Libya and the Failure of the U.S. Press: A Case Study," Barry Gan touches upon another First Amendment right: freedom of the press. Gan argues that news media professionals fall under the same obligations as other moral agents. Specifically, they have an obligation to provide information when it bears upon another's well-being, when they have the capacity to report it, and when the costs of providing it do not outweigh the costs of failing to provide it. Arguing from these premises, Gan reviews the news coverage of the 1986 attack on Libya as a case study and finds that many news media professionals did not live up to their obligations to inform a public who could have responded more intelligently, if they had known the more complete story.

In "South Africa and the Consequences of Divestment," Richard Werner undertakes an ethical study of a practical question that plagues any democracy built upon a free market economy: How does one effect one's moral values in business? Werner examines the consequentialist argument common to those who oppose divestment and sanctions against South Africa. He shows that many of the reasons why people think sanctions and divestment would not work are fallacious. Werner demonstrates that critics falsely assume the only ethically relevant consequences are their own intended actions. To overcome this fallacy, he then describes how in practical economic situations "faith in solidarity with others" creates good consequences.

THE NEED FOR A REEVALUATION OF THE TREATMENT OF CONSCIENTIOUS OBJECTION UNDER THE LAWS OF THE UNITED STATES

Michael P. Seng

The United States takes great pride in its tradition of protecting the liberties of the individual. We recently celebrated the bicentennial of our Bill of Rights. We have also celebrated the collapse of communism in Eastern Europe as a repudiation of collectivism and a reaffirmation of the importance of preserving individual liberties. We cherish freedom of conscience as one of the most basic individual liberties and as crucial to the effective working of a democratic society.[1] Yet we have only grudgingly accommodated those who are conscientiously opposed to serving in the military. As shown below, the U.S. Supreme Court has refused to uphold the right of conscientious objection under the First Amendment and Congress has given only limited recognition to the right of conscientious objection in the Selective Service Act.

This chapter argues for broader, more consistent protection for the rights of conscientious objectors. Presently the law appears to offer more protection to aliens seeking asylum in the U.S. because of their unwillingness to serve in foreign military operations than it gives to our own citizens who are opposed to serving in the military. This chapter advocates that this inconsistency should be eliminated, not by restricting the rights of refugees but by expanding the rights of our own citizens, especially by recognizing an exemption for selective conscientious objection. The traditional arguments against expanding the rights of conscientious objectors are no longer cogent and do not militate against the reforms urged here.

1. The Right of Conscientious Objection: Not Yet Fully Recognized under International Law or the U.S. Constitution

The United Nations Universal Declaration of Human Rights protects freedom of conscience.[2] However, international law has not traditionally been interpreted to require that nations respect the rights of conscientious objectors who refuse to participate in the military. This may be changing because of the efforts of the United Nations Commission on Human Rights.

In 1983, the Subcommittee on Prevention of Discrimination and Protection of Minorities issued a report that urged states to recognize an exemption from military service for conscientious objectors and to grant asylum to those who are persecuted because of their conscientious objection.[3] In 1989, the Commission passed a resolution urging the Secretary-General to transmit to member states its recommendations urging states to enact legislation recognizing exemptions for conscientious objectors.[4] As shown below, international refugee law provides some protection to those who fear persecution because of their refusal to serve in the military. These developments may portend greater international recognition for the right of conscientious objection in the future.

The First Amendment to the U.S. Constitution clearly protects the rights of Americans to speak out against the military and to engage in non-violent protest that does not trespass upon or damage private or public property.[5] However, it is most improbable that one could make a successful argument in the courts today that the Constitution requires that the government exempt conscientious objectors from military service.

In a recent case decided in 1990, *Employment Division v. Smith,*[6] the U.S. Supreme Court set forth a new, more lenient test for determining whether laws which are neutral on their face violate the free exercise of religion clause of the First Amendment. An Oregon law, which prohibited the use of certain drugs, did not grant an exemption to American Indians who ingested peyote for religious ceremonial purposes. In upholding the law, the Court noted that "the mere possession of religious convictions which contradict the relevant concerns of political society does not relieve the citizen from the discharge of political responsibilities." As examples, the Court cited the requirement that citizens pay general taxes and participate in the military even if their opposition to doing so is based on religious grounds.

More recently the U.S. Court of Appeals for the Seventh Circuit in *Department of Justice v. Ryan,*[7] upheld the dismissal of an FBI agent who refused on the basis of his religious convictions to investigate non-violent anti-war groups who were suspected of entering military bases to vandalize government property. The agent had worked for the FBI for 21 years and was only nine months short of being eligible to retire with a pension when he was sacked for his insubordination in refusing to carry out orders. The Court held that any argument that the FBI had violated the First Amendment was "untenable."

Conscientious objection should not be confused with the principle that members of the armed forces are excused from obeying unlawful orders—the so-called Nuremburg principle. That principle is predicated on the objective illegality of the order and not on the subjective judgment of the officer. A good example is that of Dr. Howard B. Levy, who was court martialed in 1967.[8] Dr. Levy refused to give medical training to "aidmen" on the ground that American troops were committing war crimes in Vietnam. Dr. Levy's defense was not that he conscientiously opposed war but that this war was illegal. He did not prevail because he did not establish the objective illegality of the war even though he clearly believed that the war was illegal and immoral.

While United States law may protect those who refuse to obey an illegal order,[9] it does not similarly protect those who conscientiously believe that an order is immoral. Although it can be argued that the Constitution should be interpreted to give protection to conscientious objectors, the present trend of the Supreme Court to give more weight to the government's concern for efficiency than to individual liberty does not portend that the Constitution will be interpreted, at least in the near future, to protect the right of conscientious objection. Thus, because of the present status of international and American constitutional law, any appeal to expand the rights of conscientious objectors in the United States must be on the basis of statutory law.

2. The Selective Service Act Gives Only Limited Recognition to the Right of Conscientious Objection

Despite the fact that there may be no international or constitutional requirement at the present time that requires the government to respect the rights of conscientious objectors, federal statutes since the Civil War have given limited recognition to the rights of conscientious objectors. The Selective Service Act exempts any person from "combatant training and service in the armed forces of the United States who, by reason of religious training and belief, is conscientiously opposed to participation in war in any form."[10] The Act defines "religious training and belief" as not including "essentially political, sociological, or philosophical views, or a merely personal moral code."

The U.S. Supreme Court first construed the term "religious training and belief" in 1965 in *United States v. Seeger*.[11] Prior to 1967, the Selective Service Act had defined "religious training and belief" as "an individual's belief in a relation to a Supreme Being involving duties superior to those arising from any human relation, but [not including] essentially political, sociological, or philosophical views or a merely personal moral code." The Court held that "a sincere and meaningful belief which occupies in the life of its possessor a place parallel to that filled by the God of those admittedly qualifying for the exemption" comes within the statutory definition.

Subsequently in *Welsh v. United States*,[12] the Court held that an applicant was entitled to conscientious objector status even if his belief was based on moral rather than "religious" grounds. The Court held that Section 456(j) exempted from military service "all those whose consciences, spurred by deeply held moral, ethical, or religious beliefs, would give them no rest or peace if they allowed themselves to become a part of an instrument of war."

However, in *Gillette v. United States*,[13] the Court refused to recognize a theory of selective conscientious objection and held that those who embraced a "just war" theory could not be exempted from military service under the Selective Service Act. To qualify as a conscientious objector the applicant must be opposed to participating in any war and all war. The Court did recognize that the determination of conscientious objection was not precluded because the applicant would be willing to use force in self-defense or in defense of his home or family. One can also qualify as a conscientious objector even though that person may belong to a religious organization that does not list conscientious objection to war as one of its tenets.

To qualify as a conscientious objector one must strictly follow the procedures set forth for doing so by Congress and the federal agencies charged with enforcing the selective service laws. Review by the courts is limited.

Prior to the ending of the draft in 1973, conscientious objectors were required to apply for an exemption prior to notice of induction. However, after registration requirements were reimposed in 1980, the procedures were reversed so that now registrants cannot apply for conscientious objection status until after they have received an order to report for induction but prior to the day they are scheduled to report.[14] Because induction can be as early as the tenth day after the order to report is issued,[15] registrants have very little time to prepare and file a written claim and the documents supporting the claim for conscientious objection.

A requirement that a citizen register for the draft has been held not to violate the First Amendment.[16] The Supreme Court has approved a Congressional measure which denies federal financial aid to male students who fail to register for the draft.[17] The Court held that the measure did not violate either the prohibition against bills of attainder or the Fifth Amendment privilege against self-incrimination.

In 1962, the Department of Defense began to allow members of the armed forces to apply for an administrative discharge on the grounds of conscientious objection.[18] The standards are the same as for preinduction registrants.[19] The Department of Defense has prescribed procedures to govern these discharges.[20] The regulations provide that persons whose conscientious objection beliefs had crystallized prior to entering military service are ineligible for reclassification as conscientious objectors. Applicants for a conscientious objection discharge are entitled to a hearing and to counsel at their own expense. Applicants must establish their claims by "clear and convincing evidence."

The regulations also provide that the military will do all that is practicable to assign applicants to duties consistent with their beliefs pending determination of their claim, but they also warn that applicants are expected to conform and perform satisfactorily the duties they are assigned. These regulations were construed very narrowly during the Gulf War when the military required persons who received a notice of alert to report to Saudi Arabia before it would allow them to file their petitions for discharge. Applicants complained that this made it harder to assemble their documentation, to secure the services of attorneys, and to call witnesses.

The law recognizes that a person's beliefs can change overnight. Therefore, a traumatic event such as the declaration of war can force persons to rethink their beliefs and become conscientious objectors. However, the sincerity of one's belief is always subject to attack and persons who undergo a midnight conversion may have a difficult time convincing their superiors that their beliefs are genuine.

The law of the United States thus gives protection to Quakers and other similarly situated individuals who hold pacifist beliefs. It does not give protection to some Roman Catholics and others who are selective conscientious objectors. Applicants for conscientious objector status must strictly follow the procedures prescribed by law. As a result of these requirements, those persons in the United States who refuse on a selective basis to participate in the military cannot qualify as conscientious objectors. They are faced with the painful choice of subordinating their beliefs or risking the penalties that can be imposed on them under the law.

3. The Refugee Act Defines Conscientious Objection More Broadly than Does the Selective Service Act

Congress provided in the Refugee Act of 1980 that aliens may be granted political asylum in the United States if they are unable or unwilling to return to their country "because of persecution or a well-founded fear of persecution on account of race, religion, nationality, membership in a particular social group, or political opinion."[21] Congress sought to bring United States law into conformity with the United Nations Convention Relating to the Status of Refugees,[22] which the United States agreed to comply with in 1968. The Convention forbids states from expelling or returning refugees when to do so would threaten their lives or freedom on account of race, religion, nationality, membership of a particular social group or political opinion.

In *I.N.S. v. Cardoza-Fonseca*,[23] the U.S. Supreme Court relied upon the Convention to interpret the Refugee Act. The Court held that applicants must show both a subjective fear that they will be persecuted and that there is an objective basis for the fear; however, the applicant does not bear the burden of showing that persecution is probable but only reasonably possible.[24]

In *I.N.S. v. Elias-Zacarias*,[25] the U.S. Supreme Court denied asylum to a native of Guatemala who feared conscription by a guerrilla organization. The petitioner claimed that the coercion practiced by the guerrilla organization necessarily constituted persecution on account of his political opinion. The Court held that the petitioner had failed to show that his refusal to join the guerrillas was politically motivated and that the guerrillas would "persecute him *because of* his political opinion, rather than because of his refusal to fight with them."[26]

Elias-Zacarias sets a strict standard for applicants seeking asylum. They must show a direct link between their beliefs and the persecution they fear. Also, unlike in *Cardoza-Fonseca*, the Supreme Court relied solely on the "ordinary meaning of the words used" in the statute and did not examine international standards governing the granting of asylum. The Court also held that courts should reverse the discretion exercised by the Attorney General in denying asylum applications only if the petitioner presented evidence "so compelling that no reasonable fact finder could fail to find the requisite fear of persecution."[27] The Court's deference to the Attorney General and its almost summary rejection of Elias-Zacarias' claim indicates that those who claim persecution because of their religion or politics bear a heavy burden if they seek judicial relief after their request for asylum has been denied by the Attorney General.

However, despite the heavy burden placed upon applicants in *Elias-Zacarias*, federal law does provide support for refugees seeking asylum because of their conscientious objection to military service. The United Nations High Commission Handbook on Refugee Status recognizes that conscientious objectors may qualify as refugees so long as their belief is not based on a mere "dislike of military service or fear of combat."[28] Religious convictions may provide the basis for conscientious objection if they are "genuine" and "are not taken into account by the authorities of [the applicant's] country in requiring [the applicant] to perform military service."[29] Unlike the Selective Service Act, this definition appears to include those whose religious views prevent them from participating in an "unjust" war. The Handbook requires that those persons who base their conscientious objection on political grounds must in addition demonstrate that the war is "condemned by the international community as contrary to basic rules of human conduct."[30]

Issues involving conscientious objectors have begun to be addressed by the federal courts of appeals, and the Handbook definition of conscientious objection has been crucial in these decisions. The Ninth Circuit Court of Appeals relied upon the Handbook and recognized that conscientious objection can be the basis for an asylum claim in *Canas-Segovia v. I.N.S.*,[31] an appeal by two brothers who claimed that their political and religious beliefs prevented them from participating in military service in El Salvador. El Salvador had a policy of mandatory military service for all males between the ages of 18 and 30 and did not exempt conscientious objectors or offer an alternative to military service. The petitioners presented evidence that those who refused military service were tortured and killed.

The Court of Appeals rejected the argument that the petitioners had not been singled out for persecution because the law applied equally to all. The Court held that the petitioners' beliefs were genuine, that the laws of El Salvador made no provision for their beliefs, and that El Salvador would likely imprison the petitioners for refusing to serve in the military because of their beliefs. Therefore, the Court held that the petitioners qualified for asylum. The Court handed down its decision prior to the more restrictive requirements imposed by the Supreme Court in *Elias-Zacarias*.

The government appealed the Ninth Circuit's decision to the U.S. Supreme Court. While the appeal was pending, the Supreme Court handed down its decision in *Elias-Zacarias*. Thereafter, the Supreme Court vacated the Ninth Circuit's order in *Canas-Segovia* and remanded the case to the Ninth Circuit for reconsideration.[32] On remand, the Court of Appeals held that the petitioner[33] had presented no evidence that he faced persecution because of his religious beliefs under the standards set forth in *Elias-Zacarias*. However, the Court found persuasive evidence that the Salvadoran government "imputed" political motives to those who refused to serve in the military and held that the petitioner had a genuine fear of persecution because of his "imputed" political motives.[34]

The Court of Appeals for the Ninth Circuit has also found that persons who are conscientious objectors to particular acts of violence can qualify as refugees. In *Barraza-Rivera v. I.N.S.*,[35] Barraza was forcibly recruited into the military in El Salvador. He was told by his commander that he was to be sent on a mission to assassinate two men. Barraza left the country because he did not want to participate in the killings and he feared persecution on his return because of his abandoning military service. He also argued that because of his association with the military, he was now a target of the guerrillas that were opposing the government.

The Court of Appeals found that Barraza demonstrated a well-founded fear of persecution based on his refusal to participate in the murders. The Court held that conscientious objector status was not limited to "those who refuse to be conscripted into the military because of dictates of conscience," but extends to "those who, after submitting to mandatory conscription, are placed in a position that requires them to betray their conscience by engaging in inhuman conduct and refuse to engage in such conduct."

The Fourth Circuit Court of Appeals has taken a more restrictive view when asylum is sought because of political as distinct from religious reasons. In *M.A. A26851062 v. I.N.S.*,[36] the Court rejected a request for asylum from an applicant who feared political persecution. The applicant based his opposition on the ground that the Salvadoran government had allowed the military to perpetrate atrocities in the course of the war. However, the Court held that atrocities committed by military units or officers could not in and of themselves be attributed to a governmental policy. It rejected evidence from such groups as Amnesty International and America Watch that showed a deliberate government policy and instead required that the applicant show that the acts of the Salvadoran government had been condemned by a recognized public governmental body and not just private human rights organizations. This requirement, of course, makes it very difficult ever to prove persecution on the basis of political opinion by a government friendly to the United States.

The decisions reached by the Ninth Circuit Court of Appeals in *Canas-Segovia* and *Barraza-Rivera* appear to apply correctly the United Nations standards on conscientious objection. The applicants had demonstrated that their beliefs were genuine and that their fears of persecution were real. The Fourth Circuit's decision in *M.A. A26851062* correctly sets a higher standard for those seeking asylum on political grounds, but its requirement that the actions of the foreign government be condemned by the international community through a recognized public government body is overly stringent. The law is satisfied if the official actions violate international law.

Although the U.S. Supreme Court has not yet decided an asylum case involving a conscientious objector, the law seems reasonably clear that if refugees genuinely fear persecution because of their religious or political opposition to military service, they qualify for asylum in the United States. The Refugee Act is broader than the Selective Service Act in that it recognizes political motivations and allows conscientious objection to be based upon opposition to specific military actions.

It is thus quite possible that one could qualify for asylum under the Refugee Act for beliefs that would not exempt that same person from military service in the United States under the Selective Service Act. The government might argue that the inconsistency is reasonable because of the different purposes to be served by the two laws, but the inconsistency makes little sense when viewed from the perspective of the liberties of the individual conscientious objector.

4. The Selective Service Act Should Be Amended To Recognize the Right to Selective Conscientious Objection

The Refugee Act of 1980, as it embodies the standards contained in the United Nations High Commission Handbook on Refugee Status and as interpreted by the Ninth Circuit Court of Appeals, provides enlightened standards for determining recognition on the basis of conscientious objection. Congress should borrow the standards contained in the Refugee Act to amend the Selective Service Act and to accord recognition to selective conscientious objectors.

As the Supreme Court has aptly recognized, "ours is a Nation of enormous heterogeneity in respect of political views, moral codes and religious persuasions."[37] To the extent practicable our nation should accommodate heterogeneity. By speaking up against war in general and specific wars, conscientious objectors caution us against blindly following our leaders into military confrontations. They also remind us that there may be alternatives to war and military action. Greater respect for conscientious objection in our society may lead us to focus on civilian-based defense systems which could provide us with greater flexibility in dealing with "internal usurpers and international aggressors."[38]

The Supreme Court in *Gillette v. United States*[39] mentioned several reasons why Congress might not want to recognize selective conscientious objection as a basis for exemption from military service, but none of these reasons is definitive today. The first reason, the government's need for manpower, probably would not be compromised by changing the law. We currently are operating under a volunteer army. Even if it becomes necessary to reinstate the draft, experience demonstrates that there is a sufficient pool of young men and women available to make groundless the fear that we would lack military personnel.[40] The present regulations that do not allow draft registrants to declare their conscientious objector status until after they receive a notice of induction[41] clearly indicate that the government is sufficiently confident of its manpower supply that it does not even need to know in advance how many persons will apply for a conscientious objector exemption when they are drafted.

The second reason, maintaining a fair system for determining "who serves when not all serve,"[42] would also not be compromised. Selective conscientious objectors would still be required to perform alternative service.[43] The alleged difficulty of sorting out the claims of selective conscientious objectors[44] is not an insurmountable barrier to recognition of the right. The burden would still be upon the applicant to establish that he or she is conscientiously opposed to serving in the military and that this opposition is sincere.[45]

The Supreme Court's third reason, that expansion of the right to conscientious objection would "open the doors to a general theory of selective disobedience,"[46] is also unfounded. The Supreme Court itself recognized that the history of the present exemption demonstrated that "it is not inconsistent with orderly democratic government for individuals to be exempted by law, on account of special characteristics, from general duties of a burdensome nature."[47] A broader exemption might well increase the respect of many persons for the law and legal process.

Procedures should also be adopted to insure that those who do claim conscientious objection status receive a fair hearing to determine their status. Our present system of registration for the draft should either be abolished or provision should be made for registrants to express their conscientious objector status at the time of registration. This would ease the consciences of many young persons and would appear not to impose any undue burden on the government.

As our nation moves into the twenty-first century, we can best insure peace by emphasizing non-violent solutions to international and domestic disputes. Giving due respect to those who conscientiously oppose the use of force and violence in general or selectively is a step in the right direction.[48]

NOTES

1. Abrams v. United States, 250 U.S. 616, 630 (1919) (Holmes, J., dissenting).

2. See *The United Nations Universal Declaration of Human Rights* (1948), Article 18.

3. "Question of Conscientious Objection to Military Service," U.N. Doc. E/CN.4/Sub 2/1983/30 (27 June 1983).

4. See Resolution 1989/59 of the Commission on Human Rights (8 March 1989).

5. See Bond v. Floyd, 385 U.S. 116, 132 (1966).

6. 110 S.Ct. 1595 (1990).

7. 950 F.2d 458 (7th Cir. 1991).

8. See Taylor, *Nuremburg and Vietnam: An American Tragedy* (Bantam Books, 1971), 163–64.

9. See Little v. Barreme, 6 U.S. (2 Cranch) 170 (1804); United States v.

Bevans, Cas. No. 14,589 (C.C.D. Mass. 1816), rev'd on other grounds, 3 Wheat. 336 (1818); Mitchell v. Harmony, 13 How. 115, 137 (1851); S. Cohen, *Arms and Judgment* (1989), 23–24.

10. 50 U.S.C. App. §456(j).

11. 380 U.S. 163 (1965).

12. 398 U.S. 333 (1970).

13. 401 U.S. 437 (1971).

14. 32 C.F.R. §1633.2(a).

15. 32 C.F.R. §1624.5.

16. United States v. Schmucker, 815 F.2d 413, 417 (6th Cir. 1987); United States v. Crocker, 308 F.Supp. 998 (D. Minn. 1970), aff'd in part, 435 F.2d 601 (8th Cir. 1971).

17. Selective Ser. Sys. v. Minnesota Public Int. Research, 468 U.S. 841 (1984).

18. D.O.D. Directive 1300.06 (21 August 1962).

19. 50 U.S.C. App. §456(j).

20. See 32 C.F.R. Part 75.

21. 8 U.S.C. §§1101(a)(42)(A) and 1158(a).

22. 19 U.S.T. 6223, 6259–6276, T.I.A.S. No. 6577 (1968).

23. 480 U.S. 421 (1987).

24. Ibid.

25. 112 S.Ct. 812 (1992).

26. 112 S.Ct. at 816. The Court noted that: "Elias-Zacarias objects that he cannot be expected to provide direct proof of his persecutors' motives. We do not require that. But since the statute makes motive critical, he must provide some evidence of it, direct or circumstantial. And if he seeks to obtain judicial reversal of the BIA's determination, he must show that the evidence he presented was so compelling that no reasonable factfinder could fail to find the requisite fear of persecution. That he has not done" (112 S.Ct. at 816–17).

27. 112 S.Ct. at 817.

28. Handbook, ch.V, B, §§168–170.

29. Handbook, ch.V. B, §172.

30. Handbook, ch.V, B, §171.

31. 902 F.2d 717 (9th Cir. 1990), vacated and remanded, 112 S.Ct. 1152 (1992).

32. 112 S.Ct. 1152 (1992).

33. One of the brothers had since married an American Citizen and thus qualified to stay in the United States on that ground. Canas-Segovia v. United States, No. 88–7444 (9th Cir., 10 July 1992).

34. Canas-Segovia v. United States, No. 88–7444 (9th Cir., 10 July 1992).

35. 913 F.2d 1443 (9th Cir. 1990).

36. 899 F.2d 304 (4th Cir. 1990).

37. Gillette v. United States, 401 U.S. 437, 457 (1971).

38. Sharp, *Civilian-Based Defense—A Post-Military Weapons System* (1990), 1.

39. 401 U.S. 437, 455 (1971).

40. Congress can and should remove gender discrimination from the Selective Service Act and require women, as well as men, to register. This would increase the pool available for service in the military. The Gulf War demonstrated that women can participate in combat equally with men.

41. 32 C.F.R. § 1633.2(a).

42. Gillette v. United States, 401 U.S. at 455.

43. See 50 U.S.C. App. § 456(j).

44. 401 U.S. at 455–56.

45. Clay v. United States, 403 U.S. 698, 700 (1971).

46. Gillette v. United States, 401 U.S. at 459.

47. 401 U.S. at 460.

48. The arguments made in this chapter are more fully discussed in Seng, "Conscientious Objection: Will the United States Accommodate Those Who Reject Violence as a Means of Dispute Resolution?" 23 *Seton Hall Law Review* 121 (1992).

LIBYA AND THE FAILURE OF THE U.S. PRESS: A CASE STUDY

Barry L. Gan

On the morning that the U.S. invasion of Panama was first reported to the American public, Tom Brokaw and Bryant Gumbel were on the *Today* show discussing the operation of the American press in Panama. Gumbel said that contrary to the Reagan Administration's view that the press could not keep a secret, "There were x number of press people who knew about this [operation] obviously in advance, and nothing was said, as has been true throughout our history." Brokaw concurred, noting that the press had known in advance of the bombing of Libya in 1986 and had kept the details of that story from the public until after the attack. In holding back such news from the public, Brokaw concluded, the press demonstrated its responsibility.

Should not Brokaw have said instead that the press's actions demonstrated to the public the *ir*responsibility of the press in *not* reporting the news? The question is perplexing. When, if ever, should the U.S. news media withhold news stories from the U.S. public? The answers to these questions hang on two issues. First, do the news media have an obligation to report information to others? Second, if they do have such an obligation, can circumstances override it? The analysis below will reveal that: (1) the news media do have a conditional obligation to report information to others; (2) some circumstances override this obligation; and (3) no such extenuating circumstances were present prior to or during the U.S. attack on Libya.

1. The Obligation to Provide Information to Others

People in the news media, business people, soldiers, doctors, in short, people who find themselves in various roles, are not subject to special applications of morality because of the distinct positions they occupy. Imagine a person with no living relatives and no occupation or role. We would agree that this person nonetheless has certain obligations with respect to her treatment of other human beings affected by her actions. Now imagine that this person marries and has children. Have her obligations to the rest of humankind changed? No, they have not. She has simply incurred some additional duties—and perhaps some additional rights—which must be weighed against her other rights and obligations. The same holds true for people in the news media, in business, or in the military. Their obligations to humankind do not change because they have elected to occupy a certain role. Rather they incur additional obligations—and perhaps rights—that must be weighed in decision-making against those obligations and rights they already have.

The news media are therefore subject to the same standards of morality that apply to other people. This is so for several reasons: the news media comprise people, and people are moral agents. Thus all actions taken by news people—the hiring decisions of the publishers, the editorial decisions of editors, the conduct of reporters and photographers—all are actions performed by moral agents. All are subject to moral evaluation. The only difference between people in the news media and others is that journalists, editors, and broadcasters often find themselves in situations unlike those of most people outside of the news media. Such circumstances, however, do not change any rules of the game. They warrant only that one must apply those rules more carefully.

All else being equal, people in general have an obligation to provide others with information (1) when that information has a bearing on others' well-being, (2) when people have the capacity to provide that information, and (3) when the costs of providing the information do not outweigh the costs of failing to provide it. These obligations follow fairly straightforwardly from Kantian notions of respect for persons, utilitarian considerations of minimizing harm, and concerns for developing a virtuous character. These considerations are all matters of degree, and the costs are not intended to be understood as financial costs alone: for example, broken promises, whether explicit or implicit, cost a great deal of trust. I do not know how to measure such costs; I know only that they should be considered.

2. The Public's Right to Know? — An Aside

From the conclusion that some people sometimes have an obligation to provide information to others, it does not follow that the U.S. public has a right to know. Nor does it follow that the news media have an obligation to provide news. Such a hasty inference ignores the ambiguity of the concept of the public's right to know. First, of course, there is the question of *right*. What sort of right is asserted here? And then, even assuming that the matter is clear, there is the question of just *what* it is that the public has a right to know. They certainly do not have a right to know anything and everything. And finally, it leaves unspecified *which* public has the right. For example, do all publics have equal moral rights to information, or are some publics more entitled than others to certain information?

To speak of a public's right to know might be to speak of a public's right to learn of certain events, ideas, decisions, and so on. Or it may be to speak of a public's right to be informed of certain events, ideas, or decisions. Clearly, if the public has a right to learn of certain events, ideas, and decisions, then the right in question is a negative right, a right not to be hindered in the pursuit of this knowledge except to the degree that it interferes with others' rights. And if the public has a right to be informed of certain events, ideas, and decisions, then the right in question is a positive right, a right to be provided with information.

It is an interesting question whether or not the public has a right to be provided with information. One might argue that representative governments must inform the public of their decisions before they are implemented so that informed public debate might ensue. But such an argument is outside the scope of this inquiry. Here we are concerned with the public's rights with respect to information gathered by the news media. With respect to the government, citizens may indeed have both positive and negative rights to know. But with respect to the news media, it is doubtful that the public has any rights—either rights to be provided with information or rights not to be interfered with in obtaining information. A public's right to receive information entails an obligation on the part of another party to seek out the public and give them the information. It is thus a very powerful right. But it is not a right that citizens may typically exercise against the news media. Legally speaking and in general, government may act on behalf of the public and require journalists to release information that, if withheld, may jeopardize the public good. And morally speaking, this is as it should be, all else being equal. But except in these special cases where the public has good reason to believe important information is being withheld, the public has no legal or moral right to be provided information by the news media.

3. The Conditional Obligation of the News Media

On the other side of this question of rights is the question of obligations. No one, of course, is obliged to make a career out of reporting news. Nor is anyone who has made a career out of reporting news obliged to continue. Thus no one, including NBC, has any absolute or categorical obligation to report the news. But once someone chooses to report information to others, that person incurs certain obligations. And because people at NBC have chosen to report news, they incur a number of obligations that fall upon anyone who provides information to others.

To begin with, they have an obligation to tell the truth. In almost all communications, there is a presumption that the truth is being told. Thus truth is regarded as a *prima facie* duty. It is also regarded as a *prima facie* duty for news reporters as well. And it may be overridden only by exceptional circumstances. Nonetheless, some people suggest that the media may slant the truth if they warn their readers of their slant. Jeffrey Olen, for example, states in *Ethics in Journalism*:

> Media organizations engage in something like an informal contract with their readers, viewers, or listeners. That is, they make explicit or implicit promises to their audiences concerning the editorial policies they will follow, and individuals will read or tune in with the expectation that these promises will be kept.[1]

There is some merit in Olen's description, but one must be cautious about accepting it as a justification for conduct. One is not freed of an obligation to tell the truth simply by proclaiming as an editorial policy that one's coverage of news stories will be slanted to the left or right, the West or East, the north or south. Blameworthiness for harm that results from slanted reporting may be mitigated when an audience has been adequately warned of the slant, but one's obligation to tell the truth is not diminished simply because one has proclaimed otherwise.

At this point it is reasonable to ask, "Well, what is truth?" While any answer to that question may be problematic, I am convinced that truth is more apt to be perceived when many sides of a story are told than when only one side of a story is told, and thus the *prima facie* obligation to tell the truth when communicating with others is in part a *prima facie* obligation to tell as much of the story as is known. Space and time constraints in daily communications as well as in news media preclude one's telling all known details, but they do not preclude telling *something* of the different sides to each story.

Second, people are obliged to tell the whole story. That is to say, not only must people reveal as much as they know about the various sides of a story; they also must not fail to include important parts of the story. Any conflict can be perceived from at least two perspectives, but truth is given short shrift when details that lend legitimacy to each of the perspectives are omitted. Libya and its leader, M. Qadaffi, may have felt wronged by the U.S., and it is important that the press express Libya's sense of having been wronged. However, without details about *why* Libya felt wronged, U.S. readers or viewers are apt to dismiss that perspective as irrational or irrelevant. Although each party to a conflict always has its own story to tell, the details help one to understand the different perspectives.

Third, people are obliged to report information in a timely manner. If my child reaches for a hot coffee pot and I wait until after he has touched it to inform him that it is hot and he will scald himself if he touches it, I have not done right by him. Similarly, if the news media do not report to the public their awareness that a candidate has engaged in wrongful activities until after her election, they have not done right by the public.

Why are people are obliged to tell the truth, the whole truth, and all sides to the truth in a timely fashion? These are *prima facie* duties precisely to the extent that it is known that others will act on the basis of the information given. Consider a few examples: jokes are often lies, but they are acceptable lies because of the context in which they occur; the parties know that the so-called information conveyed by the joke is not to be taken seriously. Similarly, information casually exchanged is not subject to strict conditions of truth-telling. This is usually because the information is not likely to alter another's course of action. When it is clear that casually reported information *will* affect another's behavior, people are generally more cautious about how they convey the information. I might say to a neighbor, "I hear it's going to rain today." And I might leave it at that. But if the neighbor responds, "Well, so much for my picnic," I might feel obliged to add, "Well, I didn't hear the forecast. I just overheard someone else saying so." And this is as it should be. The more likely that my communication with another will affect his behavior, and the greater ease with which I may communicate with another, the more care must I take to be truthful and timely in my communication.

These considerations reveal that news media are subject to these conditions more strongly than most. And they themselves are largely responsible for this circumstance. Their information has much bearing on others' well-being; their capabilities of reporting are extensive; and as a rule the costs of their failing to provide information outweigh the costs of their providing it. Perhaps more importantly, they have created a climate in which no one expects jokes or casual observations in news reporting; they have created a climate in which the public expects the whole truth in a timely fashion. The U.S. news media's explicit criticism of reporting in countries like Iraq or like the Soviet Union prior to *glasnost* and *perestroika* carries with it an implicit promise that reporting in the U.S. will be complete and truthful. This implicit or sometimes even explicit promise creates in their audiences a reasonable expectation that the promise will be met except in extenuating circumstances.

4. Extenuating Circumstances?

What were the circumstances in which NBC found itself when it learned of the planned attack on Libya? At the time this paper was written, efforts to uncover details on this matter were frustrated by NBC's overwhelming attention to the Persian Gulf crisis. Thus, assuming that Brokaw's remarks on the *Today* show were accurate, one must assume either of the only two possibilities:

1. that NBC knew of the planned attack prior to its being launched, or
2. that NBC learned of the attack after the operation began but before the actual attack took place

Both possibilities will be considered in any assessments made below. Other than these assumptions, it is important to understand events in the weeks immediately preceding the attack on Libya.

Around mid-March of 1986, the U.S. Defense Department announced plans for a military naval exercise in the Gulf of Sidra off the coast of Libya. The announced purpose of these exercises was to assert rights of sailing in these disputed waters. On 25 March the U.S. announced that its military forces damaged one Libyan patrol boat severely and disabled another completely. The U.S. also alleged that they struck a missile site. The U.S. said its actions were in response to missile attacks on its ships by Libya. On the following day, 26 March, U.S. military forces again allegedly destroyed two other patrol boats and launched another attack on the missile site. The U.S. said that the 26 March encounter was provoked by what appeared to be "hostile intentions." No reporters witnessed the hostilities on either of those two days.

There followed a period of approximately ten or eleven days during which rhetoric between the U.S. and Libya became increasingly heated. On 6 April a bomb exploded in a West Berlin discotheque frequented by U.S. servicemen. For the next nine days the U.S. government attempted to develop anti-Libyan sentiment by claiming that it had irrefutable evidence that Libya was responsible for the bombing of the discotheque. The evidence was never produced, and to this day the charges remain unsubstantiated. Nonetheless, these charges led to growing suspicion that the U.S. was planning a military strike against Libya. On 15 April the strike took place. The strike reportedly was launched from Great Britain and from two aircraft carriers stationed in the Mediterranean. Two U.S. servicemen and approximately fifteen Libyan civilians were killed; approximately sixty Libyan civilians were wounded.

Although the U.S. news media have an obligation to report news from more than one perspective, with details, and in a timely fashion, and although the media knew prior to the attack that the attack was to take place, news of the attack was deliberately kept from the American public and the world by the U.S. news media until after the strike took place. This withholding of news violates at least one of the three obligations that make up the media's general obligation to report news truthfully: they did not tell the story in a timely fashion. Furthermore, their handling of the story in the weeks prior to the attack violates the two other obligations: they did not report from more than one perspective, nor did they provide details. None of the media insisted on evidence supporting the claim of a link between the discotheque bombing and Libya; instead, they accepted at face value the U.S. government's assertions that there was such a link. None of the mainstream media were able to verify that Libyan patrol boats had in fact attacked U.S. ships in international waters; they accepted at face value the U.S. government's assertions that these events had occurred. None of the mainstream U.S. media reported the Libyan perspective on the events that spring. Furthermore, NBC (and probably all mainstream media) deliberately refrained from a timely reporting of the attack. They all cooperated fully with the U.S. government with no justification for doing so.

The media can offer no excuse for their failure to provide perspectives and details. And one can only speculate about why NBC decided not to run a story about an impending military strike against Libya. One can imagine four likely reasons for holding back the story. The first is that NBC might jeopardize its own sources of information at the Pentagon by running the story. This could occur if the story had been leaked on condition that it not be broadcast until after the attack, or it could occur simply because a broadcast of the story might anger those in the Pentagon or White House who have served as news sources in the past. The second reason is that the story might not have been run for fear that U.S. citizens or advertisers would be angered by a news organization's preemption of their government's military actions. Such anger could hurt NBC's stature as a news organization and television network. The third reason is that it is possible that the Pentagon deliberately informed NBC of the attack in advance so that NBC would be in the awkward position of possessing information that they could not use without violating the law because they had been briefed with classified information. The fourth reason is that such a story could have negative consequences for the U.S. government, and the lives of U.S. soldiers involved in a strike might have been further jeopardized; the attack itself might have been called off.

Since NBC and other news media have incurred an obligation to report news truthfully, however, these four reasons for withholding news must be weighed against that obligation.

The first possible reason—that information might have been released conditionally—is unacceptable insofar as good journalistic practice is concerned. Journalists may occasionally accept information on condition that its source not be revealed, but they should not accept information on condition that the information itself not be revealed. Nor should journalists refuse to broadcast stories for fear that doing so would anger potential sources and keep news from the public in the future. That kind of refusal guarantees that the public will not get the news and renders the media pawns in the hands of their sources.

The second possible reason—that NBC has obligations to advertisers and shareholders, but these obligations are not powerful enough to override their news division's commitment to report the whole truth in a timely fashion. Advertisers and shareholders know what they are getting into—or at least they should know. More than money is capable of buying favors, more than corporations owe shareholders a profit, news broadcasters owe their audiences the truth. Advertiser and shareholder attempts to influence news policy is just a more subtle form of killing the messenger. If the media will not deliver truth in a timely fashion, they should not deliver news.

The third reason—that the Pentagon deliberately provided NBC with classified information to prevent them from using the information without violating the laws—holds up morally only if there is good reason not to violate the law. And whether or not the law should be broken depends, in this case, on the fourth reason, on whether the story's harm to the U.S. government and the soldiers engaged in the attack is an adequate reason to withhold the story.

Clearly, NBC's decision to withhold the story served the U.S. government well. But did the U.S. government deserve to be served well? NBC News, as part of a major U.S. corporation, certainly has some obligation to the government under which it operates. But from a moral point of view "my country, right or wrong" makes no sense. The example of Socrates is of no help here: it is true that Socrates accepted the punishment that Athens gave him, but it is also true that Socrates spoke out against Athens when he thought it was in the wrong. In this instance the U.S. did not then and has not to this day produced any evidence linking the discotheque bombing with Libya. Media demands for such evidence were light, to say the least, and were brushed off at any rate. Furthermore, even were Libya responsible for the discotheque bombing, it was by no means clear that bombing was the most effective means of combating such terrorism. Evidence warranted neither a U.S. attack nor cooperation on the part of the media in that attack.

Now some might argue that the business of news broadcasters is to report the news, not to make ethical judgments about the conduct of countries. But this claim has two problems. The first is that were the claim true, were the business of news broadcasters to report the news, then NBC *should* have run the story. The second is that in choosing not to report the story, NBC *was* making a moral judgment: the wrong one.

The strongest argument that can be offered in support of NBC's decision might appear to be the argument that any other action would have jeopardized the lives of U.S. troops or the success of the mission. As shown above, the success of the mission ought not to have been a concern of the media in this situation. The lives of U.S. troops is another matter. They deserve serious consideration. However, and especially in light of the absence of evidence justifying the mission, so do the lives of Libyans. Only if NBC had good reason to believe that a report on a planned attack would jeopardize U.S. troops and not benefit Libyans should they have withheld the story. And nothing suggests that this was the case.

Finally, it might be argued that although no one of these reasons is enough to override the obligation to report the truth, all four reasons jointly override the responsibility. Even this claim fails, however. As shown above, whether or not news media should respect classified information depends not upon the law but upon the nature of the classified information. The government had produced no case against Libya; the government had hidden its case against Libya from reporters and the public. Thus the news media were not obliged to protect the government in its assault on Libya. Furthermore, as shown above, sources, advertisers, and shareholders have *no* claim upon a news organization when it comes to reporting news, for once anybody undertakes to report information to others, they incur an obligation to report that information fully and in a timely fashion. That obligation rests upon deontological considerations of respect for persons to whom one reports the information as well as utilitarian considerations of minimizing harm from failing to inform people who would act differently if informed.

In short, while it may be the Pentagon's responsibility to keep news reporters from covering all aspects of its military operations, it is not NBC's or other news media organizations' responsibility to decide which major news stories its audiences should get and when. Its audiences should get all major news stories in a timely fashion. Otherwise NBC and the other mainstream media should get out of the news business. Perhaps they already have.

NOTE

1. Jeffrey Olen, *Ethics in Journalism* (Englewood Cliffs, NJ: Prentice-Hall, 1988), 11.

SOUTH AFRICA AND THE
CONSEQUENCES OF DIVESTMENT

Richard Werner

In one of his more picturesque phrases, Hegel states, "The owl of Minerva only spreads its wings at dusk." With the twilight of sanctions against the South African government, perhaps it is the proper time to begin to evaluate the divestment movement. We can, perhaps, view the action with greater distance and detachment. Further, we can view the consequences of the movement with the advantage of hindsight.

Initially the news media, colleges, universities, and the business community generally opposed the movement on the grounds that sanctions and divestment would prove fruitless in their attempt to affect negatively the South African economy. Initially, everyone from Reagan to Bush, *The New York Times* to *The Wall Street Journal*, the trustees and CEOs of Harvard University to Hamilton College, Citibank to Coca Cola opposed divestment. While many changed their position and supported the movement once it become well known and thereby a threat to their profits or interests (for example, Coca Cola and *The New York Times*), others questioned the success of the movement after the fact, for example, George Bush and *The Wall Street Journal*, and some remained steadfast in their opposition to divestment, for example, Hamilton College.

In this paper I focus my attention on one particular argument, what I call *the consequentialist argument.* While there are other arguments against divestment that trade on the neutrality of the university and corporation or the fiduciary responsibilities of trustees and boards of directors, the consequentialist argument is my main concern.[1] I begin with an explanation of the success of sanctions. Next, I elucidate the consequentialist argument and discuss why this seemingly plausible argument proved unsound. Finally, I examine what we can learn from our inquiry into the consequentialist argument and the success of sanctions against South Africa.

Let me begin with some observations about the divestment movement. With its commitment to war and violence as the means for settling national and international problems, a commitment Duane Cady dubs *warism,*[2] western culture often ignores the successes of nonviolent approaches to these problems. So it is with the recent, highly successful divestment movement. While the world directed its attention to the successful media war waged in the Persian Gulf, it conveniently ignored the success of the international divestment movement aimed at South Africa, choosing instead to concentrate on the sporadic acts of violence of black against black. Whereas the success of the war in the Gulf is increasingly doubtful because of our failure to attain any but the most inconsequential of our goals, the success of divestment in South Africa is increasingly apparent.[3] Acting in solidarity with oppressed blacks in South Africa, individuals, colleges, universities, states, and even some nations divested their holdings in those corporations which attempted to profit from the apartheid system of South Africa.

While the black people of South Africa, along with their white supporters, practiced nonviolent *direct* action through such activities as labor strikes and demonstrations, those who joined the divestment movement practiced nonviolent *in*direct action by removing their financial support from the Pretoria government. The black people of South Africa directly and, in the main, nonviolently confronted the Pretoria government while those in the divestment movement indirectly and nonviolently acted in solidarity with their actions by divesting. The black people of South Africa, because of their history and situation, put their lives and bodies on the line while those in the divestment movement, at most, accepted a small economic risk.

Let me make two relevant points clear from the start. I do not claim that divestment *by itself* brought the Pretoria government to its knees. Indeed, it remains crucial that it was the direct actions of the black South Africans supported by the indirect effect of sanctions which accomplished that end.

Second, the vast majority of the successful actions of South African blacks were nonviolent direct actions. While the media did its best to convince us of the violence of the black people either among themselves or in their opposition to the institutional violence of Pretoria, it is clear that the vast majority of actions, and especially the most successful ones, were nonviolent direct actions. This was so even though we now know that the Pretoria government covertly paid Zulu Chief Buthelezi to use his tribe to instigate violence against the ANC in order to influence the outcome of elections in Namibia in 1989. These attacks led to the death of over 800 South Africans in black-on-black violence. Evidence suggests that the Pretoria government sponsored and financed Zulu violence against the ANC both before and after creating a tradition of violence which has caused 10,000 black deaths to date. While ANC members are not allowed to own weapons, members of the Zulu tribe were allowed to carry their "traditional" weapons in public, which made violent attacks by the Zulus that much easier and that much more successful. But it is no surprise that strikes and demonstrations did far more to change Pretoria's ways than did street riots and fire bombs. Indeed, much to the credit of the black people of South Africa, the mass media's frequent prediction of an inevitable violent and bloody civil war never occurred. The small number of white deaths from black hands speaks to my point.

The world witnessed an impressive achievement of nonviolent direct action in South Africa. The achievement was multiracial, multicultural, and international. Yet the western media often portrayed the black cause as racist, red, and violent. One is reminded of similar portrayals by the media of the civil rights movement in the U.S. By concentrating on the relatively rare acts of violence by such groups as the Black Panthers, ignoring the police brutality, disinformation and institutional violence of the U.S. government, and portraying activists such as Martin Luther King, Jr., as responsible for the violent acts of white racists against nonviolent activists, the media both inspired and fanned white racism and white fears of racial violence. The media's portrayal of events in South Africa has, in the main, accomplished the same end.[4]

It is increasingly apparent in the New World Order, where the distinction among business, government, mass media, education, and the military is increasingly blurred, that what matters most is what people can be made to believe, the illusions that are cast on the walls of our caves. What matters least is remaining true to the facts, providing the best explanation.[5] What is hidden by the illusions cast is the effectiveness of the nonviolent actions practiced by the multiracial, multicultural, and international community of solidarity evidenced by those who actively opposed apartheid both in South Africa and around the world.

1. The Success of Sanctions

I was unable to find the facts that I am about to mention in the mainstream press. Hence, my use of nontraditional sources. Indeed, even the sources I cite did not string together these facts to argue for the success of sanctions as I do. One was forced to read between the lines to find the best explanation of the events of divestment.

During his presidency, George Bush, along with the news media generally, portrayed sanctions in South Africa as less than successful, yet the facts speak for themselves. The day Bush announced the end of sanctions, Foreign Minister Botha was giving a speech in South Africa explaining that sanctions had devastated the South African economy.[6] Both President de Klerk and Prime Minister de Plussey made similar public pronouncements about the devastating effects of sanctions.[7] When sanctions began in South Africa, the GNP had an annual growth rate of +2 percent, when they ended it was -1 percent.[8] When sanctions began, the whites of South Africa enjoyed the highest standard of living in the world, when they ended unemployment in South Africa stood at 40 percent—the highest level in the history of the industrial world.[9] Consider the following from *The New York Times*:

> About $10 billion in badly needed capital has hemorrhaged out of South Africa since the mid-1980s. American assets in South Africa dwindled from $2.6 billion to $1.5 billion...[There are] estimates that an additional $2 billion was lost annually in bilateral trade and investment. And 197 American companies disinvested , leaving 129 companies still in place.[10]

Many of the arguments offered to show that sanctions were unsuccessful are *a priori* economic arguments. That is, they are arguments based on economic theory rather than the actual facts. Some argue that corporations leaving South Africa do not affect the economy there, for other corporations simply take their place. This ignores the cost to the economy of such transitions and the realization by the incoming corporation that it can take advantage of the situation. Moreover, as corporations left South Africa it became increasingly difficult for Pretoria to purchase oil on the world market as a result of the stigma and risk that came to surround corporations operating there. Consequently, South Africa could expect to spend $5 to $10 per barrel above the market price once sanctions were in full swing.[11] Further, as the stigma and cost of operating in South Africa grew, the Pretoria government found it increasingly difficult to procure either international loans or investments.[12] They were forced to pay higher interest rates for loans, if they could get them at all, while investors withheld their money because of fear of either stigma or the unstable economy.

Let me suggest that the overly simplistic *a priori* economic arguments pave the road to foolishness concerning our understanding of sanctions. In light of even the relatively few statistics concerning sanctions offered here, it is no surprise that the highest ranking officials in the Pretoria government were begging Bush to remove sanctions, speaking publicly about the devastating effects of sanctions, while at the same time Bush and the news media maintained that sanctions were less than successful.

The reaction of Bush and the media is not surprising. Bush strongly opposed sanctions from the start. To reverse himself would be to admit defeat. Bush had opted for violence in the Gulf over sanctions. The war did not realize its stated objectives. To admit the success of sanctions is to invite the observation that sanctions were the better choice against Iraq. Finally, both Bush and the news media oppose sanctions since they interfere with big business and provide an international alternative to war which threatens one of the last arenas in which the U.S. dominates: war and military sales. Simply put, for Bush or the news media to admit the success of sanctions and make the point apparent to American people would be to threaten both our economy and our warist world view.

My point here is that there is not merely a *correlation* between the fact of divestment and the beginning of the end of apartheid, but that there is adequate explanation to support the claim that sanctions *caused* the Pretoria government to move towards racial equality. I attempted to provide a causal explanation between the fact of divestment and the beginning of the end of apartheid which reasonably explains the causal connection. Within the larger picture of the politics and economics of South Africa, a conclusion for cause over correlation seems most reasonable.

In addition, the often cited argument that divestment hurt the black population of South Africa more than the white population, is beside the point. The demise of communism in the former Soviet Union and Eastern Europe also caused greater economic hardship than existed under communism. Yet no one presents the fact as an argument for communism. The inconsistency may be based on paternalism or racism, or both. Few of us believe that freedom is to be traded for greater economic security once basic needs are met.

2. The Consequentialist Argument

The central argument of those who opposed divestment is simple and direct. Hence, its popular appeal particularly to those who profited from the economic situation created by apartheid, i.e., individuals and institutions who either owned or profited from the stocks and holdings of corporations active in South Africa. The argument goes something like this:

1. Compared to the South African GNP, the holdings of any individual, college, university, corporation, or state are insignificant.
2. Hence, by divesting such holdings an individual, college, university, corporation, or state will have an imperceptible effect on the economy of South Africa.
3. Hence, divestment is incapable of affecting negatively the economy of South Africa or to cause the Pretoria government to mend its ways.
4. Moreover, when such holdings are divested, they are simply purchased by others which creates an even smaller effect than anticipated.
5. Finally, by encouraging corporations to remain in South Africa, i.e., *not* divesting holdings of corporations that do business there, we have a better chance to dismantle apartheid through these corporations.
6. Thus, the best means to change apartheid is to remain invested in corporations active in South Africa and to refrain from divesting from such corporations.

There were many problems with this argument even when it was initially advanced. For instance, corporations were active in South Africa for more than twenty years before divestment began in earnest. During that time, apartheid, if anything, became more rather than less oppressive. The reason is obvious. South Africa is a land of rich, scarce natural resources. Under the system of apartheid, black people are forced into a situation approaching slave labor. Cheap resources, cheap labor—what incentive would business have to educate and liberate a people who would surely eliminate these corporate benefits? Better, from the perspective of multinational corporate interests, to support apartheid indirectly by remaining silent, taking advantage of the situation, and making a few token gestures that help to create the illusion that progress on apartheid is real. Finally, there is little evidence that those who advanced the consequentialist argument brought any significant pressure to bear on corporations in South Africa to eliminate apartheid.

The argument also fails to take into account the supply and demand aspect of the stock market. When many investors sell a given stock and when few are willing to purchase it, the demand for the stock falls. When demand falls, so does the price. Falling stock prices are taken seriously by a corporation. So was the notoriety of involvement in South Africa. At the height of the divestment movement, many corporations feared the stigma attached to being active in South Africa. Some created shadow corporations which did not bear their name in an attempt to escape the stigma. But many corporations, as the success of divestment proved, simply left.

Yet it is not these points and counterpoints which interest me. What does is why the consequentialist argument failed. But before we turn to that, I want to consider some arguments very similar to the consequentialist argument in the belief that they will help reveal why it is unsound.

Suppose College *H* starts a large capital campaign. Suppose it asks its alumni for donations. By parity of reasoning with the consequentialist argument, we obtain the following:

1. Compared to the size of *H*'s capital campaign, my resources are relatively small.
2. Hence, my anticipated contribution to *H*'s capital campaign will have an imperceptible effect on its success.
3. Hence, my anticipated contribution to *H*'s capital campaign will not positively affect the capital campaign.
4. Thus, it is irrational for me to contribute to *H*'s capital campaign, if my goal is positively to affect the campaign.

It is interesting to note that while many colleges and universities were voicing the logically parallel consequentialist argument, they also asked for contributions from their alumni. Besides the obvious *ad hominem* contained in the charge of either ignorance or hypocrisy on the part of such college or university officials, this argument is clearly unsound since capital campaigns do work, as did divestment.

Suppose I am considering purchasing *N* shares of stock *X*. Suppose *N* is some number significantly lower than the total number of existent shares of stock *X*. Suppose I reason as follows.

1. In comparison to the existent holdings in stock *X*, my anticipated purchase of *N* shares of stock *X* is relatively small.
2. Hence, my purchase of *N* shares of stock *X* will not affect in any significant way the cost of a single share of stock *X*.
3. Hence, my purchase of *N* shares of stock *X* will not cause me to profit.
4. Thus, it is irrational for me to purchase *N* shares of stock *X*, if my goal is to profit.

Again, there is something amiss in this argument since people do profit by investing in stocks—although one suspects neither as many nor as much as they claim. Further, one wonders why these same people were willing to accept the risk of the market but not that of divestment. Again, hypotheses about ignorance and hypocrisy loom large.

Consider a third argument. Suppose it is presidential election day. Suppose I reason as follows.

1. In comparison to the number of votes which will be cast today, my single vote is inconsequential, for example, no modern presidential election was decided by anything even approaching one vote.
2. Hence, my vote will not have any effect on the outcome of today's election.
3. Hence, it matters not whether I vote.
4. Thus, it is irrational for me to vote, given that I don't want to waste my time.

Again, the argument is unsound for, if sound, the conclusion shows that voting is irrational. If voting is irrational, then so are the institutions founded upon it like democracy.

3. The Error

The problem with the consequentialist argument should be apparent. It is simply a variation of the voter's paradox as are all four of these arguments. If one continues to vote, to give to their favorite charity, invest in the market or, better yet, if one does not consider such behavior irrational, then uses of the consequentialist argument against divestment are based either on ignorance or hypocrisy.

There is an old saw in the philosophical toolbox called "Ramsey's Maxim." It advises that when several arguments on a topic seem plausible, yet all lead to implausible conclusions, that we find what the several arguments all assume in common. We deny the common assumption and begin again.

Each argument looks at the consequences of an *individual* action taken in isolation from all others. Each assumes that the only consequences worth considering are the consequences of *my* action. But in each case it is the resultant sum of people acting in solidarity which yields the *actual* consequences. By considering my action in isolation from its connectedness with the actions of similar-minded people, I erroneously predict the consequences of my action as inconsequential. Each argument errs in its enthymematic move from the second to the third premise. Let me take each example in turn.

While it is true that my relatively small contribution toward the capital campaign will not in itself fill the coffers, my action in solidarity with other similar-minded alumni will. Indeed, this is perhaps why colleges and universities work to convince us that we are not discrete individuals but members of the class of 1969, brothers of a fraternity, alumni of the University of Mars. It is one of the reasons they invest great sums in the appearance of the campus, or the football or basketball team, or in music centers or art galleries. They induce us to identify and feel solidarity with a group, so that when they ask for our money we will reason that we are acting in solidarity with our classmates, our sisters, or our university. It then becomes our belief that when we contribute we are not acting alone, but contributing with many other similar-minded individuals with whom we are in solidarity. They use such devices as employing our classmates, sorority sisters, or professors to write or call us to ask for donations in order to impress upon us this feeling of solidarity, to create a faith in the connectedness which will lead us to think beyond our mere individually. The end-in-view is to convince us to think in solidarity rather than to reason as mere individuals. If they are successful, we are more likely to give because we will find it more rational to give. We will see that our actions can have an effect—our actions in solidarity rather than our actions as mere individuals.

Similar thinking occurs when one invests in the stock market. One's belief is that similar-minded others will also appreciate the wisdom of investing in stock X at this time. If they do, demand for X will be high, the cost of an individual share of X will increase, and I will profit through my purchase of N shares. Some stockbrokers trade on this approach. They attempt to convince the buyer that stock X is about to "take off." "Get in on the ground floor," they say, "you can reap a handsome profit if you invest in X now." The goal is to get the individual not to think as a mere individual but to think in solidarity with others who will invest in X. If successful, one's trust that others will behave similarly is raised. Consequently, one sees the wisdom of the purchase of X. Through one's faith in the worthiness of X, shared with other similar-minded people, one helps to create the fact that shares of X increase in value—the fact of one's profit.

Finally, one can see similar patterns with voting. Political parties and individual candidates attempt to cause us to identify with them and their cause. They attempt to cause us to feel and to act in solidarity with other members of the party, other supporters of the candidate with whom we believe we share common interests and goals. If they are successful we will want to support *our* party, support *our* candidate by voting. Our trust in voting relies upon the fact that we act in solidarity with many others—enough others, we hope, to defeat rival candidates. If our confidence proves correct, we will have created a new fact through our trust and action. Our belief will become a self-fulfilling prophecy.

4. The Solution

Many years ago, William James wrote that confidence in certain facts may help to bring those facts into existence. All of our examples rest on this simple confidence. Whether it is trust in the charity of our classmates, faith in the prudence of investors, or confidence in the judgment of fellow citizens, our confidence may help create future facts. Yet ours is no wild leap of faith, for the proof of the pudding is in the eating. Our trust, in each case, stands to be verified or disconfirmed by the facts. In each case, if our confidence is well placed, we stand to attain our end-in-view. If it is not, we stand to fail. The confidence of which I write may, then, be either rational or irrational, either well or ill-founded.

Like the philanthropist, the investor, or the voter, those who supported divestment placed their confidence in solidarity with the actions of similar-minded individuals. They believed that the evil of apartheid which in the past helped produce the horrors of slavery, genocide, and the holocaust can no longer be permitted among civilized people anywhere. They trusted that, like them, most well-meaning people find the evil of apartheid so abhorrent that they too would entertain a small economic risk in the faith that by acting in solidarity we could stand together with the black people of South Africa and help bring an end to apartheid. They were confident that enough people believed the same. Their confidence produced action in solidarity—solidarity with a multiracial, multicultural, and international community.

In the end our confidence proved well-founded for in concert with the actions of millions of others, Pretoria got the message. Apartheid and its institutional violence will no longer be tolerated among civilized people. Not even if it is profitable to the powerful. Not even if it is white, clean, and well-dressed. Not even if it controls the images on the walls of our cave. Our confidence in basic human decency and the solidarity it can bestow helped create important future facts, among them that there is still human decency and, perhaps most importantly, that human solidarity against evil still exists and can be effective. This, I suggest, is no small change in the dismal period we call the postmodern.

Moreover, there are good consequentialist reasons for trusting in our ability to create good consequences by acting in solidarity with others. Without such confidence in solidarity, consequentialism quickly reduces to a pernicious egoism. It becomes a convenient excuse for selfishness, hypocrisy, and apathy, just as it was with divestment. If we consider only the consequences of our individual act, then many of our activities seem inconsequential: the conservation of energy and resources, the use of biodegradable products and self-restraint from pollution, our contributions to socially conscious organizations, the promotion of peace, or the boycotting of corporations which do not. If people fail to engage in such activities, the world will be a worse place than it otherwise would have been. Simply put, in the long run, it is best to believe that the consequences are better if we reason in solidarity rather than individually whenever it is reasonable to do so. Consequentialism speaks against the narrow, selfish-minded logic of the consequentialist argument.

Indeed, there is an important lesson here for moral theory. Consequentialist theories generally are instances of *microethics*.[13] Microethics takes the survival and well-being of individuals to be the highest good and considers right whatever maximizes that good. Microethics can concern itself with the good of groups or collectives, but it does so only insofar as that good is understood to consist of nothing more than the good of the individuals that make up the group. *Macroethics*,[14] by contrast, assigns highest value to the survival and well-being of collectives and groups. Such entities are said themselves to have a good or interest. Macroethics defines moral conduct (either partly or exclusively) in terms of what maximizes the good of collectives or groups.

My point is that consequentialism can best fulfill its goal of producing the best consequences by adopting the standpoint of macroethics whenever it is reasonable to do so. As illustrated, this is what we do when we invest in the market, contribute to charity, vote, or join in solidarity with a movement like divestment. The consequences we project into the future are those of the group or collective with which we identify rather than our own in isolation.

Our survival as a culture may hinge on our ability to reason in terms of macroethics, if we are to deal successfully with such problems as those of the environment, world hunger, war, oppression, and the economy. To reason solely in terms of microethics blinds us to the fact that the maximization of the value of the consequences of our acts is more complicated than simple individualism or simple holism can allow. There is no algorithm or principle which can tell us, in all cases, when to reason individually and when to reason collectively. As John Dewey recommended, we must reason with intelligence to determine when it is best to consider collective consequences and when it is best to consider individual consequences,[15] but in either case we will adopt the point of view of macroethics.

I began with a quotation from Hegel. I hope that we shed some light as sanctions move into the night. For, as an old Chinese proverb states, "It is better to light one candle than to curse the darkness."

NOTES

1. For consideration of these other arguments, see Richard Werner, "South Africa: University Neutrality and the Consequences of Divestment" in *Neutrality and Academic Ethics*, Robert Simon, ed., (Totowa, NJ: Roman & Littlefield, 1994).

2. See Robert L. Holmes, *On War and Morality* (Princeton: Princeton University Press, 1989) and Duane Cady, *From Warism to Pacifism* (Philadelphia: Temple University Press, 1989).

3. See Noam Chomsky, "The Global Protection Racket: Reflections on the Gulf War" in *Chronicles of Dissent*, edited by Noam Chomsky and David Barsamian (Monroe, ME: Common Courage Press, 1992).

4. For an excellent comparison of apartheid in the U.S. and South Africa, see George M. Fredrickson, *White Supremacy* (Oxford: Oxford University Press, 1981).

5. See David Barsamian, ed., *Stenographers to Power* (Monroe, ME: Common Courage Press, 1992) and Neil Postman, *Amusing Ourselves to Death* (New York: Viking Penguin, 1985).

6. ABC News *Nightline* (10 July 1991).

7. Ibid.

8. Ibid.

9. Ibid.

10. *The New York Times* (14 July 1991), sec. 4, p. 3.

11. National Public Radio, *All Things Considered* (10 July 1991).

12. Ibid.

13. Robert Holmes, *Basic Moral Philosophy* (Belmont, CA: Wadsworth Publishing Co., 1993), 55–57.

14. Ibid.

15. Ibid., chap. 13.

SECTION III

Desert Storm Assessments

INTRODUCTION

The American airstrike against Iraq called "Operation Desert Storm" officially began on 17 January 1991, and ended on 28 February 1991. Because the airstrike required a major mobilization of American military personnel and budget resources, military leaders attended carefully to its justification. They presented the attack publicly as a response to Iraq's 2 August 1991 invasion and subsequent occupation of Kuwait. Within that framework, American military leaders tried to justify both the ends and the means of the attack. They tried to show (1) that the purpose of the airstrike was to get Iraq to retreat from Kuwait; (2) that the retreat was necessary and beneficial; (3) that the airstrike was the best method for bringing about Iraq's retreat; and (4) that the airstrike was carried out efficiently and with minimum damage to innocent parties.

This section of the book is primarily an assessment of the justification of the airstrike, seen through the lens of the just war tradition. The just war tradition (or the "justified war tradition," as some of the authors refer to it) has developed seven criteria for evaluating the moral viability of a particular war. The war must be fought for a *just cause*, declared by the *right authority*, be conducted with the *right intention* and be the *last resort* to bring about an *emergent peace*. Warriors must exercise *discrimination* in deciding who to harm and the total evil brought about by the war must be *proportionate* to the good to be achieved. Against this background, the authors of the essays in this section raise and offer answers to such questions as: Which criteria of just war did President Bush claim the airstrike satisfied? Did the airstrike actually satisfy those criteria? What did the President's interpretation of the just war criteria reveal about his ethical development? How should we apply the criteria of just war when dealing with an enemy who evaluates war from a different ethical perspective? How should we understand and apply the standard of proportionality in the context of this conflict? How did propagandized discourse celebrating the airstrike contaminate its justification? And, if a war cannot be justified morally, how are the souls of the warriors stained? In addition to specific observations about Operation Desert Storm, each author makes a new and substantial contribution to contemporary scholarship on justified war theory, by drawing conclusions and designing analytic nets which can and should be applied in the evaluation of future military conflicts.

The opening chapter by Jerald Richards, "George Bush, Justified War Morality, and the Gulf War," presents the background information about justified war morality and Bush's appeal to it, upon which most of the essays in this section rely. Richards examines and evaluates Bush's 28 January 1991 address to the National Religious Broadcasters Convention in Washington, D.C., in which Bush defended Operation Desert Storm using the criteria of justified war morality. Richards rejects Bush's defense, arguing that Bush applied the criteria in a mechanical and unimaginative manner, in abstraction from the ethics of justice which ground just war theory and in abstraction from the socio-political context of the war.

Joseph C. Kunkel and Bruce Taylor, in "George Bush and the Gulf War: Measuring Values Maturity," use Bush's justification of the airstrike to evaluate Bush's level of moral development. Kunkel and Taylor argue that a person's level of moral development (identified using the model first set forth by Abraham Maslow and more recently expanded by Brian Hall) affects the interpretation one gives to the criteria of just war. Bush's interpretation allowed him to justify Operation Desert Storm, but his interpretation was characteristic of a relatively immature level of valuing. A person at a higher level of valuing would have evaluated Desert Storm as unjust.

In "War with Iraq: Just Another Unjust War," James P. Sterba presents his interpretation of the just war criterion of "proportionality" and argues that Operation Desert Storm did not satisfy the criterion, for two reasons. The belligerent means employed in the Operation cannot be judged proportionate because an airstrike was not the last resort for resolving the conflict. Even if it had been, the large number of Iraqi civilians who died was not proportionate to the relatively smaller number of Kuwaitis whose lives were threatened by Iraqi forces.

In "Geopolitical Realism, Morality, and the War in the Gulf," Jonathan Schonsheck argues that Operation Desert Storm can be justified, if the criteria of last resort and proportionality are applied with an eye to the future of the Mideast region. Military action might not have been the only means of forcing Iraq out of Kuwait, but eliminating the destabilizing threat posed to the region by a fully armed Iraq could only have been achieved by military action. The military action taken, including the numbers of Iraqi casualties, was proportionate to the evils prevented, which include a possible regional war involving nuclear weapons, ecological damage caused by future Iraqi military ventures, and the deaths of thousands of innocents and defenders at the hands of an aggressor nation.

Frederick R. Struckmeyer, in "Reflections on a Mass Killing," questions whether the deaths of thousands of Iraqis as a result of such an unevenly matched military conflict could ever be justified. Reacting to an editorial in *Newsweek* magazine, he wonders about the effect that remorseless support of mass killing has on the American soul.

Ron Hirschbein, in "Support our Tropes: A Critique of Persian Gulf Discourse," explains why Americans did not see Operation Desert Storm as a massacre. Writing in an angry voice, he gives three reasons: stringent, almost unprecedented censorship; a docile, popular press committed to celebrating a triumphant vision of the American military; and the uncritical, enthusiastic acceptance of the Bush administration's trope that likened Hussein to Hitler.

Such discourse, casting Saddam Hussein as evil and Americans as just warriors, continues on the lips of the new Clinton administration. This book goes to press after America's 26 June 1993 bombing of Iraq's central intelligence headquarters in Baghdad. On that day, President Clinton described the bombing as a response to Saddam Hussein's "loathsome, cowardly attack against our country" in the form of an alleged plot to assassinate former president Bush during his trip to Kuwait. According to Chairman of the Joint Chiefs of Staff Colin Powell, the American response was "designed" to be "proportionate to the attempt on President Bush's life," in that, as Secretary of Defense Les Aspin said, it was designed to "go after those responsible; [we are] not just killing people."

American interests in controlling Iraq are multifaceted, as the Mideast is a strategically as well as economically important region, and Jews, Christians and Moslems have ideological attachments to it. At this time, the end of the conflict is not in sight. The United Nations continues its siege of Iraq and its disablement of the Iraqi military (couched in the modern terms of "economic sanctions" and "deterring nuclear war"). Iraq continues to develop its military capabilities and to display those in its attempts to subdue dissident domestic populations.

GEORGE BUSH, JUSTIFIED WAR MORALITY, AND THE GULF WAR

Jerald Richards

A new national phenomenon appeared in the dialogues, discussions, and debates prior to and during the Persian Gulf War. Never before in the history of this country have so many political, civic, religious, and military leaders been so concerned, apparently, about assessing warfare in terms of the criteria of justified war morality. At the least, those responsible for initiating, and those sympathetic with, the war appealed again and again to the justness of the war (*jus ad bellum*) and the justness of the ways in which the war was being carried out (*jus in bello*). These appeals often referred explicitly to one or more of the specific criteria of justified war morality. President Bush set the tone for this approach in many of his addresses to the nation, speeches to various organizations and groups, and press conferences.

Representative of this approach was President Bush's address to the National Religious Broadcasters Convention in Washington, D.C., on 28 January 1991.[1] Although the purpose of the address was not necessarily to talk about the Gulf War, Bush had spoken only about five minutes (it was a twenty-minute address) before he launched into a defense of the war on moral grounds, and he continued his defense throughout the remainder of the address. He claimed that the war in the Gulf was a just war, and that it had to do with "...good versus evil, right versus wrong, human dignity and freedom versus tyranny and oppression." In his defense of the Gulf War, Bush appealed, in one way or another, to all the criteria of justified war morality—just cause, legitimate authority, right intention, last resort, proportionality (just means, proportionate damage), and discrimination (noncombatant immunity).[2] Toward the end of his address, Bush repeated the words with which he began his moral defense of the Gulf War, saying, "We know that this is a just war."

There are at least three possible ways one could react to or "read" Bush's address. I will call these the ways of the pessimist, the optimist, and the realist.

The pessimist would probably read the address as an attempt on Bush's part to take the offensive against those critical of the war on moral grounds and to put those sympathetic with Bush's war policy the means not only to respond to these critics but also to feel at ease about any moral qualms they may have had about the war. For the pessimist, it is highly questionable that Bush was genuinely concerned about the primacy of morality in considering the justifiability of the use of military force in the Gulf. Some pessimists see Bush's address as just another rather cunning attempt to manipulate and exploit public opinion and to rationalize a pragmatic, nonmoral effort to advance his understanding of what is in the national interest.

The optimist reads Bush's address as a sincere effort on his part to respond to the genuine moral concerns of many Americans about the moral legitimacy of the Gulf War. On this reading, Bush takes justified war morality seriously, honestly believes the criteria are satisfied by the Gulf War, and does his best to support his beliefs with arguments and evidence.

The realist reads Bush's address with some of the qualms of the pessimist, but with a willingness to suspend these qualms, at least temporarily, and to examine Bush's argumentation and the evidence with an open mind. Throughout the remainder of the paper, I shall assume the stance of the realist. In the major portion of the paper, I shall submit Bush's reasoning to critical analysis and evaluation, concluding that his argumentation fails to support his claim that the Gulf War was a just war. Then I shall make some observations about the limitations of the way President Bush used justified war morality.

1. The Realist's Examination of Bush's Argumentation

A. Just Cause

The just cause of the Gulf War, according to Bush, was to respond to Iraq's aggression against Kuwait, to seek Iraq's withdrawal from Kuwait and the restoration of Kuwait's legitimate government, and to achieve the security and stability of the Gulf. Bush added that the withdrawal must be complete, immediate, and without condition. I take it he means that the third cause (achieving the security and stability of the Gulf) will be achieved through the first two causes (Iraq's withdrawal and the restoration of Kuwait's government).

Bush calls Iraq's aggression "naked aggression." By that term, I take it he meant that the aggression was unprovoked or was not a retaliatory response to aggression or threatened aggression on the part of Kuwait. It is fairly clear that Iraq's aggression was not a response to aggression or to the threat of aggression. But it is not clear, however, that Iraq's aggression was unprovoked. Iraq allegedly charged that Kuwait was drawing oil from Iraqi territory; was exploiting disputed territory between Iraq and Kuwait; was pouring more than its quota of oil (according to OPEC guidelines) into the world market, thus reducing the price of crude and harmfully affecting the Iraqi economy; and was unwilling to negotiate with Iraq over the possibility that two small uninhabited islands in the Gulf might be ceded to Iraq, giving it safe access to the Gulf.

In addition, the U.S. ambassador to Iraq, April Glaspie, allegedly told Saddam Hussein that the U.S. was not concerned about or interested in Arab-Arab conflicts, in particular the conflict between Iraq and Kuwait.[3] Iraq plausibly could interpret the ambassador's statement as a tacit approval, maybe even encouragement of or, at the least, indifference to Iraq's takeover of Kuwait. Further, in the light of the subsequent massive U.S. military response to Iraq's aggression, a cynic might wonder if Iraq had not been "set up" by the U.S. ambassador to attack Kuwait so that the U.S. could get a military foothold in the Middle East, as well as destroy (or weaken considerably) Iraq's military forces which some persons believed were a potential destabilizing factor in that region. It also should be noted that the U.S. was partly responsible for creating Iraq's military forces and, thus, the alleged destabilizing conditions.[4]

In spite of the possible provocation of Iraq, Iraq's aggression cannot be justified on moral grounds. Iraq was not attacked by Kuwait nor was attack threatened by Kuwait. One cannot question the moral legitimacy of insisting upon Iraqi withdrawal from Kuwait. But given the possible provocations of Iraq's aggression, more careful attention should have been given by the U.S. and the United Nations to the means used to bring about the withdrawal, including the possibility of some type of negotiated settlement.

B. Legitimate Authority

For Bush, the war against Iraq was declared by legitimate or competent authority. Bush claimed essentially that the war was authorized and conducted by the United Nations and its Security Council. The war, he said, "...is supported by unprecedented United Nations' solidarity, the principle of collective self-defense, twelve Security Council resolutions and, in the Gulf, twenty-eight nations from six continents united...."

Given a number of considerations, the truth of the matter

probably is that the United Nations provided a multinational facade for the unilateral intervention of the United States. Granted, Security Council resolutions were passed[5] and some 27 other nations besides the U.S. got involved in the war in one way or another. But no United Nations peacekeeping force ever came close to commanding and conducting the war effort. Only a mechanical and abstract application of the criterion of legitimate authority could lead to the conclusion that it was satisfied, that the United Nations had indeed declared and was conducting the war, and that the U.S. was just one of the many nations cooperating together in a genuinely collective effort. Promises of massive aid (what ordinarily might be called bribes) by the U.S. to many nations, to be paid for mainly by the U.S. taxpayer, virtually guaranteed that nations with some doubts about the legitimacy and wisdom of a war against Iraq would acquiesce and/or join in the effort.[6] At no point during the war did or would the U.S. submit to the leadership of a U.N. military command.[7] Stripping off the multinational facade, the U.S. remains as the chief instigator and perpetrator of the war against Iraq.[8]

This fact raises a number of crucial issues. For one thing, was the U.S. a legitimate authority to declare and carry out a war against Iraq? There were no treaties between the U.S. and Kuwait that might make the U.S. a legitimate authority.[9] Kuwait apparently did not make a special appeal to the U.S. as such to help it resist attack, and even if Kuwait had made such an appeal, that alone would not have made the U.S. a legitimate authority. Perhaps the U.S. has a fairly consistent history of coming to the aid of nations unjustly attacked, and this history provides a kind of international precedent for U.S. intervention. Perhaps such a history might provide such a precedent, but no such history exists. The U.S. did not, for example, go to the aid of Jordan and the Palestinians, in spite of U.N. sanctions against Israel.[10] The U.S., for another example, did not go to the aid of the Cypriots against the Turks, in spite of U.N. sanctions against Turkey.[11] In fact, a strong case could be made for a very opposite history, a history of U.S. support of groups engaged in aggression against legitimate governments, as in Chile and Nicaragua,[12] as well as U.S. "naked aggression" against other nations, as in Grenada and Panama.[13]

Assuming that U.S. military action in the Gulf was essentially unilateral action, but assuming that past international humanitarian action by the U.S. might provide a precedent for this unilateral action and, thus, satisfy the criterion of legitimate authority, and assuming also that the action satisfied all the other criteria of justified war morality, this action could not be justified unless the U.S. Congress declared war on Iraq. But did the U.S. Congress declare war on Iraq? A resolution supporting the use of military force in the Gulf, should it become necessary to use it, is hardly a declaration of war. I leave the resolution of this question to constitutional scholars. At the very least, there is some doubt that the military action of the U.S. in the Gulf was constitutional.[14]

President Bush's appeal to the United Nations and U.N. Security Council resolutions gives the impression that he was a strong advocate and supporter of the U.N. and of the rule of international law and conventions. However, this is a misleading impression. The U.S. government has been, at best, a weak supporter of the U.N. It has vetoed more U.N. resolutions than any other nation.[15] It has rejected U.N. resolutions condemning the attacks on Grenada and Panama.[16] In addition, it has, at best, ignored the World Court ruling about the illegality of the mining of the harbor of Managua and other U.S. actions in Nicaragua in support of the Contras.[17]

Given all these considerations, it is questionable that the Gulf War satisfied the criterion of legitimate authority.

C. Right Intention

According to President Bush, the Gulf War was fought with the right intention (just intention, right reason, good reason). This intention was to obtain Iraq's withdrawal from Kuwait and the restoration of Kuwait's legitimate government, in short, "... to stop the rape, the pillage, the plunder of Kuwait." But over the course of weeks, other intentions were mentioned: the safeguarding of human rights, assuring adequate and affordable energy supplies to the West, advancing a new international order, overthrowing a hostile dictator, protecting national security, protecting the national interest, making sure that aggression is not rewarded, and destroying Iraq's nuclear and chemical weapons capabilities.[18] It was never made clear just exactly what the intentions of the war were. In addition, some persons are suspicious that there were hidden intentions (hidden agendas) and have suggested one or more of the following:[19] restoring U.S. pride by overcoming the so-called Vietnam syndrome; establishing a new sphere of U.S. military influence to replace the lost sphere of influence in Europe as a result of the demise of the "cold war" confrontation between the U.S. and the Soviet Union; restoring U.S. credibility and reliability; helping to bring peace to the

Middle East as a whole; providing the U.S. military an opportunity to test out a number of weapons and weapons systems in a desert environment and under wartime conditions; using planes, weapons, bombs, and shells that were overstocked in the U.S. arsenal, some of which were about to become obsolete; stimulating the war economy; supporting the multinational oil corporations; proving that Bush is not a "wimp"; and making the world safe for war.[20]

Given all the possibilities when it comes to the actual intentions for engaging in the Gulf War, it is no wonder that thoughtful persons entertain lingering doubts whether the Gulf War was fought with the right intentions.

This concern about right intentions was especially crucial for those conscientious persons in the U.S. military who were involved in the Gulf War or about to be sent to the Gulf. Given the wide range of actually stated as well as suspected motives for military action against Iraq, these conscientious persons were put in a terrible moral bind. Many of the stated and suspected motives are unjust intentions or wrong reasons for military action. If these, or some of these, unjust intentions were the actual intentions for fighting Iraq, then those participating in the military action were participating in an unjust war. Given the wide range of possible motives and the failure of President Bush to clarify his motives, the only option for the conscientious military person would seem to be refusal to participate in the Gulf War. But such refusals led to harassment, ridicule, and court martials, thus adding the injustice of this kind of treatment to the injustice (or perceived or possible injustice) of the war. Only exceptionally strong moral persons were able to dare to question the justness of the war and to face the ensuing harsh response by the military leadership.[21]

If the actual intentions of the Gulf War were to obtain Iraq's withdrawal from Kuwait and the restoration of Kuwait's legitimate government, then one is led to wonder why, among other things, the infrastructure of Iraq had to be destroyed[22] and why Iraqis clearly withdrawing from Kuwait were killed by U.S. warplanes.[23]

D. Last Resort

For Bush, the criterion of last resort was satisfied. He claims that all attempts were made to get Iraq to withdraw but these attempts failed and war became inevitable. In his National Religious Broadcasters address, Bush mentioned failed diplomatic attempts, but did not mention the embargo. But all nonpartisan assessments of the embargo concluded that it was working and that over time it would force the withdrawal of Iraq from Kuwait, and that the losses resulting from the embargo would be considerably less than the losses resulting from warfare.[24] The failed diplomatic efforts Bush mentioned could be viewed as less than genuine attempts at negotiation and more like attempts to threaten Iraq with destruction if it did not completely, immediately, and unconditionally withdraw from Kuwait.[25] Few if any attempts were made to give Hussein an opportunity to "save face," to set up the opportunity for negotiations and the consideration of Iraq's grievances after withdrawal from Kuwait, or to acknowledge Hussein's apparent gestures toward compliance with U.N. resolutions by releasing hostages and by not initiating an attack upon U.S. and other forces.

Given the ongoing success of the embargo, war was certainly far from being inevitable. What would make it inevitable was the apparent dogged determination of President Bush to resort to warfare and to refuse to negotiate. Words like "inevitability" and "necessity" when talking about warfare function as linguistic stoppers—they stop all discussion, dialogue, and debate. And they tend to excuse and justify anything that might be done in their name and under their aegis.

It is highly unlikely that the criterion of last resort was satisfied by the Gulf War.

E. Proportionality

Not mentioning them by name, Bush claims that the criteria of proportionality (just means, proportionate damage) and discrimination (noncombatant immunity) were satisfied by keeping casualties to a minimum and by avoiding harm to the innocent. He actually combines the two criteria, but I shall assume he did not combine them (or did not intend to combine them) and I shall comment on each of them separately.

For Bush, the criterion of proportionality (just means, proportionate damage) was satisfied by keeping casualties to a minimum. In Bush's words, "...we must act reasonably, humanely, and make every effort possible to keep casualties to a minimum." I assume he meant casualties on all sides. The response, he says, was proportionate to the threat. If by "the threat" Bush has in mind the harm and potential harm to the Kuwaitis, then it is highly questionable that the response of the U.S. military was proportionate.

That the U.S. response was disproportionate to the Iraqi threat is borne out by the comparative fatality data—less than 400 Americans killed,[26] upwards of 200,000 Iraqis killed.[27] U.S. casualties were kept to a minimum, but Iraqi casualties apparently were maximized. The largest air attack of human history was launched against Iraq. The U.S. in six weeks dropped 10 times the explosive power that was used on Japan during the last 14 months of World War II, and this includes the atomic bombing of Hiroshima and Nagasaki.[28] The massive attack of the U.S. military amounted to the systematic destruction of a country of only 17,000,000 people.

Sadly lacking from U.S. strategy planning were calculations regarding many probable and possible consequences—short-term and long-term—of such massive military intervention. Surely, many of these consequences were foreseeable—such things as the missile attacks upon Israel, setting fire to hundreds of oil wells with the resultant ecological damage, Iraqi retaliation against the Kurds and Shiites,[29] the creation of thousands of refugees, and the terrible suffering of Iraqi civilians (mostly but not only children) as a result of the destruction of the infrastructure of Iraq. It is quite possible that the last mentioned consequence was not only foreseeable but also intended.[30] Other possible consequences also should have been considered—the increased militarization of the Middle East, the championing of military as opposed to nonmilitary solutions to conflicts among nations, the increased militarization of American society, the continuing suffering of thousands of U.S. citizens due to the allocation of vast sums of money and resources to the military rather than to human-helping services, the stirring up of anti-American feelings among Arab peoples, the stirring up of anti-Arab feelings among Americans, and the excessive retaliation by Kuwaitis against Kuwaiti traitors. If both these highly probable and these possible (likely) consequences had been considered seriously, it is inconceivable that the U.S. strategists could have concluded a massive military response to Iraqi aggression could/would have satisfied the criterion of proportionality.

One way that Bush and his associates attempted to justify the claim that the response was appropriate was to grossly exaggerate the strength, preparedness, commitment, and determination of the Iraqi military and people. This deception (in many cases, perhaps, self-deception) was perpetrated, not only by U.S. military strategists, but also by ex-military leaders and other types of so-called military experts. There were exceptions to these overestimations, but the dissenters were not heard or were stifled. Admittedly, it is possible that military analysts originally could honestly have overestimated the strength of the Iraqi military, but once the air war against Iraq was two or three days old, it should have been clear that a reassessment was in order and a scaling down of the military response was called for. That this did not occur tends to suggest that there may have been other concerns operating in the minds of U.S. leaders rather than a concern for a proportionate response.

F. Discrimination

In talking about keeping casualties to a minimum, Bush was referring to civilians as well as to U.S. military personnel. He claimed the U.S. did everything possible to avoid hurting the innocent. The point was made again and again by Pentagon officials, government leaders, analysts, and commentators that the bombing and missile raids were against military targets only, and that the bombs used were "smart" bombs, guided unerringly to make pinpoint strikes on these military targets. The truth of the matter seems to be quite different. Only 7.4 percent of the bombs dropped on Iraq were "smart" bombs or precision-guidance ordnance.[31] Also, among the targets of the bombing raids were bridges, electrical generating plants, water facilities, and warehouses of medicine and food. It does not take much of an imagination to realize that the destruction of the infrastructure of Iraq was aimed at the total Iraqi population and not just at the military.[32] The available data on the actual destruction and the projected suffering of civilians supports the judgement that the principle of discrimination was seriously violated by U.S. military action. A Harvard Medical School Study Team, conducting one of the first systematic and comprehensive on-site examinations of public health in Iraq after the Gulf War, concluded, among other things, the following. Approximately 55,000 children under five had already died as a result of the delayed effects of the war. At least 170,000 more children under five would die in the following year because of the war. Epidemic levels of cholera, typhoid, and other diseases already existed in Iraq and would escalate through the following summer. The key to this public health disaster was the destruction of Iraq's electrical systems by U.S. bombing, which made Iraq's water purification systems, sewage treatment systems, and much hospital equipment inoperative.[33]

I conclude that, in spite of Bush's efforts to justify the Gulf War by an appeal to the criteria of justified war morality, the war failed to satisfy at least most of these criteria and accordingly was unjust.

2. Observations on Bush's Use of Justified War Morality

The case against the moral justifiability of the Gulf War through the application of the criteria of justified war morality is extremely strong. Yet President Bush, other political and military leaders, and many civic and religious leaders insisted, and continue to insist, that the criteria were satisfied and the war was just. How can this disagreement be explained?

My opinion is that the method of the application of justified war morality is often flawed. If we abstract the criteria of justified war morality from the larger morality of which they are a part, and if we apply them in a mechanical and unimaginative manner, then we are likely to get the results that we find in Bush's defense of the Gulf War. This larger morality I call the Hebrew-Christian or Western moral tradition. Central in this tradition is an understanding of and concern for the worth of persons, the moral equality of persons, and universally applicable principles designed to protect persons from harm and to promote human well-being. A major principle of this morality is the principle of nonviolence. This morality insists upon the nonviolent resolution of human conflicts, and views violence in all its forms as an indication of human failure—ultimately the failure to genuinely respect (regard) human beings as persons. According to this morality, resort to violence, let alone resort to the organized violence of warfare, is not even a live option in most conflict situations, either individual or collective. It may become a live option in order to stop violent aggression and seriously harmful actions, but only when all other means of conflict resolution have been fully applied and have failed. But even in these kinds of situations, resort to violence is not justified unless certain stringent conditions can be fully satisfied. On the level of organized response to violence is where the criteria of justified war morality come in. When these criteria are divorced or abstracted from the morality of which they are a part, it becomes much easier to use them in such ways that a resort to violence takes on an aura of moral respectability, especially if the criteria are applied mechanically and also in abstraction from the total socio-political context.

An example of this mechanical application in abstraction both from the grounding morality and the total socio-political context is the way in which the criterion of competent authority was supposedly satisfied in the Gulf War. I think this is an especially good example because most experts on justified war morality believe this criterion was satisfied. The U.N. did pass many resolutions supporting military action against Iraq. If we take these resolutions at face value, so to speak, and if we assume, contrary to fact, that U.N. forces supervised and conducted the war, then it would appear the criterion was satisfied. However, once we learn that the U.N. resolutions were passed (1) after the massive U.S. military buildup in the Middle East, and (2) only after a whirlwind campaign by Secretary Baker that involved various kinds of promises of substantial aid to many countries, we begin to wonder if this criterion was satisfied in anything approaching good faith and right intentions. Many of the votes in the U.N. may have been bought with a price and may not have reflected the true sentiments and beliefs of the nations voting. If we add to the above facts the fact that U.N. forces did not supervise and conduct the war against Iraq, then it becomes even more doubtful that the criterion of competent authority was satisfied.

In summary, I believe that President Bush abused justified war morality and that the basic reason for this abuse was the mechanical application of the criteria of justified war morality in abstraction from both (1) the larger morality within which they are embedded and out of which they emerge and (2) the total socio-political context of the Gulf War.

It could be argued that to insist that the only justifiable application of the criteria of justified war morality is an application that is grounded in and emerges out of a larger moral stance and commitment is to expect too much of President Bush, Secretary Baker, and the other related actors in the Gulf War. I do not know whether this pessimistic claim is correct or not. I do know that President Bush, whatever his actual capabilities might have been, clearly implied, if not indicated, in the National Religious Broadcasters address and in other public pronouncements, his own commitment to this larger morality. Given these pronouncements, we are surely justified in holding Bush and his associates to the requirements of the larger morality of which justified war morality is a part.

So what can be said about this phenomenon of many of our political, civic, military, and religious leaders apparently being so concerned about assessing the Gulf War in terms of the criteria of justified war morality? The optimist might think it is cause for rejoicing that finally in our more recent national history the concerns of morality are receiving their just due and are given primacy over purely pragmatic concerns. Given the ways in which morality was abused by the defenders of the Gulf War, the pessimist might wish that appeals to morality had never become a major part of that war, and that the damage to the moral point of view because of that abuse will take years to repair. For the pessimist, thoughtful, reflective, and sensitive persons will be very wary and suspicious of such appeals by our leaders for some time to come and many other persons will be cynical about them.The realist might share many of the misgivings of the pessimist, but at the same time might see the public moral debate about the Gulf War as a possibly hopeful sign for the future. Whatever one's specific response might be, there are at least *some* things about which all persons concerned about the moral point of view can agree:

1. Right actions and good results do not necessarily occur just because the actors appeal to and claim they are following principles of morality.
2. For moral principles to be effective, they must be grounded in lives genuinely committed to the worth of persons, right acting, good pursuits, and human well-being.
3. Our pressing primary task in the modern world is moral education.

Unless we restructure our priorities in this country, unless we bring about those social conditions that will enable persons to meet their uniquely human needs in cooperation with others, unless we relearn what goodness and happiness are all about, unless we rediscover the worth of ourselves and other persons, we can expect nothing other than "business as usual," no new world order but the same old thing, nothing other than the abuse of morality and the abuse of persons.

NOTES

1. "Remarks by the President to the National Religious Broadcasters Convention," press release of 28 January 1991, by the White House Office of the Press Secretary. Unless otherwise indicated, all quotations and paraphrases of President Bush's statements are from or based upon this press release.

2. President Bush referred also to the criterion of probability of success (related to or a facet of the criterion of proportionality), which was listed separately by the U.S. Catholic Bishops in their letter to Secretary of State James Baker, 7 November 1990. Bush referred to this criterion by saying, since the price of war is always high, "It must never, ever, be undertaken without total commitment to a successful outcome." He added, "It is only justified when victory can be achieved." On the Bishops' letter, see "Letter of the U.S. Catholic Bishops to Secretary of State James Baker, November 7, 1990," NISBCO Documentation Service #7, 1990, 1–2.

3. On Ambassador Glaspie's purported statements to Saddam Hussein and her appearance before the Senate Foreign Relations Committee and the House Foreign Affairs Committee, see "The Glaspie Transcript: Saddam Meets the U.S. Ambassador (July 25, 1990)," in Michael L. Sifry and Christopher Cerf, *The Gulf War Reader: History, Documents, Opinions* (New York: Random House, 1991), 122–133; *Time* (1 April 1991), 36; and *Newsweek* (1 April 1991), 17. The Glaspie transcript is the one released by Baghdad. The key statements by Ambassador Glaspie are: "But we have no opinion on the Arab-Arab conflicts, like your border disagreement with Kuwait," and "I was in the American embassy in Kuwait during the late '60s. The instruction we had during this period was that we should express no opinion on this issue and that the issue is not associated with America. James Baker has directed our official spokesmen to emphasize this instruction" (Sifry and Cerf, *The Gulf War Reader*, 130).

4. On the arming of Iraq and other Middle Eastern countries by the U.S., the Soviet Union, France, Great Britain, Germany, China, and others, see Michael T. Klare, "Fueling the Fire: How We Armed the Middle East," *Bulletin of the Atomic Scientists* 47:1 (January–February 1991), 19–26. Klare writes, "Between 1981 and 1988, Iraq purchased an estimated $46.7 billion worth of arms and military equipment from foreign suppliers, the largest accumulation ever of modern weapons by a Third World country." See also Murray Waas, "What Washington Gave Saddam for Christmas," in Sifry and Cerf, *The Gulf War Reader*, 85–95. Waas attempts to document the claim that "[t]he secret history of U.S. government approval of potentially illegal arms sales to Saddam Hussein is the story of how the Reagan and Bush administrations aided and abetted the Iraqi regime, allowing Saddam Hussein to build up the fourth-largest military arsenal in the world. It is the story of how two American presidencies assisted Saddam in obtaining chemical and biological weapons and the means of deriving them, threatening entire cities" (86).

5. "The U.N. Resolutions: The Complete Text" in Sifry and Cerf, *The Gulf War Reader*, 137–156.

6. Tom Harkin, "The Obligation to Debate," in Sifry and Cerf, *The Gulf War Reader*, 264; Alan Geyer and Barbara G. Green, *Lines in the Sand: Justice and the Gulf War* (Louisville: Westminster/John Knox Press, 1992), 117; and Jack Nelson-Pallmeyer, *Brave New World Order* (Maryknoll, NY: Orbis Books, 1992), 79–80.

7. Geyer and Green, *Lines in the Sand,* 118.

8. Pam Solo, "Talking Law, Waging War," *The Bulletin of the Atomic Scientists* 47:5 (June 1991), 25, describes the so-called coalition as "...an international coalition largely defined by the United States but including the United Nations, functioning like a committee to approve U.S. strategies after the fact." Leonard V. Johnson, "Time for Common Security," in the same issue of the *Bulletin*, claims that the war was not a triumph for the United Nations: "To the contrary, it demonstrated the dependence of that body on the power and consent of the United States. The United Nations has never been permitted to intervene against U.S. interests, nor will it be permitted to do so in the future" (28).

9. See "Transcript of House Sub-Committee Hearing on U.S. Commitments in the Gulf," in *The March to War*, edited by James Ridgeway, 57–58 (New York: Four Walls Eight Windows, 1991).

10. National Council of Churches of Christ, "On the Gulf and Middle East Crisis," in Sifry and Cerf, *The Gulf War Reader,* 231.

11. Ibid.

12. Ariel Dorfman, "Hymn for the Unsung," and Noam Chomsky, "The Use (and Abuse) of the United Nations," both in Sifry and Cerf, *The Gulf War Reader,* 327 and 308–309, respectively.

13. Dorfman, "Hymn for the Unsung," and Chomsky, "The Use (and Abuse) of the United Nations," in Sifry and Cerf, *The Gulf War Reader*.

14. Nelson-Pallmeyer, *Brave New World Order*, 80–81.

15. Chomsky, "The Use (and Abuse) of the United Nations," in Sifry and Cerf, *The Gulf War Reader*, 310.

16. Dorfman, "Hymn for the Unsung," and Chomsky, "The Use (and Abuse) of the United Nations," in Sifry and Cerf, *The Gulf War Reader*.

17. Ibid.

18. On these stated intentions, see Geyer and Green, *Lines in the Sand,* 63–69. On the speciousness of the alarm that war was the only way to keep Iraq from becoming a nuclear power since it was within a few months of producing nuclear weapons, see the following articles by David Albright and Mark Hibbs in the *Bulletin of the Atomic Scientists*: "Iraq and the Bomb: Were They Ever Close?," 47:2 (March 1991), 16–25; "Hyping the Iraqi Bomb," 47:2 (March 1991), 26–28; and "Iraq's Nuclear Hide-and-Seek," 47:7 (September 1991), 14–23. In their March 1991 article, Albright and Hibbs speculated it would take Iraq at least a decade to produce enough weapons grade uranium for one crude nuclear explosive (25). In the light of new information, in the September 1991 article, they express their belief that "...Iraq might have developed a usable nuclear arsenal in as little as two or three years" (23). Imports of key materials from other countries would have been necessary for Iraq to develop nuclear weapons.

19. On the following suspected intentions, see Geyer and Green, *Lines in the Sand,* 69–86.

20. On this last purported intention, see Marilyn B. Young, "Ruthless Intervention," *Bulletin of the Atomic Scientists* 47:5 (June 1991), 32–33.

21. For information on the cases of CO's to the Gulf War who allegedly "...received treatment that is outside the bounds of due process, humane standards,

and contrary to the express provisions of military regulations...," see *The Reporter for Conscience's Sake* 48 (February–June 1991). One of these persons, CO George Morse, was adopted by Amnesty International as a prisoner of conscience (February 1991). See also *CCCO News Notes* 43 (3).

22. Geyer and Green, *Lines in the Sand*, 140–143.

23. Nelson-Pallmeyer, *Brave New World Order*, 84.

24. William Webster, Director of the CIA, testifying before Congress in December 1990, said "...the most effective peacetime embargo ever mounted was strangling Iraq's economy, blocking 90% of its exports." Reported in John C. Polanyi, "Collective Will or Law of the Jungle," *Bulletin of the Atomic Scientists* 47:5, 23. See also Kimberly Elliott, Gary Hufbauer, and Jeffrey Schott, "Sanctions Work: The Historical Record," in Sifry and Cerf, *The Gulf War Reader*, 255–259.

25. Geyer and Green, *Lines in the Sand*, 94–100.

26. Pentagon casualty reports indicate that 385 U.S. military personnel died during the Gulf War (between 12 August 1990 and 11 April 1991). Of these persons, 148 were killed in combat and no more than 16 were killed in skirmishes or firefights with Iraqi soldiers. On these and related statistics, see the report of the Knight News Service in *The Cincinnati Enquirer* (18 August 1991), A–4.

27. Geyer and Green, *Lines in the Sand*, 148–149.

28. For a reference on the extensiveness of the bombing, see note 31 below.

29. Iraqi retaliation against the Kurds and Shiites was greatly exacerbated, if not caused, by President Bush's encouragement that they revolt against Saddam Hussein, especially without a commitment to help them and to protect them from retaliation. The belated and inadequate U.S. aid to Kurds and Shiites fleeing Iraq's wrath was not only pathetic but also unconscionable. The exploitative and often brutal treatment of the Kurds (and other Iraqis) by the West goes back as far as the 1920s, when the British army used gas shells (chemical weapons) to put down a rebellion against British rule, killing 9,000 Arabs. Some claim that some Iraqi villages were destroyed solely because their inhabitants had not paid their taxes. Arthur Harris (later "Bomber" Harris of WWII saturation bombing infamy) reported, after one raid in 1924, "...the Arab and Kurd now know what real bombing means, in casualties and damage; they now know that within 45 minutes a full-sized village can be practically wiped out and a third of its inhabitants killed or injured..." On the action of the British and the statement of Arthur Harris, see *The Catholic Worker* 58 (June–July 1991), 8, reprinted from *Conscience* (Spring 1991), citing the *Manchester Guardian Weekly*.

30. See note 32 below.

31. The rest of the 88,500 tons of bombs dropped on Iraq were highly destructive conventional weapons, including cluster bombs and fuel-air explosives. Information on the success and reliability of the precision-guided ordnance is scanty and not very reliable. For detailed information on the types of conventional weapons used in the Gulf War see Paul F. Walker and Eric Stambler, "...And the Dirty Little Weapons," *Bulletin of the Atomic Scientists* 47:4, 20–24.

32. Although many details still remain classified, some military personnel involved in the selection of Iraqi bombing targets are acknowledging that many of the targets were selected to increase the economic and psychological impact of sanctions on Iraqi society as a whole as well as to create post-war leverage over Iraq.

Thus, damage to civilians and civilian structures was sometimes neither "collateral" nor unintended. One justification given, in U.S. Air Force briefings, for this intentional bombing of civilian targets is that Iraqi citizens were not innocent but were partly to blame for Hussein's invasion of Kuwait. One Air Force officer is quoted as saying, "They do live there, and ultimately the people have some control over what goes on in their country." In spite of these revelations about the nature of Iraqi targets, Defense Secretary Dick Cheney said to reporters in June, 1991, that all Iraqi targets were "perfectly legitimate," adding, "If I had it to do over again, I would do exactly the same thing." See report from *The Washington Post*, reprinted in *The Cincinnati Enquirer* (23 June 1991), A13.

33. See "Harvard Study Team Report: Public Health in Iraq after the Gulf War," a summary published by *Out Now*, 1991. Also, see the July 1991 report of Witness for Peace, *What We Have Seen and Heard in the Middle East: Iraq/Israel/Palestine: The Human Face of the Gulf War*. A follow-up (conducted 25 August–10 September 1991) to the Harvard Study (conducted in May 1991) by the International Study Team on the Gulf Crisis (composed of 35 researchers from 13 countries and assisted by many other people from the region) announced on 22 October 1991 even more ominous findings about infant mortality and morbidity in Iraq. About this second study, the editors of *Sojourners*, "A Tragic Year Later: Infant Mortality in Post-War Iraq," 21 (January 1992), 19, wrote: "The recent study concluded that Iraq's child mortality rate has more than tripled since the end of the war. Nearly one million of Iraq's children under 5 years of age (29%) are significantly undernourished. And many children show signs of severe psychological trauma; two-thirds of school-age children believe they will not live to adulthood." See 19–21 for an interview of Dr. Tim Cote, one of the leaders of the second study team. See also Louise Cainkar, "Desert Sin: A Post-War Journey Through Iraq," in *Beyond the Storm: A Gulf Crisis Reader*, edited by Phyllis Bennis and Michel Moushabeck (New York: Olive Branch Press, 1991), 335–355.

GEORGE BUSH AND THE GULF WAR: MEASURING VALUES MATURITY

Joseph C. Kunkel and Bruce M. Taylor

Immature presidential leadership presents a particular danger in the exercise of foreign policy. In that arena, the checks and balances that operate in the domestic political culture are largely absent which means that the president of the United States has enormous military and economic power. The president not only enjoys wide constitutional latitude but also has freedom of initiative with few well-organized constituencies to oppose any given action. In the exercise of foreign policy, presidential immaturity can result in a failure of imagination, a tendency to consider security issues solely from a worst case standpoint, and an inability or unwillingness to place events in the global context of world harmony.

In the first half of this chapter we examine the level of maturity of George Bush's style of presidential leadership in light of moral development theory. In the second half we introduce moral development theory into the types of reasons given for terming a war "just" in accord with just war doctrine. We then analyze the Gulf War justifications President Bush gave for meeting the conditions set forth in just war doctrine. Based on both analyses we contend the leadership immaturity of George Bush in the exercise of U.S. foreign policy produced a tactical success but a human disaster in the Persian Gulf.

1. George Bush and the Development of Human Values

There are a number of models that describe how humans grow toward maturity. The best known are Abraham Maslow's hierarchy of needs, Lawrence Kohlberg's moral reasoning, Jean Piaget's cognitive development, and Erik Erikson's psychosocial development. Each of these researchers has contended that humans grow through a succession of stages with varying degrees of attainment, but that each person is born with the capacity to function at the moral, intellectual, and spiritual level of those outstanding individuals who are admired by most cultures. More recently Brian Hall, beginning with Maslow's schema, has developed a sophisticated model of the process of human growth toward its fullest potential. We have chosen the Hall model, which we believe to be the most powerful analytical tool with which to measure degrees of maturity, as the basis for our inquiry.[1]

Abraham Maslow believed that values can be arranged in a hierarchy from those based upon lower or basic needs stemming from our nature as animals to those based upon higher needs deriving from our particularly human nature. For Maslow, the human being grows as a personality by satisfying the basic needs of the biological self (food, water and sex) and the safety needs (security). Once these needs are met the human is ready to advance to concerns about being loved and respected by the surrounding social group, and with developing a sense of self-esteem. Passage through these lower valuing levels is necessary for all healthy human beings; absence of fulfillment causes serious biological and psychological dysfunction. Maslow called them "deficiency" needs.

After these values are internalized the person searches for meaning as a complete human being. Maslow described such an individual as "self-actualized." By this term he meant that an individual's fully human potential is being realized. Among the qualities he found in such persons are self-acceptance, self-direction, autonomy, desire to serve others, sense of mission in life, honesty, candor, openness, and sense of justice. Maslow described these as "being" values in that these traits are incorporated by the self acting independently of the surrounding social group. Meaning-making at these higher levels marks the fully human person.

Brian Hall, following Maslow, has developed a four-phase model of human growth ranging across Maslow's hierarchy. His first two phases correspond to Maslow's lower or basic needs, while Phases III and IV are in the self-actualized area. Hall's contribution has been to codify a system involving 125 value names so that they can be used in documenting personal growth. Over the past 25 years Hall and his associates have analyzed reflection diaries, normed personality inventories, organizational documents, speeches, and letters to discover the clusters of values that mark the development of maturity in individuals and organizations. Chart I summarizes the approach.[2]

According to Hall, as children in Phase I, we are concerned with our own security, seeking protection in an environment which, without warning, can inflict inexplicable pain. Our daily activities include the search for comfort, warmth, food, and pleasure.

Chart I
Personal Values And Human Growth

Phases	I	II	III	IV
How the Person Sees the World	The world is a MYSTERY over which I have NO CONTROL	The world is a PROBLEM with which I must COPE	The world is a PROJECT in which I can PARTICIPATE	The world is a MYSTERY for which WE CARE
How the Person Sees the Self	The self EXISTS at the center of a HOSTILE WORLD	The self DOES things to succeed and to belong in a SOCIAL WORLD	The self ACTS with conscience and independence on the CREATED WORLD	Selves GIVE LIFE to the GLOBAL WORLD
Values of the Person in Each Phase	self-interest self-preservation security economics/ profit property territory	family/ belonging self worth competence work/labor success being liked order friendship prestige respect tradition competition duty efficiency honor law as rule loyalty responsibility	being self human dignity discovery equality justice self-actualization service collaboration creativity growth mission mutuality empathy generosity independence personal authority search sharing trust law as guide new order honesty	transcendence global equality truth/wisdom rights (world) global justice vision synergy detachment interdependence
Personal Orientation	"Me" Self-centered	"They"	"I" as creative	"We"
Sources of Authority	Authority Outside Self	Authority Outside Self	Authority Inside Self	Authority Inside Self

As we grow older our social horizons widen to embrace the need to belong, to be liked, to be included, to feel okay about ourselves. This is the world of the teenager (Phase II) who is desperately anxious about status, sexual acceptance, competitive success, and pleasing both peers and authority figures. If our lives proceed well, we will emerge from the immaturity of worrying about our personal survival or our acceptance by others into independent, self-directed persons interested in developing initiatives which will be satisfying in their own right and will serve others as well (Phase III). Finally there is an advanced phase, attainable by a few, in which human concerns and meaning-making become global in nature. Each day is dedicated to world conflict resolution, to keeping the peace, to ecological programs. Here at Phase IV, the concept of nationality loses its relevance; the world is viewed from a transcendent perspective.

Unfortunately, for a variety of reasons, many of us reach adulthood in a state of immature development. In some cases, people are fixated on their own physical or financial survival, perhaps because of a poor or abused childhood. Others pursue a hedonistic lifestyle in compensation for a lack of warmth and affection in their early years. Most of us, however, are struggling between an apprehension for recognition and status and a desire to be inner directed, to express our own individuality. At times we are solicitous about obeying the rules, getting a raise, achieving some sort of success in life. At other times we want to be our own boss, drop out of the rat race and do something significant for ourselves and others. This tension, however, between Phase II and Phase III valuing leaves us vulnerable in times of stress. Then we tend to revert to lower levels of valuing in decision-making which serves to reduce, for the moment, our sense of risk and anxiety.

Leaders who operate in Phase I and Phase II valuing are usually autocratic, parental, or bureaucratic in their approach (see Chart II).[3] The autocratic leader's value cluster corresponds to Phase I priorities of physical and territorial security, control over others, and defense against potential rivals. Behavior includes making all the decisions, keeping physical and social distance from those who are to remain as followers, and demanding blind obedience from all those in the organization.

Parental leadership values reflect a combination of Phases I and II. Here the emphasis is upon exercising benevolent, but controlling authority. One may listen to the views of subordinates but will not extend trust far enough to enable them to have an independence of

Chart II
Values and Leadership

Leadership Style	Phases of Growth	Characteristics
Autocratic	I	Makes all decisions Demands obedience Defends territory
Parental	I/II	Controls benevolently Protects "family" Demands loyalty
Bureaucratic	II	Delegates authority only to trusted few Enforces rules/status quo Demands organizational loyalty
Transitional	II/III	Sends conflicting message: controls and empowers
Charismatic	III	Democratizes decision-making Energizes others Articulates a vision
Servant	III/IV	Collaborates on decisions Accepts societal responsibility Recognizes interdependence of people and institutions
Prophetic	IV	Decides by global democracy Seeks worldwide justice, harmony

judgment and decision-making. When parental leaders address an audience they talk down to those whom they perceive as needing their wisdom and guidance. These leaders are concerned with Phase II values of personal loyalty and with the careful observance of the rules of their "family."

Bureaucratic leaders are fully in Phase II. They demand loyalty not to themselves necessarily but to the institution, and delegate authority only to those who have repeatedly demonstrated skill and in whom they have complete trust. Maintaining the status quo, demanding law and order, viewing change as potentially troublesome, preserving one's power, prestige, and image in what they perceive to be an intensely competitive world are all characteristics of the bureaucratic leader.

While we are characterizing these leadership styles as immature, we should note that it is not immature for a leader to embody some of these traits when particular circumstances require them. For example, if one is in an emergency situation, giving and following orders is expected. When leaders, however, are preoccupied with valuing at Phases I and II they are not only interfering with the development of healthy personalities within their organizations, but they are also less imaginative and creative in responding to newer opportunities and challenges than those who are operating at more mature valuing levels.

Leaders at Phases III and IV in Hall's model are termed charismatic if their value cluster is entirely at Phase III, and servants if they begin to integrate Phase IV values with those in Phase III. A fully Phase IV leader, an extremely rare occurrence in national leadership, Hall characterizes as prophetic. A prophetic leader has as his or her primary concern not the specific welfare of a particular nation but the harmony of the world. This attitude is sometimes found in a globally democratic organization such as the United Nations which tries to reconcile opposing national views, to move toward a more equitable distribution of the world's wealth, and to enhance the earth's shared eco-system.

Leaders functioning on Phases III and IV valuing have the "vision thing." That is, they are able to articulate a direction for an organization based on a sense of shared values and are able to energize those with whom they work so that each member enthusiastically contributes. The vision not only encompasses the interest of the organization or nation but also takes responsibility for its impact on the larger society, be it national or world. These more mature leaders, however, are always concerned with the personal development and dignity of all organization members, and recognize that people and institutions are interdependent. Their management style is democratic: they collaborate rather than dictate, include rather than exclude, extend trust rather than rely on loyalty. Their leadership authority comes from proven ability rather than from the power of their office.

There is abundant evidence that George Bush operated out of a Phase II valuing stance. Andrew Rosenthall in *The New York Times* reminds us that Bush seemed to need to impress the public with his enthusiasm for competitive sports.[4] Golf was on the agenda for Sunday 26 May 1991, but the weather was foul. "It's raining; we're playing...," announced Bush. Rosenthall adds, "Mr. Bush...almost seems to delight in playing in the most inclement conditions." In a similar vein, we note that Bush's fishing craft is named "Fidelity." Loyalty, competition, and the need to present an image of fitness are Phase II values. Other indications of his level of valuing include his pride in his World War II record as a fighter pilot and, in an extension of the values of group loyalty and competition, his unusual penchant for secrecy. The latter is reinforced by his membership in Yale's Skull and Bones society and by his CIA directorship.

George Bush's immaturity appeared in the early days of the Gulf War when he adopted a Hussein-Hitler analogy which in turn drove subsequent policy formation. In a speech to employees at the Pentagon on 15 August 1991, Bush declared, "A half-century ago our nation and the world paid dearly for appeasing an aggressor. ...We are not about to make the same mistake twice."[5] Saddam Hussein may have some personal qualities similar to Hitler's, but Hussein in Iraq is in no way equivalent to Hitler in Germany. Moreover, Secretary of Defense Dick Cheney thought Bush's comment was not appropriate. According to Bob Woodward, Cheney was troubled that Bush was "ratcheting up the rhetoric" at a time when U.S. forces were outnumbered in the Gulf ten-to-one.[6]

In using the example of Hitler, Bush reverted to a Phase I value stance. Hitler, for Bush's generation, was the archetype of the forces of evil which could engulf the world, including the United States, and which were only encouraged by appeasement at Munich. Saddam's sudden invasion of Kuwait became in the President's eyes a direct threat to the security of the United States and therefore had to be stopped at all costs. Moreover, from what we now know about Bush's aid to Saddam before the latter's invasion of Kuwait, Saddam could also have loomed as a huge threat to Bush's political survival. Once locked into that Phase I security value stance, the concept of appeasement became so powerful that it blocked any possibility of dialogue with Hussein as well as any discussion of other issues in the Middle East. Saddam, for instance, at several points called for a conference on outstanding problems. To agree even to discuss those problems, such as Palestinian grievances, distribution of oil wealth among poorer Arabs, democratization, limitations on nuclear and chemical weapons, and Hussein's legitimate concern about Kuwait's improper slant drilling into a 98 percent Iraqi-owned oil field, would be appeasing the aggressor. This immature valuing phase paralyzed administrative negotiations and initiatives, and virtually assured the outbreak of war.

Bush revealed Phase II valuing as he crafted strategy during the crisis. Michael Massing, writing in *The New York Review of Books*, reports that Bush relied only on a small number of trusted advisors: "Even the Joint Chiefs of Staff would have trouble getting to see their commander in chief."[7] Bush apparently saw Middle Eastern experts infrequently and showed little interest in what they had to say. "All in all, George Bush and his aides worked in a highly insulated environment largely cut off from other perspectives."[8] Phase II leaders have difficulty extending trust beyond a small circle. Bob Woodward in *The Commanders* further conveys the impression that Bush was making decisions largely on his own without at significant times including his major advisors Cheney, Powell, or Baker. In a revealing passage about the meetings of the National Security Council, Woodward says:

> Bush liked to keep everyone around the table smiling—jokes, camaraderie, the conviviality of old friends. Positions and alternatives were not completely discussed. Interruptions were common. Clear decisions rarely emerged.[9]

If Woodward's picture is accurate, then Bush would be operating at a level of maturity lower than a full Phase II—perhaps as a benevolent parental authority who is convinced that he must rely only on his own judgment to make decisions. Contrast Bush with Kennedy, who, during the 1962 Cuban Missile Crisis, called in a varied group of advisors to present him with all his options. Woodward's passage also discloses Bush's concern with maintaining friendships so that he can always be affirmed and accepted by others. Valuing at Phase II, with lapses under stress into Phase I, makes it difficult for Bush to mature as a person and as a leader.

There is, however, one significant piece of evidence that suggests Bush may have been calling on higher values in his role as leader. In his responses to the situations in both Panama and the Persian Gulf, Bush espoused just war conditions as part of his justification for intervening militarily. Just war has its foundation in the natural law tradition, which sees humans acting in harmony with God's eternal law. World harmony is a Phase IV worldview. Just war doctrine itself, when imbued with the intention to reconcile opposing parties and to search for justice and peace in the world, is also Phase

IV valuing. We shall examine Bush's use of just war conditions in his reaction to Iraq's invasion to discern to what extent Bush was responding to these higher values.

2. Just War Doctrine: A Case in Point

Just war doctrine is a tool for morally evaluating reasons for wars that includes a set of conditions all of which have to be met in order for a war to be called "just." The conditions are just cause, right intention, last resort, discrimination, proportionate grave reason, and legitimate authority. Simply as conditions, their meaning has become somewhat elastic, subject to interpretation according to the value system of the interpreter. A Hobbesian, for instance, who stresses security in a hostile social environment and who is thereby in a Phase I valuing stance, will interpret the conditions solely in light of realpolitik. By contrast an exponent of the original just war doctrine, which has its beginnings in the medieval ethics of natural law, would view human beings as naturally in harmony with one another. Such a person, operating out of Phase III or IV values, would seek to reconcile any break from the natural order.

Take, for example, the condition of just cause. As an isolated condition, a cause for going to war can be legitimated under Phase I valuing if it provides national security, protects property, or safeguards sovereignty; these reasons form the basis for Hobbesian realism. Under Phase II valuing, just cause includes punishing lawbreakers, intervening in riot-torn areas for the restoration of order, or rescuing citizens who are endangered in foreign countries. A response within Phase III valuing, closer to the original natural law meaning, would require massive and systemic human rights violations, an unfair restructuring of an otherwise equitable distribution of resources, or, in keeping with the modern preference for citizen participation in governing, the unauthorized overthrow of an established democracy. Phase IV, which is seldom seen, shifts the focus away from individual nations toward the harmony within the universe; it uses disharmony along the lines of Gandhian principles to further a broader reconciliation of the people.

To be more specific, when President Bush called the U.S. invasion of Panama "Operation Just Cause" he gave four justifica-tions. "To defend democracy" (one might ask, "What democracy?") comes under Phase I or II; "to combat drug trafficking" is possibly Phase II; "to protect the lives of United States citizens" (that is, security) is Phase I; and "to protect the integrity of the Panama Canal Treaties" (that is, protecting property) is also Phase I.[10]

When the just war conditions are applied in a Hobbesian sense, every conflict is justified. When the conditions are applied from a higher valuing stance, most wars are deemed unjust. The difference lies in the priorities of the person making the application. We shall be mindful of this elasticity of meaning as we apply these conditions to the war in the Gulf.

George Bush, in his 28 January 1991 address before the National Religious Broadcasters Convention, set the Gulf crisis in just war terms.[11] Bush stated that the just cause was Iraq's occupation of Kuwait, and the consequent demand by the coalition for an Iraqi withdrawal. Such a cause, he said, "could not be more noble." Under right intention, the President emphasized, "Extraordinary diplomatic efforts having been exhausted to resolve the matter peacefully, then the use of force is moral." Last resort, however, was given in terms of numbers: Secretary of State James Baker has travelled "over 103,000 miles...to talk with, among others, members of the United Nations, the Arab League, and the European Community." Under discrimination, the President said every effort was being made not to harm innocent Iraqi civilians and that he was proud of the military achievement in this regard. He declared there was proportionality in fighting a war "for the greater good." And finally, he indicated there was legitimate authority in 12 UN Security Council resolutions, and in 28 nations participating in the military coalition.

We shall examine the President's arguments in more detail to see if he is correct in stating the cause "could not be more noble." In the President's viewpoint, everything hinged on Saddam Hussein's military invasion on 2 August 1990. Surely Saddam could not justify the takeover of Kuwait by claiming the disputed territory or by charging Kuwait with slant-drilling of their common oil pool. Some international response to the invasion was called for. Moreover, as the Iraqi troops were massing near the border of Saudi Arabia, the peoples of neighboring nations needed to be defended from further incursions. But does that mean the situation justified a military counteroffensive?

Was going to war to remove Iraq from Kuwait justified? Bush was primarily concerned over the loss of sovereignty (Phase I valuing) by the Emir of Kuwait. Interestingly, he never raised the question of democracy or the Kuwaiti people's right to choose their own government (Phase III values). Instead at the U.S. President's insistence, the coalition chose to restore order (a Phase II value), to remove a dictatorship in favor of a feudalistic oligarchy. The central issue for Bush was merely boundary lines in the sand. Michael Kinsley, a senior editor of *The New Republic*, expressed our point well: "Oh sure, a police state like Iraq is worse than a feudal kingdom like Kuwait. But you cannot ask Americans to die for that kind of comparative awfulocracy."[12]

Some ethicists claim that more was involved. There were serious human rights violations, and therefore saving people from the ruthlessness of a brutal military dictatorship (Phase III) was a just cause. The most visible of these human rights violations was Saddam Hussein's use of "foreign guests" inside Iraq itself as international hostages. That situation was indeed outrageous. However, under considerable international pressure on this specific issue, Saddam did renege and the hostages were released. For ethicists to ask for more, insist on a broader human rights agenda, is to ask for the removal of Saddam from Iraq, not of Iraq from Kuwait, but that was not President Bush's objective as presented to the National Religious Broadcasters. Indeed, if removing Saddam from power in Iraq were the goal, then all the conditions of just war would need to be reworked and reevaluated.

How about right intention and last resort? On the one hand, some see right intention fulfilled when a war is fought solely for the reasons specified (and in accord with the valuing phase exemplified) in the just cause, and without hatred for the people of the offending nation. In this sense, President Bush displayed right intention when he told the Broadcasters: "And let me add, we do not seek the destruction of Iraq. We have respect for the people of Iraq, for the importance of Iraq in the region." ("Respect" and "importance" are Phase II values.) On the other hand, as we indicated above, just war under natural law views all human beings as living in harmony with one another. This is a Phase IV valuing position. Under right intention, wars can only be fought defensively against a major disruption of this order and only after reconciliation by peaceful means has been seriously tried and found wanting. In this sense, right intention embodies last resort; in the former sense, last resort must be met as a separate condition.[13]

Peacemaking, of course, would have been difficult with a leader such as Saddam Hussein. Still, for the United States to have insisted almost from the outset upon "Iraq's withdrawal from Kuwait—completely, immediately, and without condition" *before* negotiations could be begun cast the United States in the role of seemingly not wanting a peaceful settlement.[14] Thus, while President Bush pointed to Secretary of State Baker's travelling 100,000 miles as assuring his commitment to peace, the Bush Administration was unwilling to negotiate a peaceful withdrawal with Iraq. The right intention for Bush should not have been that Saddam's "naked aggression will not be rewarded," but finding a way to save 100,000 Iraqi lives.

Saddam was clearly looking for a negotiated settlement. On several occasions, Iraq indicated it would withdraw from Kuwait contingent upon three factors: U.S. forces would be removed from Saudi Arabia, a Middle East conference would be convened—as is now being tried—on security and territorial disputes, and weapons of mass destruction would be negotiated out of the area.[15] Even though these conditions appear reasonable, the United States responded with "no linkage." "No linkage," like unconditional withdrawal, is a low valuing power play, not an effort at reconciling differences.

An article in *The Nation* reports a peace proposal put forth early in August 1991. Iraqi troops would be withdrawn from Kuwait in exchange for "guaranteed Iraqi access to the Persian Gulf, total Iraqi control of the Rumaila oil field, which dips slightly into Kuwait, and U.S.-Iraqi negotiations on oil prices."[16] That proposal too was rejected by the Bush Administration.

The clearest indication Saddam was willing to negotiate was his announcement in early December that the 2,000 foreign hostages would be released. Granted, he did not couple their release with a partial withdrawal of Iraqi troops from Kuwait. The latter would have seemed like a surrender in the face of the U.S. November decision to double its forces with the introduction of 200,000 offensive troops into the Gulf. As it was, Saddam's hostage release statement came one week after President Bush said on 30 November that he would "go the extra mile for peace" in receiving Iraqi Foreign Minister Tariq Aziz in Washington in exchange for U.S. Secretary of State James Baker being received by Saddam Hussein in Baghdad. This face-to-face exchange between the heads of state and the foreign ministers never occurred because both nations could not agree on "convenient" dates for the two visits. Still, the hostage release was a significant concession for Saddam, which Bush saw only for its military advantage, saying Saddam had "cleared the decks for war." With no hostages held prisoner on Iraqi military installations, there would be no limits on a coalition air attack.

Lastly there was the Gorbachev peace proposal, after the air war had devastated Iraq but before the ground offensive began. While the proposal contained no mention of any postwar conferences and only set steps for withdrawal, the United States insisted on its own conditions backed up with a 24-hour ultimatum.[17] The United States wanted to destroy the Iraqi military might, not simply to remove Iraqi forces from Kuwait. The ground war went on and the rest is history. So right intention viewed as peacebuilding was not satisfied by President Bush.

Regarding the just war condition of discrimination, President Bush told the Broadcasters, "We are doing everything possible, believe me, to avoid hurting the innocent." Once again there is a matter of interpretation regarding the meaning of the discrimination condition. Under the natural law principle of double effect innocent people cannot be killed as a means for achieving the good effect or responding to a just cause. A Kantian interpreting this clause would not allow the killing of any innocent persons regardless of circumstances. Proponents of just war generally make a distinction between intended and unintended killings of the innocent. Innocent killings are then excused when they are unintended or indirect. Here the reasoning gets nebulous. Some excuse only accidental killings and others allow whatever is contained under "military necessity." So the discrimination clause runs the gamut from no killing of the innocent (Phase III or IV valuing of the dignity and worth of all humans) to whatever falls under military necessity (which is tantamount to Hobbesian power or Phase I valuing).

The Americans hoped to avoid the Phase I extreme on this issue by their use of "smart weapons" in the Gulf War.[18] However, only 7.4 percent of the bombs used were precision-guided ordnance, and only 30 percent of all bombs dropped successfully hit their targets.[19] Citing such statistics is not intended to imply that the bulk of the bombs hit nonmilitary targets; most surely fell on vast stretches of sand. Nevertheless, nonmilitary targets were hit. Baghdad seems to have been saved from heavy damage to civilian structures. But the same was not true of Basra, a city of one million people, and other cities closer to Kuwait.[20]

In the middle of the fighting, military "necessity" was questionably extended to include electric generator plants, water and sewage facilities, and government buildings that serviced cities. The latter installations were hit after the primary targets had been mostly destroyed, and the coalition broadened its attack to include the country's infrastructure.[21] These bombings had little military value and accounted for mounting civilian casualties after the war. This decision obviously represented a very low level of moral development.

Then there was the Mutlaa "massacre" of Iraqi soldiers caught in a traffic jam on their way out of Kuwait. The latter killings may not have been functionally indiscriminate as soldiers are not civilians, but the killings were cruel since the Iraqi soldiers were retreating and trapped. The same can be said for burying Iraqi troops alive with bulldozers. And finally, for President Bush to have urged the Iraqi Kurds and Shiites to rise up against Saddam with the clear implication that the coalition would aid them and then not aid them while they were killed by the returning Iraqi military, is using innocent people as means to discredit Saddam's military regime. All was not clean, therefore, in respect to the discrimination condition.

The next condition is proportionality or, under natural law, proportionate grave reason. The issue is not body counting but an assessment of whether the killings are in proportion to the grave reason(s) for going to war. If loss of sovereignty for the Emir—and not restoration of democracy for the Kuwaiti people—is the cause, then the coalition is in effect removing from Kuwait a brutal dictatorship for a stringently controlled feudalistic oligarchy at the unacceptable cost of 100,000 lives. Otherwise we are simply talking Phase I power, first by Saddam and then by the coalition.

A modern interpretation of proportionality is weighing consequentially the beneficent and maleficent effects. Accordingly, Bush spoke of fighting a war "for the greater good." The greater good factors in Iraqi as well as coalition lives and includes a comparison with other alternatives. The most serious alternative to war was worldwide economic sanctions. A study of 115 cases since 1914 indicates that success has been achieved 40 times when sanctions were imposed against single countries.[22] Moreover, Iraq was more vulnerable because of its heavy dependence upon a single export, oil, and the UN sanctions were "by far the strongest and most complete against any country by other nations."[23] While there was some leakage, the fact that a naval and an air cargo blockade were in operation strengthened the effect. Admittedly, other nations were being hurt by this cutback of oil from the Middle East, but international efforts were being made to lessen this unwelcome adverse effect.

So why not continue the sanctions for 12-to-18 months? The main moral argument is that sanctions hurt innocent people who begin to starve. This is certainly true. But the comparison we are making is between two options each of which will hurt the innocent. A proportionate weighing of results asks which alternative benefits the most and harms the least? It hardly seems likely that an embargo would have produced more harm to the innocent than resulted from the bombing of sewage and water facilities and from the postwar civil war. Besides, as the sanctions were aimed at forcing the Iraqi military out of Kuwait, food and medicine would have been allowed through for humanitarian reasons. All in all, sanctions would have been the more morally mature route had the greater good of both the Iraqi people and the coalition forces been taken into account.

The last just war condition is legitimate authority. This condition is directed more to the question of who decides whether or not a nation ought to go to war than to whether the war is moral. The condition thus concerns the authority to send forces to war. The President mentions the votes of the United Nations. This gave an important international consent that has been lacking in other U.S. responses to foreign conflicts.

An international approval does not settle the authorization issue for American forces. Significant in this regard was the divided yet favorable vote in both Houses of Congress on 12 January 1991, before the air war began. Had Congress not so acted, it was unclear whether the President had the authority to send American forces to war in the Gulf.[24] The President, of course, felt he had the power to decide as sovereign (Phase I) and did not need the democratic (Phase III) backing of Congress. Indeed in his 28 January speech to the Religious Broadcasters Bush does not even mention the vote in Congress. With the vote, however, the question of legitimate authority is settled. Parenthetically, we might ask what level of values members of Congress were acting upon when they voted to back the President in the Gulf, but that question is beyond the scope of this paper.

In summary, if a Phase I or II level of valuing is the norm, then President Bush's application of just war conditions is arguably sound. However, if a Phase III or IV level of valuing is desirable, then right intention as peacemaking, discrimination of the innocent, proportionate grave reason, and even just cause are dubiously applicable to the Gulf War. President Bush as a person and a leader showed little inclination to rise above an immature level of valuing.[25]

NOTES

1. See, for example, Brian Hall, *The Development of Consciousness: A Confluent Theory of Values* (New York: Paulist Press, 1979); Hall, *Developing Leadership by Stages: A Value-Based Approach to Executive Management* (London: Manohar Publications, 1979); Hall and Helen Thompson, *Leadership through Values: An Approach to Personal and Organizational Development* (New York: Paulist Press, 1980); Hall, *The Genesis Effect: Personal and Organizational Transformations* (Rahwah, NJ: Paulist Press, 1986); Hall, Bruce Taylor, *et al.*, *Value Development: A Practical Guide* (New York: Paulist Press, 1982); Hall, Taylor, *et al.*, *Developing Human Values* (Fond du Lac, WI: Marian College, 1990).

2. This chart is adapted from two diagrams in Hall, Taylor, *et al.*, *Developing Human Values*, 17 and 188–89.

3. The material in this chart is adapted from Hall, Taylor, *et al.*, *Developing Human Values*, 58–62.

4. Andrew Rosenthall, "Bush's Holiday More Active than His Thyroid Ever Was," *The New York Times* (27 May 1991).

5. George Bush, "Against Aggression in the Persian Gulf," Washington: U.S. Department of State, Bureau of Public Affairs (Current Policy No. 1293).

6. See Bob Woodward, *The Commanders* (New York: Simon & Schuster, 1991), 282.

7. Michael Massing, "The Way to War," *New York Review of Books* (28 May 1991), 17.

8. Ibid.

9. Woodward, *The Commanders*, 302.

10. For an ethical analysis of the U.S. invasion of Panama see Joseph Kunkel and Bruce Taylor, "'Operation Just Cause' in Panama—Was It Just?" *Concerned Philosophers for Peace Newsletter* 10:1 (Spring 1990), 5–9.

11. "Remarks by the President in Address to the National Religious Broadcasters Convention," Washington: The White House, Office of the Press Secretary, 28 January 1991. The quotations in this paragraph are from these remarks.

12. Michael Kinsley, "Taking International Law Seriously," In *The Gulf War Reader: History, Documents, Opinions*, edited by Micah Sifry and Christopher Cerf (New York: Random House, 1991), 222.

13. The last resort condition appears to have been derived from this more comprehensive meaning of right intention, wherein the resolution of conflict is sought by peaceful means first. This is right intention as something more than a duplication of just cause. Some commentators therefore do not stipulate a last resort condition believing instead that a proper use of right intention includes efforts at peacemaking. See Kunkel, "Right Intention, Deterrence, and Nuclear Alternatives," *Philosophy and Social Criticism* 10:3–4 (1984), 145.

14. President Bush first used the term "unconditional withdrawal" in a speech at the Pentagon on 15 August 1990. See his "Against Aggression." This particular wording of the phrase is taken from his speech to the National Religious Broadcasters.

15. See Alexander Cockburn, "The Press and the 'Just War,'" *The Nation* (18 February 1991), 186–87.

16. See Robert Parry, "The Peace Feeler that Was: Did Saddam Want a Deal?" *The Nation* (15 April 1991), 480–82.

17. See the relevant documents in Sifry and Cerf, *The Gulf War Reader,* 345 and 349–52.

18. See Nicholas Fotion, "The Gulf War: Cleanly Fought," *The Bulletin of the Atomic Scientists* 47:7 (September 1991), 24–29.

19. See Paul Walker and Eric Stambler, "...And the Dirty Little Weapons," *The Bulletin of the Atomic Scientists* 47:4 (May 1991), 22. The 30 percent figure was cited by Bill Moyers in his PBS "Special Report: After the War," aired 18 June 1991.

20. See Erika Munk, "The New Face of Techno-War: Witness in Baghdad," *The Nation* (6 May 1991), 583–86, and Ramsey Clark, "Bombing Civilians: A War Crime," *The Nation* (11 March 1991), 293 and 308–309.

21. See George Lopez, "The Gulf War: Not So Clean," *The Bulletin of the Atomic Scientists* 47:7 (September 1991), 30–35.

22. See Kimberly Elliott, Gary Hufbauer, and Jeffrey Schott, "Sanctions Work: The Historical Record," Sifry and Cerf, *The Gulf War Reader,* 255–59.

23. Ibid., 255.

24. See, for example, Senator Tom Harkin, "The Obligation to Debate," in Sifry and Cerf, *The Gulf War Reader,* 260–64.

25. The authors are indebted to Laura Duhan Kaplan and Laurence Bove for their constructive criticisms of an earlier draft of this chapter.

WAR WITH IRAQ:
JUST ANOTHER UNJUST WAR

James P. Sterba

The U.S.-led war against Iraq resulted in a popular victory for President Bush and his administration. For many in the U.S., the President's ability to cope with a myriad of social problems, such as a deepening budget crunch, trade deficits, a $3 trillion national debt, inadequate health care, drug problems, homelessness, deteriorating highways and bridges, and a $500 billion savings and loan bailout, seemed less important than his ability to triumph over the military forces of Saddam Hussein.

The morality of a war, however, is never determined by whether it produces victory or whether it distracts people from the social problems they face. The morality of the war against Iraq is determined by whether it satisfies the requirements of just war theory, specifically the requirement of just cause that nonbelligerent correctives must be either hopeless or too costly, and the requirement of just means that the harm resulting from the use of belligerent means must be neither directly inflicted on innocents nor disproportionate to the military objectives to be attained. Unfortunately, neither of these basic requirements of just war theory were met in the U.S. led war against Iraq.

First, going to war against Iraq was not the last resort because there was strong evidence that the economic sanctions would have worked. In a comparative study of 115 cases where economic sanctions were employed since the beginning of World War I, economic sanctions were effective 34 percent of the time. In the case of Iraq, the estimated cost of the economic sanctions was 48 percent of its gross national product, which was three times higher than the cost imposed on any country where sanctions had been successful. So the likelihood that economic sanctions would be successful in the case of Iraq was near 100 percent if the sanctions were kept in place for about a year. The results of this study were also clearly available to the Bush administration as they were reported in *The New York Times* two days before Desert Storm began.

Second, war with Iraq also violated the proportionality requirement of just means. Intelligence sources estimated that as many as 120,000 Iraqi solders were killed during the war, and the number of civilian deaths resulting from the war is easily double that number. A recent United Nations survey of civilian damage caused by allied bombing of Iraq calls the results "near apocalyptic" and claims that the bombing has relegated Iraq to a "pre-industrial age," warning that the nation could face "epidemic and famine if massive life-supporting needs are not rapidly met." A Harvard study done in May 1991 estimated that epidemics and malnutrition—the delayed effects of the war—have already killed 55,000 children under five. These researchers say that at the very least 170,000 will die in the next year. Further evidence of the extent of collateral damage can be derived from the kinds of targets that were directly attacked, for example, bridges, electric power stations, water and sewage treatment plants, most of these within Iraqi cities. Moreover, under the just means requirement of just war theory, many of these targets would have been ruled out as objects of direct attack. There were also a number of opportunities during the war when military action could have been halted or slowed down to allow for a diplomatic solution to develop, which would have meant less damage and fewer casualties, but these opportunities were ignored in the rush to achieve a military victory.

1. The Standard of Proportionality

But can't there be honest disagreement over whether the harms inflicted in a war are proportionate or not? After all, the U.S. led war against Iraq did succeed in removing Iraqi forces from Kuwait, and it was a short war. Couldn't the harms inflicted be judged proportionate in the light of the quick military victory that was achieved? Not at all. To see why this war failed to meet any reasonable interpretation of the just means requirement of proportionality, let us begin by considering the following cases where there is general agreement among interpreters of just war theory that the just means requirement of proportionality has been met or not met. [1]

Case (1) where only the intentional or foreseen killing of an unjust aggressor would prevent one's own death. [2] In this case, there is general agreement among interpreters of just war theory that the harm (death in this case) inflicted upon the unjust aggressor is proportionate since it is the only way to save one's life. Of course, it would be better if unjust aggressors could be stopped without killing them, but when killing them is the only way to save one's life, then it is judged to be proportionate.

Case (2) where only the intentional or foreseen killing of an unjust aggressor and the foreseen killing of a relatively few innocent bystanders would prevent one's own death and that of many other innocent people. In this case, we have the foreseen killing of a relatively few innocent people as well as the killing of the unjust aggressor, but since it is the only way to save one's own life and the lives of many other innocent people, there is general agreement that the harm inflicted is proportionate. In this case, the intended life-saving benefits to many innocent people is judged to outweigh the foreseen death of a relatively few innocent people and the intended or foreseen death of the unjust aggressor.

Case (3) where only the intentional or foreseen killing of an unjust aggressor and the foreseen killing of a relatively few innocent bystanders would prevent the death of many innocent people. In this case, despite the fact that we lack the justification of self-defense, it is generally agreed that saving the lives of many innocent people in the only way possible still makes it moral permissible to kill an unjust aggressor, even when the killing of a relatively few innocent people is a foreseen consequence. In this case, the foreseen death of a relatively few innocent people and the intended or foreseen death of the unjust aggressor is judged proportionate given the intended live-saving benefits to many innocent people.

Case (4) where only the intentional or foreseen killing of an unjust aggressor and the foreseen killing of many innocent people would prevent the death of relatively few innocent people. In this case, there is general agreement among interpreters of just war theory that the proportionality requirement of just war theory is not met. Too many innocent people would have to be killed to save too few. Here the fact that the deaths of the innocents would be merely foreseen does not outweigh the fact that we would have to accept the deaths of many innocents and the death of the unjust aggressor in order to be able to save the lives of relatively few innocents.

Notice that up to this point in interpreting these cases, we have simply been simply minimizing the loss of innocent lives that would result in each case. Suppose, however, that an unjust aggressor is not threatening the lives of innocents but only their welfare or property. Would the taking of the unjust aggressor's life in defense of the welfare and property of innocents be judged proportionate? Consider the following case.

Case (5) where only the intentional or foreseen killing of an unjust aggressor would prevent serious injury to oneself or others. Since the intentional or foreseen killing of the unjust aggressor is the only way of preventing serious injury to oneself or others in such a case, there is still general agreement among interpreters of just war theory that the harm is proportionate. Of course, if there were any other way of stopping unjust aggressors in such cases short of killing them, that course of actions would clearly be required. Yet if there is no alternative, the intentional or foreseen killing of the unjust aggressor to prevent serious injury to oneself or others would be justified.

In such cases the serious injury could be bodily injury, as when an aggressor threatens to break one's limbs, or it could be serious psychological injury, as when an aggressor threatens to inject mind altering drugs, or it could be a serious threat to property. Of course, in most cases where serious injury is threatened, there will be ways of stopping aggressors short of killing them. Unfortunately, this is not always possible.

In still other kinds of cases, stopping an unjust aggressor would require indirectly inflicting serious harm, but not death, upon innocent bystanders.[3] Consider the following cases.

Case (6) where only the intentional or foreseen infliction of serious harm upon an unjust aggressor and the foreseen infliction of serious harm upon relatively few innocent bystanders would prevent serious harm to oneself and many other innocent people.

Case (7) where only the intentional or foreseen infliction of serious harm upon an unjust aggressor and the foreseen infliction of serious harm upon relatively few innocent bystanders would prevent the serious harm to many innocent people.

In both of these cases, serious harm is indirectly inflicted upon some innocent bystanders in order to prevent greater harm from being inflicted by an unjust aggressor upon other innocent people. In case (6), we also have the justification of self-defense which is lacking in case (7). Nevertheless, with regard to both cases, there is general agreement among interpreters of just war theory that preventing serious injury to many innocent people in the only way possible renders it morally permissible to inflict serious injury upon an unjust aggressor, even when the serious injury of relatively few innocent people is a foreseen consequence. In these cases, the foreseen injury of the unjust aggressor is judged proportionate given the intended injury-preventing benefits to many other innocent people.

Up to this point, there has been general agreement among interpreters of just war theory as to how to interpret the proportionality requirement of just means, but in the following case this no longer obtains.

Case (8) where only the intentional or foreseen killing of an unjust aggressor and the foreseen killing of a number of innocent people would prevent serious injuries to the members of a much larger group of people. The interpretation of this case is crucial. In this case, we are asked to sanction a loss of innocent lives in order to prevent serious injuries to the members of a much larger group of people. Unfortunately, just war theorists have not explicitly considered this case. They agree that we can inflict serious injury upon an unjust aggressor and innocent bystanders to prevent greater injury to other innocent people, as in cases (6) and (7), and that one can even intentionally or indirectly kill an unjust aggressor to prevent serious injury to oneself or other innocent people as in case (5). Yet interpreters of just war theory have not explicitly addressed the questions of whether we can indirectly kill innocent bystanders in order to prevent serious injuries to the members of a much larger group of innocent people. Rather they have tended to confuse case (9) with case (5) where it is agreed that one can justifiably kill n unjust aggressor in order to prevent serious injury to oneself or others. In case (8), however, one is doing something quite different; one is killing innocent bystanders in order to prevent serious injury to oneself or others.

Now this kind of trade-off is not accepted in standard police practice. Police officers are regularly instructed not to risk innocent lives simply to prevent serious injury to other innocents. Nor is there any reason to think that a trade-off that is unacceptable in standard police practice would be acceptable in larger scale conflicts. Thus, for example, even if the Baltic republics could have effectively freed themselves from the Soviet Union by infiltrating into Moscow several bands of saboteurs who would then attack several military and government installations in Moscow, causing an enormous loss of innocent lives, such trade-offs would not have been justified. Accordingly, it follows that if the proportionality requirement of just war theory is to be met, we must save more innocent lives than we cause to be lost, we must prevent more injuries than we bring about, and we must not kill innocents, even indirectly, simply to prevent serious injuries to ourselves and others.

Of course, sometimes our lives and well-being are threatened together. Or better, if we are unwilling to sacrifice our well-being then our lives are threatened as well. Nevertheless, if we are justified in our use of lethal force to defend ourselves in cases where we will indirectly kill innocents, it is because our lives are also threatened, not simply our well-being. And the same holds for when we are defending others.

In sum, what this shows is that the standard of proportionality required by just means:

1. allows the use of belligerent means against unjust aggressors only when such means minimize the loss and injury to innocent lives overall,
2. allows the use of belligerent means against unjust aggressors to indirectly threaten innocent lives only to prevent the loss of innocent lives, not simply to prevent injury to innocents,
3. allows the use of belligerent means to directly or indirectly threaten or even take the lives of unjust aggressors when it is the only way to prevent serious injury to innocents.

2. Applying the Standards of Proportionality

Applying this more articulated standard of proportionality to the U.S. led war against Iraq, we can conclude the following:

First, that the belligerent means employed in the war cannot be judged proportionate because it was not the last resort, nor, for that matter, were those belligerent means always directed against acceptable military targets.

Second, that even if the belligerent means employed in the war were the last resort, and would have been directed against only acceptable military targets, the large number of Iraqi civilians who died and still are dying as a result of the war cannot be judged proportionate given the relatively smaller number of Kuwaitis whose lives were threatened by Iraqi forces and given that it was possible to halt the war at various stages in order to pursue nonbelligerent means to resolve the conflict.[4]

It might be objected that if the U.S. had failed to go to war against Iraq following its invasion of Kuwait, we would have found ourselves embroiled in a still more destructive war against Iraq at some future time, even if Saddam Hussein had voluntarily withdrawn his forces from Kuwait.[5] Now a crucial bit of evidence that is appealed to in support of this contention is the Iraqi invasion of Kuwait. The invasion of Kuwait is thought to reveal the depth of the warlike intentions of Saddam Hussein, as if the war against Iran and Iraq's treatment of its own Kurdish population hadn't provided enough evidence in this regard. It is argued that these warlike intentions of Saddam Hussein would most certainly have led to war in the future if business as usual would have resumed with Iraq, following its hypothetical withdrawal from Kuwait.

Yet there is no reason why opponents of the U.S. led war against Iraq should favor business as usual with Iraq following its hypothetical withdrawal from Kuwait. Given Iraq's invasion of Kuwait, its war with Iran and its treatment of its own Kurdish population, I would favor a severe weapons and military technology embargo against Iraq as well as the establishment of a truly United Nations deterrent force in the region. I claim that if actions such as these were undertaken in the hypothetical situation in which Iraq were to withdraw from Kuwait, it would have been possible to avoid a more destructive war with Iraq in the future. So I contend that the U.S. led war against Iraq cannot be justified as the only means for avoiding a more destructive war with Iraq in the future.

Yet given the immorality of the war against Iraq, why did so many people approve of the U.S. led war against Iraq? Is it that they rejected the moral requirements of just war theory? Not necessarily. First of all, it may be that they were simply misinformed about the likelihood that an economic blockade would have been successful, although the close vote in the U.S. Senate suggests that many U.S. political leaders were well aware of that likelihood. Note also that those who favored staying with the economic blockade included such well known moderates and conservatives as Sam Nunn, Lloyd Benson, Casper Weinberger, and two former Chairs of the Joint Chiefs of Staff, Admiral William Crowe and General David Jones. Secondly, so such attention was devoted to the limited damages and the small number of casualties suffered by the U.S. and its allies, that many people failed to appreciate the widespread damage and the large number of casualties suffered by Iraq. But the proportionality requirements of just means demands that we take both types of harm into account. Thirdly, once it appeared that the casualties to the U.S. and its allies could be minimized, many people were attracted to the idea of winning this war with Iraq as though it were like winning a game. After the debacle of Vietnam, many in the U.S. wanted to show the world that their military forces could be victorious again in a large scale war. All of these simply lost sight of the fact that the only justifiable goal of any war is peace with justice.

The irony of it all is that once the full costs of this war for the

U.S. and its allies are known, it may turn out that even this war with Iraq, like so many other unjust wars in the past, has only losers.[6]

NOTES

1. It should be noted that viewed most generally just war theory is not a theory about war per se but about defense, or more specifically about just defense. It should also be noted that when I discussed this topic in my Concerned Philosophers for Peace presidential address in 1990, I only distinguished five cases, but now I see the need to distinguish eight cases in order to make clear that lethal force can sometimes be justifiably used simply to prevent serious harm to innocents. See "Reconciling Pacifists and Just War Theorists," in *Just War, Nonviolence and Nuclear Deterrence*, edited by Duane L. Cady and Richard Werner (Wakefield, NH: Longwood, Academic, 1991). For the common ground among just war theorists, see Paul Ramsey, *The Just War* (New York: Scribners, 1968); James Johnston, *Just War Tradition and the Restraint of War* (Princeton: Princeton University Press, 1981); Robert Phillips, *War and Justice* (Norman: University of Oklahoma Press, 1984); Michael Walzer, *Just and Unjust Wars* (New York, 1977).

2. By an "unjust aggressor" I mean someone who the defender is reasonably certain is wrongfully engaged in an attempt upon her life or well being or the lives and well being of other innocent people.

3. Here and elsewhere harm that is indirectly inflicted is harm an agent causes that is foreseen but not intended.

4. It is interesting to note that similar conclusions were reached by the overwhelming majority of 200 American Catholic theologians who were asked to apply just war theory to the war with Iraq. The greatest number, 97 percent, said the death, devastation, displacement, and misery resulting from the decision to go to war were "out of proportion" to the purported good accomplished by the military effort. Also, 89% said the just war principle supporting the need to discriminate between military and civilians had been seriously violated and 94 percent said the war was not pursued as a last resort. (*National Catholic Reporter*, 22 May 1992.)

5. This is the main objection to my *Concerned Philosophers for Peace Newsletter* (11:1, 4–5) version of this essay that is raised by Jonathan Schonsheck in his chapter "Geopolitical Realism, Morality, and the War in the Gulf," 155–170 in this volume.

6. I wish to thank Jonathan Schonsheck, Laura Duhan Kaplan, and Laurence Bove for their comments on earlier versions of this chapter.

GEOPOLITICAL REALISM, MORALITY, AND THE WAR IN THE GULF

Jonathan Schonsheck

A complete moral appraisal of Operation Desert Storm would, of course, require far more philosophical work than can be contained in these few pages. My focus will be limited to two of the criteria for a war's being a "just war": proportionality and last resort. Two past presidents of Concerned Philosophers for Peace—Douglas P. Lackey and James P. Sterba—have argued that Operation Desert Storm failed to meet these criteria.[1] Although deeply embarrassed to find myself philosophically aligned with President Bush[2] and opposed to Lackey and Sterba, I shall argue that Desert Storm did indeed satisfy both criteria.

Sterba and Lackey (and many others) claim that Operation Desert Storm did not satisfy the just-war criterion of "last resort." Offered as a *non*-last resort: the economic sanctions imposed by the United Nations. The proponents of this position argue that the economic sanctions ought to have been given more time to succeed; the Coalition (principally the United States) ought not have resorted to armed conflict—war—prior to a defensible judgment that the sanctions had indeed failed. However, the claim that the sanctions "ought to have been given more time to succeed" can be neither accepted nor rejected prior to a specification of the "success" of the sanctions. Once the criteria of success have been specified, I shall argue, it will be clear that economic sanctions *could* not have succeeded. Such sanctions could not have achieved that which needed to be achieved: eliminating the destabilizing military threat posed by Saddam Hussein. If this is correct, then military action was indeed the last resort; the just war criterion was satisfied.

Sterba and Lackey (and many others) claim that the evil of Desert Storm exceeded the good created (conjoined with the evil prevented)—and thus the criterion of "proportionality" was not met. However, their assessment of the good achieved—and, more importantly, of the evil prevented—is woefully inadequate. Their assessment cannot be accepted unless one adopts an incredible view of Saddam Hussein's military capabilities—and more importantly, military intentions. In light of the plausible scenario sketched in arguing that Desert Storm did indeed satisfy the criterion of last resort, I shall argue that it satisfied the criterion of proportionality as well.

I address some other clusters of issues that arise in the context of proportionality. I consider issues raised by conflicts not *within* an identifiable moral community, but *between* quite different moral communities. And I investigate the relevance of ecological damage to the argument about justification.

1. Geopolitical Realism and the Last Resort

Might the economic sanctions imposed on Iraq have succeeded? Clearly Sterba thinks so:

> ...going to war against Iraq was not the last resort because there was strong evidence that the economic sanctions would have worked. In a comparative study of 115 cases where economic sanctions were employed since the beginning of World War I, economic sanctions were effective 34% of the time. In the case of Iraq, the estimated cost of the economic sanctions was 48% of its gross national product, which was three times higher than the cost imposed on any country where the sanctions had been successful. So the likelihood that economic sanctions would be successful in the case of Iraq was near 100% if the sanctions were kept in place for about a year.[3]

Unfortunately, Sterba offers no criterion of success, does not tell us what would count as the sanctions' having succeeded. I assume, then, the widely accepted criterion of the time, a return to the *status quo ante*: Iraq returns to the border of 1 August 1990.

Lackey, too, believes that the economic sanctions could have succeeded. He is more forthcoming as regards what constitutes success—and he would be satisfied with less.

> But it is the "last resort" requirement that is the weakest link in the Presidential chain. The speed and size of American deployments, the limited time allowed for sanctions to take effect, the inflexibility of the Administration's negotiating stance, all point to a decision to use force sooner rather than later. I agree that Saddam Hussein should not profit from his crimes, but he cannot profit from oil he cannot sell. Many experts believe that, given the destabilizing effect of sanctions, Saddam might have settled for a minor change in the border and two small islands in the Persian Gulf. [4]

Could economic sanctions have achieved one or the other of these results? If sanctions could not, then by that fact alone, the criterion of "last resort" is satisfied. But could they have achieved the *status quo ante*? Perhaps—but so what? Unless we hypothesize the world's ending as the last Iraqi soldier crosses the old border (Sterba) or the new border (Lackey), it is incumbent on us to ask: And *then* what? How are geopolitical events likely to unfold *thereafter*? Of necessity, every response to this question will be speculative. Nonetheless, given what we know about the history of the region, and the history of Saddam, some scenarios are more plausible than others.

What we are imagining is that economic sanctions have succeeded—the Iraqi economy is so devastated that Saddam's regime is threatened, and consequently he retreats (partially or completely). (Not incidentally, for the sanctions to have worked [i.e., achieved this result], no small amount of suffering and death will have been inflicted on the noncombatant population of Iraq—an evil of imposing economic sanctions that the proponents of this course of action are prone to overlook.) Saddam retains the entirety of his military might: conventional weaponry, chemical and biological weapons (and the facilities which produce them), an active nuclear weapons research program, and a large standing army (an army that stands towards the front, and not towards the back, of food lines). Saddam's credibility and popularity reach an all-time high. (Even if forced to return to the old border, he will not be considered a "loser" in the Arab world. And if he retains additional territory....) Upon compliance, the sanctions are lifted: oil flows and petrodollars are earned for additional weaponry. Political instability in the region sharply increases, as pro-Saddam groups grow in numbers and influence. How does Saddam interact with his neighbors? Is he chastened, and more peaceable? I have discovered no evidence to support this hypothesis. Indeed, all the evidence points towards his being emboldened. He threatens Kuwait—and the other Gulf States as well, including Saudi Arabia—in order to attain price concessions, production concessions, and debt forgiveness. Soon thereafter, Saddam's geopolitical aspirations emerge again: in particular, fulfilling the Arab dream of pushing Israel into the sea. In pursuit of that dream—and to prevent another coalition that includes Arab states—Iraq attacks Israel. Israel, attempting to halt (or at least impede) the Iraqi ground assault, uses battlefield (tactical) nuclear weapons. And in retaliation for Iraqi chemical and biological attacks on its cities, or in hope of deterring such attacks, Israel launches nuclear weapons against Iraqi population centers. Casualties—to civilians, to military personnel, to ecosystems—vastly exceed those of Desert Storm.[5]

This, I submit, is the evil prevented by Operation Desert Storm: a far deadlier war, on a far greater scale. This result could be achieved, this greater conflict prevented, only by the military emasculation of Saddam. It could be achieved only by destruction of Iraq's chemical and biological weapons, the destruction of the facilities for producing these weapons, the destruction of Iraq's conventional armaments, and the killing of a significant number of Saddam's best-trained troops. Once Saddam Hussein had shown both the ability and the willingness to threaten Western interests, the elimination of that threat needed to be achieved. And that could not have been achieved by economic sanctions.

My argument can be summarized in the form of a dilemma. If we construe the "success" of economic sanctions as coercing Iraq's return to the *status quo ante* (or something close to that), then they would have worked, or they would not have worked. If they would not have worked, then military action would have been necessary, would have been the "last resort." If the sanctions would have succeeded, then they wouldn't have succeeded. That is, a return to the *status quo ante* would have left vital interests in peril, and was thus unacceptable. To achieve that which it was necessary to achieve required military action; nothing less would suffice. Hence, military action was indeed the last resort; that criterion of just war theory was indeed satisfied by Desert Storm.

My position receives further strength from the following thought-experiment. Imagine that, in December of 1990, Saddam calls Bush: "Allah has come to me in a dream, and has told me to leave Kuwait. I am a servant of Allah, and shall comply with Allah's wishes." Suppose further that Saddam had made good on his commitment to Allah, and had indeed withdrawn—but of course with his entire military, and his entire military-industrial complex, completely intact. Such an outcome would have been unacceptable to the Coalition. Having shown both the ability and now the willingness to use force against vital Western interests, Saddam could not be permitted to retain his extensive offensive capability. The military had to be emasculated, and the man de-mythologized.

2. Problems of Proportionality

A. Moral Myopia and Proportionality

Consider now the issue of *proportionality*. For this just war criterion to be satisfied, the evil of Desert Storm must be exceeded by the good created combined with the evil it prevented. So we need to both *identify* and *quantify* the good and the evil *created*, and the good and the evil *prevented*.

There are empirical obstacles to accurately specifying and quantifying the evils created by Desert Storm: estimates of the damage inflicted and the lives lost have a wide margin of error.[6] And several centuries of utilitarianism show us nothing if not the difficulties of quantifying good and evil. Worse, the problems of specifying and quantifying the *factual* are exceeded by the problems of specifying and quantifying the *counterfactual*: the goods and evils of what *didn't* happen. As is the case with all counterfactuals—and as was the case regarding the "last resort"—we must be content with plausibility arguments: how believable is it that various events would, or would not, have transpired?

We must guard against "moral myopia," the temptation to lower the horizon of inspection, assessing only the short-term consequences, while neglecting the long-term consequences of actions—and *in*action. So let us look at the specifications and quantifications of goods and evils, both created and prevented, offered by Sterba and Lackey—charitably bearing in mind that their pieces are quite short, and that that precludes extensive specification.

Consider Sterba's argument:

> ...war with Iraq also violated the proportionality requirement of just means. Intelligence sources estimated that as many as 150,000 Iraqi soldiers were killed during the war, and the number of civilian deaths could equal that number. A recent United Nations survey of civilian damage caused by allied bombing of Iraq calls the results "near apocalyptic" and claims that the bombing relegated Iraq to "a pre-industrial age." ...During the war, we were shown precision attacks with smart bombs. But after the war was over, we were told that only 7% of the explosives dropped on Iraq and Kuwait were smart bombs and that 70% of the 88,500 tons of bombs dropped on Iraq and Kuwait actually missed their targets, thereby causing extensive collateral damage. There were

also a number of opportunities during the war when military action could have been halted or slowed down to allow for a diplomatic solution to develop, which would have meant less damage and fewer casualties, but these opportunities were ignored in the rush to achieve a military victory.[7]

A series of comments. First, the evidence points to fewer than 100,000 Iraqi soldiers killed.[8] Second, Sterba's inference about dumb iron bombs which missed their targets is fallacious. From the fact that a bomb missed its target, it just does not follow that "extensive collateral damage" was the result: the bombs might have caused no damage at all. Given the percentage of dumb bombs dropped at Iraqi hardened positions in Kuwait, quite far from civilian population centers, this is the more likely result of missing the intended target. Third, Sterba's argument suffers from moral myopia. He does not include, in his moral assessment, the longer-range consequences of failing to oppose Saddam militarily, of permitting Saddam's aggression to succeed. Once again, we *must* ask: how would events have unfolded, were it not for Desert Storm? And once again, my answer is that an emboldened Saddam, still in possession of a large standing army and a vast array of weaponry, would have (in the fairly near future) initiated new aggression; in all likelihood, it have would involved heavily-armed Israel. This future conflict, the conflict precluded by Desert Storm, would have been far wider in scope, and far deadlier. Preventing this future war was, I submit, the ultimate goal of the Coalition. Inflicting extensive damage on the military of Iraq was therefore not a side effect, but rather the ultimate *point* of the conflict. No diplomatic solution was seriously pursued, because diplomacy, like economic sanctions, was not capable of achieving that which needed to be achieved.

Consider now Lackey's argument concerning proportionality.

The scale of the allied bombardment runs the President into trouble with the rule of proportionality, which requires that the damage caused by allied action be less than the damage it prevents. Since the damage to Iraq was nearly total, and Iraq is considerably larger than Kuwait, the restoration of Kuwait cannot counterbalance the destruction of Iraq. If Saddam is evil because he has brought so much death and destruction into the world, the moral remedy can hardly be to cause even more death and destruction. [9]

Here Lackey exhibits the same moral myopia exhibited by Sterba: his moral assessment is limited to the immediate damage done to Iraq and Kuwait, and does not include any appraisal of probable events if Iraqi aggression is allowed to succeed.

My position is this: the ultimate goal of Operation Desert Storm was the military emasculation of Iraq; an essential element of the justification for pursuing that goal was preventing a substantially worse conflict in the future. If my scenario is plausible—if "peaceable Saddam" strains credulity, is profoundly unrealistic—then the "evil prevented" by Desert Storm is far greater than the evil created. Thus, it satisfied the just war criterion of proportionality.

Neither Lackey nor Sterba has properly applied the criterion of proportionality. Or if they have: so much the worse for the criterion of proportionality, and Just War Theory generally. If the preclusion of a clearly foreseeable and clearly worse evil is not countenanced by Just War Theory, then Just War Theory ought to be abandoned as morally ludicrous.

B. Universal Universalism Run Amok

There is a deeper problem shared by Lackey and Sterba. To determine whether the damage inflicted by Coalition forces was "proportionate," one must specify just how much a fallen Iraqi combatant "counts"—and this is not easy. A tour of some possible worlds will clarify my claim.

Assume that Iraqi casualties totaled 100,000; round off Coalition casualties to the nearest thousand: zero. Thus the total number of combatants killed in the war, at the actual world, is 100,000. Now the first alternative world we visit is one in which the Gulf War claimed 60,000 Iraqi casualties, and 30,000 Coalition casualties. Casualties total 90,000, that is, 10,000 fewer than at the actual world. Is this possible world morally superior to the actual world? Visit a second possible world, one in which each side suffers 40,000 casualties; the total is 80,000. Is *this* world morally superior to both the actual world, and also the first possible world? Visit a third possible world, one in which 10,000 Iraqis die, and 50,000 Coalition combatants die. Visit a fourth possible world, one in which 1,000 Iraqis are killed, and 50,000 members of the Coalition are killed.[10]

The longer our tour continues, the lower the total casualty count. If one subscribes to "universal universalism," is one

believes that all combatants—aggressors and defenders alike—
"count" the same, then one is thereby committed to the position
that the possible-worlds tour progresses from morally inferior to
morally superior worlds, for the total casualty count is lower at
each successive world. But common-sense morality—indeed,
common sense itself—rejects this consequence. I do not believe
that we sincerely hold the position that the life of an aggressor
"counts" as much as the life of a victim of aggression, or the life
of one resisting aggression.[11] It is "universal universalism" run
amok to presume, without argument, that all combatants are to
"count" the same, that the death of an aggressor is precisely
equivalent to the death of a defender. The particular brutality of
the Iraqi invasion itself, and the subsequent array of atrocities
committed against the civilian population of Kuwait,[12] further
erode the plausibility of the position that the lives of aggressor
and defender are morally equal. Much philosophical work remains
to be done on the requirements of morality in conflicts between
distinct moral communities. "Universal universalism" might be
the conclusion of some meta-ethical argument. But it is illicit for
it to appear unargued as the first premise of a moral appraisal—or
worse, as a suppressed premise of such an argument.

If "universal universalism" is rejected, if the life of an
aggressor "counts" less than the life of a defender, then less "evil"
was created by Desert Storm than appears in the calculations of
Lackey and Sterba. In consequence, it is more plausible to hold
that Desert Storm did indeed satisfy the just-war criterion of
proportionality.

C. Proportionality and Conflicts between
Moral Communities

Just War Theory developed in the context of conflicts
between nations which were, despite those conflicts, members of a
single (broadly and loosely defined) moral community: Christianity. However, the Gulf War was not a war between two nation-
states within a single, overarching moral community—it was a
conflict between *differing* moral communities. It was a conflict
between Just War and Holy War, between Just War and *Jihad*.

Philosophers have devoted too little attention to the matter
of the constraints of morality in cases where one's opponents
subscribe to a different, and indeed competing, set of moral
precepts.[13] Perform this thought experiment. Imagine that your

nation-state is engaged in mortal combat with another nation-state, a nation-state which subscribes to a moral system quite different from your own. Imagine further that one point of divergence in the two moral systems concerns *jus in bello*, concerns justice in the actual prosecution of war. Imagine that certain actions which are *prohibited* by your own moral system are *permissible* according to the precepts of your adversary's moral system. Now suppose it is the case that, if you abide by the precepts of your own moral system—refraining from actions that, by hypothesis, your adversary is morally free to elect, and will elect—you will, as a result, be vanquished. Can a moral system require a course of conduct which entails the destruction of its adherents—and thus, in a clear sense, the elimination of the moral system itself?[14]

Certain actions of Iraq—using schools as military command headquarters, storing military equipment in residential neighborhoods, and at archaeological sites—sorely tempted the Coalition to violate the Just War principle of "discrimination."[15] The Coalition resisted the temptation—at least in part, one suspects, because the general war effort was so successful. How would the Coalition have acted, were these targets militarily decisive? More importantly: how *should* the Coalition have acted in such a case?

My point is this: if it seems, in a conflict between differing moral communities, that adherence to proportionality—or to other criteria of Just War Theory—would lead to one's destruction, then either one has misapplied the criteria, or Just War Theory ought to be rejected (as regards that conflict).

Unhappily, I cannot say what "morality" *does* require, when there is a conflict between divergent moral communities; again, this is an issue that has received too little philosophical attention. It is not unimportant, however, to reject the claim that a moral system might mandate its own elimination. I accept the possibility that "universal universalism" might be the conclusion of a sound meta-ethical argument. But it is illicit for it to appear unargued as the first premise of a moral appraisal—or worse, for it to be a suppressed premise of such an appraisal.

3. Proportionality and Paralysis:
The Relevance of Ecological Damage

Jerald Richards has also argued that Desert Storm failed to meet the criteria of Just War.[16] In arguing that it failed to meet the criterion of proportionality, Richards cited the ecological damage of the war: principally, the water pollution of crude oil dumped into the Persian Gulf, and the air and land pollution of the torching of Kuwaiti oil wells.

It would seem that some support for this position can be found in William V. O'Brien's essay "Just-War Theory" (excerpted in Sterba's *The Ethics of War and Nuclear Deterrence*). O'Brien writes,

> The probable good to be achieved by successful recourse to armed coercion in pursuit of the just cause must outweigh the probable evil that the war will produce.

> The calculation of proportionality between probable good and evil must be made with respect to all belligerents, affected neutrals, and the international community as a whole before initiating a war and periodically throughout a war to reevaluate the balance of good and evil that is actually produced by the war.[17]

The aforementioned ecological damage surely was an evil, and was, in a sense, produced by "the war." Does it thereby render Operation Desert Storm morally unjustified, for failing the criterion of proportionality?

Loosely speaking, the ecological damage was "produced by the war." But this is loose speaking in the extreme; the damage was not produced by some "agent" named "the war;" the damage was produced by one of the participants in the war. Strictly speaking, the dumping of the crude oil, and the torching of the Kuwaiti oil wells, was done by one of the combatants—Iraq. And this is morally crucial.

Suppose an aggressor credibly threatens to inflict ecological damage n if its aggression is resisted by a defender. Suppose that a defender, following Richards and O'Brien, counts ecological damage n as an evil "produced by" the war, and thus military action is justified only if the anticipated good of that action exceeds n plus the other evils of the war. Then there are two possibilities: either the anticipated good does exceed ecological damage n (plus the other evils), or it does not. If it does not, then the aggressor prevails in the conflict; the aggressor's injustice is rewarded, not punished. On the contrary, suppose that the anticipated good of military action does exceed n plus the additional evils. Then the defender's military action is justified. But wait—if the aggressor credibly threatens to do *even more* ecological damage—$n + m$, let us say—then, once again, the evil "produced by the war" exceeds the anticipated good, and the defender's military action is unjustified. And so on; if we follow the interpretation of Richards and O'Brien on this, then an aggressor can make morally impermissible *any* military action by a defender, merely by credibly threatening to do so much ecological damage that that evil outweighs the anticipated good of the contemplated military action. Thus, if we follow Richards and O'Brien, a defender can be paralyzed, frozen into inaction by an aggressor's threat to do evil. Indeed, on this interpretation, the greater the evil posed by the aggressor, the more difficult it becomes to morally justify thwarting that evil.

Were we to accept an interpretation of proportionality according to which the "evil produced by the war" includes the evil done by one's adversary, we would be committed to this bizarre result: the greater the evil one's adversary is willing to commit, the less one may morally do in resisting that evil. If one's adversary is willing to do unlimited evil in response to one's military actions, then proportionality prohibits military action. Thus proportionality entails paralysis.

This is, I submit, precisely the wrong result. An aggressor that credibly threatens to inflict extensive ecological damage is an aggressor that morally needs to be thwarted. Indeed, the greater the damage threatened, the *stronger*—and not the weaker—the moral justification of military action against the aggressor.

What is the relevance of this for Richards's argument? An analogy will help.

There are many different sorts of mistakes one can make in one's checkbook: errors of addition or subtraction, failures to record a check or a deposit. Although individual errors will vary in magnitude, the worst *sort* of error is entering a debit as a credit, for in such a case the amount of the error automatically *doubles*.

Richards and O'Brien count ecological damage as an evil that must be counterbalanced by the anticipated good of military action if that action is to be morally justified. However—and quite

to the contrary—*that* Saddam was willing to do such damage must
be entered as part of the *justification* for military action against
him. It is to be added to the moral reasons *for* military intervention, not added to the moral reasons *against* intervention.
Richards treats the ecological damage done by Iraq as a moral
debit of Desert Storm; it is, in fact, a moral credit. It counts as an
element of the evil to be resisted, not as an evil produced by the
Coalition. Thus, under proportionality, the Coalition is morally
freed to inflict even greater damage on Iraq, for the evil opposed
is that much greater.

In general, the greater the evil one's adversary is willing to do,
the stronger is one's justification for resisting that evil, and the
greater is the evil one is morally permitted to produce in resisting
that evil. Once again: either *this* is the correct application of the
criterion of proportionality, or proportionality ought to be
rejected as morally ludicrous.

4. Pronouncements and Justifications

Now, it could be objected that the justification for Operation
Desert Storm that I have offered differs from the justifications
(and there were several) offered by the United States. True
enough. However, two responses are in order.

First, it is rare for our own individual, comparatively simple
actions to have but a single justification; often, we justify our
actions by offering several, or even a *constellation* of reasons. So
too with the vastly more complex matter of the War in the Gulf:
it wasn't *only* to liberate Kuwait—though that is an element of
the justification. It wasn't *only* to assure a supply of oil for
Western economies—though that too is an element of the
justification.[18] It wasn't *only* the last chance for collective action
to prove its effectiveness—though that too is an element of the
justification. And it wasn't *only* to eliminate the threat posed by
Iraq—but that surely is an essential element of the justification.
Whether the war was justified, all things considered, does indeed
depend upon considering all things.[19]

Second, it would have been militarily stupid to have announced beforehand the whole array of justifications, that is, the
whole array of Coalition intentions. The U.S. claimed, in
undertaking Operation Desert *Shield*, the goal of preventing Iraq
from invading Saudi Arabia. Suppose the U.S. had announced,

before the deployment, its intention to eliminate the threat to the region posed by Iraq. Saddam is likely to have (correctly) reasoned that he had nothing to lose, and everything to gain, by extending the invasion to Riyadh. This he could easily have achieved. And without Saudi bases, repelling Iraqi aggression would have proved difficult, or perhaps impossible: Desert Storm could not have been launched solely from carrier decks. It was smart to not openly discuss military goals. But really—it ought not have been too difficult to foresee. Reflect again on one of the thought experiments I offered above: Saddam announces that he has made a terrible mistake, and withdraws—but keeps his entire military. Such a withdrawal would have been unacceptable—not in and of itself; it would have been a good thing to have Iraq leave Kuwait without further bloodshed. It would have been unacceptable because of the particular future it portends. The evil created by the Coalition in prosecuting Desert Storm was indeed proportional in precluding that particular future; military action was also the last resort in precluding that particular future.

5. Conclusions

Sterba and Lackey have claimed that Operation Desert Storm failed to satisfy the just-war criterion of "last resort"—the Coalition ought to have given economic sanctions more time to "work." I have argued against that position. The goal of the Coalition was not merely a return to the pre-invasion border; the goal was to eliminate the destabilizing effect that a fully armed Iraq was having on the region. *Even if* the Iraqi military had retreated to the previous border, it would have continued to pose a destabilizing threat. Since eliminating that threat could not have been achieved by economic sanctions alone, could not have been achieved by any means short of military action, the criterion of last resort was indeed satisfied.

Sterba, Lackey, and Richards all claim that Operation Desert Storm failed to satisfy the just-war criterion of "proportionality." I have argued against that position as well. If my arguments are essentially sound, each of these philosophers has failed to accurately assess the goods and evils of the war. Implicit in the arguments of both Sterba and Lackey is "universal universalism," "counting" the life of an aggressor as equal to the life of a defender. As my tour of possible worlds shows, however, this is untenable: a world in which relatively more defenders and relatively fewer aggressors die is not morally superior to the actual world, even if the total casualty count is lower.

This raises a deeper philosophical issue: the demands of morality in a mortal conflict between the adherents of differing, of conflicting, moral communities. While unable to supply a resolution of issue, I did defend one important result: it is implausible to maintain that a moral system demands that its adherents pursue a course of conduct that assures the annihilation of those adherents, and thus the annihilation of that moral system itself.

Against Richards, I argued that it is misleading to attribute ecological damage to "the war," and thus to consider it an evil that must be counterbalanced by the good produced by the war (if the war is to be shown justified). The ecological damage of the Gulf War was perpetrated by Iraq; that Iraq was willing to employ such a tactic is an addition to, and not a subtraction from, the Coalition's moral justification.

It is a mistake to think that there must be a single, simple justification for Operation Desert Storm. Quite to the contrary, we ought to expect a constellation of justifications in a matter so complex as modern warfare.

NOTES

1. Douglas P. Lackey, "Bush's Abuse of Just War Theory"; James P. Sterba, "War with Iraq: Just Another Unjust War," *Concerned Philosophers for Peace Newsletter*, 11:1, 3–5.

2. I do not approve of much else that George Bush has done; perhaps the most serious consequence of the war was his rise in popularity. However, that popularity soon waned.

3. Sterba, "War with Iraq," 4. See also Sterba in this volume, 147–154.

4. Lackey, "Bush's Abuse of Just War Theory," 4.

5. Richard Werner, who commented on my chapter, argued quite forcefully that predictions about the future of the region had Operation Desert Storm not been launched are colored by the predictor's ideology. I quite agree. Nonetheless, one can (indeed *must*) consider the actions of Saddam in the past—principally, the attack on Iran (1980) and the use of poison gas against unarmed Kurd civilians, citizens of Iraq itself (1988). And it is difficult to devise benign interpretations of other activities: the programs to develop a "supergun" and to develop nuclear weapons. Although Saddam was "demonized" by Western leaders and media, his uncontested record made this an easy task. For a sketch of that record, see *Time* Magazine Editors, *Desert Storm: The War in the*

Persian Gulf (Boston: Little, Brown, 1991), 125–34.

6. Patrick E. Tyler, "Iraq's War Toll Estimated by U.S.," *The New York Times* (5 June 1991), A5.

7. Sterba, "War with Iraq," 4–5. See also Sterba's chapter in this volume, 147–148.

8. Tyler, "Iraq's War Toll."

9. Lackey, "Bush's Abuse of Just War Theory," 3.

10. In the final world, 100,000 Coalition are killed, and (rounding off) no Iraqis are killed. Is this world morally equal to the actual world?

11. This point is discussed by Gregory S. Kavka in "Was the Gulf War a Just War?" *Journal of Social Philosophy*, 22:1, 26–27.

12. See James LeMoyne, "New Kuwait Refugees Tell of Iraqi Killings and Rapes," *The New York Times* (2 December 1990), A19; "The Thieves of Baghdad," editorial, *The New York Times* (16 July 1991), A18; *Time* Magazine Editors, *Desert Storm*, 135–54.

13. There are many important differences between these two moral communities—far more than I can mention, much less investigate. But one important difference must not be neglected. In the Just War Tradition, there is no special "reward" in the afterlife for falling in battle against infidels; in the Holy War Tradition, there are splendid rewards for service to Allah—which includes falling in *Jihad*. See *The Holy Qur'an*, translated by A. Yusuf Ali (Brentwood, MD: Amana Corp., 1983), Sec. 9: 20–23 and n.1270 and n.1271.

14. Much philosophical work remains to be done on the requirements of morality in conflicts between differing moral communities. I raise the issue in "The End of Innocents," *Journal of Social Philosophy* 28:2 and "Hostages or Shields?," *Public Affairs Quarterly* 1:2.

15. *Time* Magazine Editors, *Desert Storm*, 51, 58.

16. Jerald Richards, "George Bush, Justified War Morality, and the Gulf War," in this volume, 113–128.

17. William V. O'Brien, "Just-War Theory," in *The Ethics of War and Nuclear Deterrence*, edited by James P. Sterba (Belmont, CA: Wadsworth Publishing Company, 1985), 35.

18. The slogan "No Blood for Oil" is defective on two counts. First, it presumes that securing oil was the sole element of the justification, which it is not. Second, it underestimates the importance of petroleum and petrochemicals to modern economies. No small amount of human misery would have resulted from a steep rise in oil prices, given that the U.S. economy was already in recession. Nor have the proponents of that slogan explained just how more resources could be made available for social programs (e.g., AIDS research) in a recessionary economy further hobbled by significantly more expensive oil.

19. Consider the following analysis—which was published well after my own was written. Note its implicit but important reliance on the distinction between pronouncements and justification. "Until Election Day, the President had been sending out mixed messages about his intentions, confusing Americans, allies and quite probably Saddam Hussein himself....Some attributed the signs of vacillation to Bush's basic inability to articulate his views. But the confusion contrasted with his otherwise clear and oft-stated assertion of U.S. objectives: that Iraq withdraw completely and unconditionally from Kuwait;

that Kuwait's government be restored, that U.S. citizens be protected and regional stability achieved. There were three reasons for this ambiguity. Some was deliberate. The Administration was, in part, bluffing. If it could scare Saddam out of Kuwait without a fight, so much the better. To avoid war, however, Bush had to threaten credibly that he was ready to wage one. Until he doubled the number of U.S. troops, there were no teeth in his threat.... The second reason behind Bush's ambiguity was the necessity of addressing different audiences. For Saddam, the message had to be force. But for Middle Eastern coalition members fearful of the consequences of fighting an Arab brother, for jittery Europeans and also for Americans, who faced disproportionate risks, the U.S. had to be seen as pursuing every approach short of war. Third, Bush was really uncertain what he would have to do. He was receiving conflicting advice about the efficacy of the sanctions." (*Time* Magazine Editors, *Desert Storm*, 31.)

REFLECTIONS ON A MASS KILLING

Frederick R. Struckmeyer

In 1991 the United States engaged in a brief and highly successful war with the military forces of Saddam Hussein. The Iraqi death toll in that war now appears to be far higher than the 100,000 or so killed in the bombing—due to the destruction of water, sewage, and medical systems throughout the country.

It is certain that many of the earlier victims were simply slaughtered in what one U.S. soldier on the scene called a "turkey shoot," bombed to death with an awesome array of modern weapons. These weapons were financed by U.S. taxpayers, most of whom seem to have regarded the war as necessary and just.

In this article—which I recognize is more suggestive than argumentative—I wish very briefly to explore some ramifications of this massive and almost totally one-sided killing, using as my primary point of reference Lance Morrow's *Time* essay for 1 April 1991, "A Moment for the Dead." I find the Morrow essay interesting and instructive because, while it makes some valuable points and says some things which very much need to be said in the wake of the lopsided Gulf War victory, it seems to me not to go far enough. It is as if the author does not wish to see where his premises are leading him, does not wish to see all the logical consequences of arguments which he himself puts forth. I shall attempt to draw out some of these consequences as well as comment on what I take to be other vulnerabilities in Morrow's line of reasoning.

Morrow's basic point is that, while the overwhelming U.S. victory in the Gulf War was "as satisfying as anything Americans have done together since landing on the moon," we ought not to feel too satisfied with the results. (In suggesting that we did it "together," as if in unanimity, he does not mention that the Senate voted only 52–47 to approve the military offensive nor that two former chairmen of the Joint Chiefs of Staff were among those advising against the offensive.) "The killing was very well done," he writes. "I hope it does not give us too much pleasure." This last sentence constitutes his closing plea.

It is "human nature," Morrow contends, to "feel great" at the one-sided victory, the almost unbelievably easy triumph. Feeling psychological relief is appropriate and expected, he notes, since we had originally feared a protracted ground war which might have cost tens of thousands of American lives (tens of thousands of body bags were in fact sent to the war front, to be ready as needed).

But feeling relieved psychologically, Morrow goes on to say, is hardly the same as being exonerated morally: "...There is not, or there should not be [Is he unclear which?], such a thing as killing without guilt—especially not mass killings without guilt. When people kill without remorse, we call them insane. We call them maniacs, serial murderers."

This is, perhaps, overstated, but Morrow is totally right in saying that we normally expect remorse, when major crimes are found out. Judges look for this in courtrooms. The American public looked for it from President Nixon, when his culpability in the Watergate break-in was ascertained. In situations like this we expect an "I'm sorry," or a *mea culpa* in some form, an admission of wrong-doing. And, the greater the wrong, the more we require the confession. This is why the Nuremberg trials, after World War II were so important—and why the unrepentant attitude of the top Nazis was so perplexing. They would not admit wrong-doing nor accept personal responsibility for what they had done.

It is worth noticing that, when Morrow says (in the passage quoted earlier) that "...there is not...such a thing as killing without guilt...especially not mass killings without guilt," he is making an observation which goes beyond psychology. Whether there is remorse or not, the killer is affected by his deeds. He may claim to feel no remorse and may evidently not be feeling any—it is one of the characteristics of much psychopathology, as therapists well know, that the individual is out of touch with his or her feelings—but there are unavoidable consequences all the same. As Sartre says, I may "flee," try to run away from myself, but I cannot avoid knowing that I am the one who is fleeing. I can pretend not to know that I have done something terrible, something very contrary to my own principles, but at some level of myself I know it anyway. It has registered in my psyche. I can tell myself, if I engage in or try to justify mass killing, that I am merely eradicating a "cancer" (this medical metaphor was actually used during the Gulf War, once by a Naval Academy student who was interviewed by a newspaper reporter). But I still have to reconcile what I have done with my self-image, no matter what defense mechanism this requires me to employ: denial, rationalization, or some other.

So killers, and, perhaps, especially mass killers, are psychologically scarred by what they have done. As Raskolnikov illustrates in Dostoyevsky's *Crime and Punishment*, one cannot walk away from murder—even when the law has been escaped—and pretend that nothing has changed. One carries a definite psychological burden. A steep price is paid, not just by the victim, but by the killer as well.

It was exactly at the point in Morrow's essay about there being no "mass killings without guilt," referred to above, that I expected the writer to go on to say something like the following: "So if this nation and its leadership can sponsor mass killing and feel no apparent remorse, then perhaps this constitutes a case of mass psychopathology." However Morrow does not explicitly draw this conclusion. In fact, he immediately moves on to another line of thought and leaves his tantalizing conclusion to be drawn by the reader. It is as if he does not wish to linger on the difficult-to-swallow deduction which he himself has allowed, if not required, to be drawn: as if he does not wish to see, to face squarely, what he himself has brought into the light of day. This is perhaps because he realizes just how unpalatable to most Americans his conclusion is.

But perhaps his deduction is correct none the less. Perhaps "psychopathological" is not too strong a term to describe certain attitudes and behaviors of the U.S. in recent years. In the case of Vietnam, we prosecuted a war which left more than a million enemy dead and many more scarred either physically or emotionally. Yet we walked away, after the Paris peace accords, bitter that we hadn't won the war on the battlefield, and proceeded to isolate Vietnam, economically and politically, for the next fifteen years.

In the case of Nicaragua, which this writer visited while the Contra War was still in progress, we inflicted billions of dollars of damage and tens of thousands of deaths on a poor, underdeveloped nation—and afterwards, when elections had finally removed the government we found undesirable, we refused to pay the reparations that our own policies had made necessary (and which simple morality seemed to require). As in the case of Vietnam, we got a lot of people killed and wounded and inflicted great damage on a small, poor country, but afterward acted as if we didn't need to think about the matter any further. We had other business to attend to.

That seems evidence of national psychopathology. It is not merely the "arrogance of power," but an unwillingness to accept responsibility for our collective deeds. We don't know, or don't want to know, what the moral consequences of our actions are. We thus act in a collectively irresponsible way, which Karl Menninger says is one form of sin.[1]

Now it is true that sinfulness is not the same thing as psychopathology, though some thinkers have tried to show the link between them. Menninger, in the book cited above, talks about the "the disappearance of sin." He wants to put renewed emphasis on the moral aspects of wrong-doing, despite his professional standing as a psychiatrist, rather than on the pathological as such. So Menninger might not care for my expression, "national psychopathology." But at the very end of his book he makes the following statement: "For doctors, health is the ultimate good, the ideal state of being. And mental health...includes all the healths: physical, social, cultural, and moral (spiritual)."[2] In light of this standard, and from this standpoint, one may truly say that recent American society has been sick, unhealthy, pathological. The violence we have sponsored abroad and the violence we have allowed to proliferate at home are evidence of ill health. And the situation is worse now than twenty years ago, when Menninger was writing.

To return to Morrow: if mass killing without attendant remorse and without awareness of guilt is pathological, then the U.S. did act pathologically during and after the Gulf War. (I include the post-war period because of the trade sanctions which have had the effect of causing many additional deaths.) We are in some respects like an alcoholic who has just taken another huge drink, in Robert Bly's apt analogy, i.e., fought another war, gotten another euphoric high (witness 1991's victory celebrations), yet who at the same time denies that he has a drinking problem.[3]

But maybe the alcoholism analogy is faulty: drunken drivers don't usually try to deny the hard evidence when confronted with the automobile wreck, and possibly the destroyed lives, which their irresponsible behavior has caused. On the other hand, while we do hold drunken drivers morally and legally accountable, we recognize that their drinking problem is very much like a disease. So the same behavior, driving drunk and causing a deadly accident, may be rooted in a disordered mental/emotional state, but is still something for which the individual is morally responsible. He cannot claim nonresponsibility because of his allegedly uncontrollable drinking. In the film, *Come Back, Little Sheba*, Burt Lancaster tells his wife that he does not remember what he said and did while in his drunken stupor. But he is contrite, asks her forgiveness, and is genuinely repentant. The same is true of many or most drunken drivers who must confront their victims' families in court. But nations, when convicted of crime in the court of international opinion (and sometimes in international law), are not always willing to admit guilt. This illustrates Reinhold Niebuhr's point that groups tend to be more immoral than individuals.[4]

One possible reason why the U.S. has expressed no contrition over the Gulf War killings emerges in a part of Morrow's essay where he speaks of an "impaired humanity." We feel little or no pain at having caused so much death and destruction, he suggests, and have become desensitized.

Why? Maybe because to admit the obvious would conflict with our nation's self-image: we simply don't see ourselves as mass killers. We still hold to the "myth of America's good intentions," as Noam Chomsky puts it.[5] If we have invaded, bombed, or killed, it was for good reason and in a "just cause." There is thus no need for being sorry. The dead, or at least their government, brought it on themselves.

"If Saddam Hussein was a poisonous snake in the desert," Morrow says in another place, "and he had one million poisonous snakes arrayed around him, then it was good sense to drop bombs and kill 100,000 snakes and thus turn back the snake menace. But, of course, the 100,000 Iraqis were not snakes." Once more Morrow does not spell out his implied conclusion—that maybe it didn't make "good sense" (he clearly means morally, not militarily) to "drop bombs and kill 100,000 snakes." He does not elaborate on the moral question he has raised about U.S. strategy and chooses, once more, to move on to a different issue. Yet, in the passage quoted above, Morrow clearly believes that 100,000 Iraqis needn't have died: they weren't evil or deserving of death, unlike Saddam Hussein. They were ordinary people and probably unwilling conscripts. So to kill them while trying to get him, Saddam, was wrong. And to kill them while leaving him still in power, after the war, compounded the wrong. To knowingly kill the innocent while trying to punish the guilty is wrong.[6] But we did it anyway and felt no visible remorse.

I must pause here to comment on the question of whether 100,000 Iraqi deaths were actually unavoidable, for Morrow seems to contradict himself on this point. In the "snake" passage cited above, he tells us they didn't have to die. But a bit later in the essay, after referring to an old saying about the Texan who "needed killing," he suggests something different. "In the circumstances," he writes, the dead Iraqis did "need to be killed." (We are not told just why the circumstances required this.) So he seems to have been unable to make up his mind on this issue and tries to have it both ways.

I wish now to come back to one of Morrow's main points about the Gulf War killing: that it is not guilt-free. He makes an important observation: "All killing is unclean. It has upon it a stain that technology cannot annul or override."

This fact is recognized by the public. When a statue of Arthur Harris, who directed the RAF bombing campaign which killed tens of thousands of German civilians during World War II, was recently unveiled, there was an outcry from some in the British public who thought this unfitting. Harris' bloody deeds did not deserve such a tribute, they insisted. And in the Old Testament, King David was told that he would not be allowed to build the temple—his son, Solomon, receiving this honor—because he also had too much blood on his hands. David had been a very successful military chieftain.

The "stain" of killing referred to above has an objective, indelible quality to it, as Lady Macbeth knew all too well. The saying, "He tried to wash his hands of the whole affair," also suggests the idea of uncleanness, stain, something which defiles us and renders us impure.

The idea of stain, of the association between guilt and uncleanness, is very ancient,[7] and is not limited to Western thought. Cain, the first killer, carried a mark on his body for the rest of his life. Various New Testament writers, such as Peter, explicitly speak of sin in terms of stain. And some Christian hymns still sung today help to keep alive the association between guilt and uncleanness. In fact, evangelistic preaching often has the overt goal of forcing the listener to feel the connection between his (objective) sins and the (subjective) guilt he should be—but perhaps has not been—feeling. The immediate aim is to elicit his repentance and confession, i.e., his conversion.

In his book, *Faces of the Enemy*,[8] Sam Keen says that *metanoia*, repentance, is in fact the thing that will defuse and ultimately overcome the violent, warmaking tendency of humans, as we begin to own up to our own dark side (our repressed evil tendencies) and face the reality of who and what we are. We can then begin to view the perceived enemy more accurately and compassionately, as we look at ourselves with greater honesty.

A question comes to mind at this point, though Morrow himself does not ask it: if killing "stains" the killer, and if mass killing produces a correspondingly large stain, and if contemporary America has a lot of innocent or mostly innocent blood on its hands, then what should we do about it?

Morrow's timid conclusion to his own essay's argument is that we simply should not, in the wake of our recent victory, indulge in "too much pleasure," too much celebration. He seems to fear what he calls a "rude awakening," if we carry our euphoria too far. (Since I originally wrote these words in June of 1991, the euphoria has diminished considerably.)

I, on the other hand, would like to propose something that prophetic religion might recommend, namely national self-examination and, beyond that, some form of restitution to the victims. We need to look squarely at what we have done and we need to make amends for it, to the extent that that is possible. Given the precedent that was set by Vietnam, I realize this sounds highly implausible. But it seems morally required none the less.

The ancient Chinese sage, Lao Tzu, once wrote the following words:

> ...To praise victory is to delight in the slaughter of men. For the slaughter of the multitude, let us weep with sorrow and grief. For a victory, let us observe the occasion with funeral ceremonies.[9]

This attitude is not now characteristic of America. We do not weep over the "slaughter of the multitude" in Iraq precisely because we are sure we were doing what was right: our cause was righteous, it was just—or so various religious and secular authorities have claimed.

Morrow does not touch upon the "just war" issue. As noted, his concern is more existential: what does killing do to the killer? But if killing the innocent is as metaphysically consequential as he suggests, it would seem that much more is required than merely taking what he calls "a moment of silence for the Iraqi corpses." National self-examination, which probably will not originate in Washington, is needed. *Metanoia*, repentance, is needed. A turning away from war as a way of resolving international differences and imposing U.S. "solutions" is needed. A dismantling of the whole war system, of which we are presently the undisputed masters, is needed.

Morrow, of course, suggests none of this. He is willing to settle for a "moment for the dead." But that, surely, is just for starters. What about those who will die in future wars, if we do not begin changing the war system now? What about the American families who will grieve over their thousands of dead? And if we do not soon solve the nuclear dilemma, what about the millions of persons, whatever their nationality, who may be killed? These are questions which Morrow's interesting and provocative essay raises but does not actually deal with. By all means, let us take a "moment for the dead." But let us also take steps to assure that the dead, both theirs and ours, shall not have died in vain.

NOTES

1. Karl Menninger, *Whatever Became of Sin?* (New York: Hawthorn Books, 1973).

2. Ibid., 230.

3. G. Simon Harnak suggests that we "consider violence as an addiction and the American culture as a system addicted to violence." See his article, "After the Gulf War: A New Paradigm for the Peace Movement," *Journal of Humanistic Psychology* 32:4, 11–40.

4. See, for example, Reinhold Niebuhr, *Moral Man and Immoral Society* (New York: Scribner's, 1932).

5. A *Time* essay several years ago (18 July 1988) by Walter Shapiro,"When Bad Things Are Caused by Good Nations," made a similar point. Shapiro comments on the muted U.S. reaction to the shooting down of the civilian Iranian airliner, with the loss of 290 lives. He speaks of how America reacted by "stifling both moral responsibility and collective grief." And he concludes that "Independence weekend 1988 may be remembered as that moment when Americans declared their independence from the moral consequences of misadventure."

6. This line of reasoning is admittedly rather silly. The whole idea in war is to kill as many of "the enemy" as possible, not to distinguish between the leadership which plans the war and the men in uniform who do what they are told. We do have to distinguish between the military and civilians, though in Vietnam this was especially difficult and in the nuclear age this has become impossible.

7. Paul Ricoeur does a brilliant phenomenological analysis of this and other metaphors whereby we speak of sin and guilt in his book, *The Symbolism of Evil* (New York: Harper & Row, 1967).

8. Sam Keen, *Faces of the Enemy: Reflections of the Hostile Imagination* (New York: Harper & Row, 1986).

9. *Tao Teh Ching*, chap. 31, Chan translation.

SUPPORT OUR TROPES:
A CRITIQUE OF PERSIAN GULF
DISCOURSE

Ron Hirschbein

Discourse supplements force in several important ways, among the most important of which is ideological persuasion. In the hands of elites and of those professionals who serve them...discourse in all forms—not only verbal, but also the symbolic discourses of spectacle...and the like—may be strategically employed...to win the consent of those over whom power is exercised, thereby obviating the need for the direct coercive use of force and transforming simple power into "legitimate" authority. [1]

This chapter analyzes the role of discourse in persuading the American public to condone and celebrate the Bush Administration's recent military campaign against Iraq. The Administration relied upon discourse—language and spectacles—to persuade a public (with a will to believe) that it orchestrated a just war, not a massacre. Within this context, it is only possible to examine one important facet of this discourse: the trope—the historical analogy—that was invoked to tell the Administration's story about its actions.

Due to the pervasive comparison of Hussein to Hitler, the public came to believe that it supported a just war: an organized, violent conflict between rather evenly matched adversaries—a righteous struggle in which the outcome was not predetermined by factors such as numerical and technological advantage. The possibility that the Administration perpetrated a massacre—a one-sided conflict in which a vastly superior adversary engaged in the virtually unopposed slaughter of civilians and combatants—never entered the realm of discourse. How did the Administration exclude such a possibility?

It appears that American leaders engaged in a carefully planned campaign to construct and shape public opinion. One of its most influential advocates, Congressman Newt Gringrich, authored a booklet for key officials entitled *Language: A Key Mechanism of Control*. It suggested that when Republicans speak of themselves they should invoke terms such as "peace, freedom and flag." And, Gringrich continued, they must characterize opponents as "sick, liberal and self-serving." The Administration heeded this advice along with the recommendations of various spin controllers and impression managers. It promulgated its official version of the military campaign through a type of discourse that is the subject of this essay—narrative. In response to the probability of full scale combat in the Persian Gulf, the public quite naturally asked, "What's the story?" The Bush Administration supplied an answer: a trope that capsulized a simplistic, resonant account of events by likening Hussein to Hitler. This metaphorical narrative did not merely indicate what was happening—it conveyed meaning: it signified *why* the conflict was happening and *what was expected* of the public. (The public was expected to uncritically and enthusiastically support a costly policy that resulted in several thousand American casualties and hundreds of thousands of Iraqi casualties; it complied with alacrity.)

Of course, in order to persuade the public to accept its official version of reality, the Administration did not tell the whole story. Accordingly, before we investigate what was said, we must be attentive to what was left unsaid—the words that never could be uttered.

1. What Was Left Unsaid

How easy to kill someone we don't have to mourn because we never dared to imagine him alive.[2]

Foucault was right: those who control the discourse control the argument. What is left unsaid is often more significant than what is spoken and written. In my view, mainstream discourse eschewed the term "massacre" precisely because it described American policy.

Curiously, the media aptly characterized Iraqi actions against Kuwaitis and Kurds as a "massacre." Indeed, calling the Iraqi atrocities a "war" would divert attention—and righteous ou trage—from the fact that a vastly superior, virtually unopposed conqueror perpetrated the wholesale slaughter of these hapless peoples.

By the same token, American actions have the characteristics ordinarily ascribed to massacres. In decidedly one-sided air raids and missile attacks, thousands of Iraqis were killed. Moreover, the destruction of the infrastructure of the major cities is responsible for a slower massacre. A Harvard Medical School study, for example, concludes that approximately 175,000 Iraqi children will die as a result of the destruction of electrical, water, and sewage treatment facilities.[3] Finally, it is estimated that between 100,000 and 120,000 retreating Iraqi troops were killed in about 100 hours of combat. Total allied deaths from accident and from combat are estimated at 343 (the Americans sustained about the same number of combat deaths as they did during the invasion of Grenada: 40).[4] These estimates are shared by sources as diverse as the Saudi government and Greenpeace.

Now it could be argued that the Bush Administration did not perpetuate a massacre because it *intended* to conduct a war: i.e., it believed that Iraqi opposition was formidable and therefore it concluded that hostilities would not result in a one-sided slaughter. Its deeds, however, suggest otherwise.

1. During the January 1991 talks between American and Iraqi officials, Baker presented Aziz with an ultimatum: leave Kuwait or the people of Iraq will pay a "terrible price" and face a "certain calamity."[5]
2. The air raids and missile attacks made good on the threat. The virtual absence of Iraqi resistance to these attacks should have disabused official Washington of the notion that it faced a formidable foe.
3. Rather than invoking a cease fire and exploring diverse peace proposals, Bush ordered his forces to attack Iraqi troops. (Contrary to his rhetoric, Bush did not "go the last mile" for peace—he didn't give an inch.) It was obvious at the onset that Iraqi resistance was negligible. Yet, the slaughter of retreating, demoralized troops escalated.

These facts suggest that characterizing American actions as a massacre is descriptive, not rhetorical. Why weren't American actions called by their right name? To be sure, government censorship—virtually unprecedented in modern times—prevented journalists from telling the whole story. As Pulitzer Prize winner Sydney Schanberg observes:

> The press has been crippled, rendered unable to provide the public with a credible picture of what war is like in all its guises. What has been delivered...instead are superficial brush strokes across the sanitized surface of war. Bombs fall remotely and perfectly, and no one is bleeding.[6]

Indeed, American officialdom suppressed embarrassing facts and censored competing stories about the conflict. Media representatives were accompanied by military personnel to carefully selected areas, and subsequent dispatches were rigorously scrutinized. The

American public did not witness the carnage on the "Highway of
Death" as retreating Iraqi troops—and bewildered Kuwati civilians—were slaughtered by American aircraft. Indeed, the public did
not get the whole story.

Regrettably, the mainstream media was not exercised by such
censorship. Why? Could it be that the media did not want to reveal
the whole story? In order to sell papers, placate advertisers and stay
in the good graces of officialdom, did it dutifully circulate what the
public, corporate and government elites wanted to hear? Schanberg's
revelations suggest this is a distinct possibility: unlike maverick
publications such as the *Nation*, the mainstream media did not pursue
litigation against government censorship. For the most part, it
uncritically and enthusiastically supported Administration policies. It
seems reasonable to suspect that, even without governmental
restrictions, a docile media would have been reluctant to tell the
whole story.

2. What Was Said

> There is scarcely a society without its major narratives which are recounted,
> repeated and...recited in well-defined circumstances; things said once and
> preserved because it is suspected that behind them there is a secret or
> treasure. [7]

The Administration knowingly and unknowingly used various
discourse techniques to garner support for its campaign against Iraq.
Advocates of military action from the President on down affected a
calm, confident air that many equate with reason and truthfulness.
And, refusing to call things by their right name to protect the guilty,
they invoked congenial euphemisms and high-tech acronyms. My
concern, however, is with the narrative the Bush Administration
recounted and repeated in order to persuade the public—and possibly
itself—that it was conducting a just war, not a massacre. It relied
upon a resonant trope to tell its story.

A. Support Our Tropes

By comparing Hussein to Hitler the Administration expressed its
justification of the massacre. In 1991 the world according to
mainstream discourse had returned to the 1930s—again! And
Hussein was no longer the dictator of a fourth rate military power
surrounded by formidable opponents and threatened by the greatest
military colossus in history; somehow he had become Hitler—a

dictator who enjoyed uncontested military superiority in his region and a disarmed, isolationist United States. In legerdemain that rivals "A Thousand and One Nights," Baghdad became Munich, and Bush would be Churchill, not Chamberlain. As political analyst Christopher Matthews explains:

> While the Hussein-is-Hitler argument may strike most Americans as a relatively harmless bit of hyperbole, the Munich reference is not. It puts our country in the dangerous position of either going to war or facing national shame not known since…Chamberlain. The fact that the "Munich" comparison is palpably false has not limited its effectiveness. It has justified a…war against Iraq as the only means of avoiding a global conflict. [8]

Curiously, even critics of the Administration's reasoning and policy such as Matthews accept the claim that American forces conducted a war, not a massacre. In my view, by invoking the comparison between Hussein and Hitler, the Bush Administration was telling the public—and possibly itself—that since Hussein and his legions were the incarnation of Nazism, annihilation was a proper—if not obligatory—response. If the enormity of Hitler's crimes justified the destruction of Hamburg and Dresden, surely the crimes of a latter-day Hitler justified the destruction of Baghdad and the carnage of the "Highway of Death."

Influential columnists such as A. M. Rosenthal promulgated the historical analogy with considerable zeal. He explained:

> The West would not listen to Saddam any more than it listened to his plain-speaking models: Hitler and Stalin. The West…thought that they could stop this man, steer him away from his lifetime commitment to empire by giving him more money, more military power.…[The policy should have been] to stop a dictator before he becomes unstoppable. [9]

An equally influential columnist, William Safire, explained that a military campaign against Iraqi combatants and civilians would ultimately save lives "By moving quickly we can reduce the capacity of this generations' Hitler to put innocent lives at risk."

Finally, other pundits, such as Charles Krauthammer, urged that bombing Baghdad is no cause for guilt. On the contrary—given that Hussein is Hitler with an Arabic accent—Americans must muster the courage to condone the killing of Iraqi civilians:

> Civilian pain in war is a horror beyond words. But when a war is just, it must be faced with a kind of nerve. We demand of American soldiers on the front

the nerve to risk their lives on our behalf....We have a reciprocal and far less
onerous obligation to them to keep our nerve in the face of Saddam's cynical
strategy of broadcasting the carnage he has brought upon his own people.[10]

Unhappily, examples can be compounded. What is essential for
our purposes is the recognition and indictment of the deceptive
nature of historical analogies. Such tropes exaggerate similarities
between past and present while concealing differences. They thereby
distract attention from the unique properties of the present by
focusing attention on a version of the past reconstructed in memory
and propaganda. Such tropes represent magical thinking in which the
decidedly complicated uniqueness of the present suddenly becomes a
simplified past crying-out with a time-honored lesson. The lesson, of
course, reflects the ideology of the storyteller. In order to score
rhetorical points, Hussein could have been likened to Lyndon
Johnson invading Vietnam; Begin invading Lebanon; or even Bush
invading Panama. The most apt trope would have likened Hussein to
Assad (the neighboring Syrian despot who launched a brutal invasion
of Lebanon in October 1990). Such an analogy was not favored,
however, because Assad became a newfound American ally in its
campaign against Iraq.

In any case, it might be noted that presidents who are not
plagued by "wimp" images seem less exercised by the possibility
that they may be likened to Chamberlain, not Churchill. During the
Suez Crisis of 1956, for example, Anthony Eden (the British Prime
Minister) likened pan-Arabist Nasser to Hitler, and pleaded with
Eisenhower to intervene militarily. General Eisenhower, however,
was immune from charges of "appeasement": he rejected the analogy
and—despite considerable pressure for his allies and advisors—he
refused to go to war, and settled the crisis diplomatically.

B. Support Our Troops

Thucydides, an influential if not prescient Greek historian,
reminds us that it dangerous to uncouple words from things. What is
the danger? When words don't refer to things they become slogans
that sound good, elicit favorable visceral responses, and thereby
short-circuit critical thinking. Words decoupled from things allow
listeners to project whatever meaning they want into the slogan.
"Support our troops!" is such a slogan.

A tangible, concrete representation of Administration policy
would have been less popular. If it had advocated killing tens of

thousands of civilians in order to undermine the Iraqi infrastructure with the ultimate goal of reestablishing a medieval Kuwati monarchy, perhaps the public would have been less enthusiastic. "Support our troops!" sounded better. I suspect that for many, the resonance of the slogan and the feeling it elicited sufficed. Those who pondered its meaning could project their favored interpretation into the slogan:

1. Those who supported the Administration's tropes readily supported its troops. If Hussein was Hitler, surely the American cause was just.
2. Others questioned the analogy, but supported the troops because they interpreted the slogan to mean that the Administration was trying to establish a "New World Order." "New World Order" itself is a vacuous slogan that sounds good and feels good, but refers to nothing at all. This recognition suggests that contemporary political discourse has taken on an Alice-in-Wonderland quality in which symbols merely refer to other symbols; in other words, one fiction refers to another. Dan Quayle indicts a fictional character for undermining family values (whatever they may be), and George Bush urges that supporting the troops will promote a new world order.
3. Even critics supported the troops. They interpreted the slogan to mean that the troops should be taken out of harm's way and brought home expeditiously. Moreover, after they are brought home, they should not endure the calumny suffered by the veterans of Vietnam.
4. Other critics such as Jesse Jackson used the slogan as a pretext for imposing a political agenda. He argued that he supported the troops because he believed that when they return, they should be afforded adequate housing, nutrition and education, and the same system of socialized medicine as the one available to members of Congress. [11]

"Support our troops!" meant everything and nothing at all. No wonder Orwell observed that "in our time, political speech and writing are largely the defense of the indefensible."

NOTES

1. Bruce Lincoln, *Discourse and the Construction of Society* (Oxford: Oxford University Press, 1989), 4–5.

2. Ariel Dorfman, "Hymn for the Unsung," in *The Gulf War Reader: History, Documents, Opinions*, edited by Micah Sifry and Christopher Cerf (New York: Random House, 1991), 328.

3. Cited in *The Washington Post* (23 June 1991), 1 and 16.

4. See, for example, *The San Francisco Chronicle* (30 May 1991), 15.

5. George Bush, "Letter to Saddam," in Sifry and Cerf, *The Gulf War Reader*, 178–179.

6. Sydney Schanberg, "A Muzzle for the Press," in Sifry and Cerf, *The Gulf War Reader*, 370.

7. Michael Foucault, "The Order of Discourse," in *Language and Politics*, edited by Michael Shapiro (New York: New York University Press, 1984), 114.

8. Christopher Matthews, "The Mirage of 'Munich'," *The San Francisco Examiner* (14 January 1991), A22.

9. A. M. Rosenthal, "Saddam's Goals Were Plain," *The San Francisco Chronicle* (14 January 1991), A22.

10. Charles Krauthammer, "No Cause for Guilt," in Sifry and Cerf, *The Gulf War Reader*, 259.

11. Jesse Jackson, from his speech before the convention of the National Association of Science and Technology, Washington, D.C., 1 February 1991.

SECTION IV

Jihad, *Intifada*, and Other Mideast Concerns

INTRODUCTION

In the board game "Risk," players represent colonial powers and compete to conquer the world by amassing military strength. Because the Middle East is at the intersection of Africa, Asia and Europe, it is both the most desirable and the most difficult territory for Risk players to control. Whoever controls the Middle East controls access to all three continents. It is hardly a wonder, then, that in the real world struggles between colonial powers are battled out in the Middle East. Colonial powers have not hesitated to exploit the conflicts between the indigenous peoples of the region, a variety of ethnically related but religiously, politically, and economically estranged groups. Playing upon fierce tribal loyalties in the region, the colonial powers continually shift their military, political, and economic alliances with various nations in order to gain an advantage in the region. Foreign powers view Mideasterners as pawns. And Mideasterners, who want to distinguish themselves from inferior tribes, play the role of pawn in exchange for tribal power.

The authors of the chapters in Section IV focus on the theme of respect for persons as a prerequisite for nonviolence in the Middle East. Respect by foreign powers for the autonomy of Mideastern peoples might free Mideasterners to begin to work together to solve regional problems. Respect by Mideasterners for members of other tribes would make it impossible for foreign powers to exploit tribal rivalries. The authors in this section hold such respect as an ideal as they discuss political policies and philosophies. The first two essays describe the respect for self and others which make possible the existing Mideast nonviolent movements. The third essay argues that the Palestinian people are entitled under international law to exercise self-determination. The fourth essay presents a shocking biblical parable about violence and lack of respect, relating the lesson to the contemporary Mideast.

In "Interpreting the *Jihad* of Islam: Muslim Militarism vs. Muslim Pacifism," Robert Paul Churchill examines the potential development of pacifism within Islam. He recognizes that Islam has not tended to nurture pacifism and nonviolence as ways of life, because a commitment to follow one's individual conscience is essential to pacifism but not to Islam. Nevertheless, Churchill argues, the sacred texts of Islam, as well as the concept of "holy war," can be and have been reinterpreted as supporting peaceful and nonviolent social reforms among Muslim peoples.

In "Nonviolence and the *Intifada*," Robert L. Holmes refutes the view, widely held by Americans, that the *Intifada*, the ongoing Palestinian uprising against Israeli rule in the occupied territories, is a violent movement. Although explicit advocacy of nonviolence in the movement has been rare, Holmes argues that the movement nonetheless has been predominantly nonviolent. He discusses a model of nonviolent civil disobedience in the city of Beit Sahour.

In "Self-Determination and the Israeli-Palestinian Conflict," Tomis Kapitan argues that the message of the *Intifada*—that self-determination by Palestinians is a necessity—must be recognized by international powers if there is to be a just and lasting peace in the Mideast. Under international law, the concept of "self-determination" requires that any settlement be based on the "free acceptance of that settlement by the people immediately concerned...." The absence of such "free acceptance" by Palestinian Arabs living under Israeli occupation not only violates international law but has also led to an explosive struggle.

In "The Parable of the Levite's Concubine," Laura Duhan Kaplan suggests that political solutions are necessary but not sufficient to end violent conflict. Analyzing a Biblical parable about the relationship between political chaos and violence, and noting the similarities between biblical and current Mideastern conditions, she concludes that members of Mideastern tribes must become aware of the humanity of persons from other tribes.

As this book goes to press, the desire to end violence appears to have become strong enough for the leaders of the Palestine Liberation Organization and the Israeli government to negotiate together as equals. The editors of this volume recognize that discussion of the Israeli-Palestinian conflict will involve the leaders of a number of Middle Eastern nations, and they hope that the negotiations will lead to a viable peace plan for the region. Section VI, "Postcript: 1993," includes a discussion of the prospects for peace in the Middle East.

INTERPRETING THE *JIHAD* OF ISLAM: MUSLIM MILITARISM VS. MUSLIM PACIFISM

Robert Paul Churchill

Even if I am granted eternal life, I would not like to have it alone. May there
be no rain on me or my land, unless it rains all over the country too.

—Abu al-'la' al-Ma'rri

1. The Possibility of Pacifism in Islam

In this chapter I want to explore the potential for pacifism within
Islam. I do this in part by showing how three courageous Muslims—Bawa Muhaiyaddeen, Kamil Husain, and Ustadh Mahmoud
Taha—reinterpreted the sacred texts of Islam so that these texts
could be read as supporting peaceful and nonviolent social reform
among Muslim peoples. But equally important to this effort will be
an exploration of the characteristics of Islam, such as the militant
interpretation of *jihad*, or "holy war," which make Islam problematic
as a "carrier" or nurturer of pacifism and of nonviolence as a way of
life.

To avoid misunderstanding at the outset, it is necessary that I
clarify the kinds of persons I understand to be pacifists when I speak
of the possibility of pacifism in Islam. First, by pacifists, I am
referring not just to persons who have a doctrinal commitment to the
immorality of war and violence, but to those who choose on moral
grounds to be personally committed to opposing war and violence.
Second, I am referring to persons who have met the psychological
condition I believe to be necessary for such a personal commitment,
namely, acceptance of the belief that the commitment to oppose war
and violence must arise, for each individual, out of one's own sense
of personal responsibility. [1]

My interpretation of the character of the pacifist's commitment
is supported, I believe, by evidence from the history of pacifism,
especially evidence of dialogue within Protestant denominations
about the individual's responsibilities in relation to the religious
community. Nonviolent creeds often grow out of the painful
uncertainty of individuals over compatibility between their needs for

integrity and spiritual purity and demands for conformity in the
religious community. Pacifists who are also religious individuals
often hold themselves to standards that surpass, or even conflict
with, the requirements of their faiths as "officially" interpreted.
Indeed, in the gap, or breach, between individual aspiration and
official creed, lies the fertile ground for the growth of pacifism. It is
precisely the existence of this gap, or chasm, that allows the
individual's conscience to take a primary role in religious and moral
life, and that requires a heightened sense of personal responsibility. It
is thus not at all surprising that references to individual conscience
should be very prominent in the literature of pacifists and of
advocates of nonviolence, whether it is George Fox and the Quakers'
conception of conscience as the "spark of the divine" in each
individual, Tolstoy's reliance on the truths of conscience to support
his Christian anarchism, or even Gandhi's intuition that our
consciences bid us to engage others in *Satyagraha* to test our
conflicting "relative truths" and to seek their reconciliation in the
"absolute truth" of Brahma, or God.

I find in my reading of Islam that very little mention is made of,
and little thought given either to pacifism as a way of life or to the
role of conscience as a guide to life. It is also clear that whereas one
concept of peace, or *salam*, occurs many times in the *Qur'an*, its
associations are overwhelmingly nonpolitical. In Muslim usage,
salam denotes peace as tranquility in this world or as salvation in the
next.[2] The concept of peace is not associated with active resistance to
evil. In both *Sunni* and *Shi'a*, the main traditions of Islam, nonviolence has not been accepted as an integral doctrine.[3] The Prophet
Muhammad appears to have had no compunction about the
legitimacy of force when he believed the situation demanded it, and
he called upon the private Muslim to make over his personal
conscience to the common will.[4] Those dubious about battles and
campaigns were seen in the *Qur'an* as either slothful or cowardly,
letting their scruples weaken their nerve or allowing their love of
domestic peace to become a *fitnah*, or temptation, to them.[5]

2. *Jihad* and Islamic Militarism

From the outset, Islam divided the world between *dar-al-Islam*,
the House of Islam, and *dar-al-Harb*, the House of War. The first
was composed of Muslims and those in submission to Muslim rule,
the second was the realm of infidels.[6] Between these two "houses" a

state of war existed, ordained by God through the *jihad*, which has the literal meaning of "effort," "striving," or "struggle."[7] The basis of the obligation of *jihad* is the universality of the Muslim revelation. Because God's word and God's message are for all of humanity, it is the duty of those who have accepted them to strive (*jahada*) unceasingly to convert or at least subjugate those who have not.[8] From the beginning, a minority of *Ulama*—jurists and scholars—argued that *jihad* should be understood as a moral or spiritual striving rather than as a commitment to military violence. Nevertheless, the overwhelming majority of classical theologians, jurists, and traditionalists understood the obligation of *jihad* to mean waging war.[9] And while there was a long tradition of law limiting the causes of and the conduct of war that could be described as "fighting in the way of Allah," many Muslim scholars believe, even today, that a fighter who lays down his life for the cause of Allah achieves instant immortality.[10]

This is also the meaning of *jihad* evoked by Islamic militants, or neofundamentalists, who exhort Muslims to rise against secular governments corrupted by Western influences.[11] These neofundamentalist movements acquired most of their ideology of contemporary Islamic resurgence from the following figures: Hasan al-Banna (1906–1949), founder of the influential Muslim Brotherhood (*Jamiyyat al-Ikhwan al-Muslimin*) in Egypt in 1928, from his successor Sayyid Qutb (1906–1966), himself influenced by the Pakistani neofundamentalist theologian Sayyid Abul Al Mawdudi (1903–1979), from Sayyid Mujtaha Navvab Safavi (1923–1986), founder of the *Fidaiyan-i Islam* (Devotees of Islam) in Iran, and by Ali Shar'iati (1933–1977), the Iranian, nonclerical ideologue.

All neofundamentalists see the "world of Islam" in a state of chronic disorder. The source of disorder and decay is the contemporary West which represents an immoral culture based on false values and which has infected the indigenous Muslim societies with the twin evils of licentious materialism and godless, secular nationalism.[12] The only solution is a comprehensive re-Islamization: a restoration of all the traditional legal, social, and political institutions as originally constituted. Most or all vestiges of Western culture must be purged from the contaminated societies. To accomplish this, the resurgent organizations have attempted to repoliticize Islam and have proclaimed *jihad* as the primary mission and duty of all those participating in the struggle.[13] For example, the central concept in Sayyid Qutb's activist doctrine is that Muslims have always been confronted—perhaps more today than at any other time—with the threat of *jahiliyya* (ignorance) against which they have to wage *jihad*. For traditional Islamicists, the term *jahiliyya* connotes the age of ignorance in Arabia before the advent of Islam, and Qutb declared, "We are...surrounded by *jahiliyya* society today, which is of the same nature as it was during the first period of Islam...."[14]

Many neofundamentalist groups advocating militant *jihad* have not been loath to countenance draconian measures if necessary, or even to sanction violence.[15] They reject modernist attempts to interpret *jihad* as a purely defensive form of warfare.[16] The *Fidaiyan-i Islam* (Devotees of Islam), which strongly influenced Khomeini as did Qutb, was dedicated to violent activism.[17] Khomeini himself revived the bipolar view of conflict between *dar-al-Islam*, the realm of Islam, and *dar-al-Harb*, the realm of war.[18] Khomeini and Ali Shari'ati both reinterpreted the life of the Shi'ite martyr, Imam Hussain, as a revolutionary leading the oppressed against their oppressors. And they asserted that, rather than passively beg for his intercession, good Shi'ites should actively emulate his revolution.[19]

Among the violence of neofundamentalism, one must include the role of the Ayatollah Khomeini and Islamic resurgents in the overthrow of the Shah's regime in Iran; the subsequent brutal excesses of the Islamic revolution; the assassination of Anwar Sadat by members of the radical *al-Jihad* group which had infiltrated the Egyptian army; the conflict which began in 1963 between Assad's Baath Party of Syria and the Syrian branch of the Muslim Brotherhood which declared a "*jihad* against the enemies of God" and actively sought to unseat the ruling elite;[20] and finally, the exploits of extremist Shi'ites in Lebanon including the terrorism of *Hizb Allah* (The Party of God) and the Islamic *Jihad* for the Liberation of Palestine.

In addition to its militaristic connotations, the resurgent's call for *jihad*, as well as the traditionalist's, connotes the subjugation of the individual to the larger "good" of Islam: the unquestioning obedience of the individual Muslim in this "holy struggle" to the authority of the ruling caliph or *imam*. In fact, a defining characteristic of neofundamentalism is the insistence that all aspects of life, social as well as political, should conform to a set of sacred scriptures believed to be inerrant and immutable.[21] Thus, for neofundamentalists, renewal comes through *jihad*, or striving, which subjugates the individual to the traditional forms of Islamic authority. It is perhaps not surprising, therefore, that there are many Muslim treatises on *jihad*, or justifiable warfare, but that the treatises on peace, written from a traditional, "mainstream" Muslim perspective generally do not offer an alternative vision of peace. These treatises do not appeal to conscience, or to individual judgment and personal responsibility, and they generally ignore the possible role for the individual in promoting peace through individual initiative or active resistance. Peace is to be achieved through conformity: by faithfully following the commands of the *Qur'an* or the *shari'a*, the "holy law" presumably derived from the *Qur'an* and the *Sunna* of the Prophet (composed of his sayings, the *hadith*, and his acts, the *sira*.)[22]

3. The "Totalism" of Islam

Considerations such as these suggest that the traditional call for *jihad*, and the neofundamentalists' revival of it as a militant striving, draw upon further characteristics of Islam that block or impede the development of pacifism. These characteristics block access to the counsels of conscience and diminish the individual sense of responsibility. They make it difficult for Muslims to form and sustain moral communities that can claim to transcend Muslim identity and the ordering of Muslim life imposed by *shari'a*. Moreover, these characteristics make it exceedingly difficult to interpret the obligation of *jihad* in anything but a militant way. All of these characteristics can be summarized by what Habib Boulares, author of *Islam: The Fear and the Hope*, calls the "totalism of Islam."[23] I shall analyze this "totalism" into four elements: the all-inclusive identity of the Muslim as a member of the *Umma*, the "brotherhood" or community of Islam; the politicization of Islam and the absence of independent secular and moral domains of life; the subordination of the individual to authority; and finally, the orthopraxic character of the religion.

In most Muslim countries, Islam is still the ultimate criterion of group identity and loyalty. "The ultimate definition of the Other, the alien outsider and presumptive enemy, has been the *kafir*, the unbeliever."[24] A great many, if not most, Muslims continue to see themselves as members of a transnational community. Most neofundamentalists maintain that there is a "basic contradiction" between nationalism and "Islam as an eternal, universalist message."[25] Furthermore, as noted by Bernard Lewis, "in political life, Islam offers the most widely intelligible formulation of ideas...Islam provides the most effective system of symbols for political mobilization...."[26] Secularism, as understood in the West, does not exist in a clear manner in the psychology of the traditional Muslim.

In the emigration, or *hijra*, of the Prophet and his followers from Mecca to Medina, Muhammad became political and military leader as well as spiritual guide for his movement. The resulting *Umma* came to see all of communal life as sacral. In classical Arabic there was no vocabulary with which to draw distinctions between the spiritual and temporal, or the lay and ecclesiastical. Even in modern usage, there is no Muslim equivalent for "the Church" meaning "ecclesiastical organization," and the term "laity" is a meaningless expression in the context of Islam. Certainly for all neofundamentalists, "the very notion of a secular, jurisdiction and authority—of a so-to-speak unsanctified part of life that lies outside the scope of religious law and those who uphold it—is seen as an impiety, indeed as the ultimate betrayal of Islam...."[27]

The *shari'a*, or Holy Law of Islam, embraces the whole range of human activities. Traditional Muslim scholarship considered that all major questions of belief and law had been aired and settled by about the fourth century after the *hijra*. Until that time, Muslim jurists, known by the collective term *'ulama* ("learned"), had exercised their professional right of independent legal decision making called *ijtihad*. Today, however, consensus among Sunni Muslims regards the "gate" of *ijtihad* to be closed.[28]

Along with the absolute subjection of the individual to *shari'a*, one must consider the subjugation of the individual to *de facto* political power. The *'ulama* and *faqih* (doctor of the Holy Law) see the state primarily as a divine instrument: as a necessary part of God's providential dispensation for mankind. In the vision of Islam, the body politic and the sovereign power within it are ordained by God for the principal function of government is to enable the *Umma* to attain the good Muslim life.[29] In the traditional view, the state does not create the law, but is itself created and maintained by the law. Hence, in theory, while the ruler may legislate, to clarify and apply the law, he may in no way abrogate it.[30] In actuality, however, because he holds the final say over its interpretation and application, including the power to make regulations to supplement *shari'a*, the ruler's power may be absolute.[31] Moreover, there is no provision in *shari'a* for legal opposition and Muslim tradition recognizes illegitimacy of rule only when it is associated with apostasy, that is, with betrayal of the *shari'a*.

The subject's duty of obedience is a religious obligation. An oft-repeated comment among jurists is that "tyranny is better than anarchy" and that "whose power prevails must be obeyed." Hence, there is consensus that even an oppressive government—provided that it is Muslim—must be obeyed.[32] One observer notes, "Muslims are fond of declaring that 'humankind has no rights, only duties',"[33] and indeed, within traditional Muslim culture there is no widely accepted theory of human rights, no tradition of civil disobedience, and no higher law theory. Even the concept of citizen, with its connotation of the right to participate in the formation and conduct of government, was outside the Muslim political experience and a rough equivalent—*watan* (meaning the place of one's birth or residence)—was adopted only under the pressure of Western ideas of nationality and citizenship.[34] Therefore, in effect (and apart from the ages-old dispute between Sunni and Shi'ite Muslims) there is no firm distinction within the Muslim context between *de jure* and *de facto* power and little that is comparable to the liberal Western notion of political legitimacy.

Of course, Muslim modernists in the late nineteenth and twentieth centuries have worked diligently to bring concepts such as human rights into the Muslim context. But the solidity and conservatism of Islam, combined with its militant resurgence, have meant that, with few exceptions, these Western doctrines still struggle to gain a purchase in the mental landscape of Islam.

The absence of a secular domain of moral reflection and practice partly explains one major difference between just war theory as it has developed in the West and just war theory as it has developed in Islam. Because it is a very legalistic religion and a religion which sanctions defensive wars, and even some forms of aggression, Islamic commentary is extensive on the "laws" governing the occasion and conduct of war. This is true as well in the West and especially within Roman Catholicism with which European commentary on just war originated. As the just war tradition has advanced in the West, however, it has become increasingly secularized so that it draws heavily on principles of international law, morality, and conceptions of human rights that are not derived from Christian orthodoxy. In particular, unlike the twelfth and thirteenth centuries when the Crusades were proclaimed by the Church to be holy wars, the determination of the justice of the cause of war has become independent of religious ideology. In the Islamic tradition, by contrast, the evaluation of the justness of the cause of war is not independent of religious ideology. To be sure, there is much controversy over the justness of particular wars and, given the division of the *Umma* into different states, controversy over which caliph or *imam* has the right to declare *jihad*. But the debate remains within the boundaries of sacred texts and commentaries; it has not been significantly enlarged by independently secular or ethical argumentation.

Each of the major features of Islam discussed so far—the all-inclusive identity of Muslims as members of the *Umma*, the politicization of Islam and the absence of a secular domain, and the subordination of the individual to authority—overlaps with the "orthopraxic" character of the religion in which the acting out of basic beliefs and attitudes is central.[35] Christianity is an orthodox religion because it has traditionally placed greater emphasis on belief and its intellectual structuring in creeds, catechisms, and theologies. It may even be said to have an antilegalistic bias. Islam, by contrast and like Judaism, places fundamental emphasis on law and the regulation of community life. Indeed, the formal, ritualistic, and performative characteristics of Islam are especially pervasive in Muslim life. While Islamic traditions are vitally concerned with correct thinking, knowing the truth without *doing it* is vanity. As one scholar notes, "In fact, the truth cannot be merely known, in the sense of being brought into mental awareness; it must be fully 'known' through realization in action."[36]

The orthopraxic character of Islam sustains the *Umma* as a community of faith and secures its identity by incorporating the teachings of the *Qur'an* and *Sunna* "through intimate and indelible processes of personality formation and imprinting and habits of the mind, body, and heart."[37] The major devotional-ritual duties, known as the Pillars of Islam, emphasize individual subordination, ritual purification, and almost reflexive, automatic conformity. For example, the *Salat*—the devotional service required five times a day—is "highly formalized and minutely regulated in its precisely observed cycles of spoken formulas and bodily postures" and a primary prerequisite for performing the *Salat* is ritual purification for every individual.[38] The pilgrimage, or *hajj*, often the climactic event in a Muslim's life, is a highly ritualized series of activities in which the pilgrim must don special clothing, must abstain from normal activities (including even shaving the beard, or cutting hair), must participate in ceremonies such as the standing ceremony on the plain of Arafat, and in rites including circumambulation of the *Ka'ba* and the ritual stoning of the devil.

Defenders of traditionalism point to the degree of emotional attachment with which Muslims complete these devotional rituals. Indeed, they stress that ritual participation enables Muslims to believe that they are participating with God in history.[39] It is claimed that Muslims "'partake' of the nature of their Lord by means of reciting the *Qur'an*." Recitation of the *Qur'an*, with its emphasis on performative uniformity leads some readers to report that it feels as if the *Qur'an* is 'reading' them.[40] As one observer notes, "When the *Qur'an* is recited properly, God's presence, in the form of his *sahina* ["tranquility"] is believed to descend upon the reciter and hearers."[41] This commentator adds, "The *Qur'an* and *hadith* do not guide the Muslims primarily as books, that is, as written texts; rather the Muslims themselves become, as it were, 'textualized' and activated in such a way as to be in turn a living guide for others."[42]

The four characteristics of Islam just discussed—the inclusiveness of the *Umma*, the politicization of religion, the subordination of the individual, and Islam's character as orthopraxic—make up the "totalism" of Islam. These characteristics also explain why so many Muslims regard Islam as a complete way of life and why the striving of *jihad* can be interpreted so easily, as the neofundamentalists do, in a militant sense. Indeed, some modernist Muslim critics fear the tendencies of Islam to establish itself as a cult and to deprive individuals of self-direction. Habib Boulares refers to Islam, as traditionally practiced, as "mimetism" and decries the Muslim's abandonment of independent judgment.[43] Writing with Iran's fundamentalist revolution in mind, Boulares complains, "All life's acts being envisaged in one text or another, the candidate for Islamist activism knows that it is lawful to find in his religion an answer for anything—even if this allows him to come up with simplistic solutions."[44] He adds grimly that "[e]verything is called Islamic from the most rational decisions to the acts of pure barbarism."[45]

4. Pacifist Interpretations of *Jihad*

Given that pacifism and a nonviolent way of life are not expressly part of the teachings of the *Qur'an* and the *Sunna*, and given the "totalism" of Islam, one must expect that the seeds of pacifist thought will not alight on fertile soil in the world of Islam.

Nevertheless, as noted earlier, pacifism is surely possible, provided that individuals successfully evade the strictures of ritualistic conformity and reinterpret the message of the *Qur'an* and *Sunna* in such a way as to give a prominent place in Islam to conscience and individual responsibility. In contrast to the traditionalists and the neofundamentalists, all three of the Muslim pacifists, Bawa Muhaiyaddeen, Kamil Husain, and Ustadh Mahmoud Taha, whose thought I will explore, stress, as most pacifists do, the counsels of conscience and the need for individual choice and responsibility. Thus, in stark contrast with militant neofundamentalists, these Muslim pacifists believe that true religious purity and social renewal can be attained only when *jihad* is interpreted as the striving of each individual for personal self-mastery, a self-mastery that can be attained only when unthinking subjugation to the strictures of traditional Islamic authority is replaced by the liberating influences of conscience and reliance on individual judgment.

Some support for pacifism already may be found in the tradition of personal spirituality within Islam known as *Erfan*, or Sufism in the West. Sufism, which began very early in Islam (Hasan of Basra d. 728), emphasizes *tariqa*, which like shari'a, means "way," but connotes a spiritual discipline or path, rather than God's legislation. Sufis generally believe that others, in addition to Muhammad, may experience God directly in this life. The aim of Sufi meditation, therefore, is to complete such purification as is needed to make one's soul a fitting "vessel" for the reception of God's infinite qualities. But despite this emphasis on "inwardness" and personal spirituality, Sufism generally did not depart, as one commentator notes,

> from the universal religious duties of Muslims; rather it may be understood to have intensified them and augmented them with new rites and ceremonies...centered in remembering God by mentioning in prayerlike formulas his 'Most Beautiful Names'. [46]

Still, some Sufis drew on their personal spirituality to reinterpret key aspects of the *Qur'an* and the *Sunna* in the direction of pacifism. Already by the eleventh century, al-Qushayri (d. 1074 C.E.) claimed that *jihad* consists not in warring against the infidel but in purifying the interior state. And al-Jilani (d. 1166 C.E.) read the Prophet's words, "We have returned from the lesser *jihad* to the greater *jihad*," as meaning that the conquest of the self is far more important than the conquest of external enemies.[47] One contemporary Sufi who has expanded this interpretation of *jihad* is Bawa Muhaiyaddeen.[48]

For Bawa Muhaiyaddeen, true *jihad* means to fight the war against the satanic elements within the self. "Each person in Islam must understand where this real war must be fought, where the real battlefield exists."[49] This is a lonely "war" which each individual must wage within him or herself, for only the individual can drive selfishness, avarice and the desires for praise and sensual pleasures out of his or her own soul. Moreover, success in the struggle occurs only when one truly can say that he acts only as conscience bids.[50] In the words of Bawa Muhaiyaddeen, "Only when you open that spring within and divine water flows from it will the water of God's qualities fill your heart."[51]

Bawa Muhaiyaddeen believes that those who earnestly struggle will find the peace of Allah, for the innermost heart of the individual is His kingdom.[52] This Sufi offers no social program for promoting nonviolence, for peace can spread only by the "sword of love," only by the opening of a heart to the approach of another filled with love, compassion, faith and certitude. As Muhaiyaddeen says, speaking from his mysticism, "[f]aith alone can capture another heart....The qualities of Allah that exist within the heart of one with determined faith must reach out, enter the heart of another and give him comfort and peace."[53]

One Muslim thinker influenced by Sufism, Mirza Ghulan Ahmad (1839–1908), did found a movement, the Ahmadiyya Movement, that accepts the need to resist oppression through organized effort. The Ahmadiyya movement, claiming perhaps half a million followers, is at best a quasi-pacifistic movement, for Mirza Ghulan Ahmad rejected non-resistance and accepted only a conditional pacifism.[54] But followers of Mirza Ghulan Ahmad do disown the concept of a *jihad* directed to the expansion of Islam. Instead, like the sufis, his followers interpret the "striving" or "exertion" imposed on the Muslim as a personal striving and an obligation to assist the oppressed by active measure, including resistance, as well as by prayer and meditation. Thus the essence of *jihad* lies in an active concern for the oppressed; it "enjoins on every Muslim to sacrifice his all for the protection of the weak and oppressed whether Muslims or not."[55]

Although he was not the founder of a movement, Muhammad Kamil Husain of Cairo (1901–1977) was a pacifist and a thinker of considerable force who, like Bawa Muhaiyaddeen, rejected the traditional interpretation of *jihad* and stressed the importance of conscience. Kamil Husain concentrated on what he called "faith-

therapy." He offered a unique response to *taqwa*, the human awe
before the face of God and the call of the Prophet to follow "the
straight path." The straight path was not the *shari'a* but an inner
"road" to God that led through self-discovery and self-composure.
"The making of your own self is the most definitive thing in your
life," wrote Kamil Husain. [56]

Most important in faith-therapy was a proper understanding of
the concept of purity in the *Qur'an*. Purity Kamil Husain interpreted
as the "hallowed valley"—*al-wadi-al-muqaddas*—the state of mind
in which one can hear the voice of conscience, which Kamil Husain
describes as "the very voice of God."[57] Because of this concern for
purity, Kamil Husain was wary of collectives and communities due
to their corrosive effects.

The central argument of Kamil Husain's major work, *Qaryah
Zalimah (City of Wrong)*,[58] is that the vested interests of collectives,
of political structures, always tend towards injustice and tyranny.
Collectivities, by their nature, are incapable of acquiring a conscience and they threaten to overwhelm and stifle the scruples of
private conscience. Indeed, the greater the vested interests or the
more ambitious the collective's ends, the greater the danger. Thus in
perpetrating a massive collective evil, such as aggressive war or
economic oppression, shares of responsibility may become so
fragmentary as to be untraceable to any particular individual, or so
minuscule as to no longer connote culpability. "It follows that the
only check, frail as it must be, to the wrongdoing of states and parties
and institutions, is the resistance of the individual conscience."[59]
Kamil Husain thus insisted that the private person must refuse to do,
in the name of some collective loyalty, what he would refrain from
doing in his individual capacity.

Kamil Husain's emphasis on conscientious choice and individual
responsibility was shared by Mahmoud Mohamed Taha (1909/11–
1985), a pacifist martyr from the Sudan. Ustadh (revered teacher)
Mahmoud Taha opposed the "mimetism" of Islam: those aspects of
its orthopraxic character that blinded Muslims to the injustices
committed in the name of their religion. And Ustadh Mahmoud Taha
was especially opposed to those aspects of *shari'a* which perpetrated
manifest inequalities and injustices.

For Ustadh Mahmoud Taha, the kernel of Islam is contained in
two passages: the verse, or Sura, of the *Qur'an* that proclaims, "And
[now] you have come to Us as individuals in the same way We have
created you in the first place" (6:94) and in the "divine" *hadith* of the

Prophet, "I am neither contained in my earth nor in my heavens but rather contained in the heart of my true slave [Muslim—one who has submitted to god]."[60] Thus, for Ustadh Mahmoud Taha, one meets Allah within one's self, within what the Sufis called *sir al-sir*, the secret of the conscience, by bringing the qualities of the limited closer to the qualities of the Infinite. Consequently, individuality is the essence of the whole endeavor of religion, for it is only in the individual that such qualities of the Infinite as responsibility, honor, purity, and righteousness can develop.[61] *Shari'a* must therefore be in the service of "absolute individual freedom," a state not of lawlessness, anarchy and self-indulgence or self-assertion, but the state of the individual's own self-mastery and willing submission to God. "*Shari'a fardiyah*, individual law rather than community law, is the original principle of Islam, just as the individual rather than the community is Islam's original goal."[62] But, he argued, the *Qur'an* and the *Sunna* continued to be interpreted in *shari'a* in ways that caused oppression and injustice and therefore perverted the genuine message of Islam. He argued that many of the social practices sanctioned by *shari'a* (as well as some now superceded such as slavery) were not original precepts in Islam. These included *jihad*, private ownership of property, inequality between men and women, polygamy, divorce, and *al-hijab*—the veil. These injustices continued to be accepted by Muslims, he believed, because they failed to see that Islam, as revealed in the *Qur'an*, was not one message but two, that every verse has a dual meaning.[63] Because they continued to elaborate the first message while ignoring the second, he held that up to the present there had been no nation of true submitters (al-muslimin): Islam has not yet been achieved on earth.

The key to Ustadh Mahmoud Taha's argument in *The Second Message of Islam* is his claim that, as God's *dhat* [Self or Soul] the *Qur'an* descended, out of pure grace, to levels comprehensible by Muslims, and thereby became a written text at various levels of understanding.[64] Thus, Islam was offered first in Mecca where the Prophet preached tolerance, equality and individual responsibility between all men and women without distinction on grounds of race, sex, or social origin. But that message was rejected in practice and the Prophet and his followers were persecuted and forced to migrate to Medina. Historical Islamic *shari'a* was based on texts of the Medina period when God responded through the Prophet to the limits of human understanding and the exceptional needs of the *Umma* at that time of emergency. To that end, some aspects of the earlier level of revelation and *Sunna* were subjected to repeal or abrogation (*naskh*).[65]

Ustadh Mahmoud Taha and his followers believed that the shift in the content of the message is clearly shown on close comparison of the *Qur'anic* texts and *Sunna* dating from the Mecca stage with those following the migration to Medina. Many Muslim jurists also concede that parts of the earlier message were repealed, but they do not accept the claim that the repeals were not final but mere postponements because of the "inadequacy of the human capability to discharge properly the duty of freedom at that time."[66] Nor do they accept Ustadh Mahmoud Taha's additional claim that the texts of the *Qur'an* and *Sunna* that were the basis for *jihad* as war and for inequality, as well as for discrimination against women and non-Muslims, must now be set aside as having exceeded their temporary, transitional purposes.[67]

Despite meeting with hostility from traditional Muslims in their native Sudan, Ustadh Mahmoud Taha and his followers attempted to put their social beliefs into practice. Forming in 1951 his comprehensive vision of what he later termed the "Second Message of Islam," Ustadh Mahmoud Taha transformed a political party, the Republican Brotherhood, into an organization for the propagation of his vision. It was established also as a community to apply, as far as possible, the main tenets of this vision of Islam and it did succeed in implementing among its members the reform of marriage practices and equality between men and women. But by 1973 Ustadh Mahmoud Taha's public lectures were banned and the Sudanese government began to increase its harassment of the Brotherhood, including the occasional arrest and detainment of its founder and of members of the group. By 1983 Ustadh Mahmoud Taha had become an outspoken critic of the Islamization policy of President Numeiri, which imposed stringent *shari'a* in a manner detrimental to women and non-Muslims and which reinstituted a violent system of criminal justice based on *al-haq*, the principle of retribution. Also critical of the government's continued use of military force against rebels in the southern part of the country, Ustadh Mahmoud Taha was arrested again in 1985 and, following the most cursory of trials, executed 18 January 1985.

5. Conclusion

The fate of Ustadh Muhmoud Taha illustrates once again the terrible dangers to which pacifists become exposed when the demands of *de facto* power conflict with a course of action conscientiously chosen. But the philosophy of Ustadh Mahmoud Taha's Brotherhood, as well as the examples of Kamil Husain, and Muhaiyaddeen, (and to a more limited extent Mirza Ghulan Ahmad) demonstrate the possibilities for pacifism, not only in Islam but among devout practitioners. As these cases show, pacifism can exist in Islam when a wedge can be driven between the "totalism" of Islam and Muslims who seek an individualistic path toward moral righteousness.

The examples discussed represent different ways in which this critical gap of doubt and uncertainty may open up, and therefore, different ways in which individuals may accept greater personal responsibility for their actions. For Muhaiyaddeen this meant the rejection of the traditional and neofundamentalists' interpretation of *jihad* and the acceptance of a personal struggle for self-mastery. The faith-therapy of Kamil Husain meant not only this inner striving for purity and an "opening" to one's conscience, but also the pacifistic commitment not to commit deeds for a state or collectivity which one could recognize in one's private conscience as wrong. Thus Kamil Husain extends the Sufi emphasis on inwardness into genuine individuality, and thus, into direct conflict with *shari'a* and the fundamental ordering principles of traditional Muslim life. Ustadh Mahmoud Taha regards the objective of Islam itself as the perfection of our humanity, not in the collective *Umma*, but through our solitary individualities. Finally, Ustadh Mahmoud Taha took the ultimate and radical step of reinterpreting the sacred texts of Islam so that they would support, rather than hinder, the social reforms he considered required of Islam.

Although Ustadh Mahmoud Taha may seem to have been but a brief light in a gathering storm, his life and thoughts—like those of other Muslim pacifists—represent a hope for an Islamic future in which the militant interpretation of *jihad* falls into silence. These pacifists show that, whatever other contributions Islam makes to world civilization, it could also become a nurturer of pacifism and thus a true force for a world peace based on genuine respect for human dignity and human diversity.

NOTES

1. I have been influenced in developing this view by Peter Brock who claims that "the pacifist stands for freedom of conscience in matters of life and death" in *Twentieth-Century Pacifism* (New York: Van Nostrand Reinhold Co., 1970), 33. Brock adds that an essential part of pacifist "ideology" is formed by "conscientious objecting embodying [a] sense of personal responsibility...." See *Pacifism in Europe to 1914* (Princeton: Princeton University Press, 1972), 471.

2. Bernard Lewis, *The Political Language of Islam* (Chicago: University of Chicago Press, 1988), 78.

3. Asghar Ali Engineer, *Islam and Liberation Theology* (New Delhi: Sterling Publishers Private Ltd., 1990), 149.

4. Kenneth Cragg, *The Pen and the Faith* (London: George Allen & Unwin, 1985), 139.

5. *Qur'an*, Suras 8.28, 9.49, 64.16. Also, see commentary by Cragg, *The Pen and the Faith*, 139.

6. John Ferguson, *War and Peace in the World's Religions* (New York: Oxford University Press, 1978), 131.

7. Lewis, *Political Language of Islam*, 72.

8. Ibid., 73.

9. Ibid., 72.

10. (Ayatullah) Muhammad Hosayni Behishti and (Hujjatul-Islam) Javad Bahonar, *The Philosophy of Islam* (Salt Lake City: Islamic Publications, n.d.), 575.

11. The appropriateness of applying the term 'fundamentalism' to the Islamic context is defended by Henry Munson, Jr., *Islam and Revolution in the Middle East* (New Haven: Yale University Press, 1988), 4. Munson points out that, like 'puritanism' and 'zealotry', the term has transcended its origins. A fundamentalist in this context is one who believes that all aspects of life should conform to a set of sacred scriptures or to rules made by those identified as authoritative interpreters of those texts. I follow Alan R. Taylor in using 'neofundamentalist' to refer to those radicals who add to fundamentalism a strong anti-Western bias and the revival of the traditional conception of *jihad*. Thus, for example, the neofundamentalists of Iran are to be distinguished from the Wahhabi fundamentalists of Saudi Arabia. See Alan R. Taylor, *The Islamic Question in Middle East Politics* (Boulder, CO: Westview Press, 1988), viii. I use the term "modernists" in this paper to refer to Muslims who are opposed to the objectives of the neofundamentalists and who believe that the reform of Islamic societies need not be at odds with certain Western institutions.

12. Taylor, *The Islamic Question*, 11.

13. Ibid.

14. Sayyid Qutb, *Milestones* (Cedar Rapids, Iowa: Unity Publishing, 1981), 20, as quoted by Taylor, *The Islamic Question*, 58.

15. Taylor, *The Islamic Question*, 11.

16. Munson, *Islam and Revolution*, 15.

17. Taylor, *The Islamic Question*, 64.

18. Ibid., 67.

19. Munson, *Islam and Revolution,* 24.

20. Taylor, *The Islamic Question,* 177.

21. Munson, *Islam and Revolution,* 4.

22. Not surprisingly, pacifism appears to be quite rare and groups of professed pacifists, usually very small minorities, seem frequently to be persecuted as dissenting sects within the *Umma*—the "brotherhood," or community, of Muslim believers. The best known of these sects, the nineteenth century followers of Baha'u'llah (1817–1892), were severely persecuted and eventually broke away to form their own religion, the Baha'i faith.

23. Habib Boulares, *Islam: The Fear and the Hope* (London and New Jersey: Zod Books, 1990), 42.

24. Lewis, *The Political Language of Islam,* 5.

25. Hamid Enayat, *Modern Islamic Political Thought* (Austin: University of Texas Press, 1982), 112.

26. Lewis, *The Political Language of Islam,* 5.

27. Ibid., 3.

28. Shi'ite Muslims have never ceased exercising *ijtihad* and the law in Shi'ite communities has been considerably more flexible and adaptive than Sunni jurisprudence. But even among Sunnis, there is an increasing call from modernists for the reopening of the "gate" of *ijtihad* so that *shari'a* can be extended to meet the demands of the modern world. See Frederick M. Denny, *Islam and the Muslim Community* (New York: Harper & Row, 1987), 70. Some extreme modernists, such as Habib Boulares, argue that the individual Muslim must be allowed access to the *Qur'an* in the sense of assuming responsibility for his or her own interpretation of the text (131). This presages a cultural crisis in Islam, for even learning itself, beyond the practical needs of the faith, has very often been suspect among Muslims (Denny, 70).

29. Lewis, *The Political Language of Islam,* 29.

30. Ibid., 31.

31. Abdullahi Ahmed An-Na'im, "Introduction" to (Ustadh) Mahmoud Mohamed Taha, *The Second Message of Islam* (Syracuse, NY: Syracuse University Press, 1987), 27.

32. Lewis, *The Political Language of Islam,* 82.

33. Denny, *Islam and the Muslim Community,* 8.

34. Lewis, *The Political Language of Islam,* 63.

35. Denny, *Islam and the Muslim Community,* 47.

36. Ibid., 12.

37. Ibid., 67.

38. Ibid., 49.

39. For most Muslims, Muhammad is not the basic cause of Islam's coming into the world: "That fundamental cause is the conviction among his people that God was entering definitively into the Arabian scene and commanding their attention in novel ways" (Denny, *Islam and the Muslim Community,* 40).

40. Ibid., 88.

41. Ibid., 66.

42. Ibid., 67.

43. Boulares, *Islam: The Fear and the Hope*, 84.

44. Ibid., 60.

45. Ibid., 79.

46. This is a practice known as *dhikr*. See Denny, *Islam and the Muslim Community*, 72.

47. Ferguson, *War and Peace in the World's Religions*, 136.

48. M.R. Bawa Muhaiyaddeen, *Islam and World Peace: Explanations of a Sufi* (Philadelphia: The Fellowship Press, 1987).

49. Ibid., 60.

50. Ibid., 8 and 20–22.

51. Ibid., 40.

52. Ibid., 38.

53. Ibid., 92–93.

54. Hazrat Mirza Ghulam Ahmad, *The Philosophy of the Teachings of Islam* (Padstow, Cornwall, England: T. J. Press, 1979), 31.

55. Ferguson, *War and Peace in the World's Religions,* 136.

56. Muhammed Kamil Husain, "Muhammed Kamil Husain of Cairo," translated by Cragg in *The Pen and the Faith,* 135.

57. Husain, as quoted by Cragg, *The Pen and the Faith,* 134.

58. Muhammad Kamil Husayn [translation], *City of Wrong: A Friday in Jerusalem* (New York: Seabury Press, 1959).

59. Husain, as quoted by Cragg, *The Pen and the Faith,* 138.

60. Ustadh Mahmoud Taha, *The Second Message of Islam*, trans. and intro. by Abdullahi Ahmed An-Na' im (Syracuse, NY: Syracuse University Press, 1987), 64–65.

61. Ibid., 62.

62. Ibid., 167.

63. Ibid., 147.

64. Ibid., 149.

65. An-Na' im, "Introduction," *The Second Message of Islam*, 21.

66. Taha, *The Second Message of Islam*, 134.

67. An-Na' im, "Introduction," *The Second Message of Islam*, 23.

NONVIOLENCE AND THE *INTIFADA*

Robert L. Holmes

Speaking of Palestinian youths born under Israeli occupation, Israeli political analyst Meron Benvenisti said in June of 1987: "There is a change in attitude in this generation. There is a greater willingness to risk their lives in confrontations. They are ready to defy the authorities."[1]

His words were soon borne out. Six months later an Israeli semi-trailer crashed into two cars in the Gaza Strip, killing four Palestinians—three from the Jabalya refugee camp—and injuring ten others. Amid suspicions the killings were deliberate, 4,000 people from the camp attended that night's funeral.[2] As hundreds demonstrated the next day in the camp itself, Israeli soldiers shot and killed a Palestinian youth. Demonstrations then spread quickly throughout the occupied territories. The *Intifada* was born.

The *Intifada* began as a spontaneous, leaderless, popular uprising of men, women, and children. Only later did it acquire the properties of a movement. Even then its leadership evolved mainly from the people themselves. Israeli authorities would have preferred it to be otherwise. Had it been the work of a few radicals, or better yet, the PLO,[3] the *Intifada* could not so easily have symbolized the failure of Israeli occupation policy. The PLO would likewise have preferred the *Intifada* to be its own doing, since its claim to be sole representative of the Palestinian people carries with it a presumption of leadership. Thus the Israelis promptly rounded up and deported supposed *Intifada* leaders (to no effect in stemming the uprising), and the PLO began speaking as though it were in charge.[4] Both failed to perceive the conviction governing the *Intifada*. As that conviction was expressed by a Palestinian shortly before the uprising's outbreak: "If there is one thing 20 years of occupation has taught us, it is that we can only rely on ourselves." [5]

Although the 8 December 1987 accident unquestionably caused the following day's demonstrations, it did not cause the *Intifada*; it was no more than the precipitating incident. The causes of the *Intifada*, however, are perhaps too complex to identify other than in very general—and most likely nonneutral—terms (such as by reference to Israeli oppression). The *Intifada* itself, in fact, is difficult to characterize; partly owing to Israeli restrictions on press coverage, partly to difficulty in stating some basic facts of the Israeli-

Palestinian conflict in an unbiased way. Even neutral descriptive language is difficult come by. The occupied territories (itself a contested term) are part of Israel to some, part of Palestine to others. The Golan Heights are part of Syria to Druze and Syrians, part of Israel (by annexation) to Israelis. Until recently the West Bank (another contested term, known as Judea and Samaria to many Israelis) was to Jordanians part of Jordan, whereas it is part of Israel to its Jewish settlers and many within Israel. This makes it easy for both sides to cite as "causes" whatever features of the complex historical, political, religious, and ethical context best fit their evaluative predispositions. Be that as it may, our concern is with nonviolence and the *Intifada*, a topic that has received relatively little attention.

1. What Is Nonviolence?

Let us begin with some points of clarification. One problem in discussing nonviolence is what exactly to count as instances of it. How one resolves this problem bears upon how much evidence one believes there is for its use and effectiveness, historically and now.

If by nonviolence one means simply actions (whatever their motivation and objectives) that do not use violence, then evidence for the widespread use of nonviolence abounds. Those who believe in the use of violence rarely engage in it themselves; others, like the police or military, do that for them. And even these others typically use violence only a small percentage of the time. Modern armies, for example, train to kill on a massive scale, but for the most part they engage in such killing only infrequently (speaking now of wartime; many armies are used regularly to control their own citizenry), and when they do only a relatively few soldiers engage directly in combat. Even violent individuals like rapists and serial killers are actively engaged in violence only a fraction of the time. By this standard, practically everyone is nonviolent most of the time.

To equate nonviolence with nothing more than the absence of violence—a minimalist conception we may call formal nonviolence—makes it easy to cite extensive evidence for its practice, but does so at the cost of depriving that evidence of much relevance to the crucial questions about the effectiveness or moral desirability of nonviolence. People troubled about violence want to know whether it can or should be foregone even in those cases in which it is directly used and sanctioned, such as self-defense, police work, or war. And they want to know whether it is right to threaten its use, directly or indirectly, in ways that are formally nonviolent (as, for example, are most armed police patrols, much of international diplomacy, and all policies of conventional and nuclear deterrence). Yet to equate nonviolence exclusively with the deep spiritual commitment of a Mohandas Gandhi, a Martin Luther King, Jr., or a Mother Teresa, virtually guarantees that it will be found only rarely in human affairs. Few have, or are ever likely to have, that kind of commitment. To propose to ordinary people that they adopt a philosophy that presupposes that they make such a commitment is to consign that philosophy in advance to irrelevance.

Between these minimalist and maximalist conceptions lies considerable ground, however. Where within that ground to draw the distinction between nonviolence and its absence is a matter of judgment, reflecting a variety of ways of understanding the concept of nonviolence. For present purposes, I shall take nonviolence to be the deliberate disavowal of violence in the adopted means to social, political or moral objectives, whether on moral grounds, which I shall call principled nonviolence, or grounds of effectiveness, which I shall call pragmatic nonviolence. This gives a broad understanding of nonviolence without expanding it to the maximalist sense.

In this sense, nonviolence has characterized much of the *Intifada*, even though little of that nonviolence has been expressly advocated and defended as such.[6] But such express advocacy as there has been is of considerable significance, if only because the response it has elicited from Israeli authorities reveals the potential power nonviolence is perceived to have. The same occurs in some of the clear cases of nonviolent resistance. In the next section, I comment on two cases, one involving a prominent Palestinian advocate of nonviolence, the other involving a sustained and arguably successful use of nonviolent civil disobedience by an entire West Bank town.

2. Examples of Nonviolence

The first case is that of Mubarak Awad, founder of the Palestinian Center for the Study of Nonviolence in Jerusalem. Born in Palestine and educated in the United States, Awad is a follower of Gandhi and King. He established his center for the study of nonviolence in 1985. A Christian Arab, he and his Quaker wife, Nancy Nye, then principal of the Friends Girls' School in Ramallah, actively promoted nonviolence in the West Bank through education and direct action. He figured prominently in the documentary, "Courage Across the Divide," by Victor Schonfeld, on the Israeli occupation. At the onset of the *Intifada* he openly advocated civil disobedience against Israeli rule in the territories.[7] His following was small, but eventually the National Unified Leadership which emerged in the uprising came to recommend in its leaflets many of the tactics he advocated, including resistance to the Israeli administration through refusal to pay taxes. One Israeli official, sensing the pitfalls in the use of violence against civilian populations, remarked, "This nonviolence is a smart way to trigger Israeli violence and thus incite the uprising."[8]

Another advocate of nonviolence was Hanna Siniora, editor of the Palestinian newspaper *Al Fajr*, who along with others openly called for nonviolent civil disobedience early in the *Intifada* to protest deportation orders against nine Palestinians (five with alleged PLO connections, most of the remainder being Islamic fundamentalists).[9] His advocacy of nonviolence subsequently took the form of an article in which he cited the need to develop a strategy to keep the sacrifices of the uprising from having been in vain. He wrote, "Palestinians are now using some of the tools that have been neglected over the past twenty years. Here I am referring to the campaign that the Palestinian leadership in the occupied territories launched in early January [1988], calling for nonviolent resistance to the occupation, or civil disobedience."[10] He spoke specifically of two phases, one already underway, involving the boycotting of Israeli products like cigarettes and soft drinks, the other projecting the refusal of Palestinians to work in Israeli factories and other establishments. The second phase, he said, would require extensive financial support from the Arab world to offset the economic burden upon Palestinians. Precisely this sort of nonviolent strategy came eventually to be endorsed even by George Habash, leader of the hard-line PLO faction, The Popular Front for the Liberation of Palestine (PFLP).[11]

The possibility of widespread nonviolent action alarmed Israeli authorities even before the outbreak of the *Intifada*. The *Christian Science Monitor* reported on 24 November 1987 that "Many Israelis concede that a Gandhi-style campaign by Palestinians in the occupied territories would have a devastating effect on Israel's ability to control those areas." It quoted one Israeli as saying, "If the Palestinians all start doing what Awad proposes, the occupation will crumble in three days." American analyst of nonviolent techniques, Gene Sharp, describing a 1986 visit to the Middle East, reported that "When I asked various Israelis what would happen if the Palestinians shifted to nonviolent struggle, without exception people answered that this would make a much greater problem for the Israeli government than Palestinian violence." [12]

The authorities had initiated deportation proceedings against Awad even before the *Intifada*. Those efforts intensified once the *Intifada* got underway (his case differed from that of most other deportees in that he held an American passport, and the U.S. government openly opposed the Israeli action). The deportation order was signed by Yitzhak Shamir on 6 May 1988, and Awad was deported shortly thereafter. As an indication of the seriousness with which the Israeli government regarded the matter, its ambassador to the U.S., Moshe Arad, followed up the action with an op ed piece in *The New York Times* on 17 June justifying the deportation.

The second case is the example of the West Bank town of Beit Sahour, a small predominantly Christian town of about 12,000 near Bethlehem. Unlike many Palestinians (particularly from Gaza), who have little to lose in opposing Israeli rule, residents of Beit Sahour had a great deal to lose; theirs was a prosperous community that included many well-educated, middle class business and professional people. Radicalization of Beit Sahour began less than two months into the *Intifada* when Israeli soldiers searching for stone-throwers used rifle butts to break into the home of one of its leading families. Two of the sons were taken to a bus and beaten. According to *The New York Times* account of 7 February 1988, residents considered the house breaking "an alarming escalation of the confrontation."

By spring, Beit Sahour was becoming recognized as a symbol of a new phase of the *Intifada*—away from mass demonstrations and into community organizing. The idea, in keeping with the emphasis upon self-reliance, was to decrease dependence upon Israel. An agricultural committee was formed, and by May virtually every home in Beit Sahour had developed a vegetable garden—"*Intifada* gardens" as they came to be called—as a way of sustaining a boycott of Israeli produce. [13] On 7 July Jad Issac, a professor and former chairman of the biology department at Bethlehem University, was arrested and jailed for five months without charges for encouraging the planting of such gardens. By spring of the following year, Israeli soldiers regularly searched homes in the middle of the night. [14] Meanwhile, a nonviolent campaign of civil disobedience gained momentum, as increasing numbers of the town's residents refused to pay taxes to the Israeli authorities. They claimed the taxes violated international law and were used both to finance the occupation and to benefit Jewish settlers. As the town became a symbol of resistance, a five-day solidarity strike was called throughout the rest of the territories. On 21 September 1989, Israeli authorities laid siege to Beit Sahour, cutting phone lines to the town and declaring it a closed military area. Reporters and foreign diplomats were prohibited from entering. "If it takes a month, it will take a month," Defense Minister Yitzhak Rabin was quoted as saying, "but they will break."[15]

After the arrest of 40 residents for tax refusal failed to break the boycott, tax collectors backed by armed troops (as authorized by a 1988 military order), confiscated property to be auctioned off in Tel Aviv to compensate for lost tax revenues. They took everything from cars and machinery to sofas, tables, chairs, television sets, food and clothing. Still the residents refused to pay the taxes. Finally the Israelis lifted the six-week siege on 31 October 1989, possibly in anticipation of the arrival of a group of 120 Americans, The American Friends of Beit Sahour, who presented a statement of solidarity to the town's municipality and walked through the town on November 5, visiting four places of worship. They were joined by thousands of the town's citizens before they were dispersed by Israeli troops.[16] Though Israeli authorities claimed to have gotten value in kind through confiscated property, they did not collect the taxes, and the townspeople claimed victory. In May of 1990 Beit Sahour was awarded the annual Danish Peace Foundation prize for its commitment to nonviolence in opposing violent suppression.[17]

3. Alternative Institutional Leadership

To move beyond these express instances of nonviolence is to find less sure footing with regard to the facts. The very nature of some of other relevant developments is such that the details of how they have come about are not yet fully available. That makes it difficult to project precisely what they will lead to in the end. Yet they are of interest because they represent the kinds of efforts essential to any extensive campaign of nonviolent resistance against an occupying military power.

I refer here principally to the development of alternative institutions and the emergence of an indigenous, decentralized, democratic leadership in the territories, both of which have been essential to the continuation and vitality of the *Intifada*. The Israelis have proven superb over the years at prevailing in military confrontations. And they have proven effective at preventing the development of Palestinian political leaders within the territories. But during the *Intifada* they have been unable to prevent the development of alternative institutions and the emergence of underground leadership.

Grass roots organizations formed early in the *Intifada*, first in the refugee camps, later in the cities. They functioned initially to smuggle food to camps that were sealed off. "Smuggling food into the camps and the creation of popular committees are more important than the violence," one Palestinian said.[18] The Social Youth Movement, or Shabiba, formed in 1982 by Fatah, the largest of the PLO groups (led by Arafat), was the most important of these at the outset. It was outlawed in 1988. Such support committees became responsible for providing food, medical care, education, and other services where needed to counteract Israeli measures against the camps and other communities. According to one report from early in the *Intifada*:

> People have set up local committees to handle distribution of foodstuffs in curfew and siege conditions, to organize guard duty in villages, to promote local agricultural projects. Women working in one Ramallah neighborhood committee told us that one of their first steps was to conduct a house-to-house survey to learn special needs—elderly or infirm, number of school-age children, professional and manual skills that might be needed. One project was to compile people's blood types; this proved immensely useful as casualties mounted in the spring. They also collected donations to build up a fund for community needs.[19]

Women have become an important part of the movement. As one underground leader said:

> ...women are organizing Palestinian women who work in Israeli factories so that when we are ready to call a strike, it will be effective. Women are organized so that whenever a youth is grabbed by the soldiers, they will all start shrieking and try to get him away. They are very disciplined.[20]

From this process there eventually emerged the Unified National Leadership (UNL). As Michael Jubran reported:

> UNL cells, comprising 5 to 20 people and scattered throughout each town, village and camp, represented the four mainstream groups within the

PLO—Fateh, PFLP [Popular Front for the Liberation of Palestine], DFLP
[Democratic Front for the Liberation of Palestine] the Palestine Communist
Party and, in Gaza, the Islamic *Jihad*. Leadership of each UNL cell is
rotated, usually monthly, with a delegate from each of the four PLO groups
assuming a lead role in turn.[21]

Leaflets regularly appeared, which, combined with broadcasts
from Palestinian radio stations in Syria and Iraq, helped maintain a
communications system regarding events outside as well as inside
the territories. Graffiti and improvised Palestinian flags, moreover,
were virtually unstoppable symbols of defiance. Indeed, symbols
have become of importance throughout the uprising. The West Bank
village of Salfit has a highly developed system of popular committees handling everything from health, disputes, and problems with
the settlers down to the "*Intifada* gardens." Residents reportedly
regard army raids as symbolizing Israeli failure to control the town.[22]

While there may not be anything that could be called the
leadership of the *Intifada*, there is undoubtedly leadership at many
different levels and in different ways. Not all of it is under one
control—certainly not that of the PLO—and not all of it is of one
mind tactically, strategically, religiously or politically. On a small
scale, there are some groups like the Black Panthers in Nablus, a
violent youth group apparently uncontrolled by any other organization. On a larger scale, and of greater social and political significance, is the fundamentalist Moslem group, Hamas, which openly
opposes the PLO and has growing influence, particularly in Gaza.
Nor should it be overlooked that coercion and violence are
increasingly being directed by Palestinians against Palestinians as a
means of enforcing solidarity. In fact, for several months prior to the
8 October 1990 killing of at least 17 Palestinians in Jerusalem, more
Palestinians were killed by other Palestinians than by the Israeli
authorities. It was reported, however, that the leadership of the
Intifada has prohibited any further killing of suspects, warning that
violators will be punished.[23] The PLO has done the same.

4. New Developments

Several developments will have significant, though as yet
incalculable, effects on the *Intifada* and the likelihood of its
remaining largely nonviolent.

First is the influx of Jews as a result of relaxed emigration
policies in the former Soviet Union. This effect is twofold. On the

one hand, new immigrants are taking up many of the menial jobs previously held by Palestinians. This decreases Israeli dependence upon the Palestinian work force. At the same time it removes a source of potential economic power from Palestinians and increases their economic hardship. On the other hand, the new immigration is exacerbating problems in the occupied territories. After a storm of international protest at Shamir's statement that Soviet Jews were needed to populate the territories, the Israeli government backed off from that claim, and settled upon a less inflammatory but equally effective policy: rent subsidies to new immigrants has helped put rent prices out of the reach of many other Israelis, who are now forced to settle in the territories. Thus the settler population of the West Bank continues to rise. Combined with increased emigration of Palestinians to the United States since the beginning of the uprising, this makes all the more difficult any eventual resolution of the conflict that is likely to be acceptable to Palestinians.

Second is the aforementioned growth of the Islamic fundamentalist group, Hamas. Established at, or shortly after, the beginning of the *Intifada*,[24] Hamas refuses to recognize Israel, claims the whole of Palestine as an Islamic endowment, has issued virulently antisemitic leaflets, and has advocated violence against Israelis since the October 1990 killings at the Temple Mount. When Moshe Arens replaced Yitzhak Rabin as Defense Minister, he promptly issued orders for restraint in the use of force in the territories; Army patrols diminished in number, use of live ammunition was restricted, tax raids decreased, and some Palestinian prisoners were released in an apparent goodwill gesture.[25] As a result, prior to the Jerusalem shootings, the number of killings had dropped dramatically. Since those shootings, however, with subsequent increased violence against Israelis, the Israeli military seems once again to have toughened its policies, and by the beginning of the fourth year of the *Intifada*, Palestinian deaths at the hands of Israeli troops were again rising. While it would be unfair to attribute all the increased violence to Hamas, should the movement gain strength, it would likely transform the largely nonviolent character of the *Intifada*. It would in any event fragment Palestinian loyalties, as it presents a clear challenge to the PLO program.

Finally, the Persian Gulf War dealt a blow to the *Intifada* by alienating Palestinians from the Arab governments which had backed them financially and from supporters within the Israeli peace movement. This and a suddenly altered political picture for the entire

Gulf region will undoubtedly present new challenges for the *Intifada*.

5. Conclusions

What may we conclude about the significance of nonviolence for the *Intifada*?

It is probably true, as Norman Finklestein observes,[26] that few Palestinians adhere to nonviolence as a matter of principle. It has not been for them a moral or spiritual commitment of the sort it was for Gandhi and King and has come to be for Mubarak Awad. Their nonviolence has been pragmatic; directed at specific problems and adopted because of its effectiveness, practically or symbolically.[27] But that having been said, it should be added that the sense of empowerment that Palestinians have drawn from what are essentially nonviolent actions—particularly those involved in the institutionalization of the *Intifada*—cannot be overestimated. Whether or not the *Intifada* remains predominantly nonviolent, it has laid a foundation for effective nonviolent resistance; it has transformed Palestinian society in ways that bring into existence possibilities for creative actions that did not exist before.

There have, to be sure, been some notable failures of specific nonviolent actions. Plans to sail a ship containing Palestinian deportees to Israel from Athens was called off when the "ship of return," as it was called, was mined in its Cypress harbor. Although the Israeli government disclaimed responsibility, Shamir reportedly called the proposed sailing a declaration of war;Transport Minister Chaim Corfu warned that if the PLO chartered another ship it would meet the same fate.[28] And the civil disobedience of Gazans in resisting the order to apply for new identity cards—the order representing a deliberate attempt by the authorities to demonstrate control over Palestinians in the Gaza—eventually collapsed as the economic burden of foregoing their earnings from work within Israel became too acute.

But even failures had their positive sides. The proposed ship sailing was an idea hatched by the PLO; its initiative was from outside, not from Palestinians directly involved in the *Intifada*. As such it marked an attempt on the part of the PLO to use a largely symbolic nonviolent action to promote their cause. This departed dramatically from the violence and terrorism with which the PLO had long been associated. Although the action failed, that it was undertaken at all owed to the *Intifada*. By the same token, the issuance of new identity cards was part of a broad set of administrative measures adopted when Israelis became stymied in their efforts to quell the uprising by the use of force. In a sense, it represented a measure of success by the *Intifada*, in that the Israelis were forced to shift to a basically nonviolent tactic themselves to combat a form of resistance to which they were unaccustomed. Similarly, the cutting back of patrols, with the subsequent reduction in deaths, also represents a kind of nonviolent success for the *Intifada*, symbolizing the failure of military force to put an end to predominantly nonviolent resistance. As one Palestinian leader expressed it, "By our use of nonviolent resistance and the limits we have placed on violence, we have neutralized the Israeli atomic bomb, the air force, the tanks, and even machine guns. Now we should act so as to neutralize even the rifles."[29]

One should not minimize the extent to which there has been growing recognition within the PLO of the power of nonviolent resistance. I have already mentioned the endorsement by George Habash of the PFLP of many of the tactics advocated by Mubarak Awad and Hanna Siniora. Even more explicitly, the Voice of the PLO, a radio station broadcasting to the territories from Baghdad,[30] and representing what is now the moderate mainstream of the PLO under Yasser Arafat, has called upon Palestinians to reject the use of firearms, to practice passive resistance, and to follow the example of Beit Sahour. Arafat himself, in a broadcast commemorating the second anniversary of the *Intifada*, reportedly urged Palestinians to follow the example of the residents of Beit Sahour.[31] In this, the Voice of the PLO has come into open conflict with another Palestinian station, Al-Quds, broadcast from Syria, which advocates armed struggle and the liberation of all of Palestine.

But not only has the use of force failed to quell the *Intifada*, it has helped keep it going. In this sense the use of force has been counterproductive. At various stages when it appeared the *Intifada* was dying out, some new Israeli action would fuel it anew. The earliest of these occurred at the outset of the uprising, which seemed to be dying out after a few weeks but was revived by the killing of a Palestinian woman and the deportation order against nine Palestinians; the most notable later action occurred on 8 October 1990, with the killing of the seventeen Palestinians in Jerusalem, which thrust the Palestinian cause back into the world spotlight at a time when it had been off the front pages for months.

Thus, while the *Intifada* cannot be characterized as a fully nonviolent movement, it has nonetheless been predominantly nonviolent, and most of the power it has generated has been of an essentially nonviolent sort. Stone-throwing, as pathetically ineffectual as it is as a military tactic against heavily armed soldiers, is still a form of violence, as is the throwing of fire-bombs and the dropping of rocks from buildings. And, moral considerations aside, it would almost certainly serve the Palestinians better to renounce such acts. Stone-throwing has almost exclusively symbolic value. Other actions, like sit-ins in front of advancing Israeli patrols, could have that same value and would be less likely to foster bitterness in the Palestinian youths who engage in them, and less likely to contribute to the brutalization of young Israeli soldiers sent to contend with those youths with clubs and guns. And they would almost certainly help to minimize the damaging psychological effects that Palestinian psychologists document in Palestinian children.

The *Intifada* does, in any event, represent a milestone in the historical evolution of the idea of nonviolence. It will almost certainly provide a lasting example of the potential of nonviolent action, whether that potential is further realized in this context or not.[32]

NOTES

1. *The Christian Science Monitor* (8 June 1987).

2. The Palestinian newspaper, *Al Fajr*, published in Jerusalem, reported on 13 December 1987, that Gazans believed the killings were in revenge for the killing of an Israeli salesman in Gaza on 6 December. This claim has been neither confirmed nor disconfirmed. At his trial twenty-eight months later in an Israeli traffic court on charges of reckless driving, the driver, Herzl Bocavza, who fled the scene at the time of the accident, claimed he had lost control of his vehicle when turning into a gas station. See *Al Fajr* (26 March 1990).

3. Israeli intelligence officers reportedly concluded very soon that the uprising was indeed spontaneous and not directed from outside by the PLO. See Don Peretz, "Intifadeh: The Palestinian Uprising," *Foreign Affairs* 66:5, 973; and Ze'ev Schiff and Ehud Ya'ari, *Intifada: The Palestinian Uprising—Israel's Third Front* (New York: Simon and Schuster, 1990), 25.

4. Schiff and Ya'ari *(Intifada,* 123–124) dismiss a 17 October broadcast to the territories by Yasser Arafat, apparently calling for an uprising, as nothing more than routine. They contend that his subsequent appeal to the broadcast as evidence of his responsibility for the *Intifada* is a case of trying to rewrite history.

5. *The Christian Science Monitor* (8 June 1987).

6. The role of nonviolence is beginning to receive attention, however, in studies of the *Intifada*. See, for example, Deborah J. Gerner, *One Land, Two Peoples* (Boulder, CO: Westview Press, 1991), 96–97; Don Peretz, *Intifada: The Palestinian Uprising* (Boulder, CO: Westview Press, 1990), 52–58; and Schiff and Ya'ari, *Intifada*, 240–266.

7. The principal statement of his views may be found in Mubarak Awad, "Nonviolent Resistance: A Strategy for the Occupied Territories," *Journal of Palestine Studies* 13:4, 22–36, reprinted in *Nonviolence in Theory and Practice,* edited by Robert L. Holmes, (Belmont, CA: Wadsworth Publishing Company, 1990), 155–163.

8. *The New York Times* (7 May 1988).

9. *The New York Times* (6 January 1988).

10. Hanna Siniora, "An Analysis of the Current Revolt," *Journal of Palestine Studies* 13:3, 5f.

11. See the interview published in *The Christian Science Monitor,* 9 May 1990, in which he said: "We have to show [Israeli Prime Minister Yitzhak] Shamir and [former Defense Minister Ariel] Sharon that Israel is losing, not gaining from the occupation—by boycotting Israeli goods, stopping tourism, keeping Palestinian workers from jobs in Israel."

12. From an interview by Afif Safieh, a Palestinian Visiting Scholar at Harvard University's Center for International Affairs, published as "Gene Sharp: Nonviolent Struggle," in *Journal of Palestine Studies* 17 (1): 37–55. For a more detailed statement of Sharp's views, see his "The *Intifada*h and Nonviolent Struggle," *Journal of Palestine Studies* 19:1, 3–13.

13. Schiff and Ya'ari report that the committee's members "...taught the townsfolk how to raise vegetables in their yards and other available plots. At one stage they introduced the fad of raising rabbits and organized metal workers to turn out cheap iron cages that were snapped up in quantities, particularly by the classes that had always considered agriculture beneath their station. They also taught people how to turn old, unused refrigerators into incubators for chicks, and for a time makeshift chicken coops set up on roofs were a status symbol even in neighborhoods known for their posh villas." *Intifada*, 247.

14. *The New York Times* (15 March 1989).

15. *The New York Times* (11 October 1989).

16. A group of Israeli peace activists who had hoped to join the demonstration were reportedly prevented from entering the town, though *Al Fajr* (13 November 1989) reported that ten Israeli Jews who had spent the previous night in the town participated. According to political scientist Deborah Gerner, eyewitness and participant in the demonstration, and to whom I am indebted for this account of events in Beit Sahour, a nonviolent sit-down by a group of Americans in protest against the military break-up of the demonstration was eventually forcibly ended by the troops.

17. *Al Fajr* (4 June 1990).

18. *The New York Times* (6 February 1988).

19. Joe Stork, "The Significance of Stones: Notes from the Seventh Month," in *Intifada: The Palestinian Uprising Against Israeli Occupation*, edited by Zachary Lockman and Joel Beinin (Boston: South End Press, 1989), 71.

20. *The New York Times* (6 February 1988). On the factors drawing Palestinian women into the *Intifada*, see Jim Lederman, "Dateline West Bank: Interpreting The *Intifada*," *Foreign Policy* 72, 230–246.

21. Michael Jubran, "'Not Planned But Not Spontaneous': The *Intifada*, Its Leadership and the PLO," *The Washington Report on Middle East Affairs* 8:8, 10.

22. *The Washington Post Weekly* (16–25 June 1989).

23. *The New York Times* (1 January 1991).

24. Schiff and Ya'ari report it as being founded by Sheikh Ahmed Yassin in February of 1988 (*Intifada*, 222), but another Hamas leader, Abdel Aziz Rantisi contends it was established on 9 December 1987, implying that it was done so to ignite the *Intifada*. See *Al Fajr* (24 September 1990).

25. *The Christian Science Monitor* (26 July 1990).

26. Norman Finklestein, "Bayt Sahur in Year II of the *Intifada*: A Personal Account," *Journal of Palestine Studies* 19:2, 66.

27. This is not to say that there are not elements of nonviolence to be found in Islamic theory and practice. See Ralph E. Crow, Philip Grant, and Saad E. Ibrahim, eds., *Arab Nonviolent Political Struggle in the Middle East* (Boulder, CO: Lynne Rienner, 1990).

28. *The New York Times* (18 February 1988).

29. Cited by Gene Sharp, "The *Intifadah* and Nonviolent Struggle," *Journal of Palestine Studies* 19:1, 11. Reflecting much the same perception, Roli Rozen, writing in the Israeli newspaper, *Haaretz*, in May 1989, quotes military historian Marin Van Kerfeld as saying: "The era of conventional war is over; the battlefield of the future is the Intifada" (from *Israel Press Briefs*, No. 66, July 1989, 2, published by The International Center for Peace in the Middle East, Tel Aviv).

30. Whether these broadcasts have continued following the Gulf War I do not know.

31. As reported by Kirsten Nakjavani Bookmiller and Robert J. Bookmiller, in "Palestinian Radio and the Intifada," *Journal of Palestine Studies* 19:4, 104, n. 37.

32. An earlier version of this chapter was presented at a conference, "The Ethical Dimensions of the 'Changing Use of Force' in International Affairs: Tensions Among Politics, Military Operations and Ethics," at the University of Notre Dame, sponsored by the Institute for International Peace Studies of the University of Notre Dame and the Midwest Consortium for International Security Studies, 24–26 October 1990.

SELF-DETERMINATION AND THE ISRAELI-PALESTINIAN CONFLICT

Tomis Kapitan

In the adjustment of Jews and Arabs, one-sided bargains are to be dreaded. They spell disaster for the future.

—Alfred North Whitehead, 1937

Much of the current political instability in the Middle East stems from the conflict between Israeli Jews and Palestinian Arabs. At issue is a struggle over territory, each group claiming possession of the region traditionally known as Palestine. The West is familiar with the vision of Palestine as a "promised" land with which Jews have maintained an association for over 3,000 years, though Jews governed no portion of it from the time of the Roman conquest in 65 B.C. until 1948 when, through the success of the Zionist movement, the state of Israel was established. Yet the historical association of Palestinian Christians and Muslims to Palestine is equally deep, whether as the descendants of ancient Canaanites, Phoenicians, Jews, Philistines, or Arabs. Since the rise of Islam in the seventh century A.D., Palestine had been part of the larger Islamic world under the rule of various Islamic governments, even though no independent sovereign Arab or Muslim state was ever established there. Moreover, the strategic location of Palestine makes it a vital land bridge linking the Asian and African portions of the Arab and Islamic worlds, favoring its political linkage to larger units.

Matters are complicated by the religious significance of Palestine to three major religious traditions, Jewish, Christian, and Islamic, each claiming descent from the monotheistic faith of Abraham. Religious sentiment generates a connection to territory that transcends purely legal and political concerns and the intense emotional attachments to Palestine and Jerusalem have given the conflict between Israelis and Palestinians a significance far beyond that of usual regional disputes. As W. T. Stace wrote in "The Zionist Illusion" (*The Atlantic Monthly*, February 1947), the question of Palestine "is not an isolated issue. It touches the future of the whole world."

The notion of *self-determination* has been invoked to shed light on the struggle. Some view it in terms of rival claims by distinct peoples, each wishing to determine its destiny in Palestine, thus, as a tragic clash between competing *rights*.[1] But not all find this image appealing. Apart from the members of each group who deny that the other has any rights of self-determination in Palestine at all, a construal of the conflict as a clash of competing rights of self-determination obscures its evolution while blocking proposals for its just solution. At best, it merely dramatizes the difficulty without resolving it. Still, the concept of self-determination remains relevant in understanding the critical historical and normative dimensions, for it is employed in justifying present hostilities, explaining present obligations, and proposing viable solutions. The following is an examination of its application to this very troublesome conflict.

1. Self-Determination in International Law and Morality

There is a considerable debate about the status of self-determination in international law, a debate made even more timely by recent events in the post Cold War era, as various groups, peoples, and nationalities renew calls for self-determination within given territories. The unresolved questions are several,[2] including the following: What is self-determination? What is called for by a principle or right of self-determination? Is self-determination a right, a formative or directive principle to be used as a basis for establishing statutes, or a moral or political principle to be used in guiding debates over sovereignty in disputed territory? When, and to whom, does self-determination apply, that is, what are the proper units or beneficiaries of self-determination? What are the mechanisms for implementing self-determination?

The mere existence of a debate over self-determination does not diminish its normative or legal relevance; the concept has been prominent in efforts to secure lasting peace in the aftermaths of each of the world wars and in the subsequent breakup of European colonial empires. It is present in agreements having significance for international law, for example in Article 1 of the United Nations Charter, which calls upon member nations "to develop friendly relations among nations based on respect for the principle of equal rights and self-determination of peoples, and to take other appropriate measures to strengthen universal peace." However, the exact status accorded self-determination by this terminology remains a matter of debate. That a right is recognized is indicated in the French version "du principe de l'égalité de droits des peuples et de leur droit à disposer d'eux-mêmes," which explicitly refers to a right (*droit*). Again, the language of "right" occurs in a number of General Assembly Resolutions, for example, in GA Res. 1514 of 14 December 1960, and GA Res. 2625 of 24 October 1970, and, again, in Article 1 of the International Covenant on Civil and Political Rights passed by the General Assembly on 16 December 1966:

> All peoples have the right of self-determination. By virtue of that right they freely determine their political status and freely pursue their economic, social, and cultural development.

While not all legal scholars take these provisions to settle the issue, it remains that post World War II diplomacy has repeatedly invoked the concept of self-determination to justify independence movements in regions which had previously been under foreign domination.[3] This is enough to establish its normative importance for international relations, if not its status as a *jus cogens* principle of international law.[4]

It is at the level of *moral* foundations for international law and diplomacy that our present discussion of self-determination is anchored.[5] The concern is not whether self-determination is enshrined in international law and, if so, how, nor whether a principle of self-determination has any effect on the actual policies and practices of nations. The issue is whether there is justification for taking some such principle as a normative basis for settling questions of international law and international relations.

Some preliminary problems must be taken up. Most directly, if self-determination is to involve a people's entitlement to political autonomy or popular sovereignty within a given territory, then at least three elements stand to be clarified: (1) the group of people in question, (2) the territory at issue, and (3) the connection that makes that group entitled to self-determination there. There is considerable vagueness on each account. For example, while some might think it easiest to first delineate the group in question, there is little agreement about the identifying criteria for the appropriate collectives, for example, on what a "people" is. If not defined in regional terms, then some sort of national, cultural, or linguistic similarities might seem relevant, but these are as vague as they are controversial, as discussed below. Perhaps all that is necessary is that members of the group share enough moral ideals that would sustain their adherence to the same

political and legal institutions, thus, minimally, that the group possesses the potential for constituting a "politically coherent" community. [6]
Even if this could be determined, there remains the problem of fixing
the region in which a community is entitled to be self-determining. No
precise individuating conditions for "territories" or "regions" have
been agreed upon. Historical boundaries are no doubt important, as are
geographic-economic considerations, but so are the historic and
emotional attachments peoples have to given regions, including the
aspirations of both the minorities which dominate sub-regions of
historically recognized territories and the majorities which dominate
larger regions within which these territories fall. Could these matters
be settled, there is still the difficulty of determining the appropriate
link of community to territory; it is fair enough to demand that the
collective consist of established inhabitants or legitimate residents of
the territory in question, but deciding who is a "legitimate resident" is
a delicate matter, particularly concerning immigrants and those whose
refugee status is not voluntary. Plainly, we do not yet have a precise
formula for deciding when a given region or people is entitled to self-
determination.

Illuminating algorithms are hard to come by, but some advance
can be made by describing distinct, though overlapping, concepts of
self-determination, each emphasizing different elements in the
overall call for political autonomy or popular sovereignty. At least
three different notions and correlated principles can be identified:

1. Regional Self-Determination. A demand that inhabitants of
well-established regions, territories, or states be allowed to settle for
themselves all questions of sovereignty over that territory, even if
they should choose to be politically autonomous. Typically, regional
self-determination is demanded when a territory is under foreign
domination or, for one reason or another, unsettled or disputed, but it
is also conceived as a continuing right of peoples within established
state boundaries.

2. Democratic Self-Determination. The idea of self-government by popular consent, requiring that the inhabitants of a territory
ought to be democratically self-governing or that the social and
political institutions which regulate public life be established through
broadly "democratic" procedures. Minimally, this requires that the
institutions be both founded and sustained by democratic means,
hence, by majority preference, though it is a further step to insist that
these institutions themselves operate on democratic principles, that a
self-determining unit be a "democracy." Taking it would mandate a

democratic form of government in order for self-determination to be realized.

3. National Self-Determination. The conception that a nation or people has a right to constitute itself as an independent sovereign state, a view popularized under the nineteenth-century German socialists' call for the *Selbstbestimmungsrecht* (sovereign right) of peoples.[7] At its crux is the concept of a "nation" or a "people," namely, a group whose members self-consciously share a cultural identity that is vital in determining the self-identity of each.[8] Historically, this view has been used not only to justify the right of existing nation-states to determine their own form of government and destiny, but also to pave the way for subordinate national groups to claim rights of secession from larger political unities. It also strengthened the call for cultural, ethnic, religious, and racial homogeneity within a state as such, providing an atmosphere in which twentieth century nationalist movements could flourish.

Various combinations of these three conceptions yield still richer notions of self-determination and there are elements in each in the relevant modern discussions. But it is important not to conflate them; none requires any one of the others. Arguably, democratic self-determination must be either regional or national, though the converse is not true. Nor is national self-determination necessarily regional; a call for self-determination of a certain national group in a territory might be quite oblivious to the interests of the established inhabitants of that territory.

A combination of regional and democratic self-determination—self-government by the inhabitants of a territory through popular consent—emerged as the important principle after World War I. Embedded within his vision of enduring world peace, President Woodrow Wilson felt its observance was a natural extension of democratic theory essential for both preventing future wars and "making the world safe for democracy" :

> ...no peace can last, or ought to last, which does not recognize and accept the principle that governments derive all their just powers from the consent of the governed, and that no right anywhere exists to hand peoples about from sovereignty to sovereignty as if they were property."[9]

He first employed the term "self-determination" on 11 February 1918: "Peoples may now be dominated and governed only by their own consent. Self-determination is not a mere phrase. It is an imperative principle of action, which statesmen will henceforth

ignore at their peril."[10] A more complete statement of the relevant
principle came on 4 July 1918:

> The settlement of every question, whether of territory, of sovereignty, of
> economic arrangement, or of political relationship upon the basis of the free
> acceptance of that settlement by the people immediately concerned and not
> upon the basis of the material interest or advantage of any other nation or
> people which may desire a different settlement for the sake of its own
> exterior influence or mastery.[11]

It was in this form that Wilson's vision emerged as a "basic
principle" for negotiations in the Paris Peace Conference of 1919,[12]
despite the fact that neither the principle nor the term 'self-
determination' made its way into the Covenant of the League of
Nations.[13]

Three aspects of Wilson's principle stand to be clarified before
considering it as a possible cornerstone of international justice. First,
while it does not obviously assert a universal *right* of self-
determination, Wilson's normative language indicates that he
conceived of the principle as a moral precept rooted in the long-
standing ideal that political institutions gain legitimacy only from the
consent of the governed. Here, the principle mirrors a good deal of
Western political philosophy and indicates, at minimum, that
Wilson's concept was one of *democratic* self-determination. Second,
the wording in the last sentence of the second quote from Wilson
suggests that the principle was also offered as a maxim of political
prudence, one which should guide those "statesmen" entrusted with
making decisions about the future status of given territories.
Combining the moral and prudential in this way, the principle
imposes an obligation upon any agent, whether a state, an institution,
or an individual, which, by virtue of historic circumstance, has a
voice in resolving an issue of sovereignty.[14]

Third, the Wilsonian principle was primarily intended for use in
settling questions concerning the status of territories *unsettled* by
conflict or which are (or previously had been) under foreign
domination. It was as such that the principle was used in the Paris
Peace Conference of 1919, though its application was contested
precisely in certain "unsettled" regions, for example Alsace-
Lorraine, Upper Silesia, and, as we shall see, Palestine. After World
War II, it was in circumstances occasioned by international conflict
and colonial breakup that the paradigmatic applications of the
principle of self-determination occurred.[15] Thus, the Wilsonian

concept is also one of *regional* self-determination. Indeed, there is reason to think that the regional, not the national, concept prevails in international law and that its most obvious relevance is to decisions about the political status of unsettled regions which are not yet self-governing or are in dispute, for example, regions established under mandates and trusts. [16]

So understood, the principle of self-determination is to be invoked whenever there is a question about what political, economic, social, and cultural institutions are to prevail in a territory. Such a question is genuine when there is a potentially politically coherent community whose members are legitimate residents of a territory which either (1) is under the domination of a foreign community in a way that threatens the well-being and human rights of its members, (2) was formerly dominated by another community but is currently free from that domination and not yet self-governing, or (3) is currently under some form of internationally sanctioned trusteeship. The community of legitimate residents would then be the beneficiary of the principle's application. What the principle requires is that the said institutions be decided by the community in question, not by external communities, agencies, or nations. The preferred mechanisms for resolution are referenda, especially plebiscites, viz., community-wide votes on political proposals whose outcomes are determined by majority preference. [17]

An argument for ranking the principle of regional-democratic self-determination as a norm of international justice is available from prevailing philosophies of political legitimacy. It has become an increasingly dominant view that social, political, economic, and cultural institutions should be created and sustained through the preferences of the people whose lives they most immediately affect and, therefore, that the people be allowed to participate in the relevant decision-making processes that determine these institutions. By voluntarily binding themselves to a social-political arrangement, a people's commitment grounds a moral obligation to abide by its terms and, in this way, preferred institutions and their constitutive rules gain legitimacy. Settling a territorial dispute through self-determination increases chances that the arrangement will conform to what people perceive as just, if not to what is just, and thereby, enhance prospects for future stability, peace, and orderly development. By contrast, imposing an arrangement upon a people against their will creates resentment that is likely to nourish future instability. It is, thus, that observing self-determination—whether as a political principle for solving conflicts over sovereignty, a legal right of peoples, or a human right of individuals[18]—has become the crucial mechanism for securing a people's recognition of a state apparatus established in a region within which they are entitled to self-determination.

Two final observations. While the principle of regional-democratic self-determination imposes an obligation upon decision-makers, it also taken as conferring entitlement to self-determination upon deserving collectives. Such a "right," if this language is appropriate, should not be considered absolute.[19] There are independent considerations limiting how a people can exercise self-determination and checks upon the types of institutions they are entitled to establish. Certainly, the human rights of every inhabitant of the territory must be respected and legitimate minority interests taken into account, in which case, self-determination cannot be construed as a *carte blanche* for majorities to establish objectional forms of discrimination. Consequently, it does not provide the sole normative principle relevant to decisions concerning the political status of disputed territories.[20]

Finally, it is obvious that nations and diplomats do not always abide by recognized principles of international justice, no matter how entrenched they may be. But even if adherents of *Realpolitik* are correct in holding that nations act only in regards to promoting their self-interest, unmoved by moral considerations, it remains that some standards of international behavior are universally welcomed as means for fostering cooperation and assuring a stable predictable international order and, thus, an orderly pursuit of self-interest. More impressively, international law itself is largely the creation of powerful nations seeking a viable framework for international stability within which justification for actions and policies can be sought. Recognized norms constitute a fabric of constraints regulating a wide variety of international transactions and conditioning the sorts of responses a country makes to perceived opportunities and provocations.[21] There have been widespread violations, to be sure, and perhaps there are intrinsic limits to the effectiveness of the prevailing norms, but as long as there is a need for any countries to achieve a *modus vivendi* with each other, normative proposals for achieving international order, for example, that of self-determination, will retain their practical relevance.[22]

2. National Self-Determination: A Brief Discussion

Understood as calling for regional-democratic self-determination, the Wilsonian principle is restricted in its application to specific sorts of territories and communities; neither does it apply to all peoples or national groups, nor does it require recourse to plebiscite for all outstanding disputes about prevailing institutions in every territory.[23] It does not confer a right to national sovereignty upon all peoples, and even for those who satisfy the conditions of beneficiaries, there is no implication that an application of the principle is of overriding importance.

It may be asked, of course, whether there are also grounds for inclusion of a principle of *national* self-determination within a framework of international justice and moral decision-making. Margalit and Raz argue the affirmative, though they make no claims about recognition in international law. Briefly, their argument is that since there is value to membership in a "self-encompassing" (national) group, including participation in the political activities of that group, then there is an inherent value in that group's being self-governing.[24] A right to self-determination derives from this value and is possessed when the self-encompassing group (1) "forms a substantial majority in a territory," (2) "the new state is likely to respect the fundamental interests of its inhabitants," and (3) "that measures are adopted to prevent its creation from gravely damaging the just interests of other countries," in which case the right to self-determination is not unconditional.

That there is an inherent value in self-government cannot be disputed, but the restrictions on when this right is possessed, if ever, are perhaps more severe than Margalit and Raz recognize. Few regions of the world are culturally homogenous, and "unsettled" regions typically are not. Conscious national self-determination is likely to entail emergence of characteristic cultural values within political and legal institutions. This poses a threat to the interests and rights of minorities outside the predominant national majority within a territory—it always has and it continues to do so as ongoing disturbances in Africa, Eastern Europe, and the former Soviet Union testify. Minorities resent not only the imposition of cultural values of majorities but the threat of such, for the establishment of political institutions to reflect the preferences of national groups poses a danger to their rights and interests. Even if assurances are given to protect the human rights of these minorities, international law has not evolved to the point where there are reliable mechanisms to ensure such protection. Finally, the threat of national determination to world peace must also be considered, not only because a proliferation of claims for self-determination threatens world order,[25] but also because the call for national self-determination has often been coupled with nationalistic chauvinism, persecution of minorities, and interstate belligerency, for example, in Nazi Germany and recently in the Balkans.[26] In today's world, there is an increasing need for individuals to identify themselves as members of the global community, to work for the common interest, and to recognize that the world and its resources belong to peoples of diverse cultural backgrounds. Too frequently, the demand for national allegiance is exclusivist, pointing an individual in an opposite direction.

A right to national self-determination might seem appropriate in certain limited circumstances, such as when the "nation" in question is an overwhelming majority and there are constitutional and international safeguards for protection of minority rights. But then the principle of regional-democratic self-determination, as delineated above, is itself sufficient to secure the same ends of self-government. Additional justification in terms of national self-determination is not only of dubious worth but, quite frankly, unnecessary.

3. Self-Determination in Palestine: 1918–1948

The tragedy of the people of Palestine is that their country was 'given' by a foreign power to another people for the creation of a new state.

—Bertrand Russell, 1970

In 1917–1918, combined British and Arab forces ended over 400 years of Turkish administration in various parts of the Arab world, including Palestine. The nationalities in these territories, stated Wilson in his "Fourteen Points" speech of January 1917, "should be assured an undoubted security of life and an absolutely unmolested opportunity of autonomous development." Yet nothing of the sort took place immediately; in the aftermath of World War I, the newly formed League of Nations placed much of the region under British and French mandatory rule, Palestine going to the British.[27]

At that point, there was uncertainty in Western capitols about the precise borders of historic Palestine. It was generally agreed that the region extended at least to the Mediterranean on the west, the Jordan River on the east, the southern Golan Heights in the northeast, and the Negev and Sinai deserts in the south (there was dispute concerning the northern and eastern borders, fueled partly by Zionist aspirations).[28] This area, including the Negev, was classified as 'Palestine' by the League of Nations Mandate for Palestine granted to the British in 1922. Of the some 800,000 inhabitants in that region by 1918, Arabs outnumbered Jews ten to one. Approximately half the land was privately owned by Arabs, 2.6 percent privately owned by Jews; the remainder was State property under Ottoman law, though much of it had been farmed for generations by Arab villagers.

Given the general acceptance of Wilson's principle, it would seem that Palestine, either in itself or as part of a larger geographical unit, was a region to which regional-democratic self-determination should have been applied. Despite Arab expectations, this never occurred. Two political decisions intervened, one by the British in 1917 and another by the Americans in 1946, both eventuating in actions taken by international bodies which entailed a denial of self-determination in Palestine. Following are highlights of this well-argued assessment.[29]

During World War I, Britain promised its Arab allies independence throughout the territory liberated from the Turks,[30] but also signed two other agreements embodying contrary policies. In 1916, Great Britain and France concluded the Sykes-Picot agreement by which the Arab Middle East would be divided up into regions of British and French influence under the sovereignty of those powers, with Palestine placed under some form of international administration. This was soon superseded by a more momentous decision; in 1917, the wartime British government under David Lloyd-George issued the *Balfour Declaration* declaring British policy to establish a "national home" for the Jewish people in Palestine. The Declaration was the first significant victory for the Zionist movement initiated in the late nineteenth century. Under the persuasive and careful diplomacy of the movement's chief spokesman, Chaim Weizmann, the British Foreign Secretary, Arthur Balfour, issued the declaration in a letter of 2 November 1917, to Lord Rothschild:

> His Majesty's Government view with favour the establishment in Palestine of a national home for the Jewish people, and will use the best endeavours to facilitate the achievement of this object, it being clearly understood that nothing shall be done which may prejudice the civil and religious rights of the existing non-Jewish communities in Palestine, or the rights and political status enjoyed by Jews in any other country. [31]

In one stroke, Palestine, a land which had been peopled by an Arab majority for centuries, was now promised by a European power to the Jewish people; not to the established Jewish minority in Palestine, but to the Jewish people *per se*. Although the crucial phrases 'civil and religious rights' and 'political status' were left undefined by the Declaration, the document contrasted civil rights with political status while avoiding reference to the political status of Palestinian Arabs; the "non-Jewish communities," which comprised the substantial majority of inhabitants.[32]

The principle of self-determination was ignored here; the largest segment of Palestine's inhabitants did not participate in the making of a decision which was to have a monumental impact upon their future. They were not consulted; no referendum or plebiscite was ever held, no approval from Palestinian representatives ever secured. To the contrary, they adamantly opposed it and repeatedly voiced their opposition, as early as 1919.[33] In 1925, shortly after the Balfour Declaration had been incorporated into the terms of the 1922 Mandate for Palestine, international lawyer Quincey Wright reported that Palestinian Arabs viewed the Declaration as a political decision constituting "a gross violation of the principle of self-determination proclaimed by the Allies."[34] The United States and Great Britain were apprised of the situation in Palestine and were fully informed of Arab opposition to the Declaration. In 1919, Wilson dispatched the King-Crane Commission to report on the political situation. In their 28 August 1919, report to the Paris Peace Conference, the commissioners expressed concern about the future of Palestine, claiming that if the principle of self-determination is to rule,

> then it is to be remembered that the non-Jewish population of Palestine —nearly 9/10 of the whole—are emphatically against the entire Zionist programme. The tables show that there was no one thing upon which the population of Palestine were more agreed than upon this. To subject a people so minded to unlimited Jewish immigration, and to steady financial and social pressure to surrender the land, would be a gross violation of the principle just quoted, and of the people's rights, though it kept within the forms of law.[35]

The commissioners also noted that none of the British officers consulted felt that a Jewish National Home could be established except by force of arms. Citing Article 22 of the League of Nations Covenant, their report indicated that the inhabitants preferred that the mandate for all Syria (including Palestine) go to the United States.

But the recommendations of the King-Crane Commission fell on deaf ears. They became no part of the policy of either the U.S. or Great Britain and were ignored by the League of Nations committees which drew up the terms of the mandates. In March and again in April 1919, Wilson reiterated his October 1917, approval of the Balfour Declaration and in 1922 the U.S. Congress concurred.[36]

Wilson was apparently not pressed upon the apparent conflict of this vision with his principle of self-determination and the British took the view that he fully supported Zionism.[37] The British Government had already ruled out settlement of the Palestine question by appeal to the principle of self-determination. Lord Balfour was particularly blunt:

> ...in Palestine we do not propose even to go through the form of consulting the wishes of the present inhabitants of the country....The Four Great Powers are committed to Zionism. And Zionism, be it right or wrong, good or bad, is rooted in agelong traditions, in present needs, in future hopes, of far profounder import than the desires and prejudices of the 700,000 Arabs who now inhabit that ancient land.[38]

An official memorandum of the British Foreign Office Department to the British Cabinet contained an equally explicit suspension of the principle:

> The problem of Palestine cannot be exclusively solved on the principle of self-determination, because there is one element in the population—the Jews—which, for historical and religious reasons, is entitled to a greater influence than would be given to it if numbers were the sole test.[39]

These statements foreshadowed subsequent British policy. No mention of self-determination was made in the terms of the Mandate for Palestine and, against the wishes of the Arab majority, the gates of Palestine were opened to Jewish immigration so that by 1931 the Jews constituted 16 percent of the total population, and by 1936, 28 percent. Even at the height of World War II in 1942, Winston Churchill, echoing the sentiments of Balfour and Lloyd-George, expressed concern about the self-determination clause of the Atlantic Charter since it might obstruct Zionist settlement in Palestine.[40] By 1947, Jews constituted roughly one-third of Palestine's approximately 1.9 million people, "by the might of England, against the will of the people."[41] Despite explicit assurances from Zionist leaders like Weizmann that Jews had no intention of turning the Arabs out of their homes, Zionist political rhetoric in the streets and exclusivist policies on Jewish-owned land revealed other intentions. Only when Arabs resorted to armed insurrection against the British in 1936–1938 did policy change. In the 1939 MacDonald White Paper, Britain renounced the Balfour Declaration and declared a new policy of advocating a singular secular state throughout Palestine.[42] This met with approval among many Arabs (though not all), but was angrily rejected by the Zionist movement.[43] With the onset of World War II, the latter began to concentrate its diplomatic efforts on the United States.

In the aftermath of World War II, a weakened Great Britain thrust the issue of Palestine onto the lap of the newly formed United Nations. Western opinion was now more favorably disposed towards Zionist aspirations as the facts of Nazi persecution and genocide of European Jews became clear. In the most significant political victory for Zionism since the Balfour Declaration, President Truman endorsed Zionist proposals in August 1946, setting in motion American diplomatic efforts to secure a partition of Palestine into a Jewish and an Arab state. In September 1947, the U.N. Special Committee on Palestine (UNSCOP) acknowledged that the League of Nations Mandate had violated the Palestinian Arabs right of self-determination and that the creation of a Jewish National Home in Palestine "ran counter" to the principle of self-determination.[44] But prevailing political opinion, particularly in the U.S. and U.S.S.R., pushed the General Assembly to recommend partition of Palestine into Jewish and Arab states with Jerusalem placed under an international trusteeship (Resolution 181 of 29 November 1947). While Great Britain abstained in the voting, the United States led the fight for approval, resorting to pressure diplomacy to secure the necessary votes.[45] Officially, the Jewish Agency (the political arm of the Zionist movement in Palestine) accepted the recommendations of the partition plan; Arabs overwhelmingly rejected its provisions as constituting a gross violation of the rights of the Arab majority in Palestine. It is, as some describe it, the "original sin" which "underlies the entire Palestine conflict."[46]

In the subsequent violence of 1948–1949, Jewish military organizations outnumbered and outgunned the disorganized Palestinians and their Arab allies.[47] Massacres, like those that took place at the Arab village of Deir Yassin in early April 1948, caused thousands of Arabs to flee their homes in fear of a similar fate.[48] Outright expulsion was employed by the Israeli forces in other cases, for example in Lydda, Ramleh, Haifa, and parts of the Galilee region.[49] Self-determination took on a new meaning, with the gun rather than the ballot box as its principal instrument. By the time a cease-fire was finalized in 1949, over 800,000 Arabs fled or were driven from their homes, villages, and towns; Israel came into possession of 77 percent of mandated Palestine. The refugees were never permitted to return to their homes which, in many cases, no longer exist, since Israel has destroyed 385 Arab villages.[50] Today, they and their descendants number over 3 million, and on land that was once theirs, Jewish immigrants from Europe and other parts of the Middle East, are settled. Chaim Weizmann, who earlier assured the Arabs of Jaffa that it had never been anybody's intention "to turn anyone out of his property" now proclaimed that the events of 1948 constituted "a miraculous clearing of the land: the miraculous simplification of Israel's task."[51] Here, then, the seeds of violence in the Middle East took root and germinated.

Let us conclude with these observations. After World War II, the Atlantic Charter and U.N. Charter made the principle of regional-democratic self-determination a clearly acknowledged norm of international diplomacy, and there are powerful arguments that it existed as a norm of international law by the time of the U.N. Resolution 181 in 1947.[52] With U.N. Resolution 181, however, Palestinian Arabs were denied input into the decision-making process that would determine their fate, despite the fact that by 1947 they still outnumbered Jews by two to one. Although Jews owned only about 6 percent of Palestine, nearly 56 percent of the territory was allotted to the proposed Jewish state, while the Arab state was to be established on 43.7 percent, the remainder being in Jerusalem. Adherence to the concept of regional-democratic self-determination would have called for a plebiscite on the partition proposal. As it was, Resolution 181, the establishment of Israel on 14 May 1948, and subsequent violence and refusal of repatriation constituted an unmistakable denial of self-determination for the Arab residents of Palestine.

Some have tried to justify Resolution 181 by claiming that the Jewish inhabitants of Palestine secured self-determination[53] and, indeed, that the very existence of a democratic Israel represents a paradigmatic exercise of that right. Yet, however strong the case for a Jewish state was in 1947, it could not be anchored on the type of self-determination discussed above, namely, regional-democratic self-government. The Jews lacked a majority in Palestine in 1947; over half of the 650,00 Jews in Palestine had immigrated since 1920, at least 10 percent classified as "illegals" by the British authorities.[54] The Zionist claim to be exercising a right to self-determination in 1947–1948 could only reduce to a plea for self-government by a specific national group within a certain territory, that is, for *national* self-determination. The existence of such a right is questionable (as argued above), but even if it did exist, the belief that it would override the call for regional-democratic self-determination is an implausible repudiation of the Wilsonian principle.[55]

Finally, considering the demographic, historic, and legal circumstances prevailing in 1947–1948, Arab Palestinians cannot be faulted for failing at that time to recognize another people's claim for nationhood in a territory which they (the Palestinians) regarded as their own. Given standing international norms, Palestinians and Arabs in general were under no obligation to either accept Resolution 181 or to recognize the state of Israel. How could they? The imposition of Israel was not only against their will, it defied all standards of international behavior in directly assaulting their rights to land, homes, and heritage in their traditional domain. On this score, David Ben-Gurion, Israel's first Prime Minister, was candid:

> Why should the Arabs make peace? If I was an Arab leader I would never make terms with Israel. That is natural: we have taken their country...why should they accept that? [56]

4. A Continued Denial of Self-Determination: 1948–1992

In the years since Israel's declaration of statehood, Israeli Jews have enjoyed a considerable measure of self-determination: they have constituted themselves as a nation-state, are self-governing in the territory controlled by that state, and enjoy democratic rights of political participation. At the same time, the vast majority of Palestinians have been denied the most elemental form of self-determination by being excluded from the negotiations that have taken place to resolve the Israeli-Palestinian conflict, not only those in areas under Israel's control, but also those in the surrounding Arab countries to which Palestinians fled or were expelled in 1947–1948. This denial has persisted despite numerous resolutions by the U.N. General Assembly that the right of self-determination be accorded the Palestinian people.[57] Let us see how it has been manifested.

1. Although Resolution 181 called for the establishment of an Arab state in 43.7 percent of Palestine, it never materialized. Instead,

from May 1948 to June 1967, Israeli, Jordanian, and Egyptian forces occupied that area and Palestinian Arabs were never given the opportunity to create a state, but were precluded from so doing by force of arms. Similarly, under Jordanian rule, Palestinians of the West Bank were accorded no rights of democratic participation in their own governance.

2. Throughout Israel's occupation of the West Bank, Gaza Strip, and Golan Heights (since June 1967), Arab residents have been denied any right of self-determination and any democratic rights, save for municipal elections in 1972 and 1976. Instead, they have been governed by patchwork of Turkish, British, Jordanian law, and Israeli Military Orders which includes a stringent set of Defence Regulations, introduced into Palestine by the British, which sanction deportations, house demolitions, land expropriation, and detention without charge. Israel has annexed East Jerusalem, taken direct control of over 55 percent of land in the Bank and 40 percent of land in the Gaza Strip. Currently, there are some 140,000 Israeli Jews in East Jerusalem and its outer belt and approximately 100,000 in the rest of the Occupied Territories, each of whom are governed by Israeli law, not the regulations governing Palestinians.[58] The Palestinian *Intifada* (uprising) is a direct response to these facts and to the Military Government's arbitrary taxation without representation, harassment and closure of Palestinian institutions, collective punishment, and systematic brutality. The very existence of these practices, and the ongoing occupation itself, argue Palestinians, constitute a continual violation of their human rights and entitlement to self-determination.

3. Several attempts to resolve the Palestinian problem in the international arena have failed to include Palestinian participation, most notably, the deliberations leading up to the framing of the important Security Council Resolutions 242 and 338 and of the so-called "Framework for Peace in the Middle East" contained in the celebrated Camp David Accords. The latter document, signed by Israel, Egypt, and the United States, goes some distance in providing Palestinians an opportunity to "participate in the determination of their own future," by entering into negotiations "on the resolution of the Palestinian problem in all its aspects." Palestinians charged, however, that the Accords violated their right to self-determination; they were excluded from the negotiations which led to the Framework, and no provision were made for their exercise of self-determination. The General Assembly concurred on the latter (GA

Res. 34/65, 29 November 1979). More explicitly, the Accords were an unusual means of securing peace between belligerents since they (a) failed to address the concerns of Palestinians outside the Occupied Territories (over 3 million of the roughly 5.2 million Palestinians); (b) excluded participation by the PLO—the political organization supported by the overwhelming majority of Palestinians both inside and outside Palestine—in the projected negotiations over the status of the Territories; and (c) offered only a temporary "autonomy" to Palestinians with Israel retaining control of resources, public land, security, and foreign trade. Also, the Accords allow Israel to continue its controversial settlement program, an explicit violation of the Fourth Geneva Convention governing territories occupied as a result of war and of the preferences of the inhabitants of the territories. Perhaps this, more than anything, discredited the entire Framework in Palestinian eyes.[59]

4. In the celebrated peace negotiations which began in November 1991 in Madrid and have been carried on intermittently since that time, only Palestinians from the Occupied Territories (excluding Arab East Jerusalem) have been permitted representation. As with the Camp David Accords, the majority (roughly two-thirds) of all Palestinians and the PLO are excluded. For this reason, any proposals for peace issuing from these negotiations unacceptable to this larger community would not constitute an exercise of self-determination; implementation would be yet another violation.[60]

5. Concluding Remarks

...once you appeal to the principle of self-determination both Arabs and Zionists are prepared to make every use of it they can. No doubt we shall hear a good deal of that in the future, and, indeed, in it we may find a solution of our difficulties.

—Lord Curzon, 1918[61]

The systematic violation of the principle of regional-democratic self-determination in Palestine is at once a failure to observe and apply a recognized moral norm as well as a continuing source of the ongoing conflict between Israelis and Palestinians, Jews and Arabs. In this sense, Wilson's warning of the "peril" of ignoring the principle of self-determination was prophetic. Yet the principle remains relevant, for the struggle over Palestine continues to pose a severe threat to world peace.

To some degree, the majority in Palestine today does exercise self-determination, for Israel has been a sovereign state for over four decades, recognized by a large number of countries and a member of the United Nations. One might argue that Israel's legitimacy can *currently* be based upon the principle of regional-democratic self-determination; it would be sanctioned by a plebiscite held today among the six million plus persons currently residing in the territory of mandated Palestine, most of whom can reasonably claim to be legitimate residents. But deciding sovereignty by this simple procedure would be to ignore past and present violations of self-determination and to bypass the difficult question of exactly which parties are entitled to self-determination there now. In plain fact, Israel exists only because Palestinian Arabs have been systematically denied self-determination during the period 1917–1992—and Palestine is the *only* territory placed under a League of Nations Mandate in which the established inhabitants were not granted this privilege. Given Palestinians' persistent attachment to their ancient homeland, their unresolved grievances, and repeated international recognition of their entitlement to self-determination in Palestine, the status quo in Palestine cannot be sanctioned by appeal to regional-democratic self-determination. To do so would be a mockery of the principle. On the contrary, since the 5 million plus Palestinians constitute a politically coherent group with an acknowledged connection to the land, yet without having been the beneficiary of self-determination, they retain an entitlement. That force was used against them has not erased the fact that they are, and are recognized as being, a legitimate unit entitled to self-determination. [62]

But the clock cannot be turned back to 1947, nor to 1917, and it must be asked what the principle of regional-democratic self-determination *currently* requires in Palestine or Israel. Much depends on who now counts as a legitimate resident of that territory, and there is no clear criterion for settling this sticky normative question. It seems clear that entitlements, including legitimate residency, change with the passage of time; what was the case in 1947 or 1917 is not necessarily so in 1992. But how much do they change and over what periods of time? At present, large numbers of both Israeli Jews and Palestinian Arabs can legitimately claim entitlement to self-determination in Palestine or Israel. Yet, as time passes, this assessment is likely to change if the status quo is not altered. Current Zionist insistence that Jews as such need a safe haven and are entitled to self-determination in their ancient homeland can be matched by Palestinian claims for reestablishing themselves in their homeland, and for similar reasons. Their position is supported by even more comprehensive Arab and Islamic interests in sovereignty throughout the Fertile Crescent and Arabian Peninsula—and was in this region that Sheriff Hussein of Mecca sought self-determination in 1915—if not throughout the Near East and North Africa combined. Indeed, population numbers, historical association, and the current economic, political, and military threats to the Middle Eastern peoples by aggressive Western powers lend force to arguments that the legitimate interests of Arabs require a measure of political and geographical unity throughout their traditional domain. Plainly, at this point in time, there is nothing in the principle of regional-democratic self-determination itself—as articulated above and as set forth in the relevant international documents—which decisively settles the rival claims.[63]

The normative discussion must not be stalemated by these observations, otherwise the door is opened to political chaos, violence, and the temporary rule by the strongest. A solution must be found and articulated, and if any is to be acceptable the principle of regional-democratic self-determination must be followed. Some have proposed creation of a single binational state under a democratic constitution throughout Palestine; others argue that the proper place for Palestinian self-determination is in Jordan. A more widely accepted compromise, one which would permit both Jews and Arabs a degree of self-determination in Palestine, is the two-state solution as originally envisioned in U.N. Resolution 181.[64] In this respect, the Palestine National Council's acceptance of U.N. Resolution 181 (November 1988), coupled with its appeal to self-determination, is significant. The majority of Palestinians, in supporting the Council's decision, have effectively conceded to Israeli Jews a right to self-determination in Israel, and in calling for their own state they are not only reasserting their right to self-determination in Palestine but delimiting the region within which it is to be exercised (officially, the 43.7 percent of Palestine allotted them by Resolution 181).

If compromise of this sort fails, radicals among the Palestinians, and perhaps within the Arab and Islamic world in general, will assume control of the other half of the Palestinian/Israeli c onflict—just as those who refuse territorial compromise have dominated the Israeli Government for much of the past fifteen years. The prospects are sobering. Whitehead's admonition in 1937 remains timely; one-sided bargains are to be avoided, the ideal visions of zealots must be curtailed. Unless Palestinians, like Israeli Jews, are allowed some exercise of self-determination in choosing the political institutions they wish to be governed by *in* Palestine, whether as an independent democratic state or in affiliation with some other state (Jordan or Israel), then, for the foreseeable future, there is utterly no chance for a just and lasting peace in the Middle East. War and genocide would become the increasingly likely consequences—a prospect which the world should find difficult to tolerate.

NOTES

1. For example, Y. Dinstein, "Self-Determination and the Middle East Conflict," in *Self-Determination: National, Regional, and Global Dimensions*, edited by Y. Alexander and R. A. Friedlander (Boulder, CO: Westview, 1980), and Deborah Gerner, *One Land, Two Peoples: The Conflict Over Palestine* (Boulder, CO: Westview, 1991). This was also the conclusion of Great Britain's Palestine Royal Commission in 1937, which stated that the dispute between Jews and Arabs is "fundamentally a conflict of right with right." According to W. T. Stace, however, this is "a crude piece of ethical analysis," since Zionist claims to Palestine were based on unjust promises by the British, specifically, the Balfour Declaration discussed below (W. Khalidi, ed., *From Haven to Conquest* [Beirut: Institute for Palestine Studies, 1971], 637–8).

2. The question of the precise status of self-determination in international law, specifically, whether it is a legal right, has sparked considerable discussion. See R. Emerson, *Self-Determination Revisited in the Era of Decolonization* (Cambridge, MA: Center for International Affairs, Harvard University Press, 1964), who cites representatives from both sides of the controversy. Several argue that self-determination is recognized by international law as a right of certain collectives, for example, E. Suzuki, "Self-Determination and World Public Order: Community Response to Territorial Separation," *Virginia Jr. of Int'l. Law* 16 (1976): 828; W. Ofuatey-Kodjoe, *The Principle of Self-Determination in International Law* (New York: Nellen, 1977), 160–7; M.C. Bassouni, "The Palestinians' Rights of Self-Determination and National Independence," *Information Paper No. 22* (Association of Arab-American Graduate Students, 1978), 2–4; and W.T. Mallison and S.V. Mallison, *The Palestine Problem in International Law and World Order* (Essex: Longman Academic, 1986), 193. Citing Lung-chu Chen ("Self-Determination as a Human Right," in *Toward World Order and Human Dignity*, edited by M. Reisman and B. Weston [New York: Free Press, 1976]), J. Paust ("Self-Determination: A Definitional Focus," in *Self-Determination: National, Regional, and Global Dimensions*, edited by Y. Alexander and R. A. Friedlander [Boulder, CO: Westview, 1980], 8–9) observes that a case can be made for ranking self-determination as a human right, given Article 21 of the "Universal Declaration of Human Rights" (adopted by the U.N. General Assembly on 10 December 1948). R.A. Friedlander ("Self-Determination: A Legal-Political Inquiry," in *Self-Determination: National, Regional, and Global Dimensions*, edited by Y. Alexander and R.A. Friedlander

[Boulder, CO: Westview, 1980], 309) concludes that self-determination is a "principle" of international law. On the other hand, Emerson argues that there is no legal right of self-determination, Feinstein (1979, 462) denies that its inclusion in the U.N. Charter converts the principle into a "norm of international law," and M. Pomerance ("Self-Determination Today: The Metamorphosis of an Ideal," *Israel Law Review* 23 [1984], 337) denies that there is any "single right to self-determination in all cases." J. Crawford (*The Creation of States in International Law* [London: Oxford University Press, 1979], 84–118), while granting self-determination status within international law, vacillates between the language of 'principle' and 'right'.

3. H.G. Espiell, *The Right to Self-Determination: Implementation of United Nations Resolutions* (New York: United Nations, 1980), 46–48, lists regions in which the exercise of self-determination has been granted, in many cases yielding national independence. See also U.O. Umozurike, *Self-Determination in International Law* (Hamden, CT: Archon Books, 1972), 193.

4. On the other hand, Crawford, *The Creation of States*, 81 and 365–367, states that it is "much less certain" that self-determination has *jus cogens* status, though allows that it may be protected by other means within International Law.

5. W.T. Stace, "The Zionist Illusion," *The Atlantic Monthly* (February 1947), 82–86, for example, discusses self-determination at this level: "The principles of law and justice do not change, or at least change very slowly. Now the main principle of international justice is that which was laid down in the Atlantic Charter. Nations should have the right of determining their internal affairs without aggression from outside nations....It has always been, for that matter, the fundamental idea of democracy. For the self-determination or democracy of a nation means that its affairs are governed by the wishes of its own people" (quoted in Khalidi, *From Haven to Conquest*, 632).

6. Ofuatey-Kodjoe, *Principle of Self-Determination*, 156–159.

7. Umozurike, *Self-Determination in International Law*, 3.

8. A. Margalit and J. Raz, "National Self-Determination," *The Journal of Philosophy* 87, 439–461.

9. As quoted in M. Pomerance, "The United States and Self-Determination: Perspectives on the Wilsonian Conception," *Amer. Jr. of Int'l. Law* 70 (1976), 2.

10. H.W.V. Temperley, *A History of the Peace Conference of Paris*, Vol. 2 (London: Oxford University Press, 1920), 266.

11. Ibid., 264–265.

12. Ibid., 266–268, 357–364.

13. R. Lansing, *The Peace Negotiations* (Boston: Houghton-Mifflin, 1921), 93–105.

14. By combining the political mandate with the moral principle, Wilson took a step towards satisfying Kant's call for a merger of politics with morality: "Men can no more escape the concept of right in their private relations than in their public ones; nor can they openly risk basing their politics on the handiwork of prudence alone, and, consequently, they cannot altogether refuse obedience to the concept of public right (which is particularly important in the case of international right)." (Immanuel Kant, *Perpetual Peace and Other Essays on Politics, History, and*

Morals, translated by Ted Humphrey [Indianapolis: Liberty, 1983], 131, from the essay "To Perpetual Peace: A Philosophical Sketch," written in 1795). Also, see Friedlander, "Self-Determination," (314–318) on self-determination as a political principle.

15. See Espiell, *The Right to Self-Determination,* 46–48; Umozurike, *Self-Determination in International Law,* 14; and Crawford, *The Creation of States,* 87–88.

16. Crawford, *The Creation of States,* 84–106, and Ofuatey-Kodjoe, *Principle of Self-Determination,* Chapter 7.

17. See A. Cobban, *National Self-Determination* (London: Oxford University Press, 1944); L.T. Farley, *Plebiscites and Sovereignty* (Boulder, CO: Westview, 1986); H.S. Johnson, *Self-Determination Within the Community of Nations* (Leyden: A. W. Sijtoff, 1967); Umozurike, *Self-Determination in International Law*.

18. Chen, as cited by Paust, "Self-Determination," 8–9.

19. Emerson, *Self-Determination Revisited,* 466–467; Pomerance, "Self-Determination Today," 332–337.

20. Umozurike, *Self-Determination in International Law* (192), includes the mentioned constraints among the "characteristics" of self-determination, thereby adding something to the meaning of 'self-determination' beyond the idea of self-government or popular sovereignty. This is more idiosyncratic than standard.

21. C. Joyner, "The Reality and Relevance of International Law," in *The Global Agenda,* edited by C.W. Kegley and E.R. Wittkopf (New York: Random House, 1988), 196.

22. The case for the practical relevance for a code of international law is made forcefully in Kant, *Perpetual Peace,* especially in "Idea for a Universal History With a Cosmopolitan Intent" (29–39) and "On the Proverb: That May Be True in Theory But Is No Practical Use" (85–89). There are abundant examples illustrating Kant's point about the relevance of the concept of right in justifying public policy. Even the leadership of so powerful a country as the United States has found it expedient to offer justification for its recent military actions in foreign arenas. Thus, the invasion of Panama in December 1989 was dubbed "Operation Just Cause," and, in his State of the Union Address of January 1991, President George Bush repeatedly emphasized the correctness of the armed action in removing Iraqi forces from Kuwait, stating the "our cause is just, our cause is moral, our cause is right."

23. Crawford, *The Creation of States,* 101.

24. Margalit and Raz, "National Self-Determination," 451, 456, 457, 459–461. See also Chen, as cited by Paust, "Self-Determination," 8–9.

25. The U.S. Secretary of State in 1919, Robert Lansing, reacted to President Wilson's call for self-determination in this way: "The more I think about the President's declaration as to the right of 'self-determination', the more convinced I am of the danger of putting such ideas into the minds of certain races. It is bound to be the basis of impossible demands on the Peace Congress and create trouble in many lands. What effect will it have on the Irish, the Indians, the Egyptians, and the nationalists among the Boers?...How can it be harmonized with Zionism, to which the President is practically committed? The phrase is simply loaded with dynamite. It will raise hopes which can never be realized. It will, I fear, cost thousands of lives. In the end it is bound to be discredited, to be called the dream of an idealist who

failed to realize the danger until too late to check those who attempt to put the principle in force. What a calamity that the phrase was ever uttered! What misery it will cause!" (Lansing, *The Peace Negotiations*, 97–98). This passage suggests that Lansing interpreted self-determination along national lines.

26. Particularly important here is whether a given minority in a self-determining territory has strong cultural and political links to communities on the outside. This was an important factor in Nazi propaganda, and is relevant to understanding the conflict among Palestinians and Israelis, since both parties have strong links to external communities giving it the international dimension it has.

27. Article 22 of the League of Nations Covenant established the mandate system which called for tutelage by "advanced nations" over "peoples not yet able to stand by themselves" in the modern world "…until such time as they are able to stand alone" including certain communities formerly belonging to the Turkish Empire. It also specified that the "wishes of these communities must be a principal consideration in the selection of the Mandatory."

28. David Lloyd-George, *Memoirs of the Peace Conference* (New Haven: Yale University Press, 1939), 721–773, relates some of the controversies concerning the borders of Palestine that occurred during the years 1917–1921.

29. See Bassouni, "The Palestinians' Rights"; Mallison and Mallison, *The Palestine Problem*; H. Cattan, *Palestine and International Law* (New York: Longman Academic, 1973); J. Quigley, *Palestine and Israel* (Durham: Duke University Press, 1990).

30. British promises to Arabs were conveyed to their ally, Sheriff Hussein, the Emir of Mecca, by Sir Henry MacMahon, British High Commissioner in Cairo. See F. Khouri, *The Arab-Israeli Dilemma*, 2nd ed. (Syracuse, NY: Syracuse University Press, 1976), 405. J. Stone in *Israel and Palestine* (Baltimore, MD: Johns Hopkins University Press, 1981), 146–147, cites a 1937 letter by MacMahon to *The Times* in which he claimed that Palestine "was not or was not intended to be included in the territories in which the independence of the Arabs was guaranteed in my pledge" and that this was understood by Sheriff Hussein. This interpretation does not agree with the description of Hussein's views by David Lloyd-George, Prime Minister at the time. Lloyd-George mentions that MacMahon himself was then (in 1915) "very reluctant" to discuss boundaries despite the insistence of Hussein to include all the area along the eastern Mediterranean coast up to Mersina, an area which includes Palestine even though it was not mentioned by name (Lloyd-George, *Memoirs of the Peace Conference*, 660–662).

31. Mallison and Mallison, *The Palestine Problem*, 427–429.

32. This aspect of the Balfour Declaration is not accidental, as argued by J. M. N. Jeffries, "Analysis of the Balfour Declaration," in Khalidi, *From Haven to Conquest*, 173–188. The role of Zionist leadership in drafting the document is discussed in Jeffries and F. Manuel, "Judge Brandeis and the Framing of the Balfour Declaration," in Khalidi, 165–172.

33. Khalidi, *From Haven to Conquest*, 213–21.

34. Quigley, *Palestine and Israel*, 18.

35. The text of the King-Crane report is in Khalidi, *From Haven to Conquest*, 213–218. Zionists are fond of citing a 3 January 1919, agreement between the Emir Feisal of Mecca, a leader of the Arab resistance in 1915–1918, and Chaim

Weizmann. It called for large-scale Jewish immigration into Palestine provided that the rights of Arab farmers be protected and "no religious test shall ever be required for the exercise of civil or political rights" (Stone, *Israel and Palestine*, 147–8). However, Feisal added that the agreement shall be void unless the Arabs achieve independence as promised by the British; in a subsequent letter to Felix Frankfurter, an American Zionist, Feisal made it clear that Arabs would not accept a Jewish state as such but only a possible Jewish province in a larger Arab state (Khouri, *The Arab-Israeli Dilemma*, 12). There was no popular representation of nor support by Palestinian Arabs in the making of this agreement, as the King-Crane report pointed out. See W. E. Hocking, "Arab Nationalism and Political Zionism," *The Moslem World* 35, 216–23, reprinted in Khalidi, *From Haven to Conquest*, 502. To the contrary, there was outright opposition (see M. Muslih, *The Origins of Palestinian Nationalism* [New York: Columbia University Press, 1988], chap..5).

36. A. Heckscher, *Woodrow Wilson* (New York: Scribner's, 1991), 340; Stone, *Israel and Palestine*, 151–2.

37. Khalidi, *From Haven to Conquest*, xxxii; Lansing, *The Peace Negotiations*, 104–5; Lloyd-George, *Memoirs of the Peace Conference*, 734–5.

38. Khalidi, *From Haven to Conquest*, 208.

39. Lloyd-George, *Memoirs of the Peace Conference*, 750.

40. Letter to President Franklin D. Roosevelt, quoted in Khalidi, *From Haven to Conquest*, 49.

41. Arnold Toynbee, *A Study of History*, vol. 8 (London: Oxford University Press, 1954), 306.

42. Khalidi, *From Haven to Conquest*, 461–475.

43. D. Hirst, *The Gun and the Olive Branch*, 2nd. ed. (London: Faber & Faber, 1984), 96–7, and see A. Gal, *David Ben-Gurion and the American Alignment for a Jewish State* (Jerusalem: The Magnes Press, 1991).

44. Quigley, *Palestine and Israel*, 33. A subcommittee of a General Assembly Ad Hoc committee to consider the UNSCOP proposals concluded that the proposed partition is contrary to Article 1 of the U.N. Charter (Khalidi, *From Haven to Conquest*, 655).

45. Khalidi, *From Haven to Conquest*, 709–730.

46. A.M. Lilienthal, *The Zionist Connection II* (New Brunswick, NJ: North American, Inc.), 97.

47. Khalidi, *From Haven to Conquest*, 861–871.

48. Hirst, *The Gun and the Olive Branch*, 123–129; Khalidi, *From Haven to Conquest*, 761–766 and 795–806.

49. S. Flapan, *The Birth of Israel* (New York: Pantheon Books, 1987); B. Morris, *Origins of the Palestinian Refugee Problem* (London: Cambridge University Press, 1988).

50. Lilienthal, *The Zionist Connection II* , 159.

51. Hirst, *The Gun and the Olive Branch*, 143.

52. Quigley, *Palestine and Israel*; Bassouni, "The Palestinians' Rights"; Cattan, *Palestine and International Law*; Mallison and Mallison, *The Palestine Problem*.

53. Stone, *Israel and Palestine*, 14–15.

54. Anglo-American Committee of Inquiry, *A Survey of Palestine* (1946) and *Notes Compiled for the Information of the United Nations Special Committee on Palestine* (Supp. 1947), reprinted (Washington: Institute for Palestine Studies, 1991), 17–23.

55. Had the principle of regional-democratic self-determination been observed in Palestine in 1918–1948, the world would not be saddled with the current conflict among Israelis and Palestinians and its ominous potential for massive destruction. Of course, the state of Israel might never have come into being, but such would have been the consequences of strict adherence to the principle.

56. N. Goldmann, *The Jewish Paradox* (New York: Grosset & Dunlap, 1978), 99.

57. See, for example, United Nations General Assembly Resolutions 2535 B of 10 December 1969; 2649 of 30 November 1970; 2672 C of 8 December 1971; 2792 D of 6 December 1971; 3210 of 14 October 1974; 3236 of 22 November 1974; 3376 of 1975. A more complete list of resolutions on the Palestinian–Israeli conflict is given in Mallison and Mallison, *The Palestine Problem,* 459–484.

58. *Report on Israeli Settlement in the Occupied Territories* (Washington: Foundation for Middle East Peace, 1991). This report also cites a number of U.N. Security Council Resolutions which have condemned Israel's settlement program as contrary to Article 49 of the fourth Geneva Convention. Concurring discussions are found in Mallison and Mallison, *The Palestine Problem*; Quigley, and A. Roberts, "Prolonged Military Occupation: The Israeli-Occupied Territories Since 1967," *Amer. Jr. of Int'l. Law 84* (1990), 44–103. Israelis have contested these judgments (Stone, 177–181), but they stand alone on this matter. Eugene Rostow cites Stone in a letter to *The American Journal of International Law 84* (1990), 717–720, in defending Israeli settlements. Robert's response (720–722) is gentle, but, for the most part, decisive.

59. Mallison and Mallison, *The Palestine Problem,* Chapter 6; Quigley, *Palestine and Israel,* Chapter 24. The issue of settlements has been a matter of utmost concern to Palestinians in the Occupied Territories. The Palestinian delegation currently (January 1992) engaged in peace negotiation with Israelis has repeatedly called for an immediate halt to construction of settlements. See, for example, the statement by the Palestinian representative, Dr. Haidar Abdel Shafi in *The New York Times* (1 November 1991), A7.

60. At the same time it is highly unlikely that Palestinians inside the Territories would break ranks with those outside of Palestine—a fact that Israel has itself assured through its deportation policy, since many West Bank and Gaza Strip deportees now occupy important positions within the PLO.

61. Lloyd-George, *Memoirs of the Peace Conference,* 739–40

62. Crawford, *The Creation of States,* 117. It is doubtful that the status quo can be justified by any other aspects of international justice or law, as Cattan, Mallison and Mallison, Quigley, and Roberts have argued.

63. Dinstein, *Self-Determination*, 255.

64. Jaffee Center, *Towards a Solution* (Tel Aviv: The Jaffee Center for Strategic Studies, 1989).

THE PARABLE OF
THE LEVITE'S CONCUBINE

Laura Duhan Kaplan

Thomas Hobbes's description of the problem of human nature—violence—and its solution—a sovereign government—expresses a faith many people have in the stabilizing power of government. However, as Thomas L. Friedman points out, in a context of clashing tribal loyalties such as in the contemporary Mideast, the mere institution of a central government does not bring about the hoped-for peace. Rather, as I suggest by interpreting the biblical parable of the Levite's concubine, that government must help its people think beyond the mores of tribalism.

1. Tribalism and Government

According to Hobbes, in the absence of a sovereign government, humanity's lawless nature displays itself and people compete amorally for scarce resources. Specifically, Hobbes lists "three principal causes of quarrel [among people in the state of nature]. First, competition; secondly diffidence; thirdly glory." The first cause of quarrel is competition for scarce resources. The second cause of quarrel, diffidence, is a direct result of the existence of such competition. Once people know that others are out to harm them in order to steal their possessions, they harm others preemptively. The reputation for harming others protects a person from attack. Thereby that person gains the power to amass resources without threat from others. The third cause of quarrel is the result of the accumulation of power. Out of a desire to enjoy or expand power, a person who has been proven more powerful does not hesitate to use violence to ensure that others show proper respect for that power. Life under the threat of violence is, as Hobbes recognizes, unpleasant and unproductive. He says that people prefer peace and will find a way to eliminate the three causes of quarrel. Therefore, they contract with one another to follow a sovereign government which allocates resources and honors and which protects citizens against attacks by others. [1]

Hobbes's description of life without a sovereign government parallels Friedman's description of Mideastern tribal interaction, except that in the Mideast the competing units are tribes rather than individuals. Tribal mores, says Friedman, have evolved in the context of nomadic desert life. In the desert, the resources which sustain human life are scarce. Impartial mediators are not available to distribute resources equitably or to resolve disputes over resources. Hence, violence becomes an important tactic of acquisition as well as a response to the acquisitiveness of others. A family punishes attempts at competition as brutally as possible in order to signal to other families to beware. Powerful individuals and families are those who have proven their intellectual, physical and moral abilities to carry out brutal threats. A seemingly endless cycle of violence is built into the social fabric. Successful competition leads to the need to protect against competition; successful self-protection amasses power which in turn has to be protected.

However, Friedman goes on to say, the formation of nation-states in the contemporary Mideast has done little to break the cycle of violence. The boundaries of the states were drawn by the colonial powers to suit their "foreign policy, communications and oil" needs. Little attention was paid to "ethnic, tribal, linguistic or religious communities." Therefore, many modern Middle Eastern nations are collections of clashing tribes uneasily led by a member of one of the tribes. Therefore, the institution of a sovereign government can be seen as the beginning of another round in the state of war. The three causes of quarrel identified by Hobbes underlie the methods that some Mideastern leaders use to gain and maintain power over a citizenry composed of diverse, often antagonistic, tribes. Leaders may operate out of a competitive motive: to gain access to the resources of others. They may act out of diffidence, to prevent possible future conflicts which would weaken their assets. Finally, they may, out of an enjoyment of power, act simply to expand their base of power. Given the mores of tribalism, violence arising out of diffidence and violence designed to prevent trifling with an established base of power are particularly meaningful demonstrations to which Mideastern rulers often resort. The image of the modern Mideastern nation-state masks the tribal reality when rulers use their resources to build such institutions as hospitals, schools and roads. However, rulers see the building of such institutions as a way to gain legitimacy for their regimes in the eyes of diverse tribes. Should the demands of the preservation of their power require it, those hospitals, schools and roads can be destroyed.

An example which Friedman presents and analyzes in detail is Syrian President Hafez al-Assad's treatment of the Syrian city of

Hama, headquarters of the Sunni Muslim brotherhood. In February 1982 Assad, an Alawite Christian, destroyed the city of 180,000. In a battle that lasted twenty-five days, between 10,000 and 25,000 people, mostly civilians, were killed. Virtually every building in the city was damaged. After the battle, neighborhoods were bulldozed and flattened. The road through Hama was re-opened before the city was cleaned up. Assad's regime subsequently exaggerated the number of deaths, claiming they killed 38,000 persons.

Friedman claims that it is not possible to understand Assad without acknowledging the influence of tribalism and the authoritarian rule to which the ruler of a tribal nation resorts. Assad was not merely eliminating but also punishing his competitors in a way that unequivocally signalled other Syrians to beware. Out of his awareness that his country was too ethnically fragmented to be controlled by ideology and consensus, Assad resorted to violence as a method of control. Friedman analyzes Saddam Hussein's massacre of the Kurds using the same principles. Friedman adds that both Assad and Hussein believed that their use of tribal violence was justified by their role as modernizing politicians "trying to stave off retrogressive [tribal] elements aiming to undermine" their efforts at developing twentieth-century republics.[2]

Perhaps the killing of tens of thousands of civilians can be justified according to the logic of a world wherein nothing matters except power. Friedman hints that in the desert, power ensures survival and survival is all that matters. But the Mideast is no longer an uncultivated desert and the vast majority of the population are no longer nomads. The carrying of old notions into a new context represents a failure to rethink. I would like to suggest that if a government is to prevent intertribal conflict, it must be led by persons willing to rethink what they will do in the name of tribal loyalty. I make that suggestion with the aid of the story of the Levite's Concubine.

2. The Story of the Levite's Concubine

The story of the Levite's Concubine,[3] which appears in the last three chapters of the book of Judges in the Hebrew Bible, tells of the events leading to a large-scale regional military conflict between Israelite tribes in ancient Palestine. The story can be read as a parable about preventing violent conflict between competing tribes. Explicitly, the story presents a political proposal, suggesting that a central government can check the spread of violent conflict. However, the next book in the Hebrew Bible, the book of Kings, shows clearly what Friedman's analysis of contemporary Mideast politics shows: that a strong central government often exacerbates violent conflict. Therefore, I propose a deeper reading of the story, one which reveals the lesson that thoughtful moral leadership is necessary to prevent regional conflict. My telling of the story is followed by a brief discussion of its message.

During the time when there was no king in Israel, a concubine was unfaithful to her husband, who was a member of the tribe of Levi and living in the land of the tribe of Ephraim. She moved to her father's house in the land of the tribe of Judah. After four months, her husband came to win her back. Her father celebrated with his son-in-law for several days. Each time the son-in-law was ready to leave, the father enticed him to stay longer. Finally, the father let his son-in-law leave with his daughter late on the fifth day.

At sunset, the Levite, his concubine and his servant found themselves in the strange city of Gibeah in the province of the tribe of Benjamin. Only one old man, who was originally from the tribe of Ephraim, offered the travellers food and lodging.

Later that evening, while the guests and host were eating and drinking, a mob surrounded the old man's house. The mob demanded that the old man surrender the Levite, so that it could rape and beat him. The old man offered the mob his daughter and the Levite's concubine instead. The mob refused. The Levite shoved his concubine out the door.

The mob raped and beat the woman all night long. In the morning, the Levite found his concubine lying across the threshold, arms outstretched. "Get up," he said, but she did not. He carried her body home on his donkey. When he got home, he dismembered her body and sent one piece to the leaders of each of the tribes of Israel.

At a summit meeting of all the tribes except Benjamin, the Levite told his story. The twelve Israelite tribes immediately mobilized for war. They threatened the Benjaminites to extradite the mob or face attack. The Benjaminites refused to extradite the members of the mob. The Israelite leaders appealed to God, who told them to attack the tribe of Benjamin.

Four hundred thousand Israelite soldiers moved against the Benjaminite city of Gibeah. In two battles, 40,000 Israelites were killed. The Israelites consulted God, who instructed them to regroup for a final effort. The Israelites set fire to the entire city of Gibeah, which caused the Benjaminite army to scatter. A total of 25,000 Benjaminite soldiers were slain even as they retreated, but 600 escaped to the mountains. The Israelites went on to destroy every Benjaminite city.

After the war, the Israelites regretted having cut out a part of Israel. They initiated a peace treaty with the surviving Benjaminite soldiers. The terms of the treaty included the provision of wives for all surviving Benjaminite soldiers, in order to ensure the continuation of the tribe of Benjamin. However, the Israelites found themselves at a loss to supply the women. When they had declared war on Benjamin, the Israelites had sworn never to give their daughters in marriage to a Benjaminite family. However, the city of Jabesh-Gilead had not participated in the military offensive and so its inhabitants were not bound by the oath. So Israelite soldiers entered the city of Jabesh-Gilead, killed every man, married woman and child and kidnapped every virgin young woman. However, more wives were still needed. The Israelites instructed the Benjaminites to go to Shiloh and kidnap young women as they danced together in a religious festival. The Israelite leaders told the families of these women not to worry about their daughters because the kidnapping was not really a stain on the family's honor.

These were the days when there was no king in Israel.

3. Tribalism and Thinking

The story of the Levite's Concubine certainly dramatizes amoral competition between tribes for scarce resources. All three of Hobbes' "causes of quarrel" are operative. The Gibean mob's attack on the old man's house may be seen as an example of the second cause of quarrel, a preemptive strike motivated by diffidence. The Levite's calculated response to the rape and murder of his concubine may be understood as motivated by the third cause of quarrel, the desire for glory. The violence that was used in enforcing the peace treaty (paradox duly noted) may be seen as motivated by the first cause of quarrel, competition for scarce resources. By framing the story with the statement, "There was no king in Israel," the narrator of the story of the Levite's Concubine seems to agree with Hobbes. Perhaps the institution of a sovereign government (in the narrator's view, a monarch) could prevent people from quarreling violently over resources, honor and power. But the narrator's theory is refuted in short order by subsequent stories in the Hebrew Bible.

The book of Kings describes the life of the thirteen tribes of Israel united under the reign of a succession of kings. Unfortunately, the three causes of quarrel come to motivate violent actions on the part of the monarchy against its citizens, often against those with different tribal affiliations. For example, King David used violence to compete for resources, arranging for the death of Uriah, the husband of Bathsheba, in order to take possession of his wife. Queen Jezebel used violence preemptively, executing the prophets of Jehovah in order to discourage citizens from worshipping that God. As Phyllis Trible put it, "...in these days there is a king in Israel, and royalty does the right in its own eyes."[4]

Here I shall make the unsupported assumption that if the need for monarchy were the only lesson of the story, the editors of the Hebrew Bible would not have allowed it to be immediately refuted. Therefore, I shall look more deeply into the story. What do I miss by focusing on the narrator's political frame? By focusing on political theory, I ignore some of my strongest responses to the story of the Levite's Concubine. I do not speak about the physical pain I imagine the victims felt, the emotional pain of the survivors, the moral pain of the aggressors. I sidestep the frustrated fury I feel on behalf of the concubine, who was brutalized to death due to the impulse of her frightened, selfish husband; on behalf of the civilians and soldiers of Benjamin, decimated in a frenzied bloodlust; on behalf of the people of Jabesh-Gilead, murdered because they had refused to take part in an idiotic and unjustified military offensive; and on behalf of the families of the young women of Shiloh who had insult added to their injury when the Israelite leaders told them that the kidnapping of their daughters was no insult. I suppress my disgust at the moral and intellectual shallowness of the Israelites' remorse, after reading of their crocodile tears and their stupid attempts to correct their sins by committing further atrocities.

The fact that I am ignoring my reactions is related to the content of what I am ignoring. The language which describes my suppressed reactions reveals a certain theme: I use the words "impulse," "frenzy," "idiotic," "shallow," and "stupid." All of these words denote thoughtlessness, the absence of self-reflection. Beginning with the concubine's extramarital affair, and ending with the Benjaminites' kidnapping of the virgins, the characters in this story fail to think. They forget to think about the human cost of their actions: lives lost and shattered. They do not think about the moral costs of their actions: numbing themselves to the use of violence.

They even fail to engage in clear-headed tactical thinking. They seem only to calculate the short-term odds of personal and tribal survival, thoughtlessly killing and kidnapping when they believe it increases their odds.

Several twentieth-century philosophers have discussed the types of thinking that are necessary to bring about and sustain peaceful coexistence between diverse groups. Martin Heidegger traces the threat of nuclear omnicide to the dominance of mere "calculative" solving of human problems. He calls upon people to begin to engage in "meditative" thinking, asking of each problem and solution what its implications are for humanity as a whole.[5] Trying to understand what prevents such global thinking, Susan Griffin has observed that persons sequester parts of themselves from other parts. She recommends that people examine the emotional patterns of repression and revelation taught by their families, cultures, and communities.[6] Griffin's recommendation is particularly applicable to tribal clashes, wherein the suppression of selected aspects of experience makes it possible to perceive members of other tribes as less than human. Hannah Arendt identifies the suppression of experience as the motor driving administrators of great evil. She suggests that "the habit of examining whatever happens to come to pass or to attract attention...[may] be among the conditions that make men abstain from evil-doing or even actually "condition" them against it."[7] In particular, people must be open to experiences which have the potential to refute the dehumanizing stereotypes of others which make immoral behavior seem merely "expedient." The major experience of this sort suggested to me by the story of the Levite's Concubine is the awareness and appreciation of the suffering of other people. Only this awareness on the part of leaders and followers can stop the "three causes of quarrel" from becoming occasions for violent conflict. I call upon Mideastern political actors to cultivate, communicate, and respond to this awareness, thereby putting a crack into the preeminence of the ancient drive to own a piece of the desert.

The full text of the Parable of the Levite's Concubine is included as an appendix to this chapter.

Appendix
Text of "The Levite's Concubine"[8]

During the time when there was no king in Israel, a man [from the Israelite tribe] of Levi who lived in the land of [the Israelite tribe of] Ephraim took a concubine from Bethlehem [in the land of the Israelite tribe of] Judah. His concubine committed adultery and went away from him to her father's house in Bethlehem, Judah. She was there four months. Her husband got up and went after her to speak to her heart and to bring her back. His servant was with him and several donkeys. When he came to her father's house, the young woman's father saw him and greeted him happily. His father-in-law, the young woman's father, held on to him and he stayed with him for three days, eating, drinking and sleeping there. On the fourth day he arose in the morning and got up to go. The young man's father said to his son-in-law, "Feast your heart on a piece of bread and then you'll go." The two of them sat together eating and drinking. The young woman's father said to the man, "Please yield and sleep. It will be better for you." The man got up to go but his father-in-law urged him so he came back and slept there. He rose on the morning of the fifth day to go and the father of the young woman said, "Feast to your heart's content." They dallied until the very end of the day and they ate together. The man got up to go, he and his concubine and his servant. His father-in-law, father of the young woman said, "Look, the day has sunk into evening. Sleep here. Look, it is the time of the day to make camp. Sleep here. It will be better for you and tomorrow morning you'll get on your way to your tent." But the man refused to sleep and he got up and left, coming to the stronghold of Jebus [a non-Israelite tribe], now Jerusalem, with his saddled donkeys and his concubine.

They were with the Jebusites and the sun was way down. The servant said to his master, "Let's go and turn towards this Jebusite city and let's sleep in it." But his master said, "We will not turn towards a foreign city which has no Israelites in it. We will cross the land to Gibeah." He said to his servant, "We will get close to one of these places and sleep in Gibeah or Ramah." They crossed and they walked and the sun set when they were near [the city of] Gibeah in [the land of the Israelite tribe of] Benjamin. They turned off the road there to to come to sleep in Gibeah. They came and sat down in the street but nobody came to offer them hospitality. Finally, at evening, an old man came in from working in the field. The man was of the Israelite tribe of Ephraim, although he lived in a Benjaminite city. He raised his eyes and saw the guest in the street. He said, "Where are you going and where did you come from?" The Levite said, "We are travelling from Bethlehem in the land of the tribe of Judah to the land of the tribe of Ephraim where I am from. No one has taken me in. Our donkeys have straw and fodder. I have wine and bread for us and your handmaid and your servants. Nothing is lacking." The old man said, "Peace be with you. I will take care of everything you need. Only don't sleep in the street." The old man brought them to his house where he fed the donkeys, and where the travellers washed, ate and drank.

Later that evening, as they were eating, drinking and making merry together, a group of wicked men from the city surrounded the old man's house and beat on the door. They said to the old man, "Bring us the man who is staying at your house, so that we can rape him." The old man went outside and said to them, "Please don't do such evil towards me. This man is staying at my house. Here is my virgin daughter and my guest's concubine. I will bring them out to you and you may violate them and do anything you see fit." The men refused, so the Levite grabbed his concubine and put her outside. The men raped her and tortured her all night long. They let her go at dawn. Just before morning the woman fell down at the door of the house where her master was and remained there until it became light. Her master got up in the morning and opened the doors of the house. He went out to go on his way and he saw the woman, his concubine, fallen down at the door with her hands on the threshold. He said to her, "Get up and let's go," but she did not answer. He picked her up, put her on the donkey, and went home. When he got to his house, he took a knife and cut his concubine apart at the bones into twelve pieces and sent them throughout the land of Israel. All who saw said, "Such a thing has not happened and has not been seen since the Children of Israel came up out of Egypt. Put yourselves on it, take counsel and speak."

All of the Israelites, from Dan to Beersheba to the land of Gilead, assembled as one man before God in Mizpah. The leaders of all the tribes of Israel assembled before God, including four hundred thousand footsoldiers armed with swords. (The Benjaminites heard that the Israelites assembled in Mizpah.) The Israelites said, "Tell us how this terrible thing happened." The Levite man, husband of the murdered woman answered and said, "I came to Gibeah, the Benjaminite city, I and my concubine, to spend the night. The men of Gibeah surrounded my house in the night. They made as if to kill me. My concubine they tortured and she died. I took hold of my concubine and pulled her apart and sent her all through the land of Israel because they did a shameful and degrading deed in Israel. Here are all of you Israelites. Have a word with each other and come up with a plan." As one man, the Israelites arose and said, "No one will go to his tent and no one will return home. Ten percent of us will fetch the provisions we will need when we bring upon Gibeah of Benjamin the degradation it brought upon Israel." And all the men of Israel gathered at the city as one man, as friends.

The tribes of Israel sent men to the tribe of Benjamin, saying, "What is this evil that has happened among you? Now give us the wicked men of Gibeah so that we may kill them and remove this evil from Israel." The Benjaminites refused to listen to the voices of the Israelites their brothers. The Benjaminites from all the cities gathered in Gibeah to go to war against the Israelites. That day the Benjamites called up from the cities 26,000 soldiers armed with swords. Seven hundred chosen men from Gibeah were called up. All drew their swords left-handed and could sling stones at a hair-breadth and not miss.

The Israelites numbered 400,000 men, without the Benjaminites, and all were men of valor. They went to Bethel to ask God which tribe should go out first against Benjamin and God said, "Judah first." The next morning the Israelites camped outside Gibeah. The Israelites went to war against the Benjaminites and made plans to fight in Gibeah. The Benjaminites came out of Gibeah and killed 22,000 Israelites that day. The Israelites fortified themselves and prepared to continue the battle as they had started the first day. They wept before God until evening and asked God, "Should I continue in battle against my brother Benjamin?" And God said, "Go up against him." The Israelites approached Benjamin on the second day. Benjamin came out of Gibeah to meet them and killed another 18,000 Israelite soldiers. Then the Israelite soldiers and all the people came to Bethel where they wept, fasted and made burnt offerings and peace offerings before God. They asked of God, "Shall I go out to battle again against the children of Benjamin my brother or shall I cease?" And God said, "Go, because tomorrow I shall give him to you."

The Israelites went up again against the Benjaminites on the third day, arranging themselves as they had done before. The Benjaminites came out to meet the Israelites, drew them away from the city and began to wound them, as they had done before, on the roads to Bethel and Gibeah. They hit about thirty men and said, "They are defeated, as they were from the beginning." The Israelites said, "Let us retreat and draw them away from the city towards the roads." All the Israelites moved and arranged themselves at Baal-tamar while those Israelites who were to wait in ambush also moved. Ten thousand chosen Israelite soldiers moved against Gibeah. The battle was heavy and they did not know of the evil that was coming. God defeated Benjamin before Israel that day and 10,000 Israelite soldiers killed 25,000 Benjaminites. The Benjaminites saw that they were defeated. The Israelites fell back because they trusted in those who lay in ambush outside Gibeah. Those in ambush came out, spread out across the city and hit the whole city with the sword. The sign between the Israelites and the ambushers was that the ambushers would send up a column of smoke from the city. The battle turned against the Israelites and the Benjaminites wounded about thirty Israelites and said, "Again they are defeated, as they were from the beginning." The column of smoke began to rise from the city. The Benjaminites turned and saw their entire city rising up to the sky. The Israelites turned and the Benjaminites were frightened because they saw that something terrible had happened. They tried to retreat from the Israelites to the desert but the battle stuck with them. Israelite soldiers came out of the city and destroyed them. They surrounded Benjamin, followed him to his resting place and came opposite

Gibeah from the east. Eighteen thousand Benjaminite soldiers were killed. The Benjaminites retreated to Rimmon but the Israelites killed 5,000 on the road. The Israelites chased the Benjaminites to Gidon and killed 2,000 more. A total of 25,000 Benjaminite soldiers were killed that day. Six hundred Benjaminite men escaped to the Rock of Rimmon, where they lived for four months. The Israelites returned to the land of Benjamin, killed any remaining inhabitants of the city with the sword, killed the cows and everything they found. And they set fire to all the cities they found.

The Israelites had sworn at Mizpah not to give any of their daughters in marriage to Benjaminites. The nation came to Bethel and sat there before God until evening. They raised their voices and cried bitterly. They said, "Why, God, did this happen in Israel? Why did you call one tribe out of Israel today?" The next day the people got up, built an altar to God and sacrificed burnt offering and peace offerings. The Israelites asked, "Who did not join the congregation of the tribes of Israel before God? We had sworn that anyone who did not go up to Mizpah would surely die." The Israelites had pity on the Benjaminites their brothers and they said, "Today one of the tribes of Israel has been entirely decimated. What shall we do about wives for the survivors, when we swore before God not to give them wives from among our daughters?" And they said, "Which one of the tribes of Israel did not come before God in Mizpah? No one from the city of Jabesh-Gilead came to the assembly." A census was taken and in fact no one from Jabesh-Gilead was there. The assembly sent 12,000 soldiers to Jabesh-Gilead and commanded them to kill every inhabitant of Jabesh-Gilead with the sword, their wives and children. "This is what you will do: Destroy every male and every woman who has lain with a male." The soldiers found 400 young virgins, whom they brought to the camp at Shiloh in the land of Canaan.

Then the Israelites sent messengers to the Benjaminites at the Rock of Rimmon, spoke to them and declared peace. The Benjaminites returned at that time and the Israelites gave them the women from Jabesh-Gilead that they had left alive. But they were not enough. And the Israelites took pity on the tribe of Benjamin, because God had split apart the tribes of Israel. The elders of the congregation said, "What shall we do for wives for the rest of them, because the women of Benjamin are extinct?" They said, "An inheritance of deliverance is due to Benjamin, for no tribe of Israel should be wiped out. But we cannot give them wives from among our daughters, for we swore that he who gives a woman to Benjamin is cursed." They said, "Look, a religious festival takes place in Shiloh every year." They gave orders to the Benjaminites, saying, "Go lie in ambush in the vineyards. See if the daughters of Shiloh come out to dance. Then come out of the vineyards and each of you snatch a wife from the daughters of Shiloh and go to the land of Benjamin. And if their fathers or brothers come to quarrel with us, we will say to them, 'Be gracious, because we didn't take the women in battle and you didn't give them willingly. You are not at fault.'" The Benjaminites did this and they married women according to their numbers from the dancers that they kidnapped. They went back to their land, rebuilt their cities and lived in them. At that time, each Israelite returned to his tribe and family.

In those days there was no king in Israel, and each man did what seemed right in his own eyes.

NOTES

1. Thomas Hobbes, *Leviathan*, in *Classics of Western Philosophy* 2nd ed., edited by Steven M. Cahn (Indianapolis: Hackett, 1977), 360–361.

2. Thomas L. Friedman, *From Beirut to Jerusalem* (New York: Doubleday, 1989), 99–100.

3. In titling the story told in Judges 19-21 "The Levite's Concubine," I have followed Bill Whedbee, "The Levite's Concubine," lecture delivered at Pomona College, Claremont, CA, 1988.

4. Phyllis Trible, *Texts of Terror: Literary-Feminist Readings of Biblical Narratives* (Philadelphia: Fortress Press, 1984), 54.

5. Martin Heidegger, "Memorial Address," in *Discourse on Thinking*, trans. John M. Anderson and E. Hans Freund (New York: Harper & Row, 1969), 43–57.

6. Susan Griffin, *A Chorus of Stones: The Private Life of War* (New York: Doubleday, 1992).

7. Hannah Arendt, *The Life of the Mind* (New York: Harcourt Brace Jovanovich, 1971), 5.

8. This version of the story is my (mostly) original translation of the Hebrew as it appears in *Torah, Neviim, Ketuvim* [Torah, Prophets, Writings] (Jerusalem: Koren Press, 1967). The translation is faithful to the original Hebrew. In preparing the translation, I used the following resources: *The Holy Scriptures According to the Masoretic Text* (Philadelphia: Jewish Publication Society, 1955) and Zevi Scharfstein and Rose Scharfstein, eds., *The Contemporary Shilo Pocket Dictionary* (New York: Shilo, 1963).

SECTION V

Latin American Issues

INTRODUCTION

The conflicts among ideology, repressive regimes, political support and economic freedoms spawned death and confusion in both North and Central America during the late seventies and early eighties. In the name of democracy, the United States supported repressive Nicaraguan, Salvadorian, Guatemalan, and Panamanian regimes that flagrantly violated human rights. In the name of fighting Communism, American military support flowed into Central America. At the same time, the witness of many United States priests, ministers, nuns, and lay volunteers provided the American people with a witness and a story that told a tale of the suffering and victimization of the poor. In the United States, the crisis reached a climax with the Iran-Contra scandal and the covert war against the successful Sandinista revolution in Nicaragua. In Central America, the crisis came to an end when Oscar Arias's Peace Plan succeeded in providing a nonviolent self-determined process to end the conflicts. This section explores how the philosophy of peace can help reconcile conflicts in Latin America which rest upon the deep-seated divisions between North and South, and between developed and developing nations. The first essay examines moral resistance to violence and the second examines political resistance.

In "From Nonviolence to a Just Revolutionary?," Laurence F. Bove examines whether violent resistance to an unjust regime is as moral as it claims to be. He explores the correspondence between the peace activist Daniel Berrigan and newly turned revolutionary Ernesto Cardenal, showcasing Cardenal's narrative about why violence can more effectively bring about peace and justice than nonviolence can. Bove concludes that Cardenal's story does not transform killing into a justified or Christian activity. Berrigan's defense of nonviolent resistance and Socrates' rejection of retaliation show that the violent action of revolution is never a good but, when used as a last resort, may be the lesser of two evils. At best, Bove argues, violence operates as a form of moral triage.

Celina Garcia, in "Political Idealism, Feminism, and Peace Studies: Lessons from Central America," reviews the historical status of violence and nonviolent conflict resolution in Central America. Tracing the development of Oscar Arias' Peace Platform and its relationship to feminist peace analysis, she demonstrates the ability of Arias' plans to end conflict without the intervention of international bodies. Garcia develops the notion of political action as *Idealpolitik* and suggests that philosophers of peace pay special attention to the reconciliation process developed in Central America. She calls for a practical rationality that builds society and eliminates the damage and disillusionment of wars "fought for peace."

FROM NONVIOLENCE TO A JUST REVOLUTIONARY?

Laurence F. Bove

In the late 1970s, as Nicaragua's Sandinista revolution gained momentum, the relationship between two friends, Daniel Berrigan and Ernesto Cardenal, became a casualty of war. Both men were priests, Jesuits, poets, and activists who tried to heal the wounds of the human family through nonviolent means; but now things changed. Berrigan, a well known activist against war, continued protesting, and Cardenal, leader of the alternative Soletiname community in rural Nicaragua, joined the revolution. The resulting open letters between Berrigan and Cardenal illustrate the tensions between proponents of nonviolence and justified violence. In this chapter, I describe the conflicts between Berrigan and Cardenal and explore the philosophical issues of the immorality of justified violence, the principle of the lesser of two evils, and the Socratic rejection of retaliation.

1. Ernesto Cardenal—Priest Revolutionary

On 13 November 1977, Ernesto Cardenal, leader of the Soletiname community in southern Nicaragua, went into exile. In early December, he wrote an open letter to the people of Nicaragua telling them why he had become the first priest-revolutionary in Central America.[1]

The Soletiname community had attracted worldwide attention for its peaceful alternative lifestyle and its production of arts and poetry. For over twelve years, Soletiname represented "a place where poetry, painting and the harvest do not divide men into poets and farmers, but constitute the solidarity of one life."[2] Visitors came from all reaches of the world. Films detailed the life of this community that lived in peace, cooperation, and simplicity. What led Cardenal to his fateful declaration, "Now all that is over"?[3]

In his open letter, Cardenal tells that he and his community members took up arms and decided to use violence "for the ardent desire that a just society be implanted, a real and concrete kingdom of God here on earth."[4] He adds that they thought sincerely about the use of violence only after they witnessed the savage and repeated brutality of their Somozan persecutors. He declares that they only defended themselves and their people and that, after they made up their minds, the actual wounding and killing came slowly, inevitably, though they earnestly tried to avoid it.

Cardenal maintains that Soletiname members wounded and killed without hate. He tells of the first blood:

> They fought with valor, but they also fought as Christians. That morning at San Carlos, they tried several times with a loud speaker to reason with the guards so they might not have to fire a single shot. [5]

As one reflects on Cardenal's narrative, the implications become clear: Christians kill and wound justifiably, if they fight with valor and reason, without hate and for a just cause. Even in the context of a "Christian revolution," these often repeated assertions reveal much about the inextricable logic of violence. "The guards responded to their reasoning with submachine gunfire. With great regret, they (Soletiname members) also were forced to shoot."[6] To his account, Cardenal now adds regret and perceived lack of alternatives, thus sealing the fate of pacifists who became revolutionaries on the claim of justified, even Christian, violence. The Oxford dictionary's primary definition of violence shows the irony involved in any so-called Christian violence:

> The exercise of physical force so as to inflict injury on, or cause damage to, persons or property; action or conduct characterized by this; treatment or usage tending to cause bodily injury or forcibly interfering with personal freedom.[7]

Though the ultimate choices and violent consequences of a few rebels apparently pale in comparison to the web of violence surrounding the world, we must not forget that the choices of a few can mirror moral issues that affect us all.

2. Immorality of Justified Violence

Daniel Berrigan, in his open letter to Cardenal, strikes at the heart of the Soletiname option, when he says,

> What is of import finally is whether we are able to salvage something in the open season on humans. I do not mean salvage our lives; I mean our humanity. Our sense of one another, of compassion—our very sanity. [8]

Berrigan raises the question that even so-called just revolutions may be immoral: not because they fail to conform to theoretical requirements, but because they inevitably damage the human family. He grants Cardenal's sincerity and says "the guns may bring on the kingdom. But I do not believe it."[9] He goes on—both leftists and rightists "given time and occasion, kill the children, the aged, the ill, the suspects. Given time and occasion, they torture prisoners. Always, you understand, inadvertently, regretfully."[10] This reality of the act of violence becomes strong ground for us not to choose violence. Justified violence may still be immoral, not because of broken contractual or treaty obligations, but because violence always wounds or kills members of the human family.

Our analysis yields a strong moral sanction that something justified, even though culturally approved, may still be immoral because of what it does to the human family—both victim and perpetrator. When Cardenal alludes to the regretability, to excellent intentions to do good, to being forced to kill, Berrigan poignantly responds: "Alas, I have never seen anyone morally improved by killing; neither the one who armed the bullet, nor the one who received it in his flesh."[11]

3. Lesser of Two Evils

Neither Cardenal nor Berrigan explicitly recognize a corollary that derives from their different analyses of justified violence: choosing justified violence, because of what it does to the human family, is at best the lesser of two evils. As a person or group anguishes over choice, last resort, grave injustice, and the continued spilling of blood, the situation becomes *prima facie* an occasion of seriousness and moral degradation. Consequently, choosing "justified violence," choosing to act violently to others, is, *a priori*, not a moral good. In some cultures, choosing the lesser of two evils may become so commonplace as to go unnoticed. Cultures may even encourage the illusion of violence's good, but those who mindfully participate in, or observe, warfare and the effects it has on people, know its great evil. Though one generation of observers may be silent, while yet another cheers, the political aggrandizement of the martial spirit, the corruptive effects of violence, do not change what lurks beneath the myths and social aggrandizements.

Accepting the "lesser of two evils" approach to justified violence does not necessarily stop people from choosing violence, but it keeps killing and wounding in its proper perspective.

4. Socrates and the Law of Retaliation

The reality of the violence that surrounds us must be balanced with our longing for peace. As Berrigan states, "We recoil. Perhaps, in shock, perhaps in a change of heart, we begin to savor on our tongues phrases like 'legitimate violence', 'limited retaliation,'... And the phrases make sense—we have crossed over...."[12] With this, Berrigan alludes to my third claim: violence, if chosen, raises the question of retaliation.

Ultimately, one wounds and kills to get back at others for what they have done. One may do so without undue emotion and with extreme care, but wounding and murdering are done because somehow someone deserves it. The Soletiname members chose to wound and kill the soldiers at San Carlos because they wouldn't listen to reason, because they represented Somoza, because they somehow deserved it, because they killed children. But as Gregory Vlastos, in his book *Socrates: Ironist and Moral Philosopher*, states:

> if someone has done a nasty thing to me this does not give me the slightest moral justification for doing the same nasty thing, or any nasty thing, to him. So far as we know, the first Greek to grasp in full generality this single and absolutely fundamental moral truth is Socrates.[13]

Socrates' reasoning and moral insight lend the highest source of credence to philosophers of nonviolence. Vlastos's explanation of Socrates' position deserves long study because Socrates' recognition that the law of retaliation (*lex talionis*) is unjust obviates many bases for theories of justified violence. It cuts to the quick Augustine's defense of just wars and presents a radical criticism of the just war tradition. If followed consistently, Socrates provides the bases for the ascendancy of philosophies of nonviolence. I am realistic enough to know that this intellectual respectability will not end the common acceptance of justified violence, but it does disenfranchise the intellectual bases of a system that aggrandizes violence.

For our present purposes, let me summarize Vlastos's presentation, comment on how it undercuts Cardenal's position and adds the highest intellectual credibility to Berrigan's poignantly poetical defense of nonviolence. Socrates in the *Crito*[14] presents five principles:[15]

1. We should never do injustice.
2. Therefore, we should never return an injustice.
3. We should never do evil to anyone.
4. Therefore, we should never return evil for evil to anyone.
5. To do evil to a human being is no different from acting unjustly to him.

Socrates answers, "Therefore, we should never return a wrong—or do evil to a single human being no matter what we may have suffered at his hands."[16] Here, Vlastos uncovers the radical distinction between proponents of nonviolence and justified violence; here Berrigan's "crossing the line" is explained philosophically; here projects to align just war proponents with proponents of nonviolence stumble unfulfilled.

5. The Gulf between Nonviolence and Justified Violence

Vlastos tells us that, according to Socrates' position, if agreement cannot be reached on principles two and four, "there can be no common deliberation: The gulf created by this disagreement will be unbridgeable when it comes to deciding what is to be done."[17] Socrates concludes

> that true moral goodness is incapable of doing intentional injury to others, for it is inherently beneficent, radiant in its operation, spontaneously communicating goodness to those who come in contact with it, always providing benefit instead of injury, so that the idea of a just man injuring anyone, friend or foe, is unthinkable. [18]

At this point Berrigan and Socrates sound alike. Cardenal's appeal to injustice, his "I thought it was better to wait (to answer Berrigan) until the reality showed that we were right,"[19] has the hollow ring of Thrasymachus. Cardenal's "their arms were used not to kill, but to give life"[20] sounds like so many clanging cymbals.

How varied Socrates' analysis is to Cardenal's "Those who have taken up arms have done it for compassion."[21] Rejection of the law of retaliation undercuts justified wars or justified revolution from their foundations. Men may judge acts of violence and killing as necessary, but they are not moral goods. They are times of moral triage or convenient expediency. Through Socrates' principles one, two, and four, we understand the divide that separates proponents of nonviolence and justified violence. Though principle five cannot be fully explained through Plato's presentation, we come to a closer realization that reason and moral character prohibit doing something nasty to someone who has done something nasty to me or mine.[22]

This foundational argument merits further study by philosophers of nonviolence and justified violence alike. It is the point of absolute disagreement, the place that separates yet calls for us "to agree to disagree." On the practical plane, it is where Berrigan says to Cardenal:

> And who would regard you, an exile, a priest who must now anoint your forehead with the ashes of your dream—regard your convictions, your choices, with anything but the utmost respect? All this is implicit in friendship itself.[23]

NOTES

1. Ernesto Cardenal, "Solentiname Remembered," *National Catholic Reporter* (3 February 1978), 11.

2. Ibid.

3. Ibid.

4. Ibid.

5. Ibid.

6. Ibid.

7. "Violence," *Oxford English Dictionary*, 1990.

8. Daniel Berrigan, "Guns Don't Work," *National Catholic Reporter* (5 May 1978), 12.

9. Ibid.

10. Ibid.

11. Ibid.

12. Ibid., 18.

13. Gregory Vlastos, *Socrates: Ironist and Moral Philosopher* (Ithaca, NY: Cornell University Press, 1991), 190.

14. Plato, *Crito*, 48 B–C.

15. Vlastos, *Socrates*, 194.

16. Plato, *Crito*, 49 C10–D5.

17. Vlastos, *Socrates,* 195.

18. Ibid., 197.

19. Ernesto Cardenal, interview, *National Catholic Reporter* (14 September 1979), 1.

20. Ibid., 34.

21. Ibid.

22. Vlastos, *Socrates,* 195.

23. Berrigan, "Guns Don't Work," 12.

POLITICAL IDEALISM, FEMINISM, AND PEACE STUDIES: LESSONS FROM CENTRAL AMERICA

Celina Garcia

The role of true philosophy is to vanish as philosophy, that is, to be adapted into people's daily routines. And the role of philosophy for peace is to vanish into daily and constant actions for peace.

—Fernando A. Leal, Philosopher, University of Costa Rica

It is estimated that Central American wars and political violence have claimed the lives of a quarter of a million persons in the past 25 years.[1] "We would need [a monument] five or six times the size of your Vietnam Monument to write down the names of our victims," said Dr. Oscar Arias, former president of Costa Rica, while visiting Washington, D.C. At that time, Dr. Arias refused an offer to continue the war and instead launched the peace initiative that earned him the 1987 Nobel Peace Prize.

The Central American Peace Plan[2] offers the concerned philosopher for peace an excellent source of inspiration. With the dramatic impact of a new David against Goliath, the Plan proves to the skeptic that nonviolent principles can be successfully translated into praxis, when there is a willingness to live with the initial anger and misunderstanding of the superpowers and other lesser gods. Although Central America has lost its important status as a dangerous "U.S. backyard," it could regain importance as a peaceful front yard. This would be ideal indeed, for many philosophers have been inspired by peaceful gardens! Perhaps philosophers will be inspired to leave the world of *Realpolitik* for the world of *idealpolitik*, as Central America has done. Against an historic background of violence and military interventions, Central Americans are developing the politics of peace.[3]

In August 1984, the Contadora Peace Process (negotiations for peace in Central America initiated by the foreign ministers of Mexico, Venezuela, Columbia and Panama, meeting on the island Contadora[4]) produced a peace plan, but the *Washington Post* published minutes of a meeting in which members of the U.S. National Security Council congratulated themselves on having sabotaged the agreement after it was signed by Nicaragua. In 1986 Contadora again drew a Peace Agreement, but when Nicaragua was ready to sign it, the United States would not discuss it further. Therefore it is understandable that President Arias's first peace proposal, made at a meeting of four Central American Presidents in San Jose on 15 February 1987, seemed more like an impossible dream out of Boulding's imaging exercises.[5] The world did not expect anything concrete to come from the proposal. It came as a surprise for all, and there were reasons for pessimism.

The 7 August 1987 accord called for signatory governments to hold talks with unarmed opposition groups, to issue amnesties, to form national reconciliation commissions including opposition and church representatives, to "take all the necessary actions in order to achieve an effective cease-fire," for democratization (including complete freedom for television, radio and the press; full political party freedom to organize, move and proselytize; the lifting of states of emergency and the guarantee of constitutional timetables and elections in 1988 to a new Central American parliament.) The accord requested all governments to cease open or covert military, logistical and financial aid to insurgent groups; and all the signatories were to deny use of their territory to insurgents. 5 November was originally set as the date for simultaneous implementation of most facets of the agreement. In fact, by 5 November all five signatory nations had begun taking significant steps towards implementation, which they have continued.[6]

Of course, it is taking time to achieve all our objectives, as numerous obstacles and difficulties are being encountered. For one, we are not finding the same support and enthusiasm [from the United States] for peace as we found for war. Limelights gone, we are being forced to turn to ourselves and to the United Nations in search of our own light and inspiration. And this has been most constructive: in strengthening our own resources we realize every painful step is history of nonviolence in the making.

But since contemporary history offers very few examples of successful international nonviolent conflict management, the Central American Peace Plan should not be ignored by scholars concerned about regional conflicts. What is pedagogically attractive is the fact that *idealpolitik* (political idealism) was tried and that success can happen in international relations when people act with mutual respect and recognition of common needs.

As many diplomats have noted, failures have most often been brought about by the narrow-minded whose interests are generally self-centered.[7] For example, open debate on disarmament has been a turning point in Central America, as it has channeled resources for industry instead of for the military. And this reallocation of resources will make a difference: Costa Rica with a history of 100 years of democracy has proved that investments in roads, industry, health, and housing equals lasting prosperity, and that wars and militarism spell disaster sooner or later.[8]

1. Peace Studies Redefined

The West has for the last several centuries, imposed its 'models', its notions of development and progress, its science and technology all wrapped up in an ideology of domination on the third world. They speak of human rights, of technology transfers, of concessions, of crumbs, all the while refusing to admit the need for a real transformation of their economic and political institutions.

—Corinne Kumar-D'Souza, India, "A New Time Beginning" [9]

As would researchers in any growing academic field, peace researchers have been continuously redefining their object of study. Depending on how ambitious peace researchers have been to end all forms of violence, "peace" has been identified with aims as various as nuclear disarmament and absolute nonviolence. The abundance of philosophical positions represented by the various definitions make one feel as though she or he is floating in a sea of blandness. In this sea, all conceptions of the good human life are equally valid and equally acceptable. From this sea of blandness, it is not possible to make clear criticisms of violence and other crimes against women as well as entire races and nations. Within the past ten years, however, members of the International Peace Research Association (IPRA) have been willing to challenge the complacency of peace studies. IPRA members have risked offering social criticism beyond safely defined limits. Not satisfied with war prevention and disarmament, they have questioned educational, religious and military institutions. They have inquired into the primary sources of violence and challenged the individual's relationship to society by encouraging decision-making based on a totally new perspective on human relations.[10]

Following IPRA's lead, how could we define the philosophical inquiry that can nurture peace studies? First, we need to develop the capacity to distinguish violence in its multitude of variations, manifestations, and interrelations in ourselves and our societies. Next, we need to create nonviolent strategies to resist social, cultural and economic pressures that encourage collaboration with or creation of social structures which encourage violence. The goal of social transformation from violence to nonviolence is *idealpolitik* (political idealism).

The philosophy of *Realpolitik* often implies the denial of the human rights of the weaker and a distortion of the right to protest and criticize. Philosophers who embrace *Realpolitik* often say that we can measure the value of such actions by their outcome: if protest and criticism produced justice and peace, they would be good. But some scholars concerned with regional conflicts seem to believe that unqualified collaboration with stronger powers is the only way to produce peace. To these scholars, the euphoric solution to the latest events in Eastern Europe seems to be unqualified collaboration with the west.

But measuring actions solely by their immediate outcomes is irrelevant to the oppressed, as well as deceptive and dangerous. Lasting peace, i.e., ridding ourselves of all forms of violence, is costly and difficult. It requires time and much patience. We can view the last decades as only the beginning of the next centuries of peace. The view that unqualified collaboration is the only route to peace is also wrong. As philosophers and educators, we should be eloquent about our right to struggle for human rights as a universal human possession, the cultivation of which is a central human need.

To break the routine of violence, peace education should not teach people to adapt to violence. Ideally, it should teach people to identify violence and transform it. Peace education should be based on active critical argument as well as nonviolent resourcefulness and creativity. Nonviolence is one of the most difficult principles to understand and fully accept, even by peace educators. It is the most important tool for social transformation and it should be an intrinsic part of peace education, because it does not contradict human rights. Two Quaker-inspired programs, Children's Creative Response to Violence (CCRC) and Alternatives to Violence Project (AVP) are good examples of this transformation so desperately needed in contemporary society.[11]

As educators, we constantly provide our students with clues not only of what we see but also how we are to respond to "reality." And the "reality" of traditional philosophical education is its concern with revealing fixed eternal truths. Because its main preoccupation is with justifying and glorifying the status quo, philosophy actually trains its professionals to despise the search for peace and justice. Going beyond mere indifference to justice and human rights, a traditional philosophical education, according to Burns, produces a paralysis of will.[12]

However, when we question the validity of policies traditionally made by the power elites; when we question the validity of accepting the use of violence to solve our problems; when we refuse a scientific, technological or military career because it is potentially violent and brings suffering to others; when we instead develop alternative forms of security; and when we resist oppression, the philosophy of peace systematically engenders paradigms of morality and ethics that stimulate peaceful change and move humanity into a new era. This activity is *idealpolitik*.

2. Importance of Feminist Analysis in Peace Studies

And what can men do?
Not a lot.
They have invented war,
suffering, despair and the groans of the wounded.
They know how to construct insane guns,
turn cities into rubble
and in so doing proudly display
their pitiful manly courage.

You're Asking: What Can Women Do?
Janoslav Seifert, Czechoslovakia, 1984 Nobel Prize for Literature

In relation to peace and violence, there is a ubiquitous difference between women and men. It is men and not women who traditionally institutionalize violence. Even during peacetime, a variation on the theme of violence and dominance is played on women in "peace" time as well. Is this a coincidence?

No, said several groups of women, including a group of women from IPRA, and the War Resisters International. There is a definite link between sexism and militarism, although we may not fully understand it yet.[13] This link has some profound implications, until recently unexplored under the Peace Studies microscope. Perhaps the subordination of women is the first step towards the institutionalization of violence. Peace is an obstruction to the potential conqueror. Yet the world of women is a world of peace. Therefore, there may be a "rationale" to keeping women powerless, to ridiculing their voices, to denying their existence and their right to create philosophy and policy. Feminist peace research points at persistent patterns of oppression women in general share with Third World countries. Once we attend to the needs of women we begin to see common denominators, some of which are explained below.

1. **The language commonly used to refer to both.** Both women and third world peoples are called "emotional, undisciplined, treacherous, deceitful, unpredictable, political and economic eunuchs, and incapable of making their own decisions." Therefore, they must be dominated and owned!

2. **Constant conflict between economic dependents and dominants.** This results from an insatiable need for the resources and cheap (or free) labor of the dependents. Both women and third world peoples seem to be caught in a wheel within a wheel that is ridiculed and demeaned while being exploited. Both become perpetual supplicants because their labor and resources never acquire "true" value. Yet without their labor and resources, the dominants who ridicule them could not survive.

3. **Loss of self-esteem and lack of confidence in one's own values and traditions.** Having lost the power to define themselves, both women and third world peoples are victims of the raw end of double standards whereby what is "proper" and "acceptable" is either male or first or second world. This double standard allows the dominants to do what is not proper and acceptable, such as flagrantly violate treaties and laws.[14]

4. **Status as toys.** Like women in the midst of a macho dispute, countries are tossed aside when the superpowers lose interest.

3. *Una Costa Rica Con Alma de Mujer* (A Costa Rica With a Woman's Soul): From a Political Campaign Slogan to a Central American Peace Agreement

For no other male peace activist is the connection between militarism and sexism so clear as it is to Oscar Arias.

During the four years previous to Arias's election, Costa Rica had changed from a truly civilian society to a center of illegal arms traffic and a refuge for military activities. It had been accused of armed aggression by Nicaragua in the International Court of Justice. It had played host to Contras; government officials were connected with the 1986 construction of a Contra airfield in Guanacaste. Peace activists and marchers were insulted and vilified. The time for presidential elections arrived with traditional values eclipsed and with increasing pressure to use the country to attack Nicaragua or to help the Central American left.

Arias launched his campaign on a Peace platform: demilitarization, nonintervention in Nicaragua's affairs, and more justice for women and the poor. Arias called these qualities part of "the soul of a woman" he wished Costa Rica to regain. Like Figueres, who abolished the army in 1949, Arias interpreted Costa Rican "weaknesses"—no army, no arms, and the use of resources for public education and health—as strengths. He saw the true nature of the statesperson as a peacemaker, not as an aggressor. Arias's plan included the introduction of an innovative bill to counteract the underrepresentation of women in government. If passed, Costa Rican women will be the first in the world to hold elected posts in proportion to the number of women voters. Banks will have to provide the same credit facilities to women and men. Public housing will consider women on equal terms. The bill also seeks to abolish sexual stereotypes taught in schools, by modifying school textbooks.

4. An Appeal to Rationality

For President Arias, the rational part of human beings seeks peace. Irrationality leads us to violence and death. When Arias presented his Peace Proposal to the other Central American presidents, he made an appeal to their rationality. To continue to kill brothers and sisters, he said, was irrational. To continue to use resources for death, he said, was irrational. Wasn't it time, he argued, to develop Central American economies by establishing peace? This was the moment, the historic opportunity to open a true peace dialogue. "It is here in front of us," he said, in search of the political will to initiate peace.

As we read the peace accord, it is clear that there cannot be a war to gain peace in Central America. Peace is the only way to peace, to what preserves human rights and human values, human dignity and human hopes. In many instances, wars of liberation are excused or seen with romantic eyes by some peace movements. But there is no holiness in holy wars, as there is no human justification for wars. Active, practical reasoning begs for life for all human beings. Peace should not be an abstruse contemplation that excuses killing under certain sanctioned circumstances. Practical rationality calls for Central Americans to build a new society based on the politics of peace.

NOTES

1. In Nicaragua alone, war lasted 7 years with a cost of 50,000 lives, wrecking an economy already weakened by the Somoza dynasty. In El Salvador, war lasted 11 years.

2. The official name of the Peace Plan signed by the Central American presidents in Esquipulas, Guatemala, on 7 August 1988, is "Procedure for the Establishment of the Firm and Lasting Peace in Central America." See *Procedure for the Establishment of the Firm and Lasting Peace in Central America* (La Uruca, Costa Rica: Oficina de Apoyo de la Presidencia de la Republica, 1987).

3. See, for example, Edelberto Torres and Maria Eugenia Gallardo, *Para entender Centroamerica: Resumen Bibliografico 1960–1984* (San Jose: ICADIS, 1985); Katherine J. Gedorn, *Contadora and the Central American Peace Process: Selected Documents* (Boulder, CO: Westview Press).

4. Jordan Jelic, "Contadora Dossier: The General Situation in Central America" *Review of International Affairs* 38 (1987), 11–21.

5. Elise Boulding *et al.*, "Imaging the Future," *Friends Journal* (15 April 1983). Boulding's exercises involve imagining a peaceful solution to a problem in the future and working backwards towards the present.

6. Linda Robinson, "Peace in Central America?" *Foreign Affairs* 66:3, 600.

7. Brian Urquhart, *A Life in Peace and War* (New York: Harper & Row, 1987). Urquhart is the only living person to have served continuously in senior political positions in the United Nations Secretariat since 1946. He insists that moral principles must count in the affairs of the world and that decent behavior towards the powerless, the poor and the homeless would advance the interests of the nations.

8. See, for example, the following sources on Costa Rica: Richard Biesanz, Karen Biesanz, and Mavis Biesanz, *The Costa Ricans* (New York: Prentice-Hall, 1982); Tony Avirgan and Martha Honey, eds., La Penca: *On Trial in Costa Rica: The CIA vs. the Press* (Editorial Porvenir, SA. P.O. Box 447, 2050 San Pedro, Costa Rica).

9. Corinne Kumar D'Souza, *Sangharsh* (Bangalore, India: Vimochana Ed. Collective, undated).

10. See, for example: Hanna Newcombe, *Alternative International Security Systems* (Dundas, Ontario: Peace Research Institute), 1982; Newcombe, *Cooperation in the Light of Peace Research* (Dundas, Ontario: Peace Research Institute), n.d.; Martin Patchen, *Resolving Disputes Between Nations: Coercion or Conciliation?* (Durham, NC: Duke University Press Policy Studies).

11. Both programs were developed in New York City in the early seventies and have been implemented in Costa Rica for almost two years. Expansion to other Central American countries is expected.

12. Robin Burns, "Development, Disarmament and Women: Some New Connections," *Social Alternatives* 2:5.

13. See for example, the following references on feminist peace studies. Brigit Brock-Utne, *The Role of Women and Mothers and Members of Society in the Education of Young People for Peace, Mutual Understanding and Respect for Human Rights* (Oslo: Peace Research Institute, 1981); Brock-Utne, *The Role of Women in Peace Research* (Oslo: Peace Research Institute), 1982; Brock-Utne, *Feminist Perspectives on Peace Research*, PRIO Report (Oslo: Peace Research Institute, 1986); Burns, "Development, Disarmament and Women"; Joan Didion, *Miami* (New York: Simon and Schuster, 1987); Celina Garcia, "Androgyny and Peace Education," IPRA Conference, 1978; Garcia, "Latin American Traditions and Perspectives," *International Review of Education* 29 (1983), 369–389; Corinne Kumar D'Souza, "Research as Re-Vision: Towards a New Feminist Scholarship," IPRA Conference, April 1986; Betty Reardon, *Sexism and the War System* (New York: Teachers College Press, 1986); Reardon, "A Gender Analysis of Militarism and Sexist Repression: A Suggested Research Agenda," *International Peace Research Newsletter* 21:2.

14. For example, when Nicaragua won its case against the United States in the International Court of Justice in 1986, the U.S. declared the verdict "non-binding."

SECTION VI

Postscript: 1993

INTRODUCTION

While the chapters for the first five sections of this book were being written, American attention was directed toward conflicts in the Persian Gulf, the West Bank, and Central America. As this book goes to press, U.S. interventions into Iraqi, Kuwaiti, and Latin American politics have faded into the background of American popular consciousness. Instead, American citizens are debating whether U.S. leaders should have bombed Bosnia-Herzegovina with the aim of ending the vicious ethnic war between Bosnian Serbs and Muslim Croats. American citizens are shaking their heads after watching a humanitarian mission to end hunger in Somalia evolve into a political mission to force out local leaders. They are passionately divided on the issue of whether the U.S. should absorb refugees fleeing political violence in Haiti. On a positive note, however, U.S. citizens are watching in amazement as the Israelis and Palestinians finally face one another in peace negotiations.

Section VI, "Postscript: 1993," includes five brief chapters that offer comments on these most recent developments in regional conflicts of interest to the U.S. In "Peace in the Middle East?" Jack Perry, professor and former U.S. Ambassador, sketches the historical factors which led into and could lead out of conflict in the Middle East. In "Bosnia: Resurgent Nationalism and the Need for Nonviolent Responses," Robert L. Holmes provides a similar analysis of the conflict in Bosnia, warning against interventions which would internationalize the conflict. In "Somalia: Humanitarian Aid or Business as Usual?" Joseph C. Kunkel recapitulates recent Somalian political history and argues that U.S. intervention, as it is now conceived, cannot end the economic inequalities which led to civil war in Somalia. In "Accepting Responsibility for U.S. Action Abroad," Duane Cady reminds readers that weapons sales by the U.S. government exacerbated the very situations in Somalia and Iraq which U.S. officials now claim to be healing. Finally, in "Bosnia and Somalia: Why Is It so Hard to Stop Massacre and Genocide?" Robert Paul Churchill juxtaposes the international laws designed to prevent human rights abuses with the psychological dynamics that encourage those abuses. He calls upon philosophers to use their tools to bring about an end to human cruelty, reminding us that in many ways, "We are all Bosnians. We are all Serbians."

PEACE IN THE MIDDLE EAST?

Jack Perry

For many years, the Middle East was the most dangerous part of the planet. Men and women of good will who hoped for peace in the region had to cringe and flee when hatreds and rivalries burst into armed conflict, as they did with sad frequency. Then in recent months, following the end of the Cold War, fresh diplomacy began, fresh hopes arose, and long-prayed-for events occurred, to the world's astonishment. Can we begin truly to hope for peace in the Middle East?

Let us briefly consider the region as it was after 1948, the changes in regional diplomacy wrought by the demise of the Cold War, and, finally, things as they are today.

The "old order" in what we now term the Middle East was for a long time a slowly decaying Ottoman Empire and a gradually encroaching European colonialism. What should have been the last European conquest, the French occupation of Morocco, came just as the Ottoman Empire ceased to exist and the Turks, after World War I, retreated to their present borders. "What should have been" did not happen, however, for the British, French, and Italians managed, despite the Fourteen Points and all the Wilsonian talk of self-determination of nations, to rule important pieces of Arab land until the end of World War II.

After Hitler's downfall in 1945, European colonialism began a precipitant withdrawal from nearly all of its territories, including the Middle East, although the process was in some places slow and painful, including in the Arab lands of North Africa. In the Middle East proper, France quit Syria and the Levant, Britain quit the Gulf and Egypt, the Suez Canal became Egypt's, the immediate Soviet threat to Iran and Turkey was removed, and, most importantly, Israel was born in 1948.

In the post-1948 era in the Middle East, there were at least the following interrelated dimensions to the regional security picture which prevented the nations of the Middle East from working out a workable security system for the region as a whole. First, there was blood enmity between Israelis and Arabs, with war to the death spoken of constantly and the idea of compromise apparently unimaginable. Second, there were sharp regional rivalries—for example, between Baath regimes in Syria and Iraq

and between Iran and Iraq—for preeminence in certain areas or in
the region as a whole. Third, there was the ideological rivalry
between the more radical states and the more moderate states, for
example between radical Iraq, Libya and (after the Shah's fall)
Iran, and more moderate Egypt, Saudi Arabia, and Morocco.
Finally, over the area as a whole there was the very big and dark
shadow of the U.S.-U.S.S.R. Cold War rivalry.

After the healing of the Berlin running sore in the seventies,
the Middle East was clearly the most dangerous candidate for
conflict between Moscow and Washington. Both Super Powers
lined up their client states and furnished them with lavish amounts
of arms. The possession of nuclear weapons by the two Super
Powers cast a strange contradictory light on this whole chapter of
history. On the one hand, East-West enmity was superimposed on
the Middle East scene, making peace less attainable, compromise
less thinkable, and the whole area much more flammable. On the
other hand, the East-West nuclear standoff imposed a ceiling on
("put a lid on") Middle East conflict. The imperative first task of
both American and Soviet foreign policy—the sine qua non of all
policy, in fact—was the avoidance of nuclear war with each other.
In the Middle East, this meant that when Israel and its Arab
neighbors got close to war or when war began and threatened to
get out of hand—in short, whenever America and the USSR
started to move towards a collision course themselves—then all
else became unimportant except keeping peace between the two
Super Powers. Curiously, the alien Cold War shadow over the
Middle East had as its ultimate effect the setting of limits to war.
And yet it almost guaranteed that enmity among states would
continue. Even had the Arabs been willing to include Israel in a
regional security system, the system could not be constructed
because the artificiality of the Cold War kept it from happening.

How then have a "peace process" in such a situation? For
there was a "peace process" before the end of the Cold War, even
if its successes were limited. The task was made terribly difficult
by the hatreds and blood feuds about Palestine, a tragic cause in
which all Arabs joined to some extent. The hard-liners, as they
were often called, had much to gain from the Arab-Israeli conflict,
for they could use it as an attaching place for all their own
aspirations and jealousies. (Thinking of the anti-Israeli stances of
Nasser, Assad, Saddam Hussein, Qadaffi, and the Ayatollah
Khomeini, one recognizes that the existence of Israel was as

helpful for Middle East politicians as the existence of the Soviet threat was for conservative American politicians.) In the Arab-Israeli core conflict itself, there was too much denial of reality on both sides. Arab radicals dreamt of expelling the Jews from Palestine; some Jews thought that the Palestinian people in the region could be ignored, wished away, or forgotten. Tragically, there was also a conscious turning to terrorism, which may have gained notoriety for the Palestinian cause but which shed much innocent blood, caused much unnecessary suffering, and surely put off the approach to peace.

During the tragic two-score years following 1948, two things kept peace hopes alive. First, and little credited, were the people, both in the Holy Land and around the world, working constantly to bring the need for justice for the Palestinian people to the attention of a caring public. Whether one speaks of Palestinian efforts like Mubarak Awad's non-violence movement, of the strong and continuing consciousness-raising efforts of certain Christians and Christian groups, or of outspoken voices among the intellectuals of Europe and America, there were many courageous things done to help prepare the ground for peace. Second, there were leaders who were willing to put their reputations, their careers, and even their lives in the way of harm so as to advance peace. One thinks immediately of Sadat and his historical trip to Jerusalem. But there were also the Camp David Accords of Carter and Sadat and Begin. And there was the long line of devoted American diplomats who refused to accept defeat and who kept working for a lasting peace in the Middle East: Rusk, Rogers, Kissinger, Vance, Shultz, Baker, and, most recently, Christopher, plus a host of diplomats at lower levels who made signal contributions. A great amount of preparatory work had been done by the time that history provided the opening to peace.

That opening came, of course, with the end of the Cold War.

When Gorbachev came to power in Moscow in 1985, he began what he thought was a thorough-going reform which led (no doubt to his astonishment) to the end of Moscow's hegemony in Eastern Europe, to the end of Communist Party rule in Moscow, and then to the end of the Soviet Union itself—and in the process, to the end of the Cold War, the global American-Soviet rivalry. In the Middle East, the erasure of the whole U.S.-U.S.S.R. dimension lifted the artificial "lid" that had been present since shortly after the Soviets moved into the region in the 1960s. This redefinition of the strategic balance in the area left regional forces free to come to the fore (just as in Eastern Europe the artificial freeze was ended and, as Vaclav Havel said, "history resumed"). The effacement of Soviet power, at least for a time, meant that the region was no longer divided up between the Super Powers and the way to a true regional security system was at last opened.

The bad part of this was that regional rivalries became potentially more destructive and even disastrous, owing to the removal of the U.S.-U.S.S.R. "lid"—as was seen in living red-and-white in the terrible Iran-Iraq war and then the terrible Iraqi annexation of Kuwait and the Gulf War that followed. These could hardly have happened during the Cold War: the risk of American-Soviet nuclear war would have made it imperative to find a way to stop those wars before they became so calamitous.

The good part of the new post-Cold War situation was that Washington was freed from its stifling embrace with Israel and the distance created between Washington and Tel Aviv opened up a path to American-Arab rapprochement. The peace process gained new standing. Into this changing scene moved the diplomacy of the peace-makers, including Americans like Baker and Christopher, moderate Arabs, and, very importantly, the newly elected Labor Party coalition in Israel under Rabin and Peres. With pushing and prodding from all sides, all the Arab and Israeli leaders in the region (with a few exceptions like Saddam Hussein or the Iranian and Libyan leaders) and certainly all those directly involved began to see that peace was in everybody's interest. Even the very weakening of the PLO by its backing of Saddam Hussein in the Gulf War, paradoxically, made diplomatic dialogue more possible. So with a strong push from Washington, ideas once thought of as unimaginable, such as "negotiating face to face with the PLO" or "recognizing Israel," became imaginable because advantageous. Labels like "terrorists" began to be set aside. At Madrid, direct talks started. And the rivulet became a stream.

What are Middle East prospects now?

In addition to post-Cold-War diplomacy and in addition to pushing away certain old habits of speech and thought, after 1985 Middle East leaders were brought into confrontation with hard facts of life that gradually began to seem as tall and as threatening as the old Arab-Israeli conflict. These were the facts about population, water resources, pollution, impoverishment, and the hopes for economic rebirth. Leaders who looked beyond the Arab-

Israeli horizon saw terrible problems that arms and political victories could not solve. This glimpse of a tough future drove the more far-sighted towards a desire for peace. The hope of turning the Middle East region into a blooming, greening, prospering part of the world lies before Middle East statesmen and their friends like a stream in the desert.

However, alongside this hopeful scene—at times making it seem more like mirage than reality—is the arising of those who would make the tribe their future. Various terms are used and always objected to, such as "fundamentalists," "Islamists," and "radicals," but we mean those who would use ideology or faith to rally the masses against both external and internal enemies, enemies who are all too often modern, non-traditional, liberal, and cosmopolitan. When the Muslim Brotherhood kills tourists in Egypt, when the Hezbollah launches raids from Lebanon into Israel, when fanatics attack Bahai faithful in Iran or Coptic Christians in Egypt, or when seceding from the twentieth century is seen as a way forward, then these forces are at work. They do not concern themselves very seriously with the prosperity of the Middle East. They are not afraid of war. They are popular and dangerous.

Good sense, good diplomacy, and good statecraft now seem to proclaim that the movement towards a true security system in the Middle East—for that is the operational equivalent of peace—is now more possible and more imperative than ever before since the passing of the Ottoman Empire. Egypt and Israel made peace, bringing Israel into the Arab diplomatic world. Israel and the PLO have recognized each other and are on the path that ought to lead eventually to a sane solution of "the Palestinian problem." Syria and Jordan should be at peace with Israel soon. Lebanon ought to be able to reclaim its own territory and rejoin the family of nations in the Middle East soon. And with those political happenings, the way is certainly open to an economic renaissance that would increase the security and the prosperity of every people in the whole region.

That is the good sense scenario. There are others. Egypt, with its dramatically increasing population and its severely limited resources, may fall prey at some point to fanaticism. Radicals may come to power in countries now ruled by moderates. People called on to rebel against modernism and Westernism may do so. Hatred of Israel or of fellow Arabs living next door may be stirred up. Territorial or hegemonical ambitions may call forth new, aggressive leaders. And one can picture a Middle East that would be nasty, brutish, and frightening.

But the way to peace in the Middle East has been forged. It is attainable. Some would say that surely the Holy Land deserves peace, finally. Just now, it would take a great prophet to say which will win, the joys of peace or the joys of war.

BOSNIA:
RESURGENT NATIONALISM
AND THE NEED FOR
NONVIOLENT RESPONSES

Robert L. Holmes

The site was Sarajevo, the issue Serbian claims on Bosnia-Herzegovina, the date 28 June 1914.

On that day Gavrilo Princip fired the shots that killed the Archduke Ferdinand and touched off World War I. A Bosnian Serb, Princip belonged to a group of young Serbian nationalists hoping to see Bosnia, annexed by Austria-Hungary in 1908, become part of a greater Serbia. They thought the Archduke, heir to the Austro-Hungarian throne, would obstruct those plans.

Those shots still reverberate in the events unfolding in Bosnia, events rooted, as were those of 1914, deeply in the region's history.

The Serbs, Croats, and Slovenes—all Slavic peoples—migrated to the Balkan Peninsula in the sixth century. Most eventually converted to Christianity (Croats and Slovenes becoming predominantly Catholic, Serbs, Orthodox). But when they came under the domination of the Turkish Ottoman Empire in the fifteenth century, many adopted Islam, particularly in Bosnia, giving Bosnian Muslims a relatively privileged position *vis-à-vis* the Christian Croats and Serbs.

Nationalist sentiments grew among the Slavs during the nineteenth century, with Serbia winning independence from the Turks in 1878. Following the demise of the Ottoman Empire during World War I, the Slavic peoples united to form the Kingdom of the Serbs, Croats, and Slovenes, which was renamed Yugoslavia in 1929. The monarchy ended with World War II. Germany and Italy occupied the country and established a fascist puppet state in Croatia, which, aided by Bosnian Muslims, exterminated more than 300,000 persons—mostly Serbs, but including gypsies and Jews.

Both Chetniks (supporting a return of the monarchy) and Partisans (socialists under Tito) took up arms against the occupation. The Partisans provided the only effective resistance and Tito emerged at the end of the war as leader of a communist Yugoslavia that proceeded to steer an independent course from the U.S.S.R.

With the collapse of Soviet and Eastern European communism, nationalistic aspirations flared anew. The Republics of Slovenia and Croatia seceded in 1991, followed by Macedonia and Bosnia, leaving only Serbia and Montenegro as part of the original Yugoslavia.

But longstanding Serbian claims on Bosnia were pressed with a vengeance: directly by Serbs living in Bosnia, indirectly by the Serbian government in Belgrade. And with the same passion that drove 1914's conspirators.

Although only 31 percent of the population before the succession, Bosnian Serbs seized more territory by force, laying siege to the Bosnian capitol of Sarajevo as well. Serbian farmers had already occupied much of the land, so it is difficult to know precisely how much was taken through fighting. But the Serbs came to control more than 70 percent of the territory. Though originally 44 percent of Bosnia's population, Muslims—those not killed or driven out by the "ethnic cleansing"—were left holding only 10 percent of the land, the rest being held by Croats. It is widely suspected that Croatia and Serbia, despite warring over Croatian independence, secretly had agreed to carve up much of Bosnia for themselves.

Thus, at a time of historic moves toward unity in Western Europe, resurgent nationalism in Eastern Europe threatens world peace, much as it did in the late nineteenth and early twentieth centuries.

There are no simple, long-term solutions. But military intervention by the United States or the United Nations—the simple solution of choice by many—almost certainly would worsen the situation, at best putting a temporary lid on the violence, at worst drawing outside powers into a larger conflict.

With Serbian leaders having fanned the flames of religious hatred by raising the specter of a radical Islamic state emerging in Bosnia, other Muslim countries may feel compelled to come to the aid of Bosnia's Muslims. Iranian weapons and volunteers have reportedly been intercepted en route to Bosnia, and some Saudi volunteers have taken part in the fighting. On the other side, Russian volunteers have joined with the Serbs; and some in Russia, an historical ally of the Serbs, have called for more active support of Serbia, a prospect that could quickly become a reality were the Yeltsin government overthrown by extreme nationalists. Muslim Albania, moreover, could be drawn into the conflict in response to Belgrade's repression of Kosovo (Serbia's southern province, which is 90 percent ethnic Albanian and mostly Muslim).

Of immediate importance, for this reason, is to keep the conflict from becoming internationalized, particularly along Christian-Muslim lines. To that end, a concerted effort should be made by the international community to forestall the spread of violence, particularly to Kosovo.

Kosovo's Muslims have been engaged in an unheralded campaign of nonviolent resistance. When the Belgrade government dismissed more than 100,000 teachers, professors, physicians, and others, Muslims responded by developing alternative institutions and social services—patiently laying the foundation for a protracted struggle. Their efforts deserve recognition and support.

The status quo prior to the conflict can never be restored—as unjust as that may be. Bosnia's short-lived independence as a nation-state is at an end. The need now is to design a new social-political arrangement with a decentralization of power, safeguards for religious and ethnic diversity, and a higher premium on the preservation of peoples than governments.

Outsiders cannot do this. In the end, only the Serb, Croat, and Bosnian peoples can. But others can help to facilitate the process, provided they begin with a balanced judgment of the fundamental issues, something that is difficult to achieve in the face of the atrocities, particularly by Serbs. It is unclear, for example, why the Bosnian Serbs had less of a right to independence from the newly independent Bosnia (in which they suddenly found themselves a minority) than the Bosnians had to independence from Yugoslavia in the first place. It is also unclear why the only long-term solution should be thought to lie in replicating the socio-political features of the nation-state on a smaller scale, as virtually all of the proposed solutions have done. It is, after all, fear of domination by others that has helped fuel the crisis throughout the former Yugoslavia, and the nation-state by its nature institutionalizes the capacity for such domination.

The challenge of our time is to view all the peoples of the former Yugoslavia as our brothers and sisters, and to find creative, nonviolent ways of helping them to devise new, respectful, and secure ways of living together. Only then will a new world order worthy of the name even being to materialize.

SOMALIA: HUMANITARIAN AID OR BUSINESS AS USUAL?

Joseph C. Kunkel

Much has been written about whether President Bush should have sent troops into Somalia in December 1992. With fighting out of control and with relief shipments not reaching the starving, the President's gesture seemed humanitarian. Perhaps it was. My worry is that in storming the beaches the United States may be concealing its complicity in inducing the famine.

The issue is not whether troops should be used as police officers to enhance peacemaking endeavors. The line between pacifists and just warists ought not be drawn here. The deeper question asks: is the United States committed to peacemaking which includes the creation of democratic procedures and the elimination of chronic hunger, or to *Realpolitik,* which continues the rich-poor global division that sows the seeds for future wars? The case of Somalia is instructive.[1]

Somalia is one of the United Nation's least developed countries. If superimposed on the U.S., it would range from the Gulf of Mexico to Albany, New York, and westward across Pennsylvania, Northern Ohio, and lower Michigan. Its estimated four million people, mostly Sunni Muslims, have limited literacy and mainly lead a nomad and semi-nomad, camel-transporting existence. Somalia sits across the narrow Gulf of Aden from Yemen and Saudi Arabia. Its deep-water port at Berbera is ideally located for access to the Red Sea and the Indian Ocean.

The North and the South won independence from Britain and Italy, respectively, in 1960 and united as the Somali Republic. "United" is a euphemism for joining two groups of cities miles apart in customs, distance, and especially clan loyalty. When democratically approved in 1961, the new Republic had its capital in the south with a southern president and prime minister; a majority of northerners voted against the constitution.

There are six major clans in Somalia. Their elders are the recognized moral and paternal authorities. Clan members protect their own kin, and when someone commits a murder the whole clan becomes guilty in the eyes of the aggrieved. There is no sense of political parties cutting across clan loyalty. Government positions mean patronage to one's own clan. Indeed when 64 clan and sub-clan parties vied for political office in the Assembly in 1969 the democratic government was in paralysis. Said Samatar, a Somali and historian, argues that a way out for the future would be to establish a two-chamber Assembly, one of which would be a House of Lords composed of clan elders.2

The army was small and insignificant at the time of independence. Unfortunately, the country's political borders, established in the late nineteenth century, divided the Somali grazing lands of Ethiopia and northern Kenya from the watering holes of Somalia, splitting the clans between two nations. Two million Somalis thus form an ethnic minority in Ethiopia. One of the few things the new Somalian Assembly agreed upon was a larger army to defend Somalis (on both sides of the borders). The United States, on account of its alliance with and heavy military aid for Emperor Haile Selassie of Ethiopia, refused to authorize more than a modernized police force. So the Somalis turned to the Soviet Union which provided tanks, personnel carriers, and aircraft. This refurbished army then took advantage of the weak Assembly and staged a coup in 1969 to bring in the dictator General Mahamed Siad Barre.

Barre, a member of a southern clan, ruled Somalia until 1991. At first he offered a socialistic agenda that looked promising for the people of all clans. Cooperatives were created particularly to help nomadic groups share scarce resources. Some effort was also made to reduce the rich-poor dichotomy in the cities. A fundamental change introduced the Latin script for the hitherto only oral Somali language. This allowed the beginnings of a literacy campaign among urban and nomad peoples. Women too were given greater admission to education on all levels. The 1974 serious drought, however, forced Barre to substitute foreign aid, particularly from the Soviet Union and China, for agricultural growth.

By 1975 these social innovations collapsed further. Barre lost interest and started to focus on uniting all Somalis under one nation. Selassie had been overthrown by a military coup in 1974, and here too the military leaders turned toward Moscow. Barre sought to use his growing army as the Somali peoples living in the Ogaden region of Ethiopia began to revolt. The Somali army invaded Ethiopia in 1977. Barre presumed Moscow would side with Somalia and was greatly dismayed when the Soviet Union with Cuban troops backed Ethiopia. Turning capitalist, the capricious Barre called on Saudi Arabia and the United States for help. Military aid poured in; nevertheless, by 1978 Somalian troops were pushed back to their previous borders by the much larger Ethiopian army.

With its energy and resources directed toward war and military planning, Somalia's economy nose-dived. Deficits mounted and Somalia became indebted to and dependent upon first Saudi Arabia and then the International Monetary Fund (IMF). Drought, a regularly recurring phenomenon in East Africa, hit again in 1982–85 and killed some 300,000 people in Ethiopia. A million refugees from the Ogaden war and the later drought poured into Somalia, taxing its already limited resources.

Somalia is not without arable land. Twenty million acres are available in the South between the Shabeelle and Juba rivers. This is enough farmland to feed the entire population and to have food left over for export, if proper irrigation and farm management were introduced. Of these acres, however, only about five percent are cultivated. The capitalist IMF model concentrates on food for exports as a means to cut back a nation's deficits. However in Somalia the IMF did not insist on a reduction of military expenditures or on the reform of government along democratic lines. It did force Barre to reduce socialistic programs, which allowed the few rich to get richer. Child education and literacy were ignored.

Indeed the entire global free enterprise system is geared against the world's hungry. The marketplace responds to money, not to need, and tends to concentrate economic power in the hands of a few.[3] Somalia has to import equipment in order to export manufacturing goods; the net result is generally a loss in overall income. The net loss is even worse when servicing the deficit loans is figured into the equation. In other words, whenever a new government is finally formed in Somalia it will have to pay the indebtedness incurred by the Barre regime. Hence instead of a trickle down effect there is a trickle up process. In 1990, for example, the world's Southern nations gave $35 billion more to the rich Northern nations than the North gave in aid and finances to the South, with the servicing of their debts amounting to $140 billion.[4]

There have been a number of uprisings against Barre by other clans and sub-clans, while his own sub-clan has continued to support him. The difference, of course, resides in his tremendous military power. Between 1979 and 1989 the United States supplied Barre over half a billion dollars in arms; this amounted to 93 percent of the U.S. aid to Somalia.[5] In 1988 rebels from the main northern clan attacked two of their own cities in the beginning of a civil war against Barre. The army responded with heavy artillery and bombing. Hargeisa, a city of half a million and the former capital of the North, was one of the cities reduced to rubble. Alexander Cockburn says the U.S. provided "logistical backup and diplomatic protection."[6]

Within a year, a southern clan other than Barre's own started to revolt. The fighting was ruthless. On 27 January 1991, Barre and his troops fled the capital city of Mogadishu. Afterwards the victorious clan set up one of their own, Ali Mahdi, as president. However General Mohamed Farah Aidid, a member of an alternate sub-clan, opposed Mahdi and began an internecine clan war for control of Somalia. Fighting swept back and forth across Mogadishu. This allowed Barre to reassemble his forces and reattack. After Barre had ravaged the countryside, General Aidid drove him out of Somalia in May 1992.

Needless to say, there is no recognized government in Somalia today. There is also no desire to let one of the clans take over the military and the country. Sending in U.S. troops may temporarily decrease the level of fighting, but it will not rebuild the cities or create a just Somalian state. The latter will require a new political, military, and economic policy in Washington.

NOTES

1. There are a number of good studies on the history and present condition of Somalia. Those I have used in preparing this essay are Harold D. Nelson, ed., *Somalia: A Country Study* (Washington: U.S. Government Printing Office, 3rd ed., 1981); David D. Laitin and Said S. Samatar, *Somalia: Nation in Search of a State* (Boulder, CO: Westview Press, 1987); Said S. Samatar, "Somalia: A Nation in Turmoil" (London: Minority Rights Group Report, 1991); and Richard Swift, ed., "Horror & Hope: The Horn of Africa," *The New Internationalist* 238 (December 1992).

2. See Samatar, "Somalia: A Nation in Turmoil," 30.

3. See Frances Moore Lappe and Joseph Collins, *World Hunger: Twelve Myths* (New York: Grove Weidenfeld, 1986), 77–94.

4. For these facts, see Lester R. Brown, Christopher Flavin, and Sandra Postel, *Saving the Planet: How to Shape an Environmentally Sustainable Global Economy* (New York: Norton, 1991), 150–51.

5. Quoted by Swift, "Horror & Hope," 18–19.

6. Alexander Cockburn, "Beat the Devil," *The Nation* (21 December 1992), 762.

ACCEPTING RESPONSIBILITY FOR U.S. ACTIONS ABROAD

Duane Cady

The Bush administration went out with the same bang that characterized its foreign policy for four years: U.S. military intervention. From Panama through Iraq to Somalia and back to Iraq, the solution was always, "Send in the Marines."

Perhaps the Clinton administration will pause to reflect on just how we got ourselves into Iraq and Somalia before continuing the Bush policies and committing troops to Bosnia or elsewhere. It's time the U.S. began taking responsibility for its role in causing these international crises so that others may be precluded. The media and the Congress put their energy into supporting the troops and praising the righteousness of Bush policies on Iraq and Somalia—and on questioning Clinton's resolve over Bosnia. What they should be doing is asking hard questions about why these situations arose.

We are reminded time and again that Saddam Hussein is an evil tyrant and a threat to stability in the Middle East. Widespread gloating over the U.S. victory in the Gulf was interrupted only to regret failing to finish off Saddam. Rarely are we reminded that the U.S. created this monster with millions of dollars of military aid, largely in an effort to use Iraq to check the threatened expansion throughout the Middle East of the Ayatollah's brand of Islamic fundamentalism. The price was arming Saddam to the point that the U.S. military has not been able to keep him under control, even with the weight of the United Nations behind the effort—and with more bombs dropped than in World War II. My point is that U.S. policy helped create Saddam's dangerous army by supplying much of the sophisticated weaponry now faced by U.S. troops monitoring the "peace" and enforcing the "no fly" zone.

U.S. policy played a major role in creating the situation in Somalia as well. When war broke out in a land dispute between Somalia and Ethiopia in 1977, the U.S. saw an opportunity to get a strategic foothold in the Horn of Africa. Both Somalia and Ethiopia had been aligned with the Soviet Union, but when the U.S.S.R. gave Ethiopia substantial military aid, General Mohammed Siad Barre turned to the U.S. for weapons and economic support.

Somalia lost the war with Ethiopia but to avoid Soviet domination of the region the U.S. sent large amounts of military aid to Somalia during the Reagan years. By the late 1980s, Siad Barre's rule depended heavily on the Marehan clan to keep him in power. In May of 1988, civil war broke out in the north with an uprising by the anti-Barre Somali National Movement, dominated by the Issak clan.

Siad Barre used his military against the guerrillas and killed thousands of civilians for their alleged support of the rebels. The war spread south and a second opposition group arose under the support of Hawiye and allied clans. According to Africa Watch, the government again committed atrocities against Somali civilians.

Siad Barre was overthrown in late January 1991. By then the U.S. was at war with Iraq. With the collapse of the Somali government, millions of dollars of weapons were seized by competing clans among rebel forces. These are the weapons being used against the U.S. and U.N. occupation forces today.

Our government sells its citizens on the humanitarian use of Marines to feed starving children—how can critics object to that? And our government sells its citizens on the necessity of putting down a dangerous rogue in Iraq who threatens the political stability of the Middle East and the world economy as well—and how can critics object to that? But our government fails to take responsibility for having helped create these deplorable situations through manipulative economic and military "aid." And today we hear calls for sending more weapons and even troops to Eastern Europe.

There is another thing our government sells: weapons. I read in the Twin Cities press that the U.S. has sold weapons to 142 of the 180 members of the United Nations; presumably the former U.S.S.R. sold to the other 38. Very often such weapons are paid for by U.S. taxpayers in the form of foreign aid. A lot of money has been made in the weapons industry—in the mid-to-late 1980s, the profit margin in the U.S. weapons industry was nearly double that of the rest of the economy. But while weapons contractors were making money, the proliferation of arms throughout the world helped create the very problems our government then calls upon our military to fight. This requires even more sophisticated weapons, not to mention risking lives of young Americans. Even now Clinton is under pressure to send arms to Islamic forces in Bosnia so they can "defend themselves."

The situations in Iraq and Somalia are very complex. I do not want to oversimplify them by pointing out the role of U.S. weapons sales in creating them. But I do want to call for accepting responsibility for the consequences of U.S. economic and military aid policies.

The starvation of hundreds of thousands in Somalia is not just because of famine, poor food distribution, or clan rivalries. Iraq is not just a mess because a "madman" has come to power. U.S. foreign policy has played major and direct roles in creating both situations. And the Serb atrocities in the former Yugoslavia are not only ethnic rivalries; superpower politics during the cold war only deepened resentments and armed competing factions.

Perhaps all of this in fact "justifies" U.S. involvement in these countries. Since kindergarten we've all been told, "Clean up after yourself when you make a mess." But we've also been told, "Better still, try not to make a mess in the first place." As simplistic as it may sound, we would take a big step in the right direction if the U.S. government quit supplying so many governments with weapons. U.S. foreign policy and arms industries have helped make the world a deadly place. National Rifle Association fans are fond of saying, "Guns don't kill people; people kill people." While there may be some truth to this, U.S. policy and U.S. weapons producers have certainly made the killing more efficient, more frequent, and more likely.

BOSNIA AND SOMALIA: WHY IS IT SO HARD TO STOP MASSACRE AND GENOCIDE?

Robert Paul Churchill

The hell to be endured hereafter, of which theology tells, is no worse than the hell we make for ourselves in this world by habitually fashioning our characters in the wrong way.

—William James, *The Principles of Psychology*, 1890

Historians have persuaded us, not without reason, to designate certain periods of the past as ages of particular distinction. Thus, for example, we speak of the "Classical Age of Greece" or the "Age of Pericles," of the "Age of Exploration," of the "Age of Renaissance and Reformation," and of the "Age of Enlightenment." But how will our successors look back on the second half of the twentieth century? Will our era be known as the age of genocide and terror, or perhaps the "Age of Atrocity"? The philosopher Camus was prepared to call the twentieth century an age of murder. And, indeed, it has been estimated that politically sanctioned mass murder in this century has claimed the lives of men, women, and children totaling more than 60 million, 20 to 40 million of which must be regarded as due to genocide, depending upon the definition of "genocide" employed.[1]

But will the twenty-first century brook an end to mass slaughter and genocide? Will this age of atrocity be succeeded by an age of greater respect for life and human rights? This is our hope and dream, of course, but you must forgive me for not feeling very optimistic. Already we are witnessing resurgent nationalists calling for the creation of fictive homelands purified of "alien peoples" in many parts of former Eastern Europe as well as within the remnants of the former "Soviet Empire." Actual genocide or its real potential is already present in the Serbian nationalists' "ethnic cleansing" in Bosnia and in conflicts between Armenians and Azerbijanis. New civil wars and acts of aggression tragically similar to events in Bosnia are already underway or imminent in Macedonia, Moldovia, Georgia, and some of the new Republics of Central Asia. Nor is the threat of genocide and political massacre restricted to lands recently under the shadow of Soviet repression. We need only remember the continuing threat of crimes against humanity committed against the

Kurds by the Ba'athist regime in Baghdad; the north-south civil war in Somalia and the massacres of northern civilians that led to massive starvation and the present crisis; chronic warfare and persistent repression in Sudan and Myanmar (Burma); serious risks of renewed warfare along ethnic or religious lines in Ethiopia and Sri Lanka, India, Nigeria, and Pakistan; and the continued threats of extinction of indigenous groups in places such as Guatemala, Brazil, Ecuador, Peru, Bolivia, and Paraguay, either through direct assault or by the process of "genocide by ecocide." In *Minorities at Risk*, a study of 200 minorities since the end of World War II, Ted Gurr finds that violent ethnic conflicts in the Third World have steadily increased in frequency and intensity since the 1960s.[2] Even the recent political measures taken in Germany against Gypsies and Rumanian "guest-workers," as well as the violence of neo-Nazi skinheads, are causes for grave concern.

Why does it look as though the toll in human life from genocide, mass murder, and torture will continue to be high in the twenty-first century? Why is it so difficult to rid the world of the specter of torture, mass murder, and genocide?[3] This question must itself be divided into two further questions:

1. Why is it so difficult to stop torture and genocide when it is known by the international community to be occurring?
2. Why is it so difficult to end or prevent the processes by which target groups become the victims of mass torture and genocide?

In connection with the inability to stop known and ongoing genocides, we must wonder why the U.S. government continued to support Indonesia during the "politicide" of 1965–1967 when as many as half a million supposed communists were slaughtered; why it was so difficult for the international community to stop the "autogenocide" led by Pol Pot and the Khmer Rouge in Kampuchea from mid-1975 to 1978; and why the United Nations and the European Economic Community seems virtually paralyzed in the face of present Serbian-led genocide in Bosnia-Herzegovina. In connection with the second question, we must wonder what it is about the human psyche, and about the group psychology of collectivities, that makes it so easy for a people to turn a target population into "the enemy," to legitimize the murder of members of this target group, and to proceed with mass murder in what is often a methodical and apparently rational and conscientious manner.

Many people believe that there is a readily evident answer to the first question: "Why is it so hard to end genocide and torture once it is undertaken as a state policy?" They believe the answer has to do with the failure of the state system and the "legitimist" instruments created by this system—notably the United Nations and non-governmental organizations (NGOs) operating in coexistence with it—to adequately protect human rights.

This is the view taken by such leading authorities as sociologists Helen Fein in *Accounting for Genocide* and Leo Kuper in a number of works, most notably *The Prevention of Genocide,* and by political scientist Barbara Harff in *Genocide and Human Rights*.[4] All three authors note a fundamental conflict within international law itself: the Genocide Convention forbids governments to take steps to destroy any distinct national, ethnic, or religious group, and Article 3 of the Universal Declaration of Human Rights asserts that "everyone has the right to life, liberty, and security of person." Such treaty provisions demanding that fundamental rights be regarded as superior to the laws of sovereign states collide with the long-standing principles in international law of "self-determination" and "non-intervention."

This conflict of principles is itself embedded in the Charter of the United Nations. The latter principles are enshrined in Article 2 which prohibits intervention in matters that are within the domestic jurisdiction of a state, while Article 34 empowers the Security Council to investigate disputes that cause international friction; Article 51 and Chapter VIII of the Charter offer regional organizations the legal justification for collective intervention. The present situation in Bosnia well illustrates the paralysis of the United Nations resulting from conflicting international law. If Bosnia is to be regarded as an independent state (as the U.N. did in granting Bosnia a seat in the General Assembly), then, under Article 51, the Bosnians have the right of self-defense, including the right to ask for outside assistance. If one denies that Bosnia is an independent state, as does the Serbian successor to the federal Yugoslav government, then the situation is one of civil war between a state and a secessionist region. In the latter case, the Security Council is still empowered to execute collective measures in virtue of ample evidence that the Serbian state has committed crimes against humanity. But the specific actions to be taken are to be decided by the Security Council, with the assistance of the Military Staff Committee, an archaic structure in which the former imperial powers play a predominant role. It is hardly surprising that Serbia-Montenegro claims to be victimized by a new brand of imperialism under the guise of the "new world order."

Unblocking this impasse would require that U.N. member states, with the capacity to enforce sanctions, assert that the protection of international human rights should prevail over assertions of national sovereignty. But, as Barbara Harff notes, "What has been lacking time and time again, on the part of states with the capacity to act is the political will to take a strong stand and accept the consequences of boldness."[5]

But even very powerful states, such as the United States, the lonely super power, are not likely to attack directly the principle of national sovereignty, especially not under circumstances which would establish a clear precedent for international law. The simple truth is that recognition of the limited national sovereignty of one member, in a state system premised on basic equality among sovereign territorial states, requires, as the price of logical consistency, recognition of the limited sovereignty of every other state. It is hardly surprising, therefore, that the historical precedents for humanitarian intervention to end genocide (India in East Pakistan, Bangladesh in 1971; Vietnam in Kampuchea in 1978; and Tanzania in Uganda in 1977) have been unilateral, have not been undertaken under international auspices, and have involved the pursuit of the intervenor's own national interests.[6]

In his *Agenda for Peace*, issued 17 July 1992, the new U.N. Secretary-General, Boutros Boutros-Ghali, insists that the U.N. focus more on threats to international security arising from "ethnic, religious, social, cultural, or religious strife."[7] And there may be ways in which the international state system will evolve away from dependence upon fundamental assumptions of state sovereignty and towards acceptance of human rights priorities as its new foundations. Both Barbara Harff and Helen Fein have some useful suggestions, which if implemented would facilitate this process of "evolution," such as setting-up an early-warning system of impending danger (perhaps taking the form of an UN sponsored news bureau with instant access to satellite telecommunications to assure global distribution of news and reports—a CNN for Peace); establishing an independent human rights data bank headed by scholars, journalists, lawyers, and others who are skilled at weighing contested evidence and committed to making judgments about risks to target groups; reinvigorating and inventing more daring and aggressive means for intervention by NGO human rights groups, e.g., such "conscience constituencies" as Amnesty International and the International Commission for Justice (ICJ); training members of potential target groups in the strategies and tactics of nonviolent resistance as practiced by Gandhi and King; and increasing reliance on limited, selective, and "interdictive" applications of military force.[8] Certainly there is a desperate need for the invention of new, creative methods of thwarting the efforts of genocidal states. As Helen Fein grimly notes, "It is ironic that the organized defenders of animals subjected to mass slaughter are so much more daring, aggressive, and inventive than are the NGO's protecting people. Can we imagine nonviolent intervenors using the same techniques employed to protect endangered species protecting peoples by 'shaming', confronting the killers, moving into the region where the kill takes place, and interposition?"[9]

But while some "legitimist" scholars believe that the state system can be salvaged so as to more effectively prevent or end genocidal practices, other commentators believe that the state is the crucial link between the two questions: "Why can't we stop genocide when it happens?" and "Why can't we prevent it from happening in the future?" For this second group, it is axiomatic that the state system is itself the culprit. In his Introduction to *State Violence and Ethnicity*, Pierre L. van den Berghe argues that the state "has been the prime killer in human history" and that states are "killing machines."[10] The historian Dwynne Dyer quotes Dwight MacDonald to the effect that "We must get the modern national state before it gets us," and argues in *War* that the state came into existence to define enemies and to wage war. Dyer says, "States are principally organizations for the accumulation of power in the pursuit of security, and their most significant distinguishing characteristic is the possession of military forces." Dyer adds, "What makes the government of a sovereign state like Greece different in kind from the government of a large city like New York...is Greece's ability and even its right (in War) to kill foreigners." Dyer insists that the end of military atrocity, if not the preservation of our species, requires the transformation of the state system into a single global culture.[11]

I am hopeful that the "legitimist" efforts of Helen Fein, Barbara Harff, and others to "make the state system work the way it ought to work" will lead to the ending of genocidal practices actually attempted by states. This would be a most important advance, although it would not strike at the root of the problem itself, the social psychological dynamics—the processes—that lead to the formation of the capacity to commit or accept genocide. Moreover, I reject as utopian the view that genocide would end if we ended the state system itself. One reason to be skeptical about the brightness of a future without states is the very real possibility that the state system is now in its death throes, but rather than experiencing a diminution of the sense of the legitimacy of a collectivity to kill those under its power who do not "fit in," we may be wandering into newer and different, but more lethal "killing fields." Human beings do not need states to divide up into bonded groups that conceive themselves ideologically as homogeneous and that feel it legitimate to rid themselves of humans in their midst who do not fit their concept of exclusive "we-ness." The historical origins of the modern state system can be dated to the end of the bloody Thirty Years' War and the Treaty of Westphalia in 1643. But before that time Roman Catholics did not need an identity as citizens of a political state to attempt the destruction of the Huguenots or to annihilate centuries earlier the Cathars and Albigensians; nor did the Crusaders need such an identity to commit massacres that approached genocide in their consequences. Alternatively, if the state is, in its fundament, just an organization the members of which believe it legitimate to kill those designated by the collectivity as "enemies" or misfits, then humans shall never be rid of the state, even if the process of balkanization now occurring in Eastern Europe and the former Soviet Empire continues almost *ad infinitum*. So much seems to be conceded by Pierre L. van den Berghe who defines the state as "those individuals who, singly or collectively, manipulate to whatever ends the coercive apparatus for which they claim legitimacy."[12]

Turning to the second question about the origins of torture and genocide in the human psyche, there is now a large body of literature in psychology, psychotherapy, history, and sociology on genocide, the Holocaust, the psychological bases for cruelty and obedience to authority, moral inhibitions against violence, and the psychological and social functions of political torture.[13] Much of this literature suggests the following thesis: human beings are, in short, natural enemy-making animals, but it is terribly important that humans do not "get stuck" in this enemy-making process. More specifically, this thesis can itself be divided into two parts.

First, it can be argued that the formation of individual self-identity and the need for self-esteem make individuals prone to temporarily devalue others who are defined as "different" from oneself or one's selected peers. When the process of identity-formation is completed without serious distortion, then the resulting individual is an autonomous "extensive person" who is no longer prone to devalue other persons and who finds it relatively easy to empathize with persons different from him or herself. But when the formation of self-identity is severely disturbed and the development of self-esteem thwarted, then the resulting individual is a dependent, "constricted person"[14] who, severely wounded in his or her sense of self-worth, remains highly vulnerable to the temptation to devalue and victimize others. These persons might be regarded collectively as potential perpetrators, for under certain circumstances they will self-select or be easily co-opted into collective processes of degradation and victimization of a designated scapegoat group. Others, not so deeply wounded in their sense of self-worth, might be regarded as "bystanders" or, depending upon their degree of "extensivity," as resistors or as rescuers, for they will not find themselves so easily drawn into socially organized processes of victimization and may actually resist or even assist those selected as victims.

The second part of the thesis maintains that, because this process of identity formation is replicated in all persons, it can on occasion be represented symbolically and ideologically for a collectivity as a whole. More specifically, there may be shocks to the sense of the security, esteem, or well-being of the collectivity as a whole that mobilize potential perpetrators to form parties or groups that accept the degradation and victimization of an "outgroup" as legitimate and that seek to rationalize the destruction of "outgroup" victims as necessary for self-defense or as required to promote interests the perpetrators view as indispensably linked to their own identity and sense of self-worth. In this latter case, the collectivity—whether state, nation, tribe, or some other affinity group—takes on, at an abstract and symbolic level, this process of enemy-making; in other words, the state or collectivity itself becomes a representation of its people's need for enemies, and its own resources of bureaucratic organization, technological infrastructure, and military coercion become available for mass murder. Hence the increased lethality of genocide in the modern, bureaucratic, and technological state.[15]

In summary, this thesis about genocide thus claims the conjunction of two sets of processes:

1. psychodynamic difficulties of self-identity and self-esteem that result in a population of potential perpetrators with continuing needs for the degradation of others, and
2. the convergence of the interests and energies of "self-selecting" potential perpetrators on abstract, symbolic, cultural, and social expressions of the "collectivization" of these needs for enemy-making.

These two processes, together with well known tendencies toward obedience to authority and moral indifference,[16] result both in the legitimation of the degradation of others and in the ease with which the victimization of "outgroups" leads to genocide.

There is now, more than ever, the need for philosophers to participate more actively in the process of understanding the causes of genocide. Hannah Arendt's 1964 study *Eichmann in Jerusalem*[17] was a dramatic demonstration of the contribution of philosophy toward understanding the "banality of evil" involved in the Holocaust. Other philosophers, notably Alan Rosenberg and Abigail Rosenthal, also have made major contributions.[18] What is now needed is a more concerted effort made by philosophers to explore and evaluate the thesis outlined above, for the practitioners of no other discipline are better poised than philosophers to employ analytical techniques in assessing the adequacy of explanatory hypotheses. Philosophers are needed to assess the adequacy of the concepts formed in these explanations, to question the logical consistency and coherence of various claims, to evaluate the reliability of the evidence, and to establish criteria for the testing of explanatory hypotheses. I see no reason, for example, why philosophers cannot occupy a role in testing hypotheses in the "human sciences" analogous to those usually adopted by natural scientists in testing hypotheses in the physical sciences. Why not regard the above thesis about genocide as an explanatory hypothesis and ask what we would predict, i.e., expect to discover (e.g., in the historical record, as a result of psychological experimentation), if this hypothesis is correct?

In addition, by relying on the tools of synthesis, philosophers can contribute to a new "syncretism": to a possible understanding of human cruelty and destructiveness available only in the overview of generalists. On the one hand, psychologists and social scientists have given us new, hard won insights into the human capacity for cruelty displayed in genocide. On the other hand, it seems surprising that, given its frequency, genocide should seem so alien and therefore that understanding it should be so taxing to scholars. The ancient philosopher Heraclitus noted that humans "are estranged from what is most familiar and they must seek out what is in itself evident."[19] So perhaps the major task before us is not so much to grasp what is inherently difficult to understand as it is to see more familiar things in a new way, and to take a new attitude toward them. In its "syncretic" role, philosophy may help us understand how grave brutality and unspeakable horror may arise from what is common, even unremarkable, in personal and social existence. Perhaps we will discover that it is true, as J. Glenn Gray believed, that "the impulses that make killers are not so different in kind from those that make lovers."[20] More important, perhaps we will discover what to do with such "truths." But whatever the outcome, we cannot stand aside cultivating our philosophical "gardens" and watch the innocent devoured by the flames of hatred. We are all Bosnians. We are all Serbians.[21]

NOTES

1. Roger W. Smith, "Human Destructiveness and Politics: The Twentieth Century as an Age of Genocide," *Genocide and the Modern Age*, edited by Isidor Wallimann and Michael N. Dobkowski (New York: Greenwood Press, 1987), 21–39.

2. *Minorities at Risk: A Global View of Ethnopolitical Conflict* (United States Institute of Peace Press, 1993).

3. I cannot here discuss difficulties with the definition of genocide. The concept has been highly politicized both by those who have sought to extend its meaning to protect potential victims as well as by states denying that genocide has occurred within their borders. For present purposes, I rely on a modified version of the definition proposed by Raphael Lemkin, who coined the term in his pioneering study of 1944 called *Axis Rule in Occupied Europe* (Washington: Carnegie Endowment for International Peace, 1944). For Lemkin, genocide was essentially a coordinated and planned effort to destroy a national, religious, racial, or ethnic group with the aim of annihilating it physically or culturally. I push the extension of the concept to include "politicide" (the massacre of a group based on its political affiliation), "autogenicide" (the physical liquidation by the state of its own citizens as occurred among the Khmer Rouge in Kampuchea), and mass torture (as in the "disappearances" of Argentina in the 1970s). For a very helpful discussion of the difficulty of defining genocide, see Kurt Jonassohn and Frank Chalk, "A Typology of Genocide and Some Implications for the Human Rights Agenda," in *Genocide and the Modern Age*.

4. See Helen Fein, *Accounting for Genocide* (New York: Free Press, 1979);

Leo Kuper, *The Prevention of Genocide* (New York: Yale University Press, 1985); and Barbara Harff, *Genocide and Human Rights* (Denver: University of Denver Press, 1984).

5. Barbara Harff, "Bosnia and Somalia: Strategic, Legal, and Moral Dimensions of Humanitarian Intervention," *Report from the Institute for Philosophy & Public Policy* 12:3–4 (Summer/Fall, 1992, 3.

6. More hopeful recent precedents are the Liberian case, in which a West African peacekeeping force, operating under international auspices, temporarily stabilized the country and facilitated negotiations among the principal factions (although fighting has recently been renewed); the establishment under international auspices of security zones for the Iraqi-Kurdish and Iraqi-Shiite populations (probably possible only because Iraq is a pariah state with a long history of genocidal actions and human rights abuses); and the presence in Somalia of UN sanctioned military forces of member states—principally the United States—and the probable role of the UN in establishing interim, internationally sponsored trusteeships to rebuild civil administration and basic services.

7. Cited by Harff, *Genocide and Human Rights*, 5.

8. See Helen Fein, "Scenarios of Genocide: Models of Genocide and Critical Responses" in *Toward the Understanding and Prevention of Genocide*, ed., Israel W. Charny (Boulder, CO: Westview Press, 1984), 3–31; and Harff, "Bosnia and Somalia," *Genocide and Human Rights*.

9. Fein, "Scenarios of Genocide,*"* 27.

10. Pierre L. van den Berghe, ed., *State Violence and Ethnicity* (Niwot, CO: University Press of Colorado, 1990), 1.

11. Gwynne Dyer, *War* (New York: Crown, 1985), 157. See especially Chapters 1, 7, and 11. The MacDonald quotation is at 253.

12. Ibid., 1.

13. The following are among the most important works making up the body of this literature: Israel W. Charny, *How Can We Commit the Unthinkable?* (Boulder, CO: Westview, 1982); Israel W. Charny, ed., *Toward the Understanding and Prevention of Genocide* (Boulder, CO: Westview, 1984); Gwynne Dyer, *War* (New York: Crown, 1985); Sam Keen, *Faces of the Enemy: Reflections of the Hostile Imagination* (San Francisco: Harper & Row, 1986); Herbert C. Kelman and V. Lee Hamilton, *Crimes of Obedience* (New York: Yale University Press, 1987); Frank Graziano, *Divine Violence: Spectacle, Psychosexuality, and Radical Christianity in the Argentine 'Dirty War'* (Boulder, CO: Westview, 1992); Robert Jay Lifton, *The Nazi Doctors: Medicalized Killing and the Psychology of Genocide* (New York: Basic Books, 1986); Alice Miller, *For Your Own Good: Hidden Cruelty in Child-Rearing and the Roots of Violence* (New York: Noonday Press, 1990); Samuel P. Oliner and Pearl M. Oliner, *The Altruistic Personality: Rescuers of Jews in Nazi Europe* (New York: Free Press, 1988); David Paskins, ed., *The Anthropology of Evil* (London: Basil Blackwell, 1985); M. Scott Peck, *People of the Lie* (New York: Simon and Schuster, 1983); Edward Peters, *Torture* (London: Basil Blackwell, 1986); Elaine Scarry, *The Body in Pain: The Making and Unmaking of the World* (New York: Oxford University Press, 1985); Ervin Staub, *The Roots of Evil: The Origins of Genocide and Other Group Violence* (Cambridge, England: Cambridge University Press, 1989); Vamik D. Volkan, *The Need for Enemies and Allies: From*

Clinical Practice to International Relations (Dunmore, PA: Jason Aronson, 1986); Isidor Wallimann and Michael N. Dobkowski, eds., *Genocide and the Modern Age* (New York: Greenwood Press, 1987).

14. I borrow the concepts of "extensive persons" and "constricted persons" from Oliner and Oliner, *The Altruistic Personality*; see especially 142–260.

15. In this connection, it is telling that Hitler remarked to Hermann Rauschning that had the supply of Jewish victims given out, he, as *Führer*, would have been forced to "invent" new "Jews." Quoted by Irving Louis Horowitz, "The Exclusivity of Collective Death," *Genocide in the Modern Era*, 70.

16. See Stanley Milgram, *Obedience to Authority* (New York: Harper & Row, 1969); Herbert Kelman and Lee Hamilton, *Crimes of Obedience;* Robert Jay Lifton, *The Nazi Doctors*; and Rainer C. Baum, "Holocaust: Moral Indifference as *the* Form of Modern Evil" and George M. Kern, "The Holocaust: Moral Theory and Immoral Acts," both in *Echoes from the Holocaust,* edited by Alan Rosenberg and Gerald E. Myers (Philadelphia: Temple University Press, 1988), 53–90 and 245–261, respectively.

17. Hannah Arendt, *Eichmann in Jerusalem: A Report on the Banality of Evil* (New York: Viking Press, 1964).

18. See Rosenberg and Myers, *Echoes*, and Abigail L. Rosenthal, *A Good Look at Evil* (Philadelphia: Temple University Press, 1987).

19. Heraclitus, frag. B72, in *Die Fragmente der Vorsokratiker*, 10th ed., edited by Hermann Diels and Walter Kranz (Berlin, 1953), translated by Jonathan Barnes, *Early Greek Philosophy* (Harmondsworth: Penguin Books, 1978), 155.

20. J. Glenn Gray, *The Warriors: Reflections on Men in Battle* (New York: Harper, 1959), 232–233.

21. This chapter is a revision of an address delivered to the William James Forum at Washington College, Maryland, on 24 February 1993, and represents research for my forthcoming book, *The Evil that 'Good' Men Do.*

ABOUT THE AUTHORS

LAURENCE F. BOVE is Professor of Philosophy at Walsh University, North Canton, Ohio. Born in Brooklyn, New York, he received his B.A. in Philosophy at St. John's University in 1969. He served two and a half years in the U.S. Air Force. Resuming his philosophical studies in 1972, he concentrated on the philosophy of the human person and the relationship between human love and being. He received his Ph.D. from St. John's University. A member of the executive committee of Concerned Philosophers for Peace, Bove's publications examine issues concerning the philosophy and practice of nonviolence.

DUANE CADY is Professor of Philosophy and Department Chair at Hamline University, St. Paul, Minnesota. He received his Ph.D. from Brown University. Cady is the author of *From Warism to Pacifism: A Moral Continuum* and various journal articles on ethics and history of philosophy. He was President of Concerned Philosophers for Peace in 1991.

ROBERT PAUL CHURCHILL is Professor and Chair of the Department of Philosophy at George Washington University. His research interests include social and political philosophy, applied ethics, philosophical psychology, and philosophy and public policy. His special interest in pacifism and nonviolent resistance began with his dissertation research on civil disobedience; he received his Ph.D. from The Johns Hopkins University in 1975. In addition to editing *The Ethics of Liberal Democracy*, Churchill is author of *Becoming Logical* as well as numerous articles including "Vaclav Havel's The Power of the Powerless and the Philosophy of Nonviolent Resistance," "Public and Private Choice: A Philosophical Analysis," and "Nonviolent Resistance as the Moral Equivalent of War." He is currently preparing a monograph on the philosophical foundations of nonviolent resistance.

LINDA RENNIE FORCEY, Professor in the School of Education and Human Development at Binghamton University (SUNY), teaches courses in women's and peace studies. She is author of *Mothers of Sons: Toward an Understanding of Responsibility* and editor or co-editor of *Disarmament, Economic Conversion, and the Management of Peace*; *Yearning to Breathe Free: Liberation Theologies in the U.S.*; and *Peace: Meanings, Politics, Strategies*. She is currently working on a study, "Women Thinking about Peace," which will include her reflections on women and peace in India, based on her recent experiences as a Fulbright scholar.

BARRY L. GAN is an Associate Professor of Philosophy at St. Bonaventure University, where he has taught since 1984. He coordinates the university's program in Justice, Peace, and Conflict Studies and teaches courses in news media ethics as well as war and morality. He is editor of *The Acorn: Journal of the Gandhi-King Society* and occasionally serves as a volunteer mediator in his community. He received his Ph.D. in philosophy from the University of Rochester in 1984.

CELINA GARCIA coordinates the Latin American Peace Studies Program (Programa Latino Americano de Estudios Para la Paz) at the University of Costa Rica. She lives in San Jose, Costa Rica.

WILLIAM C. GAY is Associate Professor of Philosophy at the University of North Carolina at Charlotte where he teaches courses dealing with issues of war, peace, and justice. He is coauthor of *The Nuclear Arms Race*, coeditor of *On the Eve of the 21st Century: Perspectives of Russian and American Philosophers*, editor of a special 1984 issue on "Philosophy and the Debate on Nuclear Weapons Systems and Policies" of *Philosophy and Social Criticism*, and current editor of *Concerned Philosophers for Peace Newsletter*. He has also published over a dozen articles and several bibliographies on nuclear weapons and nonviolence and lectured on these topics in the U.S., Canada, Germany, and the former Soviet Union.

WARREN HARRINGTON is Professor of Theology at Walsh University, North Canton, Ohio. He received his Ph.D. in Theology from Fordham University and has taught at Salve Regina University, Newport, Rhode Island, and Sacred Heart

University, Bridgeport, Connecticut. His dissertation was "Conversion as Foundation of Theology: An Interpretation of Bernard Lonergan's Method." Other writings on method have been published in *Cross Currents: Religion and Intellectual Life*; *Living Light*; and *Journal of Ecumenical Studies*.

RON HIRSCHBEIN coordinates a concentration in War and Peace Studies at California State University, Chico. He has also served as Visiting Research Philosopher at the University of California's Institute on Global Conflict and Cooperation in La Jolla. His *Newest Weapons/Oldest Psychology* analyzes the interplay of the rational and irrational forces that inform American strategic theory and practice. He has also published numerous essays on topics such as deterrence and the balance of power. He is currently developing a hermeneutical account of the narratives political actors invoke to conceptualize and manage international crises.

ROBERT L. HOLMES received his A.B. from Harvard University and his Ph.D. from the University of Michigan. He is currently Professor of Philosophy at the University of Rochester. He served as a Fellow at the National Humanities Institute at Yale University from 1976–1977, Senior Fulbright Lecturer at Moscow State University in 1983, and Faculty Fellow at the Kroc Institute for International Peace Studies at the University of Notre Dame in 1991. He is editor of *Nonviolence in Theory and Practice* and author of *On War and Morality* and *Basic Moral Philosophy*.

DAVID E. JOHNSON, Professor of Philosophy at the U.S. Naval Academy since 1971, has taught at the University of Iowa, Augustana (Illinois) College, and in the undergraduate and graduate programs of St. John's College, Annapolis. He was a visiting lecturer in the Department of Philosophy, University of Gothenburg, Sweden, during 1966–1967. In addition to ethical issues of peace and war, his teaching and research focus on philosophy of religion and philosophy of mind. He has served as the only civilian member of the board of the Joint Services Conference on Professional Ethics and is currently an A.P.A. Eastern Division representative for Concerned Philosophers for Peace. He chairs the Philosophers' Committee of the Bertrand Russell Society. In fall 1990, he was a visiting fellow at the Centre for Peace Research at Australian National University, Canberra.

TOMIS KAPITAN is Associate Professor of Philosophy at Northern Illinois University, DeKalb. After receiving his doctorate from Indiana University, he spent five years teaching at Birzeit University in the Israeli-occupied West Bank before returning to the United States in 1986. Within his primary field of research, metaphysics, he has worked on the alethic, practical and attitudinal modalities, particularly as these concern action, practical freedom, and responsibility. He has also conducted research on reasoning, reference, and the philosophy of religion. His work has appeared in *American Philosophical Quarterly, Analysis, Erkenntnis, Logique et Analyse, History and Philosophy of Logic, The Monist, Noûs, Philosophical Studies, The Philosophical Quarterly, Religious Studies*, and other journals. An avid student of Middle Eastern history, he has frequently lectured on Islam and the Middle East and is currently editing a volume of philosophical essays on the Israeli-Palestinian conflict.

LAURA DUHAN KAPLAN is Assistant Professor of Philosophy at the University of North Carolina at Charlotte, where she teaches philosophy and women's studies. Her essays in the areas of feminist peace studies and philosophy of education have appeared in *Hypatia, Educational Theory*, and *Teaching Philosophy*, as well as in various anthologies. She is currently writing on the phenomenology and ethics of self-reflection.

JOSEPH C. KUNKEL is Professor of Philosophy at the University of Dayton, where he teaches courses in ethics, ethics and modern war, and philosophy of peace. He is coeditor of *Issues in War and Peace: Philosophical Inquiries* and *In the Interest of Peace: A Spectrum of Philosophical Views*. He is also author of a number of essays that examine various ethical approaches to issues of modern warfare. He has been a member of Concerned Philosophers for Peace since its inception in 1981 and has served as Executive Secretary from 1989–1995.

STEPHEN NATHANSON was educated at Swarthmore College and The Johns Hopkins University. Since 1972, he has taught at Northeastern University, where he is Professor of Philosophy. He is the author of *The Ideal of Rationality*; *An Eye for an Eye?*; *The Immorality of Punishing by Death*; *Should We Consent to be Governed?*; *A Short Introduction to Political Philosophy*; and *Patriotism, Morality and Peace*.

JACK PERRY is Professor of Political Science and Director of the Dean Rusk Program in International Studies at Davidson College in North Carolina. He began his academic career in 1982, after retiring from a twenty-four year diplomatic career. From 1959 through 1983, Perry worked as a U.S. Foreign Service Officer, serving in Moscow, Paris, Prague, Stockholm, and NATO. From 1978–1979, he was Deputy Executive Director of the State Department and from 1979–1981 was Amassador to Bulgaria. He has authored chapters in books on the U.S.S.R., Eastern Europe, arms control, and public diplomacy and published articles in *The American Scholar, Armed Forces Journal, Publishers Weekly,* and numerous newspapers. He is author of *Light From Light,* a meditation on The Sermon on the Mount.

JERALD RICHARDS teaches philosophy and is Coordinator of the Philosophy and Religious Studies Programs at Northern Kentucky University. He teaches courses in ethics, social and political philosophy, and peace studies and has published articles on justified war morality, nuclear deterrence, nonviolence, and criminal punishment.

JONATHAN SCHONSHECK is professor of philosophy at Le Moyne College in Syracuse, New York. His areas of specialization include philosophy and public policy, philosophy and biology, and the philosophy of law. His work has appeared in *The Journal of Social Philosophy, Public Affairs Quarterly, The Philosophical Forum, Law and Philosophy,* and *Philosophy and Public Affairs. On Criminalization: An Essay in the Philosophy of the Criminal Law* is forthcoming in the Law and Philosophy Library, Kluwer Academic Publishers.

MICHAEL P. SENG is a professor at The John Marshall Law School where he teaches in the areas of Constitutional Law, Federal Jurisdiction and Comparative Law. He received his B.A. from the University of Notre Dame and his J.D. from the Notre Dame Law School. He was a Fulbright Professor at the University of Maiduguri in Nigeria in 1983-1984. Prior to his academic career, he was a civil rights attorney in Cairo, Illinois. He has written on a variety of legal subjects.

JAMES P. STERBA is professor of philosophy at the University of Notre Dame in Indiana, where he teaches political philosophy and applied ethics. He has written more than 100 articles and published 11 books, including *How to Make People Just; Morality in Practice* 4th ed.; *The Ethics of War and Nuclear Deterrence; Justice: Alternative Political Perspectives* 2nd ed.; *Contemporary Ethics; Feminist Philosophies;* and *Earth Ethics.* He is the past president of both the North American Society for Social Philosophy and Concerned Philosophers for Peace.

FREDERICK R. STRUCKMEYER is a professor of philosophy at West Chester University, West Chester, Pennsylvania. He has taught there since 1966. Since 1985, he has taught courses in peace studies, including a course on the philosophy of nonviolence. Presently he directs the university's minor in peace and conflict studies. As a peace activist, he has in recent years visited Nicaragua, the former Soviet Union, and Cuba.

BRUCE M. TAYLOR received his Ph.D. from Fordham University, where he concentrated in Modern European and Latin American history. He is Associate Professor of History at the University of Dayton and specializes in Latin America and in the application of value theory to the analysis of United States foreign policy leadership. He has collaborated in the writing of *Developing Human Values, Value Development: A Practical Guide*, and *Readings in Value Development*. Recent papers include value analyses of the decision to send U.S. forces into Panama and of the U.S. efforts to restrict drug traffic from South America. He is editorial consultant to Stack-Vaughn publishers for their series on Latin America for secondary school students.

RICHARD WERNER is Professor and Chair of Philosophy at Hamilton College. He is the author of "Ethical Realism," "Nuclear Deterrence and the Limits of Moral Theory," "South Africa: University Neutrality and Divestment," and other articles. He is co-editor, with Duane Cady, of *Just War, Nonviolence and Nuclear Deterrence*. Werner served as Eastern Division Representative to the American Philosophical Association for Concerned Philosophers for Peace during 1987–1991. At present, he is at working on the implications of pragmatism for social inquiry, the distortion of communication in America, the hidden cost of "winning" the cold war, and how these issues relate to democracy in the late twentieth century.

REFERENCE
BIBLIOGRAPHY

This reference bibliography is designed to assist scholars and others interested in carrying out further research in the philosophy of peace, especially on the issues and events discussed in this book. The bibliography includes the books, book chapters, and journal articles cited in the chapters of *From the Eye of the Storm*, as well as additional works recommended by the editors and authors. Legal cases, articles in the daily press, and government documents are cited in full in the Notes following each chapter and are not included in this bibliography. The references have been organized into the following subject headings:

1. General Works on War, Peace, Nonviolence, International Relations
2. Ethics, Morality, and Just War Theory
3. Feminism and Peace
4. Religion and Peace
5. Loyalty and Patriotism
6. Economic and Racial Justice
7. Genocide
8. Nuclear Weapons
9. International Law
10. Peace History
11. Specific Regional Conflicts
    A. The Persian Gulf War (U.S. Operation "Desert Storm")
    B. Palestine and Israel
    C. Latin America
    D. Bosnia and Somalia

1. General Works on War, Peace, Nonviolence, and International Relations

Althusser, Louis. *Lenin and Philosophy and Other Essays*. London: New Left Books, 1971.

Barsamian, David, ed. *Stenographers to Power*. Monroe, ME: Common Courage, 1992.

Benoit-Smullyan, Émile. "An American Foreign Policy For Survival." *Ethics* 56, 280–290.

Boulding, Elise *et al*. "Imaging the Future." *Friends Journal*, 15 April 1983.

Bourne, Randolph. *War and the Intellectuals: Collected Essays, 1915–1919*, edited by Cal Resek. New York: Harper & Row, 1964.

———. "The State." In *War and the Intellectuals*.

Bove, Laurence F. "Malcolm X and the Enigma of Martin Luther King, Jr.'s Nonviolence." *The Acorn: Journal of the Gandhi-King Society* 1992–1993: Fall–Winter, 18–23.

———. "Camus Revisited: Neither Victim nor Executioner." In *In the Interest of Peace*, edited by Kenneth H. Klein and Joseph C. Kunkel. Wakefield, NH: Longwood Academic, 1990.

———. "On Stories, Peacemaking, and Philosophical Method: Toward a Pluralistic Account of Nonviolence." In *Issues in War and Peace*, edited by Joseph C. Kunkel and Kenneth H. Klein. Wolfeboro, NH: Longwood Academic, 1989.

Cady, Duane L. *From Warism to Pacifism: A Moral Continuum.* Philadelphia: Temple University Press, 1989.

Churchill, Robert Paul. "Hobbes and the Assumption of Power." In *The Causes of Quarrel*, edited by Peter Caws. Boston: Beacon, 1989.

———. "Nonviolent Resistance as the Moral Equivalent of War." In *In the Interest of Peace*, edited by Kenneth H. Klein and Joseph C. Kunkel. Wakefield, NH: Longwood Academic, 1990.

———. "Vaclav Havel's *The Power of the Powerless and the Philosophy of Nonviolence.*" In *Just War, Nonviolence and Nuclear Deterrence*, edited by Duane L. Cady and Richard Werner. Wakefield, NH: Longwood Academic, 1991.

Dyer, Gwynne. *War.* New York: Crown, 1985.

Forcey, Linda Rennie, ed. *Peace: Meanings, Politics, Strategies.* New York: Praeger, October, 1989.

Gandhi, M. K. *Non-Violent Resistance.* New York: Schoken, 1951.

Gay, William C. "The Prospect for a Nonviolent Model of National Security." In *On the Eve of the 21st Century: Perspectives of Russian and American Philosophers*, edited by William C. Gay and T. A. Alekseeva. Lanham, MD: Rowman & Littlefield, 1993.

Gay, William C., and T. A. Alekseeva, eds. *On the Eve of the 21st Century: Perspectives of Russian and American Philosophers.* Lanham, MD: Rowman & Littlefield, 1993.

George, Jim. "International Relations and the Search for Thinking Space." *International Studies Quarterly* 33, 270.

Heller, M., and S. Nuseibeh. *No Trumpets, No Drums.* London: Tauris, 1991.

Hobbes, Thomas. *Leviathan.* In *Classics of Western Philosophy*, 2nd ed., edited by Steven M. Cahn. Indianapolis: Liberty, 1977.

Hollins, Harry *et al. The Conquest of War.* Boulder, CO: Westview, 1989.

Huxley, Aldous. *An Encyclopedia of Pacifism.* New York: Garland Publishing, 1972.

Kant, Immanuel. *Perpetual Peace and Other Essays on Politics, History, and Morals*, translated by Ted Humphrey. Indianapolis: Liberty, 1983.

Kellett, Christine Hunter. "Draft Registration and the Conscientious

Objector: A Proposal To Accommodate Constitutional Values." 15 *Colum. Hum. Rts. L. Rev.* 167 (1984).

Klein, Kenneth H., and Joseph C. Kunkel, eds. *In the Interest of Peace: A Spectrum of Philosophical Views.* Wakefield, NH: Longwood Academic, 1990.

Kunkel, Joseph C., and Kenneth H. Klein, eds. *Issues in War and Peace: Philosophical Inquiries.* Wolfeboro, NH: Longwood Academic, 1989.

Lapid, Yosef. "The Third Debate: On the Prospects of International Theory in a Post-Positivist Era." *International Studies Quarterly* 33, 235–254.

Lincoln, Bruce. *Discourse and the Construction of Society.* Oxford: Oxford University Press, 1989.

Lopez, George A. "Strategies for Curriculum Development." In *Peace and World Order Studies,* edited by Daniel Thomas and Michael Klare. Boulder, CO: Westview, 1989.

Musalo, Karen. "Swords into Ploughshares: Why the United States Should Provide Refuge to Young Men Who Refuse to Bear Arms for Reasons of Conscience." 25 *San Diego L. Rev. 849 (1989).*

Nelson-Pallmeyer, Jack. *Brave New World Order.* Maryknoll, NY: Orbis Books, 1992.

Newcombe, Hanna. *Alternative International Security Systems.* Dundas, Ontario: Peace Research Institute, 1982.

———. *Cooperation in the Light of Peace Research.* Dundas, Ontario: Peace Research Institute, n.d.

Patchen, Martin. *Resolving Disputes Between Nations: Coercion or Conciliation?* Durham, NC: Duke University Press Policy Studies, 1988.

Reardon, Betty A. "Toward a Paradigm of Peace." In *Peace: Meanings, Politics, Strategies,* edited by Linda Rennie Forcey. New York: Praeger, 1989.

Ridgeway, James, ed. *The March to War.* New York: Four Walls Eight Windows, 1991.

Russell, Bertrand. *History of Western Philosophy and Its Connection with Political and Social Circumstance from the Earliest Times to the Present Day.* Boston: Unwin, 1979.

Roseanu, Pauline. "Once Again into the Fray: International Relations Confronts the Humanities." *Millennium* 19, 83–105.

Safieh, Afif. "Gene Sharp: Nonviolent Struggle." *Journal of Palestine Studies* 17:1, 37–55.

Thomas, Daniel C., ed. *Guide to Careers and Graduate Education in Peace Studies.* Amherst, MA: Five College Program in Peace and World Security Studies, 1987.

Tolstoy, Leo. *Tolstoy's Writings on Civil Disobedience and Non-violence.* New York: New American Library, 1968.

Urquhart, Brian. *A Life in Peace and War*. New York: Harper & Row, 1987.

Vlastos, Gregory. *Socrates: Ironist and Moral Philosopher*. Ithaca, NY: Cornell University Press, 1991.

Vogel, Lise. "The Earthly Family." *Radical America* 1973: July–October, 9–50.

Walker, R. R. J. "Genealogy, Geopolitics and Political Community: Richard K. Ashley and the Critical Social Theory of International Politics." *Alternatives* 13, 86.

Walzer, Michael. *Interpretation and Social Criticism*. Cambridge, MA: Harvard University Press, 1987.

Whitehead, A. N. *Science and Philosophy*. New York: Philosophical Library, 1948.

Woito, Robert. *To End War: A New Approach to International Conflict*. New York: Pilgrim, 1982.

2. Ethics, Morality, and Just War Theory

Berrigan, Daniel. "Guns Don't Work." *National Catholic Reporter*, 5 May 1978, 12.

Cady, Duane L., and Richard Werner, eds. *Just War, Nonviolence, and Nuclear Deterrence*. Wakefield, NH: Longwood Academic, 1991.

Churchill, R. Paul. "Humanism, Pacifism and the Dilemma of Defense." *Contemporary Philosophy* 7:9, 11–17.

_____, ed. *The Ethics of Liberal Democracy: Morality and Democracy in Theory and Practice*. New York: Berg Publishers, 1993.

_____. "Public and Private Choice: A Philosophical Analysis." In *Moral Dimensions of Policy Choice*, edited by John Martin Gillroy and Maurice Wade. Pittsburgh: University of Pittsburgh Press, 1993.

Dewey, John. "Dualism and the Split Atom: Science and Morals in the Atomic Age." *The New Leader* 28: 1, 4.

Foucault, Michel. *The Birth of a Clinic*. London: Tavistock, 1973.

_____. *Discipline and Punish*. Harmondsworth: Penguin, 1979.

_____. "The Order of Discourse." In *Language and Politics*, edited by Michael Shapiro. New York: New York University Press, 1984.

Hall, Brian. *Developing Leadership by Stages: A Value-Based Approach to Executive Management*. London: Manohar Publications, 1979.

_____. *The Development of Consciousness: A Confluent Theory of Values*. New York: Paulist, 1979.

_____. *The Genesis Effect: Personal and Organizational Transformations*. Mahwah, NJ: Paulist, 1986.

Hall, Brian, and Bruce Taylor et al. *Value Development: A Practical Guide*. New York: Paulist, 1982.

_____. *Developing Human Values*. Fond du Lac, WI: Marian College, 1990.

Hall, Brian, and Helen Thompson. *Leadership through Values: An Approach to Personal and Organizational Development*. New York: Paulist, 1980.

Hartle, Anthony. *Moral Issues in Military Decision Making*. Lawrence, KS: University of Kansas Press, 1989.

Holmes, Robert L. *On War and Morality*. Princeton: Princeton University Press, 1989.

———. *Basic Moral Philosophy*. Belmont, CA: Wadsworth, 1993.

Johnson, David E. "Terror Tactics: A Conceptual Analysis." In *Moral Obligation and the Military*. Washington: National Defense University Press, 1988.

Johnston, James. *Just War Tradition and the Restraint of War*. Princeton; Princeton University Press, 1981.

Kaufmann, Walter. *Without Guilt and Justice*. New York: Dell Publishing, 1973.

Keen, Sam. *Faces of the Enemy: Reflections of the Hostile Imagination*. New York: Harper & Row, 1986.

Kunkel, Joseph C. "Just-War Doctrine and Pacifism." *The Thomist* 47:4, 501–512.

Miller, Alice. *For Your Own Good: Hidden Cruelty in Child-Rearing and the Roots of Violence*. New York: Noonday, 1990.

Nathanson, Stephen. "Kennedy and the Cuban Missile Crisis: On the Role of Moral Reasons in Explaining and Evaluating Political Decision-Making." *Journal of Social Philosophy* 22, 94–108.

Niebuhr, Reinhold. *Moral Man and Immoral Society*. New York, Scribner's, 1932.

Olen, Jeffrey. *Ethics in Journalism*. Englewood Cliffs, NJ: Prentice-Hall, 1988.

Paskins, David, ed. *The Anthropology of Evil*. London: Blackwell, 1985.

Peck, M. Scott. *People of the Lie: The Hope for Healing Human Evil*. New York: Simon & Schuster, 1983.

Peters, Edward. *Torture*. London: Blackwell, 1986.

Postman, Neil. *Amusing Ourselves to Death: Public Discourse in the Age of Show Business*. New York: Viking Penguin, 1985.

Ramsey, Paul. *The Just War*. New York: Scribner's, 1968.

Ricoeur, Paul. *The Symbolism of Evil*. New York: Harper & Row, 1967.

Rosenthal, Abigail L. *A Good Look at Evil*. Philadelphia: Temple University Press, 1987.

Scarry, Elaine. *The Body in Pain: The Making and Unmaking of the World*. New York: Oxford University Press, 1985.

Shue, Henry. "Mediating Duties." *Ethics* 98, 687–704.

Sterba, James P. "Reconciling Pacifists and Just War Theorists." In *Just War, Nonviolence and Nuclear Deterrence*, edited by Duane Cady and Richard Werner. Lanham, MD: Longwood Academic, 1991.

Volkan, Vamik D. *The Need for Enemies and Allies: From Clinical Practice to International Relations*. Dunmore, PA: Jason Aronson, 1986.

Wall, James M. *Winning the War, Losing Our Souls*. Chicago: Christian Century, 1991.

Walzer, Michael. *Just and Unjust Wars*. 2nd ed. New York: Basic Books, 1977.

_____. *The Company of Critics: Social Criticism and Political Commitment in the Twentieth Century*. New York: Basic Books, 1988.

Werner, Richard. "South Africa: University Neutrality and the Consequences of Divestment." In *Neutrality and Academic Ethics*, edited by Robert Simon. Totowa, NJ: Roman & Littlefield, 1994.

3. Feminism and Peace

Benson, Margaret. "The Political Economy of Women's Liberation." *Monthly Review* 21, 13–25.

Brock-Utne, Brigit. *The Role of Women and Mothers and Members of Society in the Education of Young People for Peace, Mutual Understanding and Respect for Human Rights*. Oslo: Peace Research Institute, 1981.

_____. *The Role of Women in Peace Research*. Oslo: Peace Research Institute, 1982.

_____. *Education for Peace: A Feminist Perspective*. New York: Pergamon, 1985.

_____. *Feminist Perspectives on Peace Research*. Oslo: Peace Research Institute, 1986.

_____. *Feminist Perspectives on Peace and Peace Education*. New York: Pergamon, 1989.

Belenky, Mary *et al*. *Women's Ways of Knowing*. New York: Basic Books, 1986.

Burns, Robin. "Development, Disarmament and Women: Some New Connections." *Social Alternatives* 1982, 2–5.

Chodorow, Nancy. *The Reproduction of Mothering*. Berkeley; University of California Press, 1978.

Cohn, Carol. "Sex and Death in the Rational World of Defense Intellectuals." In *Peace: Meanings, Politics, Strategies*, edited by Linda Rennie Forcey. New York: Praeger, 1989.

Daly, Mary. *Gyn/Ecology*. Boston: Beacon, 1978.

de Beauvoir, Simone. *The Second Sex*. New York: Random House, 1974.

D'Souza, Corinne Kumar. *Sangharsh*. Bangalore, India: Vimochana Ed. Collective, n.d.

Duhan, Laura. "Feminism and Peace Theory: Women as Nurturers vs. Women as Public Citizens." In *The Interest of Peace: A Spectrum of*

Philosophical Perspectives, edited by Kenneth Klein and Joseph C. Kunkel. Wakefield, NH: Longwood Academic, 1990.

Easlea, Brian. *Fathering the Unthinkable: Masculinity, Scientists and the Nuclear Arms Race*. London: Pluto, 1983.

Echols, Alice. *Daring to Be Bad: Radical Feminism in America, 1967–1975.* Minneapolis: University of Minnesota Press, 1989.

Elshtain, Jean Bethke. *Women and War*. New York: Basic Books, 1987.

Enloe, Cynthia. *Does Khaki Become You? The Militarization of Women's Lives.* Boston: Pandora, 1988.

Flax, Jane. "Theorizing Motherhood." *Women's Review of Books* 1:9, 13.

Forcey, Linda Rennie. *Mothers of Sons: Toward an Understanding of Responsibility*. New York: Praeger, 1987.

———. "Mothers of Sons and Uncle Sam." In *Women and the Military System*. Peace Union of Finland, 1988.

———. "Making of Men in the Military: Perspectives from Mothers of Sons." *Women's Studies International Forum* 7:6, 477–486.

———. "When Women Fight." *Women's Review of Books*, May 1988, 8–9.

———. "Women as Peacemakers: Contested Terrain for Feminist Peace Studies." *Peace & Change* 16:4 (October 1991), 331–354.

Fourtouni, Elene. *Green Women in Resistance*. Chicago: Lake View, 1986.

Friedan, Betty. *The Feminine Mystique*. New York: Dell, 1963.

Gilligan, Carol. *In a Different Voice*. Cambridge, MA: Harvard University Press, 1982.

Gimenez, Martha E. "Structuralist Marxism on 'The Woman Question.'" *Science and Society* 42, 301–323.

Gioselfi, Daniela. *Women on War*. New York: Simon & Schuster, 1988.

Hartsock, Nancy. *Money, Sex, and Power*. New York: Longman Academic, 1983.

Hoagland, Sarah Lucia. *Lesbian Ethics*. Palo Alto, CA: Institute of Lesbian Studies, 1988.

hooks, bell. *Feminist Theory from Margin to Center*. Boston: South End, 1985.

[Kaplan] Laura Duhan. "Feminism and Peace Theory: Women as Nurturers vs. Women as Public Citizens." In *The Interest of Peace: A Spectrum of Philosophical Perspectives*, edited by Kenneth Klein and Joseph C. Kunkel. Wakefield, NH: Longwood Academic, 1990.

Kaplan, Laura Duhan. "Women as Caretaker: An Archetype Which Supports Patriarchal Militarism." *Hypatia: A Journal of Feminist Philosophy* 9: 2, 123–133.

———. "A Liberal Feminist Critique of Political Realism." In *On The Eve of The 21st Century: Perspectives of Russian and American Philosophers*, edited by William Gay and T.A. Alekseeva. Lanham, MD: Rowman & Littlefield, 1993.

Kristeva, Julia. *The Kristeva Reader*. Oxford: Blackwell, 1986.

Milkman, Ruth. "Women's History and the Sears Case." *Feminist Studies* 12, 394–395.

Molyneux, Maxine. "Beyond the Housework Debate." *New Left Review,* July–August 1979, 3–27.

Noddings, Nel. *Caring: A Feminine Approach to Ethics and Moral Education.* Berkeley: University of California Press, 1984.

Omolade, Barbara. "We Speak for the Planet." In *Rocking the Ship of State: Toward a Feminist Peace Politics,* edited by Adrienne Harris and Ynestra King. Boulder, CO: Westview, 1989.

Pateman, Carole. "'God Hath Ordained to Man a Helper': Hobbes, Patriarchy and Conjugal Right." In *Feminist Interpretations and Political Theory,* edited by Carole Pateman and Mary Lyndon Shanley. University Park, PA: Pennsylvania State University Press, 1991.

Patmore, Coventry. *The Angel in the House.* New York: E. P. Dutton, 1876.

Phillips, Anne., ed. *Feminism and Equality.* New York: New York University Press, 1987.

Reardon, Betty A. *Sexism and the War System.* New York: Teachers College Press, 1986.

———. "A Gender Analysis of Militarism and Sexist Repression: A Suggested Research Agenda." *International Peace Research Newsletter* 21: 2.

Ridd, Rosemary, and Helen Callaway, eds. *Women and Political Conflict: Portraits of Struggle in Times of Crisis.* New York: New York University Press, 1987.

Ruddick, Sara. *Maternal Thinking: Toward a Politics of Peace.* New York: Ballantine Books, 1989.

Sapiro, Virginia. *Women in American Society.* Palo Alto, CA: Mayfield, 1986.

Scott, Joan Wallach. *Gender and the Politics of History.* New York: Columbia University Press, 1988.

Segal, Lynne. *Is the Future Female?* London: Virago, 1987.

Snitow, Ann. "A Gender Diary." In *Rocking the Ship of State: Toward a Feminist Peace Politics,* edited by Adrienne Harris and Ynestra King. Boulder, CO: Westview, 1989.

Sylvester, Christine. "Patriarchy, Peace and Women." In *Peace: Meanings, Politics, Strategies,* edited by Linda Rennie Forcey. New York: Praeger, 1989.

Trible, Phyllis. An Unnamed Woman: The Extravagance of Violence." In *Texts of Terror: Literary-Feminist Readings of Biblical Narratives.* Philadelphia: Fortress, 1984.

Weedon, Chris. *Feminist Practice and Poststructuralist Theory.* New York: Blackwell, 1987.

4. Religion and Peace

Ahmad, Hazrat Mirza Ghulam. *The Philosophy of the Teachings of Islam.* Padstow, Cornwall, England: T. J. Press, 1979.

An-Na'im, Abdullahi Ahmed. "Introduction." In *The Second Message of Islam* by (Ustadh) Mahmoud Mohamed Taha. Syracuse, NY: Syracuse University Press, 1987.

Anga, Salaheddin Ali Nader Shah. *Peace.* Verdugo City, CA: M.T.O. Shahmaghsoudi Publication, 1987.

Arberry, Arthur J., trans. *The Koran Interpreted.* New York: Macmillan, 1964.

Behishti, (Ayatollah) Muhammad Hosayni, and (Hujjatul-Islam) Javad Bahonar. *The Philosophy of Islam.* Salt Lake City: Islamic Publications, n.d.

Boulares, Habib. *Islam: The Fear and the Hope.* London: Zod Books, 1990.

Buber, Martin. *A Land of Two Peoples: Martin Buber on Jews and Arabs,* edited by Paul Mendes-Flohr. Oxford: Oxford University Press, 1983.

Cassidy, Richard J. *Jesus, Politics and Society: A Study of Luke's Gospel.* Maryknoll, NY: Orbis, 1978.

Cragg, Kenneth. "Muhammud Kamil Husain of Cairo." In *The Pen and the Faith: Eight Modern Muslim Writers and the Qur'an.* London: George Allen & Unwin, 1985.

Denny, Frederick M. *Islam and the Muslim Community.* New York: Harper & Row, 1987.

Enayat, Hamid. *Modern Islamic Political Thought.* Austin: University of Texas Press, 1982.

Engineer, Asghar Ali. *Islam and Liberation Theology: Essays on Liberative Elements in Islam.* New Delhi: Sterling, 1990.

Ferguson, John. *War and Peace in the World's Religions.* New York: Oxford University Press, 1978.

Forcey, Linda Rennie, Robert Fredrick Hunter, and Mar Peter-Raoul, eds. *Yearning To Breathe Free: Liberation Theologies in the U.S.* Maryknoll, NY: Orbis, 1991.

Ford, J. M. *My Enemy is My Guest: Jesus and Violence in Luke.* Maryknoll, NY: Orbis, 1984.

Gibb, H. A. R., J. H. Kramers, E. Levi-Provencal, and J. Schacht. *The Encyclopedia of Islam.* Leiden, The Netherlands: E. J. Brill, 1960.

Goldmann, N. *The Jewish Paradox.* New York: Grosset & Dunlap, 1978.

Graziano, Frank. *Divine Violence: Spectacle, Psychosexuality, and Radical Christianity in the Argentine 'Dirty War'.* Boulder, CO: Westview, 1992.

Khadduri, M. *War and Peace in the Law of Islam.* Baltimore, MD: Johns Hopkins University Press, 1955.

Lewis, Bernard. *The Political Language of Islam.* Chicago: University of

Chicago Press, 1988.

Little, David, John Kelsey, and Abdulaziz Sachedina. *Human Rights and the Conflict of Cultures: Western and Islamic Perspectives on Religious Liberty*. Columbia, SC: University of South Carolina Press, 1988.

Menninger, Karl. *Whatever Became of Sin?* New York: Hawthorn Books, 1973.

Muhaiyaddeen, M. R. Bawa. *Islam and World Peace: Explanations of a Sufi*. Philadelphia: The Fellowship Press, 1987.

Munson, Henry, Jr. *Islam and Revolution in the Middle East*. New Haven, CT: Yale University Press, 1988.

Nasr, Seyyed Hossein. *Traditional Islam in the Modern World*. London: Kegan Paul, 1987.

Pickthall, Mohammed M., trans. *The Meaning of the Glorious Koran*. New York: New American Library and Mentor Books, n.d.

Political Issues in Luke-Acts. Maryknoll, NY: Orbis, 1983.

Qutb, Sayyid. *Milestones*. Cedar Rapids, IA: Unity Publishing, 1981.

Ruether, Rosemary R., and Marc H. Ellis, eds. *Beyond Occupation: American Jewish, Christian, and Palestinian Voices for Peace*. Boston: Beacon, 1990.

Taha, (Ustadh) Mahmoud Mohamed. *The Second Message of Islam*, translated and introduced by Abdullahi Ahmed An-Na'im. Syracuse, NY: Syracuse University Press, 1987.

Taylor, Alan R. *The Islamic Question in Middle East Politic*. Boulder, CO: Westview, 1988.

The Holy Scriptures According to the Masoretic Text. Philadelphia: Jewish Publication Society, 1955.

Trible, Phyllis. "An Unnamed Woman: The Extravagance of Violence." In *Texts of Terror: Literary-Feminist Readings of Biblical Narratives*. Philadelphia: Fortress, 1984.

5. Loyalty and Patriotism

Axinn, Sidney. "Honor, Patriotism, and Ultimate Loyalty." In *Nuclear Weapons and the Future of Humanity*, edited by A. Cohen and S. Lee. Totowa, NJ: Rowman & Allenheld, 1986.

———. "Loyalty and the Limits of Patriotism." In *Political Realism and International Morality*, edited by K. Kipnis and D. Meyers. Boulder, CO: Westview, 1987.

Baron, Marcia. *The Moral Status of Loyalty*. Dubuque, IA: Kendall/Hunt, 1984.

———. "Patriotism and 'Liberal' Morality." In *Mind, Value, and Culture: Essays in Honor of E. M. Adams*, edited by D. Weissbord. Northridge, CA: Ridgeview Publishing, 1989.

Cottingham, John. "Partiality, Favoritism, and Morality." *Philosophical Quarterly* 36, 357–373.

Dietz, Mary G. "Patriotism." In *Political Innovation and Conceptual Change*, edited by T. Ball, J. Farr, and R. Hanson. Cambridge, England: Cambridge University Press, 1989.

Feshbach, Seymour. "Individual Aggression, National Attachment, and the Search for Peace." *Aggressive Behavior* 13, 315–325.

Gomberg, Paul. "Patriotism Is Like Racism." *Ethics* 101, 144–150.

Goodin, Robert. "What Is so Special about Our Fellow Countrymen?" *Ethics* 98, 663–686.

Hayes, Carlton. *The Evolution of Modern Nationalism*. New York: Macmillan, 1931.

Janowitz, Morris. *The Reconstruction of Patriotism*. Chicago: University of Chicago Press, 1983.

Jensen, Kenneth, and Kimber Schraub, eds. *Pacifism and Citizenship: Can They Coexist?* Washington: U.S. Institute of Peace, 1991.

MacIntyre, Alasdair. "Is Patriotism a Virtue?" *The Lindley Lecture*. Lawrence, KS: University of Kansas Press, 1984.

Nathanson, Stephen. "Patriotism and the Pursuit of Peace." In *In the Interests of Peace,* edited by K. Klein and J. Kunkel. Wakefield, NH: Longwood Academic, 1990.

——. *Patriotism, Morality, and Peace*. Lanham, MD: Rowman & Littlefield, 1993.

——. "In Defense of 'Moderate Patriotism'." *Ethics* 99, 535–552.

——. "Is Patriotism Like Racism?" APA *Newsletter on Philosophy and the Black Experience* 91:2, 9–11.

——. "Must Patriotism Be an Obstacle to Peace?" *International Journal of Group Tensions*, forthcoming.

——. "On Deciding Whether a Nation Deserves Our Loyalty." *Public Affairs Quarterly* 4, 287–298.

Navasky, V. "Patriotism." *The Nation*, 15–22 July 1991.

Oldenquist, Andrew. "Loyalties." *Journal of Philosophy* 79, 173–193.

Smith, Anthony. *Theories of Nationalism*. London: Duckworth, 1983.

6. Economic and Racial Justice

Brown, Lester R., Christopher Flavin, and Sandra Postel. *Saving the Planet: How to Shape an Environmentally Sustainable Global Economy*. New York: Norton, 1991.

Chatterji, Manas, and Linda Rennie Forcey, eds. *Approaches to Disarmament, Economic Conversion and the Management of Peace*. New York: Praeger, 1992.

Forcey, Linda Rennie. "Coming to Terms with Two Cultures: Approaches to Peace Studies." In *Approaches to Disarmament, Economic*

Conversion and the Management of Peace, edited by Manas Chatterji and Linda Rennie Forcey. New York: Praeger, 1992.

Fredrickson, George M. *White Supremacy*. Oxford: Oxford University Press, 1981.

King, Martin Luther, Jr. *Stride Toward Freedom*. New York: Harper & Row, 1958.

Lappe, Frances Moore, and Joseph Collins. *World Hunger: Twelve Myths*. New York: Grove Weidenfeld, 1986.

Nagel, Thomas. *Equality and Partiality*. New York: Oxford University Press, 1991.

Phillips, Kevin. *The Politics of Rich and Poor*. New York: Random House, 1990.

Phillips, Robert. *War and Justice*. Norman, OK: University of Oklahoma Press, 1984.

Sharp, Gene. *Social Power and Political Freedom*. Boston: Porter Sargent, 1980.

Singer, Peter. "Famine, Affluence, and Morality." *Philosophy and Public Affairs* 1, 229–244.

United States Institute of Peace. *Minorities at Risk: A Global View of Ethnopolitical Conflict*. Washington: U.S. Institute of Peace Press, 1993.

7. Genocide

Arendt, Hannah. *Eichmann in Jerusalem: A Report on the Banality of Evil*. New York: Viking, 1964.

Baum, Rainer C. "Holocaust: Moral Indifference as the Form of Modern Evil." In *Echoes from the Holocaust,* edited by Alan Rosenberg and Gerald E. Myers. Philadelphia: Temple University Press, 1988.

Charny, Israel W. *How Can We Commit the Unthinkable?* Boulder, CO: Westview, 1982.

_____, ed. *Toward the Understanding and Prevention of Genocide*. Boulder, CO: Westview, 1984.

Fein, Helen. *Accounting for Genocide*. New York: Free Press, 1979.

_____. "Scenarios of Genocide: Models of Genocide and Critical Responses." In *Toward the Understanding and Prevention of Genocide*, edited by Israel W. Charny. Boulder, CO: Westview, 1984.

Harff, Barbara. *Genocide and Human Rights*. Denver, CO: University of Denver Press, 1984.

Horowitz, Irving Louis. "The Exclusivity of Collective Death." In *Genocide and the Modern Age*, edited by Isidor Wallimann and Michael N. Dobkowski. New York: Greenwood, 1987.

Jonassohn, Kurt, and Frank Chalk. "A Typology of Genocide and Some Implications for the Human Rights Agenda." In *Genocide and the*

Modern Age, edited by Isidor Wallimann and Michael N. Dobkowski. New York: Greenwood, 1987.

Kelman, Herbert C., and V. Lee Hamilton. *Crimes of Obedience*. New York: Yale University Press, 1987.

Kern, George M. "The Holocaust: Moral Theory and Immoral Acts." In *Echoes from the Holocaust*, edited by Alan Rosenberg and Gerald E. Myers. Philadelphia: Temple University Press, 1988.

Kuper, Leo. *The Prevention of Genocide*. New York: Yale University Press, 1985.

Lifton, Robert Jay. *The Nazi Doctors: Medicalized Killing and the Psychology of Genocide*. New York: Basic Books, 1986.

Milgram, Stanley. *Obedience to Authority*. New York: Harper & Row, 1969.

Oliner, Samuel P., and Pearl M. Oliner. *The Altruistic Personality: Rescuers of Jews in Nazi Europe*. New York: Free Press, 1992.

Rosenberg, Alan, and Gerald E. Myers, eds. *Echoes from the Holocaust*. Philadelphia: Temple University Press, 1988.

Smith, Roger W. "Human Destructiveness and Politics: The Twentieth Century as an Age of Genocide." In *Genocide and the Modern Age*, edited by Isidor Wallimann and Michael N. Dobkowski. New York: Greenwood, 1987.

Staub, Ervin. *The Roots of Evil: The Origins of Genocide and Other Group Violence*. Cambridge, England: Cambridge University Press, 1989.

Wallimann, Isidor, and Michael N. Dobkowski, eds. *Genocide and the Modern Age*. New York: Greenwood, 1987.

8. Nuclear Weapons

Churchill, Robert Paul. "Nuclear Deterrence and Nuclear Paternalism." In *Freedom, Equality, and Social Change*, edited by Creighton Peden and James P. Sterba. Lewiston, NY: Edwin Mellen, 1989.

Gay, William C. "Nuclear War: Public and Governmental Misconceptions." In *Nuclear War: Philosophical Perspectives*, edited by Michael Allen Fox and Leo Groarke. New York: Peter Lang, 1985.

———. "Philosophical Bibliography on War and Peace in the Nuclear Age." In *Issues in War and Peace*, edited by Joseph Kunkel and Kenneth Klein. Wolfeboro, NH: Longwood Academic, 1989.

———. "The Russell-Hook Debates of 1958: Arguments from the Extremes on Nuclear War and the Soviet Union." In *In the Interest of Peace*, edited by Kenneth H. Klein and Joseph C. Kunkel. Wakefield, NH: Longwood Academic, 1990.

———, ed. "Special Issue: Philosophy and the Debate on Nuclear Weapons Systems and Policies." *Philosophy and Social Criticism* 10:3–4.

Gay, William C., and Michael Pearson. *The Nuclear Arms Race*. Chicago:

The American Library Association, 1987.

Green, Dorothy, and David Headon, eds. *Imagining the Real: Australian Writing in the Nuclear Age.* Sydney: ABC Enterprises, 1987.

Harvard Nuclear Study Group. *Living With Nuclear Weapons.* Cambridge, MA: Harvard University Press, 1983.

Heidegger, Martin. *Discourse on Thinking*, translated by John M. Anderson and E. Hans Freund. New York: Harper & Row, 1969.

Holmes, Robert L., ed. *Nonviolence in Theory and Practice.* Belmont, CA: Wadsworth, 1990.

Kunkel, Joseph C. "Right Intention, Deterrence, and Nuclear Alternatives." *Philosophy and Social Criticism* 10:3–4, 143–155.

Neyer, Joseph. "Is Atomic-Fission Control a Problem For Organizational Technique?" *Ethics* 57, 289–296.

Schell, Jonathan. *The Fate of the Earth.* New York: Knopf, 1982.

———. *The Abolition.* New York: Knopf, 1984.

Sharp, Gene. *The Politics of Non-Violent Action.* Boston: Porter Sargent, 1973.

Toynbee, Arnold. *A Study of History,* Volume 8. London: Oxford University Press, 1954.

Weinberg, Arthur, and Lila Weinberg, eds. *Instead of Violence: Writings by the Great Advocates of Nonviolence throughout History.* New York: Grossman, 1963.

9. International Law

Alexander, Y., and R. A. Friedlander, eds. *Self-Determination: National, Regional, and Global Dimensions.* Boulder, CO: Westview, 1980.

Barnet, Richard. "The Twilight of the Nation-State." In *The Rule of Law*, edited by R. P. Wolff. New York: Simon & Schuster, 1971.

Chen, Lung-chu. "Self-Determination as a Human Right." In *Toward World Order and Human Dignity,* edited by M. Reisman and B. Weston. New York: Free Press, 1976.

Cobban, A. *National Self-Determination.* London: Oxford University Press, 1944.

Crawford, J. *The Creation of States in International Law.* London: Oxford University Press, 1979.

Emerson, R. *Self-Determination Revisited in the Era of Decolonization.* Cambridge, MA: Center for International Affairs, Harvard University Press, 1964.

Espiell, H. G. *The Right to Self-Determination: Implementation of United Nations Resolutions.* New York: United Nations, 1980.

Farley, L. T. *Plebiscites and Sovereignty.* Boulder, CO: Westview, 1986.

Feinberg, N. *Studies in International Law.* Jerusalem: Magnes, 1979.

Friedlander, R. A. "Self-Determination: A Legal-Political Inquiry." In *Self-*

Determination: National, Regional, and Global Dimensions, edited by Y. Alexander and R. A. Friedlander. Boulder, CO: Westview, 1980.

Johnson, H. S. *Self-Determination Within the Community of Nations.* Leyden: A. W. Sijtoff, 1967.

Joyner, C. "The Reality and Relevance of International Law." In *The Global Agenda*, edited by C. W. Kegley and E. R. Wittkopf. New York: Random House, 1988.

Kinsley, Michael. "Taking International Law Seriously." In *The Gulf War Reader: History, Documents, Opinions*, edited by Micah Sifry and Christopher Cerf. New York: Random House, 1991.

Lippman, Matthew. "The Recognition of Conscientious Objection to Military Science as an International Human Right." 21 *Cal. W. Int'l L. J 31 (1990)*.

Margalit, A., and J. Raz. "National Self-Determination." *The Journal of Philosophy* 87, 439–461.

Ofuatey-Kodojoe, W. *The Principle of Self-Determination in International Law.* New York: Nellen, 1977.

Paust, J. "Self-Determination: A Definitional Focus." In *Self-Determination: National, Regional, and Global Dimensions*, edited by Y. Alexander and R. A. Friedlander. Boulder, CO: Westview, 1980.

Pomerance, M. "The United States and Self-Determination: Perspectives on the Wilsonian Conception." *Amer. Jr. of Int'l. Law* 70, 1–27.

———. "Self-Determination Today: The Metamorphosis of an Ideal." *Israel Law Review* 23, 310–339.

Ronen, D. *The Quest for Self-Determination.* New Haven, CT: Yale University Press, 1979.

Suzuki, E. "Self-Determination and World Public Order: Community Response to Territorial Separation." *Virginia Jr. of Int'l. Law* 16, 779–862.

Umozurike, U. O. *Self-Determination in International Law.* Hamden CT: Archon Books, 1972.

10. Peace History

Addams, Jane. "Personal Reactions During War." In *Nonviolence in America: A Documentary History*, edited by Staughton Lynd. Indianapolis: Bobbs-Merrill, 1966.

Brock, Peter. *Twentieth-Century Pacifism.* New York: Van Nostrand Reinhold, 1970.

———. *Pacifism in Europe to 1914.* Princeton: Princeton University Press, 1972.

Gray, J. Glenn. *The Warriors: Reflections on Men in Battle.* New York: Harper & Row, 1973.

Heckscher, A. *Woodrow Wilson.* New York: Scribner's, 1991.

Lansing, R. *The Peace Negotiations*. Boston: Houghton-Mifflin, 1921.
Lemkin, Raphael. *Axis Rule in Occupied Europe*. Washington: Carnegie Endowment for International Peace, 1944.
Lloyd-George, David. *Memoirs of the Peace Conference*. New Haven, CT: Yale University Press, 1939.
Temperley, H. W. V. *A History of the Peace Conference of Paris*, Vol. 2. London: Oxford University Press, 1920.
Woodward, Robert. *The Commanders*. New York: Simon & Schuster, 1991.

11. Specific Regional Conflicts

A. The Persian Gulf War (U.S. Operation "Desert Storm")

Albright, David, and Mark Hibbs. "Hyping the Iraqi Bomb." *Bulletin of the Atomic Scientists* 47:2, 26–28.
———. "Iraq and the Bomb: Were They Ever Close?" *Bulletin of the Atomic Scientists* 47:2, 16–25.
———. "Iraq's Nuclear Hide-and-Seek." *Bulletin of the Atomic Scientists* 47:7, 14–23.
"A Tragic Year Later: Infant Mortality in Post-War Iraq." *Sojourners* 21:1, 19.
Bennis, Phyllis, and Michael Moushabeck, eds. *Beyond the Storm: A Gulf Crisis Reader*. New York: Olive Branch, 1991.
Bush, George. "Letter to Saddam." In *The Gulf War Reader: History, Documents, Opinions*, edited by Micah Sifry and Christopher Cerf, New York: Random House, 1991.
———. "Against Aggression in the Persian Gulf." *Current Policy* 1293. Washington: U.S. Department of State, Bureau of Public Affairs.
Cainkar, Louise. "Desert Sin: A Post-War Journey Through Iraq." In *Beyond the Storm: A Gulf Crisis Reader*, edited by Phyllis Bennis and Michel Moushabeck. New York: Olive Branch, 1991.
Chomsky, Noam. "The Use (and Abuse) of the United Nations." In *The Gulf War Reader: History, Documents, Opinions*, edited by Micah Sifry and Christopher Cerf. New York: Random House, 1991.
———. "The Global Protection Racket: Reflections on the Gulf War." In *Chronicles of Dissent*, edited by Noam Chomsky and David Barsamian. Monroe, ME: Common Courage, 1992.
Clark, Ramsey. *The Fire This War: Crimes in the Gulf War*. New York: Thunder's Mouth, 1992.
Clark, Ramsey *et al*. *War Crimes: A Report on United States War Crimes Against Iraq*. Washington: Maisonneuve, 1992.
Cockburn, Alexander. "Beat the Devil." *The Nation*, 21 December 1992, 762.
———. "The Press and the 'Just War.'" *The Nation*, 18 February 1991, 186–187.

Decosse, David E., ed. *But Was It Just? Reflections on the Morality of the Gulf War*. New York: Doubleday, 1991.

Dorfman, Ariel. "Hymn for the Unsung." In *The Gulf War Reader: History, Documents, Opinions*, edited by Micah Sifry and Christopher Cerf. New York: Random House, 1991.

Elliott, Kimberly, Gary Hufbauer, and Jeffrey Schott. "Sanctions Work: The Historical Record." In *The Gulf War Reader: History, Documents, Opinions*, edited by Micah Sifry and Christopher Cerf. New York: Random House, 1991.

Fotion, Nicholas. "The Gulf War: Cleanly Fought." *The Bulletin of the Atomic Scientists*, 47:7, 24–29.

Geyer, Alan, and Barbara G. Green. *Lines in the Sand: Justice and the Gulf War*. Louisville, KY: Westminster/John Knox, 1992.

Harkin, Tom. "The Obligation to Debate." In *The Gulf War Reader: History, Documents, Opinions*, edited by Micah Sifry and Christopher Cerf. New York: Random House, 1991.

Harnak, G. Simon. "After the Gulf War: A New Paradigm for the Peace Movement." *Journal of Humanistic Psychology* 32:4, 11–40.

Heyen, William. *Ribbons: The Gulf War*. St. Louis: Time Being Books, 1991.

Johnson, James Turner, and George Weigel. *Just War and the Gulf War*. Washington: Ethics and Public Policy Center, 1991.

Johnson, Leonard V. "Time for Common Security." *The Bulletin of the Atomic Scientists* 47:5, 28.

Klare, Michael T. "Fueling the Fire: How We Armed the Middle East." *Bulletin of the Atomic Scientists* 47:1, 19–26.

Krauthammer, Charles. "No Cause for Guilt." *The Gulf War Reader: History, Documents, Opinions*, edited by Micah Sifry and Christopher Cerf, New York: Random House, 1991.

"Letter of the U.S. Catholic Bishops to Secretary of State James Baker, November 7, 1990." NISBCO Documentation Service #7 (1990): 1–2.

Lopez, George. "The Gulf War: Not So Clean." *The Bulletin of the Atomic Scientists*, 47:7, 30–35.

Massing, Michael. "The Way to War." *New York Review of Books*, 28 May 1991, 17.

Meek, Jay, and F. D. Reeve, eds. *After the Storm: Poems on the Persian Gulf War*. Washington: Maisonneuve, 1992.

Munk, Erika. "The New Face of Techno-War: Witness in Baghdad." *The Nation*, 6 May 1991, 583–586.

National Council of Churches of Christ. "On the Gulf and Middle East Crisis." In *The Gulf War Reader: History, Documents, Opinions*, edited by Micah Sifry and Christopher Cerf. New York: Random House, 1991.

Parry, Robert. "The Peace Feeler that Was: Did Saddam Want a Deal?" *The*

Nation, April 15, 1991, 480–482.

Peretz, Don. *Intifada: The Palestinian Uprising.* Boulder, CO: Westview, 1990.

Polanyi, John C. "Collective Will or Law of the Jungle." *Bulletin of the Atomic Scientists* 47:5, 23.

Schanberg, Sydney. "A Muzzle for the Press." *The Gulf War Reader: History, Documents, Opinions,* edited by Micah Sifry and Christopher Cerf, New York: Random House, 1991.

Sifry, Michael L., and Christopher Cerf, eds. *The Gulf War Reader: History, Documents, Opinions.* New York: Random House, 1991.

Solo, Pam. "Talking Law, Waging War." *The Bulletin of the Atomic Scientists* 47:5, 25.

"Transcript of House Sub-Committee Hearing on U.S. Commitments in the Gulf." In *The March to War,* edited by James Ridgeway. New York: Four Walls Eight Windows, 1991.

Vaux, Kenneth L. *Ethics and the Gulf War: Religion, Rhetoric, and Righteousness.* Boulder, CO: Westview, 1992.

Waas, Murray. "What Washington Gave Saddam for Christmas." In *The Gulf War Reader: History, Documents, Opinions,* edited by Micah Sifry and Christopher Cerf. New York: Random House, 1991.

Walker, Paul F., and Eric Stambler. "...And the Dirty Little Weapons." *Bulletin of the Atomic Scientists* 47:4, 20–24.

Young, Marilyn B. "Ruthless Intervention." *Bulletin of the Atomic Scientists* 47:5, 32–33.

B. Palestine and Israel

Anglo-American Committee of Inquiry. *A Survey of Palestine* (1946) and *Note Compiled for the Information of the United Nations Special Committee on Palestine* (Supp. 1947). Reprinted. Washington: Institute for Palestine Studies, 1991.

Awad, Mubarak. "Nonviolent Resistance: A Strategy for the Occupied Territories." *Journal of Palestine Studies* 13:4, 22–36.

Bassouni, M. C. "The Palestinians' Rights of Self-Determination and National Independence." *Information Paper No. 22.* Association of Arab-American Graduates Students, 1978.

Bookmiller, Kirsten Nakjavani, and Robert J. Bookmiller. "Palestinian Radio and the Intifada." *Journal of Palestine Studies* 19:4, 104.

Buber, Martin. *A Land of Two Peoples: Martin Buber on Jews and Arabs,* edited by Paul Mendes-Flohr. Oxford: Oxford University Press, 1983.

Cattan, H. *Palestine and International Law.* New York: Longman Academic, 1973.

Crow, Ralph E., Philip Grant, and Saad E. Ibrahim, eds. *Arab Nonviolent Political Struggle in the Middle East.* Boulder, CO: Lynne Rienner, 1990.

Dinstein, Y. "Self-Determination and the Middle East Conflict." In *Self-Determination: National, Regional, and Global Dimensions*, edited by Y. Alexander and R. A. Friedlander. Boulder, CO: Westview, 1980.

Finklestein, Norman. "Bayt Sahur in Year II of the Intifada: A Personal Account." *Journal of Palestine Studies* 19:2, 66.

Flapan, S. *The Birth of Israel*. New York: Pantheon Books, 1987.

Friedman, Thomas L. *From Beirut to Jerusalem*. New York: Doubleday, 1989.

Gal, A. *David Ben-Gurion and the American Alignment for a Jewish State*. Jerusalem: The Magnes Press, 1991.

Gerner, Deborah. *One Land, Two Peoples: The Conflict Over Palestine*. Boulder, CO: Westview, 1991.

Hirst, D. *The Gun and the Olive Branch*, 2nd. ed. London: Faber & Faber, 1984.

Hocking, W. E. "Arab Nationalism and Political Zionism." *The Moslem World* 35, 216–223.

Jaffee Center. *Towards a Solution*. Tel Aviv: The Jaffee Center for Strategic Studies, 1989.

Jubran, Michael. "'Not Planned But Not Spontaneous': The Intifada, Its Leadership and the PLO." *The Washington Report on Middle East Affairs* 7:8, 10.

Khalidi, W., ed. *From Haven to Conquest*. Beirut: Institute for Palestine Studies, 1971.

Khouri, F. *The Arab-Israeli Dilemma*, 2nd ed. Syracuse, NY: Syracuse University Press, 1976.

Lederman, Jim. "Dateline West Bank: Interpreting The Intifada." *Foreign Policy* 1988:Fall, 230–246.

Lilienthal, A. M. *The Zionist Connection II*. New Brunswick, NJ: North American, Inc., 1982.

Mallison, W. T., and S. V. Mallison. *The Palestine Problem in International Law and World Order*. Essex: Longman Academic, 1986.

Morris, B. *Origins of the Palestinian Refugee Problem*. London: Cambridge University Press, 1988.

Muslih, M. *The Origins of Palestinian Nationalism*. New York: Columbia University Press, 1988.

Peretz, Don. "Intifadeh: The Palestinian Uprising." *Foreign Affairs* 1988:Summer, 973.

Quigley, J. *Palestine and Israel*. Durham: Duke University Press, 1990.

Roberts, A. "Prolonged Military Occupation: The Israeli-Occupied Territories Since 1967." *Amer. Jr. of Int'l. Law* 84, 44–103.

Rozen, Roli. "Haaretz." *Israel Press Briefs*, July 1989, 2.

Ruether, Rosemary Radford and Marc H. Ellis, eds. *Beyond Occupation: American Jewish, Christian, and Palestinian Voices for Peace*. Boston: Beacon, 1990.

Schiff, Ze'ev and Ehud Ya'ari. *Intifada: The Palestinian Uprising—Israel's Third Front.* New York: Simon & Schuster, 1990.

Segal, J. *Creating the Palestinian State.* Chicago: Lawrence Hill, 1988.

Sharp, Gene. "The Intifadah and Nonviolent Struggle." *Journal of Palestine Studies* 19:1, 3–13.

Shehadeh, R. *Occupier's Law.* Washington: Institute for Palestine Studies, 1985.

Siniora, Hanna."An Analysis of the Current Revolt." *Journal of Palestine Studies* 17:3, 5f.

Smith, C. D. *Palestine and the Arab-Israeli Conflict.* New York: St. Martin's, 1988.

Stace, W. T. "The Zionist Illusion." *The Atlantic Monthly*, February 1947, 82–86.

Stone, J. *Israel and Palestine.* Baltimore: Johns Hopkins University Press, 1981.

Stork, Joe. "The Significance of Stones: Notes from the Seventh Month." In *Intifada: The Palestinian Uprising Against Israeli Occupation*, edited by Zachary Lockman and Joel Beinin. Boston: South End, 1989.

Walzer, Michael. "What Kind of State is a Jewish State?" *Tikkun* July/August 1989.

Witness for Peace. *What We Have Seen and Heard in the Middle East: Iraq/ Israel/Palestine: The Human Face of the Gulf War.* July, 1991.

C. Latin America

Agosin, Marjorie. S*craps of Life: Chilean Arpilleras.* Toronto: Williams-Wallace, 1987.

Avirgan, Tony, and Martha Honey, eds. *La Prenca: On Trial in Costa Rica: The CIA vs. the Press.* San Pedro, CR: Editorial Porvenir.

Biesanz, Richard, Karen Biesanz, and Mavis Biesanz. *The Costa Ricans.* New York: Prentice-Hall, 1982.

Didion, Joan. *Miami.* New York: Simon & Schuster, 1987.

Garcia, Celina. "Latin American Traditions and Perspectives." *International Review of Education* 29, 369–389.

Gedorn, Katherine J. *Contadora and the Central American Peace Process: Selected Documents.* Boulder, CO: Westview, 1985.

Jelic, Jordan. "Contadora Dossier: The General Situation in Central America." *Review of International Affairs* 38, 11–21.

Kunkel, Joseph C., and Bruce Taylor. "'Operation Just Cause' in Panama—Was It Just?" *Concerned Philosophers for Peace Newsletter* 10:1, 5–9.

Procedure for the Establishment of the Firm and Lasting Peace in Central America. La Uruca, Costa Rico: Oficina de Apoyo de la Presidencia de la Republica, 1987.

Robinson, Linda. "Peace in Central America?" *Foreign Affairs* 66:3, 591–613.

Torres, Edelberto, and Maria Eugenia Gallardo. *Para entender Centroamerica: Resumen Bibliografico 1960–1984*. San Jose, PR: ICADIS, 1985.

D. Bosnia and Somalia

Harff, Barbara. "Bosnia and Somalia." In *Toward the Understanding and Prevention of Genocide*, edited by Israel W. Charny. Boulder, CO: Westview, 1984.

Institute for Philosophy and Public Policy. "Bosnia and Somalia: Strategic, Legal, and Moral Dimensions of Humanitarian Intervention." *Reports* 12.

Laitin, David D. and Said S. Samatar. *Somalia: Nation in Search of a State*. Boulder, CO: Westview, 1987.

Nelson, Harold D. ed. *Somalia: A Country Study*. Washington: U.S. Government Printing Office, 1981.

Samatar, Said S. "Somalia: A Nation in Turmoil." *Minority Rights Group Report*, 1991.

INDEX

VIBS

26. Avi Sagi and Daniel Statman, **Religion and Morality.**

27. Albert William Levi, **The High Road of Humanity: The Seven Ethical Ages of Western Man,** edited by Donald Phillip Verene and Molly Black Verene.

28. Samuel M. Natale and Brian M. Rothschild, Editors, **Work Values: Education, Organization, and Religious Concerns.**

29. Laurence F. Bove and Laura Duhan Kaplan, Editors, **From the Eye of the Storm: Regional Conflicts and the Philosophy of Peace.** A volume in **Philosophy of Peace.**